"Our Native Antiquity"

Archaeology and Aesthetics
in the Culture of Russian Modernism

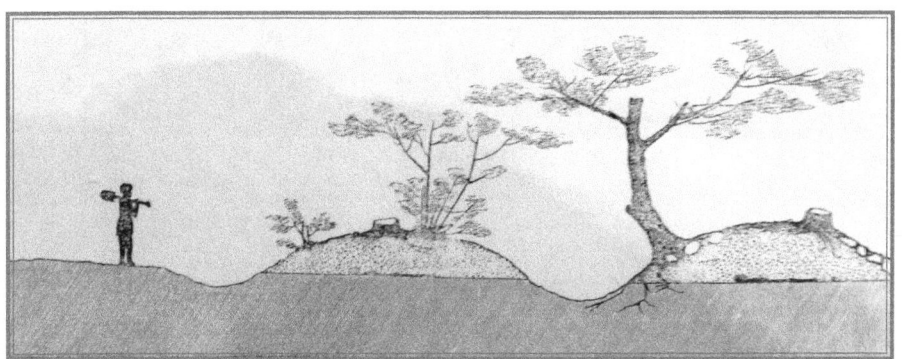

STUDIES IN RUSSIAN AND SLAVIC LITERATURES, CULTURES, AND HISTORY

Series Editor

Lazar FLEISHMAN (Stanford University, Palo Alto, California)

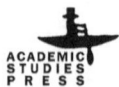

ACADEMIC
STUDIES
PRESS

"Our Native Antiquity"

Archaeology and Aesthetics in the Culture of Russian Modernism

Michael KUNICHIKA

Library of Congress Cataloging-in-Publication Data:
A bibliographic record for this title is available
from the Library of Congress.

ISBN (cloth) 978-1-61811-441-9
ISBN (electronic) 978-1-61811-442-6
ISBN (paper) 978-1-61811-664-2

Cover design by Ivan Grave
On the cover: Detail of A. S. Uvarov, "Svedeniia o kamennykh babakh,"
    Trudy pervogo akheologicheskogo s"ezda v Moskve
    (Moscow: V Sinodal'noi tipografii, 1871), 501-20.

Title page: Vignette from A. P. Bogdanov, ed., *Antropologicheskaia vystavka*
    (Moscow: Tipografiia M. N. Lavrova, 1878-), 4:2:54.

Published by Academic Studies Press in 2015, paperback 2018
28 Montfern Avenue
Brighton, MA 02135, USA
press@academicstudiespress.com
www.academicstudiespress.com

This book is dedicated to my teachers,
my parents first among them.

Table of Contents

Acknowledgments 8

Note on Translation and Transliteration 11

Introduction 12
   i. Archaic Mirrors 15
   ii. Elective Antiquities 19

Chapter One 27
The Archaeology of the Stone *Babas*
and the Modernist Inheritance
   i. "Rough Hewn Statues" 34
   ii. Idols Destroyed, Idols Displaced, 49
      and the Steppe Denuded
   iii. The Modernist Peregrinations of the Stone *Babas* 57

Chapter Two 62
A Cultural Poetics of the Kurgan
   i. How to Excavate a Kurgan 62
   ii. Gnedich, *Iliada* 69
   iii. Vantage Points, ca. 1850 80
   iv. 1876—The Grave Becomes a Cradle: 90
      Zabelin contra Chaadaev
   v. Archaeological Defamiliarization 96
   vi. Steppe Archaism and the Stratification of Time 100

Chapter Three 107
Ancient Statues, Ancient Terrors
   i. Archaic Simplicity 110
   ii. Primitive Rudeness 120
   iii. "No Ordinary Stone Woman" 128

Chapter Four 139
How a Modernist Artifact Is Made:
The "Native Antiquity" of the Stone *Babas*
and the Indigenization of Cubism
   i. The Stone *Baba* and the Bronze Horseman 147
   ii. Indigenous Cubism 162

Chapter Five   173
Velimir Khlebnikov, Poet of the Stone *Babas*
     i. "The Stone Woman" (1919): Modernist Metamorphosis 178
     ii. The Steppes of Time: "A Night in a Trench"   190
     iii. The Grave of Khlebnikov   201

Chapter Six   204
The Landmarks of Time: Burial Mounds,
     Eurasian Necropolises, and Modernist Form
     in Boris Pil'niak's *The Naked Year*
     i. Volga "Pompeiis"   211
     ii. Scythianism, 1918   217
     iii. Modernist Stratigraphy: Uvek, Site of Time   222
     iv. Modernist Topography: "Loop Station Mar"
        and the Poetics of Adjacency   234

Chapter Seven   243
Areas of Deformation
     Part One: Dziga Vertov and the Scythian   243
     i. Areas of Deformation   247
     ii. The Shooting Log   261
     iii. The Archaeology of the Superimpositions   271
     iv. Archaeology with a Hammer   275

     Part Two: Boris Pil'niak's *The Volga Falls*   280
        to the Caspian Sea and the Courage of Farewell
     i. All That Was Solid Did Not Melt into Air: 287
        Persisting Things
     ii. The Fluids of History: 291
        Archaeology and Antiquarianism
     iii. The Courage of Farewell: 297
        The Return of the Stone Women
     iv. Coda   307

Bibliography   312
Index   326

A C K N O W L E D G M E N T S

I did not know upon entering the Russian Department at Reed College and, later, the Slavic Department at the University of California, Berkeley, how fortunate I would be, then and thankfully still now, in my teachers there. Justin Weir and Elena Bogdanovich at Reed College encouraged the first steps. So, too, did Lena Lencek, mentor and friend, who gave me a language to think about literature, and certainly about life, and she has watched over everything since with grace. And then at Berkeley, Robert Hughes, Liza Knapp, Lisa Little, Olga Matich, Hugh McLean, Anna Muza, Eric Naiman, Anne Nesbet, Irina Paperno, Harsha Ram, Alan Timberlake, the late Viktor Zhivov, and the visitors with whom I was also lucky to study while there— Katerina Clark, Gregory Freidin, and Andrew Kahn—scholar-teachers all, I hope these pages reflect—Eric would probably say "pervert"—what they continue to teach me.

At Berkeley, it seemed that everyone helped with the dissertation from which this book partially draws, but I thank especially Harsha, Eric, Anne, and Yuri Slezkine for advising it. With Harsha, I poured over every sentence and idea of the dissertation; with Anne, who taught me how to watch silent Soviet film, I saw Dziga Vertov's "Scythian" in a theater in Sacile and the idea for the dissertation was born; with Yuri, at Ned's, I realized the dissertation was actually about the steppe. And it was at the Neues Museum with Irina and Joachim Klein where I saw the *kamennye baby* for the first time and was encouraged that the book could actually become a book.

Without Irina this book would never have found a home. I thank her and especially Lazar Fleishman for his editing and support, and for accepting it into his series. Penelope Burt and Jane Friedman edited the manuscript and improved it in every way. Irene Masing-Delic, the manuscript's "anonymous" reader, reviewed it with remarkable care and expert counsel. I thank Kira Nemirovsky, Sharona Vedol, and Meghan Vicks, the editors at Academic Studies Press, for their meticulous oversight of the entire publication process.

Many friends and colleagues commented on early versions of these chapters, and I thank them for their tremendous help and suggestions: Richard Anderson, Polina Barskova, Evgenii Bershtein, Molly Brunson, Catherine Ciepiela, Anne Dwyer, Devin Fore, Victoria Frede, Toral Gajarwala, Sergey Glebov, Luba Golburt, Lilya Kaganovsky, Edward Kasinec, John MacKay—whose help with the chapter on Vertov was an extraordinary act of scholarly generosity—Boris Maslov, Miriam Neirick, Tatiana Nikitina, Dale Peterson, Jennifer Presto, Stanley Rabinowitz, Tom Roberts, Gabriella Safran, Jane Sharp—whose work on Natal'ia Goncharova and the *kamennye baby* helped me to realize what the literary side of the story could involve—Irina Shevelenko, Jon Stone, Jane Taubman, and Jane Tylus. Serguei Oushakine, Marina Mogilner, and Ilya Kukulin commented on an early version of chapter six that transformed and sharpened the claims of that chapter. And throughout, Robert Hughes and Olga Matich read, reread, and improved many of these chapters.

My colleagues in the Department of Russian and Slavic Studies at New York University deserve a special word of thanks. The department has been a great place to teach these past seven years, and I thank Eliot Borenstein, Jane Burbank, Yanni Kotsonis, and, in particular, Anne Lounsbery, for her encouragement on an early version of the manuscript, and Ilya Kliger, the best office neighbor and interlocutor on deep time, among much else.

All the mistakes that remain are mine.

I am grateful to Jane Tylus and the Humanities Initiative, NYU (2008-09), for a year spent in the urban pastoral Jane creates there every year, during which I reconceived the book. And to Terry Martin and Stephanie Sandler, co-directors of the Seminar on Eurasian Subjectivities (2013-14), I am especially indebted for a Senior Fellowship at the Davis Center for Russian and Eurasian Studies, Harvard University, which allowed me to complete the revisions of the manuscript. I thank Joy Connolly, Dean for the Humanities at NYU, for supporting that leave.

Portions of the book have benefitted from audiences at various institutions. I thank for their invitations and their comments the departments and audiences at: Amherst College; the Davis Center for Russian and Eurasian Studies; the Five College Slavic Seminar; the New Scholars Series at Reed College; the NEH Seminar on Russian Modernism at the New York Public Library; the NYU Slavic Colloquium; the Poetics Workshop and Slavic Department of the University of Chicago; the Slavic Colloquium at Stanford University; the Slavic Seminar and the Slavic Department of Columbia University; and the Slavic departments at the University of California, Berkeley, the University of Wisconsin-Madison, the University of Oregon, Eugene, and Yale University.

Along with these many debts, I thank friends and family who've provided support and distraction in tandem and in equal measure these past several years: Michael Allan; David Alsdorf; Kaveh Askari; Sylvan Brackett; Caroline Byfield; Bryan Cook; Judy Goldstein; Sarah Hamill; Louise Hornby; Joost Keizer; John Kunichika; Chris Lakey; Amnon Lev; Heather Lord; Anne Lorraine-Bujon; Grant, Lexi, and Jasper Mainland; Jeremy Melius; Kelly Miyata; Ricardo Montez; Maya Portner; Paull Randt; Sally and Moxie Rudoy; Sam Schaeffer; Eva Schuss; Mariko Silver; Lizbet Simmons; Meghan Sutherland; Lisa Wakamiya; Amanda Walling; Jenny Wapner; Patrick Weil; and Boris and Benjamin Wolfson.

Then, again, there's Boris Maslov and Devin Fore to thank for their many acts of friendship and faith. And, lastly, I thank my parents, Kenneth and Janice Kunichika, whose support has sustained me throughout the writing of this book.

The publication of *"Our Native Antiquity"* was enabled by the financial support of the Humanities Initiative at NYU; The Jordan Center for the Advanced Study of Russia, NYU; and the Office of the Dean of the Humanities, NYU. An earlier version of chapter six appeared as "'The Scythians Were Here': On Nomadic Archaeology, Modernist Form, and Early Soviet Modernity," *Ab Imperio* 2 (2012): 229-57.

I would like to note my conceptual debts, as acknowledged in the subtitle of my book, to Leonard Barkan's *Unearthing the Past: Archaeology and Aesthetics in the Making of Renaissance Culture* (New Haven, CT: Yale University Press, 1999), which helped me formulate the relations between art, literature, and archaeology examined in the pages to come.

Note on Translation and Transliteration

Russian names, places, and titles are transliterated according to the Library of Congress simplified system, which I have modified for surnames of familiar authors (e.g., Leo Tolstoy, Osip Mandelstam, Fyodor Dostoevsky). For certain names, I have used an established variant (e.g., Nicholas Roerich instead of Nikolai Rerikh; Alexandre Benois instead of Aleksandr Benua). In the scholarly apparatus, however, I follow the LOC transliteration system for all citations to authors and titles. Citations in the text and in the apparatus preserve the transliteration systems used by other authors. For the sake of space, the majority of citations from Russian are given only in translation, except in the cases of poetic texts and specific passages from prose works. Unless otherwise indicated, all translations are mine. As I explain in greater detail in chapters one and two, I have opted to transliterate the words *baba* or *baby* (as in *kamennaia baba* and *kamennye baby*) in the majority of cases where the term appears, except when the statue in question is clearly gendered feminine, in which case it is translated as "stone woman" or "stone women." I also follow the source text in deciding when to capitalize the word. Throughout, "kurgan" has been preserved.

Introduction

You drive on for an hour, and another . . . Along the way you come across a silent old man-*kurgan* or stone *baba*, erected God knows when and by whom; a night bird flies noiselessly above the earth, and little by little the legends of the steppe, the tales of travelers you've met, the stories told by nannies from the steppe, everything you've managed to see and to appreciate in your soul come to mind. And then in the chirring of insects, in the suspicious figures and kurgans, in the deep sky, in the moonlight, in the flight of the night bird, in all that you see and hear, the exultation of beauty, youth, the blossoming of vigor, and the passionate thirst for life begin to be apparent: the soul responds to the call of the beautiful, austere native land, and one longs to fly over the steppes with the night bird. And in the exultation of beauty, in the excess of happiness, you feel yearning and anguish, as though the steppe realizes she is alone, that her wealth and inspiration are being wasted on the world, praised in song by no one, necessary to no one; and through the joyful clamor you hear her anguished, hopeless call: Singer, a Singer!

—Anton Chekhov,
"The Steppe" ("Step'"), 1888[1]

It was after I read this passage in Anton Chekhov's "The Steppe" that this book found its subject. What are these objects that loom

---

[1]   Anton Chekhov, "Step'," *Polnoe sobranie sochinenii i pisem v tridtsati tomakh* (Moscow: Nauka, 1974), 7:46. For my translation, I have drawn several phrases from the classic translation by Constance Garnett. Anton Chekhov, "The Steppe" (1888), in *Anton Chekhov: Early Short Stories, 1883-1888*, ed. Shelby Foote, trans. Constance Garnett (New York: Modern Library, 1999), 541-42.

before the narrator—this "old man-*kurgan*" and this "stone *baba*" erected "God knows when and by whom"? The narrator perceives the objects—initially inscrutable—as artifacts of unknown origin, and thus of unknown age, but they quickly awaken memories of stories and storytellers, of legends and tales told to him by nannies from the steppe and passing travelers. And then, as the narrator turns from the "suspicious figures" of the statuary and the kurgan (the Russian word of Turkic origin for a burial mound) and toward the steppe itself, other questions arise: What of that vast, austere field, "unsung and unwanted," denigrated in Russian cultural history as a boundless monotony of unyielding flat space? Had the steppe's "riches," such as they were, found their singer?

These questions animate the central aim of this book, which is to trace how these artifacts and this vast and often maligned space became the quintessential objects and the locus for the Russian modernist creation of an indigenous antiquity, or, as it was called at the time, *nasha rodnaia starina—our native antiquity*. Each chapter focuses on exemplary episodes in which the statuary known in Russian as *kamennaia baba*, (alternatively translated in the coming pages as "stone *baba*," "stone woman," or "stone statuary") and the kurgan became objects of sustained aesthetic and archaeological attention. To that end, the chapters narrate how both were transformed into literary and artistic artifacts of Russian modernism, in line with the period's preoccupation with archaeology, and, in particular, the archaeology of the Eurasian steppe.

While there are precedents for the modernist appropriation of these artifacts—indeed, one great predecessor we have just seen is Chekhov—it was roughly in the first three decades of the twentieth century that the idea of an indigenous antiquity reached its greatest florescence, conceptual coherence, and polemical force. It was during this period that an indigenous antiquity came to constitute a nexus of cultural, political, and aesthetic values, formal features, and behaviors systematically elaborated within modernist artistic and literary practice.

The statuary and the kurgan were the remarkable, if embattled, sources of that native antiquity. Some formidable obstacles stood in the way of their promotion to the cultural stature of art, among the most prominent being their uncertain provenance. Along with the frequent denigration of their formal features, the questions of who made the statuary and who buried whom in the kurgans had generated endless speculation from at least the end of the eighteenth century.[2] But this ambiguity of origins and cultural affiliations became fertile ground for the imagination. And each imaginative act brought to bear upon these artifacts made their transvaluation into antiquities all the more polemical. This meant, in turn, that they also served as arenas for the contention over literary tradition, aesthetic values, cultural identities, and ideologies.

The Russian modernist creation of a native antiquity mounted, then, a significant challenge to the old cultural verities by opposing them with a new conception of Russian identity, landscape, and arts and letters. What enabled the modernists to accomplish this task were the shifting aesthetic and cultural values of modernism itself. To deem these artifacts aesthetically or culturally valuable, and to designate their makers as precursors to the modernists' own experience of modernity or as idealized archaic artists, revealed Russian modernism's departures from such things as the normative concepts of neoclassical beauty or civilizational ideals rooted in settled communities like cities. This antiquity, furthermore, challenged prevailing attitudes and prejudices about Russia's absent or dubious cultural patrimony, which had kept steppe artifacts and the steppe itself—that grandest of all margins—languishing as mere curiosities or as testaments to a cultural void, obscured not only by sediment but by cultural ideologies and poetic commonplaces. In the modernist imaginary, the discovery and new valuation of these artifacts meant that the steppe could no longer be deemed a continent-ocean devoid of culture, depth, and, in some accounts,

---

[2] General histories of archaeology in Russia that have been of particular value to the pages to come include: G. A. Fedorov-Davydov, *Kurgany, idoly, monety* (Moscow: Nauka, 1968); A. A. Formozov, *Ocherki po istorii russkoi arkheologii* (Moscow: Izd-vo Akademii Nauk SSSR, 1961); G. S. Lebedev, *Istoriia otechestvennoi arkheologii, 1700-1917 gg.* (St. Petersburg: Izd-vo S.-Peterburgskogo universiteta, 1992); I. V. Tunkina, *Russkaia nauka o klassicheskikh drevnostiakh iuga Rossii (XVIII—seredina XIX v.)* (St. Petersburg: Nauka, 2002). Studies on specific topics or types of archaeology are cited in subsequent chapters.

time itself. Instead, modernists found in this space the site of their antiquity. Russian history and culture, for them, was forged out of, and sometimes ripped apart by, this conjunction of the deep past and the present within the steppe. The episodes examined in the pages to come mark a turning inward into the vast space of Eurasia to find "riches" in the form of kurgans, stone *babas*, Scythian artifacts, and Eurasian necropolises. It was a turning inward that broadened the sources relevant to Russian modernist arts and letters and the very idea of Russian cultural identity.

i. Archaic Mirrors

The propensity of modernists to find in archaeology not only an expanded world of objects but also models of temporality, of the psyche, and aesthetics prevailed throughout the early twentieth century on an international scale.[3] The Russian modernist period itself furnishes us with its own vivid account of the modernist encounter with archaeology by the poet and art critic Maksimilian Voloshin. In his essay "Archaism in Russian Painting (Roerich, Bogaevskii, Bakst)," published in the leading journal *Apollon* in 1909,[4] Voloshin locates the Russian turn toward the archaic within a broader European tendency that emerged in response to new archaeological discoveries:

> The dream of the archaic is the last and most cherished dream of the art of our time, which looked into all historical epochs with such inquisitiveness, searching within them for what was rare, heady, and secretly similar to it. . . . Like a multifaceted mirror, artists and poets spun world history, in order to see in each facet a fragment of their own particular face. The love for the archaic

---

[3]   For an overview of archaeology's influence on various disciplines, see Julian Thomas, *Archaeology and Modernity* (London: Routledge, 2004).

[4]   Maksimilian Voloshin, "Arkhaizm v russkoi zhivopisi (Rerikh, Bogaevskii, Bakst)," *Apollon*, no. 1 (1909): 43-53; reprinted in *Liki tvorchestva* (Leningrad: Nauka, 1988), 274-81. All future citations will be to the latter edition and given in the text. For more on the concept of "archaism" in Russian modernism, see Irina Shevelenko, "Modernizm kak arkhaizm: Natsionalizm, russkii stil' i arkhaiziruiushchaia estetika v russkom modernizme," *Wiener Slawistischer Almanach* 56 (2005): 141-83.

was created by the discoveries of archaeological excavations at
the end of the nineteenth century. (275)

What Voloshin refers to here as the "dream" or "love" for the archaic
finds an echo in what the American critic Guy Davenport would
describe, some sixty years later, as the "passion for the archaic,"
which he observed in a range of modernists, from James Joyce and
Hilda Doolittle, to Vladimir Tatlin and Velimir Khlebnikov.[5] That
passion, Voloshin keenly observes, was also a passion for oneself.
His striking metaphor of a "multifaceted mirror" discloses how
the present discerns in the past that which is "secretly similar" to
it.[6] Encounters with archaic artifacts transform them into archaic
mirrors. Categories such as discovery and rarity are significant
here, but so, too, are those of similarity and necessity; the latter
categories highlight how archaeological artifacts find their value
not from what they introduce into the present, but rather from what
they validate and confirm.[7] As such, some questions that we can

---

[5]   Guy Davenport, "The Symbol of the Archaic" (1974), in *The Geography of the Imagination: Forty Essays* (Boston: David R. Godine, 1997), 24.

[6]   Voloshin's insistence on "similarity" and the transformation of artifacts into "multifaceted mirrors," anticipates several recent scholarly accounts of what was a pan-European concern. See, for example, Cathy Gere, *Knossos and the Prophets of Modernism* (Chicago: University of Chicago Press, 2009); Theodore Ziolkowski, *Minos and the Moderns: Cretan Myth in Twentieth-Century Literature and Art* (Oxford: Oxford University Press, 2008).

[7]   The art historian William Rubin, for instance, has challenged the standard interpretation of the role that "discovery" played in accounts of the aesthetic tendency known as primitivism in Western European art: "the changes in modern art at issue were already under way when vanguard artists first became aware of tribal art. In fact, they became interested in and began to collect primitive objects only because their own explorations had suddenly made such objects relevant to their work. At the outset, then, the interest in tribal sculpture constituted an elective affinity. . . . The 'discovery' of African art, one must conclude, took place when, in terms of contemporary developments, it was needed." William Rubin, "Modern Primitivism: An Introduction," in *"Primitivism" in 20th Century Art: Affinity of the Tribal and the Modern*, ed. William Rubin, exhibition catalogue, 2 vols. (New York: Museum of Modern Art, 1984), 10-11. The concept of "affinity" has, in turn, been critiqued on two fronts: critical and political. In art-critical terms, it fails to recognize both morphological and structural influences, which highlight "the principle of semiological arbitrariness and, in consequence, the nonsubstantial character of the sign" rather than mere formal resemblance (Yve-Alain Bois, "Kahnweiler's Lesson," in *Painting as Model* [Cambridge, MA: October Books, 1990], 71-75; and for the political critique of "affinity,"

ask in the coming pages, to follow Voloshin's lead, are: What of the present were these artifacts seen to reflect? What did these *archaic mirrors* bring with them?

Voloshin goes on to reveal several other reasons why archaeological discoveries made such an impact on the modernist imagination, while also pointing to a way that we can distinguish the efforts to recuperate a native antiquity from this pan-European concern. On one level, he observes how archaeological discoveries transform what was once thought of as myth into palpable matter:

> It seems that the twentieth century, the first year of which coincided with the beginning of Evans's excavations on Crete, is fated to transgress the last borders of our isolated circle of history; to glance already into the other side of the archaic night; to see the crimson sunset of Atlantis. Since the very minute when the eye of a European saw on the wall of the palace of Knossos the representation of the Minoan king in the form of a red-skinned man, with a crown of feathers, reminiscent of the headdress of the North American Indian, the first connection between a secret legend and historical authenticity was established; and the first tangible evidence of the existence of Atlantis was gripped in our hands. (275-76)

Voloshin here anticipates what, in Hugh Kenner's words, members of this generation experienced as "a growing awareness that since about 1870 men had held in their hands the actual objects Homer's sounding words name."[8] This sense of the thrill generated by archaeology was confirmed by Voloshin: "When the heroic dream of thirty centuries, Troy, became suddenly graspable and material thanks to the excavations at Hissarlik; when the tombs of the Mycenaean kings were opened, and we could palpate the remains of Aeschylus's heroes, and insert our fingers [like those] of Doubting Thomas into the wounds of Agamemnon—it was

---

see James Clifford, "Histories of the Tribal and the Modern," in *The Predicament of Culture: Twentieth-Century Ethnography, Literature, and Art* (Cambridge, MA: Harvard University Press, 1988), 189-214.

8   Hugh Kenner, *The Pound Era* (Berkeley and Los Angeles: University of California Press, 1971), 29.

then that something new opened up in our souls" (275). Part of this haptic thrill was the corroboration of myth by matter, and this thrill can be found in the work of a range of writers throughout the twentieth century. As Seamus Heaney, for example, remarked on the pertinence of the discoveries at the burial mounds of Sutton Hoo: "there is something terrifically corroborating about seeing at Sutton Hoo the actual things mentioned in [*Beowulf*]."[9]

One central dilemma Russian modernist culture faced as it sought to recuperate a "native antiquity," however, was the putative absence of "sounding words" for the objects it valorized. The stone statuary and the kurgans were objects that allegedly corroborated nothing and were corroborated by nothing. In this sense, what the modernists and their precursors do is to provide, at last, the "sounding words" for objects, a process that made them reflect the concerns of the present. To understand which particular cultural ideology may have structured a given work's account of these artifacts, or which discursive framework gave shape to the perceptions of a given writer or artist, we need to reconstitute the network of associations in which the artifact operated and the discourses for which they served as metonyms. But they were only partial mirrors: while writers alleged that these objects lacked a literary past—indeed, that is also a commonplace—these objects came in tow with both a wealth of speculation by archaeologists, ethnographers, and laymen and -women, and with a literary past this book also excavates. Time and again throughout this book, these discourses will refer us to a "native antiquity" and to a range of other "isms" and archaic and cultural "mirrors": nomadism and Scythianism will be among the most prominent, but so, too, will be period discourses on primitivism and archaism. What gives even more force to the modernist reclamation project, however, was not only the projection of contemporary concerns into the deep past, but also the polemical place of antiquity in Russian modernism specifically, and Russian culture generally.

---

9   Jon Pratty, "Sutton Hoo Centre Opened by Seamus Heaney," http://www.culture24.org.uk/history+%26+heritage/time/art12007, accessed December 1, 2010. See also Sam Newton, *The Origins of Beowulf and the Pre-Viking Kingdom of East Anglia* (Cambridge: D. S. Brewer, 1993).

ii. Elective Antiquities

> This is a book about a group of objects that actually
> *did* emerge from the ground into the light of day.
> The objects, as it happens, are not new, but they are
> radical, which is to say that they appear literally
> and figuratively at the root level of the civilization
> that unearths them and provide a fundamental
> alternative that must be encountered.
>
> —*Leonard Barkan,*
> *Unearthing the Past:*
> *Archaeology and Aesthetics*
> *in the Making of Renaissance*
> *Culture*

When Walter Benjamin observed that, "among all the relations
into which modernity enters, its relation to antiquity is critical,"[10]
he elevated the kinds of encounters with the archaeological past
examined in the chapters to come to a central feature of modernity.
But from the perspective of Russian modernity (as a term that names
the experience of the post-Petrine period) and Russian modernism
(as an overarching category for literary and artistic tendencies from
around 1890 to 1930), one question that immediately arises is: *Which*
antiquity? For Russian modernists, there were myriad antiquities of
different provenance and varying degrees of prestige from which
to choose. Some found their models in Greece or Rome, others in
Byzantium, still others in Egypt or in pre-Petrine Rus'. Indeed, one
way to distinguish these camps, with their different aesthetic values
and aspirations, is to identify the elective antiquity, as it were, to
which they laid claim and whose legacy they claimed as their
heritage.

A native antiquity was but one of the elective antiquities
conjured by Russian modernists. The tally of examples is quite
vast: Andrei Bely and the Argonauts; Viacheslav Ivanov's vision
of ancient Greece and Rome; Osip Mandelstam's "Hellenism";

---

10   Walter Benjamin, *The Arcades Project*, trans. Rolf Tiedemann (Cambridge, MA: Belknap Press,
      1999), 236.

Alexandrian Egypt for Mikhail Kuzmin; the varieties of Scythianism espoused by Ivanov-Razumnik, Velimir Khlebnikov, and
Aleksandr Blok.[11] What all these choices arguably share is that any
affiliation carried along with it a distinct cultural ideology and
a certain amount of polemical charge. To select any given past was no
less difficult for the "Alexandrian" Kuzmin than it was, say, for the
"Eurasian" Khlebnikov (a major figure in the following chapters);
to do so entailed aligning Russia with a particular mythological or
cultural matrix, and thereby recapitulating the accursed questions
of Russian cultural identity. The modernists variously challenged
Westernizers and Slavophiles; the pagan, the Orthodox, and the
secular; the foreign and the indigenous; and (especially after the
Revolution) they positioned themselves between the retrospective
impulse to construct a past and the prospective visions of a utopian,
technologically oriented future.

To better appreciate what invigorated the Russian modernists'
interest in antiquity in general, and what led them to valorize
one particular antiquity over another, we could single out some
of the most agonized views of Russian culture. As one cultural
mythology powerfully asserts, the reforms of Peter the Great in
the early eighteenth century forced Russia into a radical present,
with no past and no future, and severed the country's ties with its
own autochthonous traditions by forcibly adopting cultural models
borrowed from Europe. We might recall how this view, codified
by Petr Chaadaev in his *Philosophical Letters* (1829-30) and his later
"Apologia of a Madman" ("Apologie d'un Fou," 1837), took aim at

---

[11]   See, for example, Judith Kalb, *Russia's Rome: Imperial Visions, Messianic Dreams, 1890-1940*
(Madison: University of Wisconsin Press, 2008); Alexander Lavrov, "Andrei Bely and the Argonauts'
Mythmaking," in *Creating Life: The Aesthetic Utopia of Russian Modernism*, ed. Irina Paperno and
Joan Delaney Grossman (Stanford, CA: Stanford University Press, 1994), 83-121; L.G. Panova,
Russkii Egipet: Aleksandriiskaia poetika Mikhaila Kuzmina (Moscow: Vodolei, 2006); Michael
Wachtel, *Russian Symbolism and Literary Tradition: Goethe, Novalis, and the Poetics of Vyacheslav
Ivanov* (Madison: University of Wisconsin Press, 1994); Peg Weiss, *Kandinsky and Old Russia:
The Artist as Ethnographer and Shaman* (New Haven, CT: Yale University Press, 1995). See also
the essays in Boris Gasparov, Robert P. Hughes, and Irina Paperno, eds., *Cultural Mythologies
of Russian Modernism: From the Golden Age to the Silver Age* (Berkeley and Los Angeles:
University of California Press, 1992). The bibliography on Scythianism can be found in
chapter eight.

Russian history, at its geography—a barren land to match Russia's barren soul—and at its archaeology:

> From time to time *in their diverse excavations, our fanatic Slavicists will, of course, still be able to exhume curios for our museums*, for our libraries, but one may doubt if out of the depths of our historical soil they can ever draw something to fill up the emptiness in our souls, something to condense the vacuity in our minds.[12] (Italics mine.)

When the intellectual historian Mikhail Gershenzon republished these lines in his study of Chaadaev in 1908, he perhaps enabled them to speak again with a special, immediate force to the generation of writers and artists central to this study. In his summary of Chaadaev's views, Gershenzon added a few choice metaphors of his own. "Such is our present," he writes:

> It is not surprising that our past is like a desert. Everything within it is mute; colorless; cheerless; no enchanting remembrances, no poetic images, no eloquent fragments (*krasnorechivykh oblomkov*), no monuments inspiring reverence. For all our long lives we have not bequeathed a single idea to humanity; we only perverted ideas, borrowing them from others. And for us, the past is dead. Between it and our present there is not a single connection; what ceases to be present, suddenly falls away from us, disappearing without a trace.[13]

"No eloquent fragments" could have been an alternate—if perhaps inauspicious—title for this book. The Russian land provides no real traces, nor are any traces inscribed in the Russian spirit. The central figures of *"Our Native Antiquity"* might be seen as the spiritual heirs of the *Slavons fanatiques* whom Chaadaev dismisses, inasmuch as they likewise express a deep attraction toward the excavations (which they also sometimes conducted) of these "curios" (*curiosités*)—

---

12   Peter Chaadaev, "The Apologia of a Madman," in *The Major Works of Peter Chaadaev*, trans. Raymond T. McNally (Notre Dame, IN: University of Notre Dame Press, 1969), 206.

13   M. O. Gershenzon, *P. Ia. Chaadaev: Zhizn' i myshlenie* (1908; reprint, The Hague: Mouton, 1968), 84.

or, as the Russian translation of Chaadaev had it, *dikovinki*—that they transvalued and promoted to the cultural stature of art.

What distinguished the Russian modernists from the previous efforts of "fanatic" Slavophiles and any previous enthusiasts of appropriation was their embrace of objects from that alleged void of Eurasia—which meant nothing less than an alignment of Russian culture with figures who were *not* of Slavic origin, with the steppe nomads from the remote and recent past.[14] What, in essence, this means for the strain of Russian modernism examined in this book is that it sought to discover and illuminate new sites in the cultural topography of the Russian Empire in an effort to recast a cultural identity and patrimony. It was out of the disparaged, cheerless stuff they found throughout that vast space that they created a native antiquity, and through it, a bridge over the yawning gap between the past, present, and, in some cases, the future.

But there was another prevailing view, based on a cultural paradigm of rupture, which has served to make the very idea of antiquity not just untenable but effectively unnecessary for the realization of Russia's cultural aspirations. On the one hand, this paradigm of rupture construes the Christianization of Rus' in 988, the imposition of the Tatar-Mongol yoke in the fourteenth century, the Petrine reforms in the early eighteenth century, and the Russian Revolution of 1917, as a series of breaks that consigned the past to oblivion. Hence, Russian culture is understood as perpetually subject to upheaval and violent reorientation, and thus the very idea of recuperating a past is not only deemed impossible,[15] but also radically incoherent since one can never be sure that one particular past isn't just another cultural import or the aftermath of

---

14   This is a significant contrast with the previous generation of Slavophiles, who, as David Schimmelpenninck van der Oye argues, "were opposed to Western Modernity, but they did not suggest that Russia was Asian. What they championed instead was Orthodox, Slavic Europe rather than its Romano-German variant" (*Russian Orientalism: Asia in the Russian Mind from Peter the Great to the Emigration* [New Haven, CT: Yale University Press, 2010], 225).

15   The locus classicus consolidating this view in twentieth-century criticism is Boris Uspensky and Yuri Lotman's "Binary Models in the Dynamics of Russian Culture," in *The Semiotics of Russian Cultural History*, trans. Alice Stone Nakhimovsky (Ithaca, NY: Cornell University Press, 1985).

a previous rupture. Indeed, when Chaadaev goes on to argue that Russia's proverbial poverty (cultural, historical, and geographical) forms the very conditions for its future achievement, even this alteration of his worldview, which conjoins the story of privation to that of Russian messianism, still dismisses the possibility of a meaningful deep past, and a fortiori of a space in which meaningful fragments from that deep past could be found.

Thus, on the other hand, as David Bethea has observed, rupture can also be conjoined to eschatological release, a prospect that has led figures as diverse as the religious thinker Nikolai Berdiaev and the semiotician Yuri Lotman to share the view of "the relentlessly eschatological shape of those cultural models (of history, of life, and of the two as presented in literature) that have been the focus of Russia's popular and literary imagination for centuries."[16] Or, as Berdiaev argued in his *Russian Idea (Russkaia ideia)*: "Russians are either apocalypticists or nihilists. Russia is an apocalyptic revolt against antiquity. . . . This means that the Russian people, according to their metaphysical nature and calling in the world, are a people of the end."[17] The very discourse of antiquity—however much it ramified into distinct and competing tendencies—operates against this model of apocalypse and eschatology by locating in the deep past sources of value for the formation of a Russian cultural identity. This book, in essence, tracks how it was archaeology, not eschatology—and thus the beginnings, rather than ends of history and of culture—that formed a no less powerful source of attraction for particular modernist camps.

In this light, we might turn to one of the painters whom Voloshin included in his range of figures representing the various retrospective tendencies we find throughout the period: Nicholas Roerich. Roerich was well positioned to indicate clearly that choosing a particular past was a central question facing artists and writers, having evinced a broad interest in a multiplicity of

---

[16] David M. Bethea, *The Shape of Apocalypse in Modern Russian Fiction* (Princeton, NJ: Princeton University Press, 1989), 12.

[17] Nikolai Berdiaev, *Russkaia ideia* (Paris: YMCA Press: 1946), 195, as cited in ibid.

pasts, from the Varangians onward, leading up to his collaboration with Igor Stravinsky on the premier work of Russian modernist primitivism, *The Rite of Spring* (*Le Sacre du printemps*, 1913). In 1908, in his essay "Joy in Art" ("Radost' iskusstvu"), he furnished one of the central formulations of the Russian modernist retrospectivist impulse and its desire to elect or invent one antiquity over another:

> Whither will we turn? Toward a new reinterpretation of classicism? Or will we descend into antique sources? Or will we delve into the depths of primitivism? Or will our art find the new, bright path of "neo-nationalism," covered by the sacred grasses of India, sturdy with Finnish charms? For now, I will not pause on what is perhaps a mysterious word: "neo-nationalism." It is necessary, if still early, to write a manifesto for this word. From whence will the joy of the future art come—this question ceaselessly agitates all of us? The joy in art, about which we have forgotten, is coming. In past searches, we feel the traces of this joy.[18]

As we see time and again, various modernist tendencies were staking their claim to these particular pasts. Indeed, the standard division of Russian modernist tendencies into "futurists" and "retrospectivists" is often, in Katerina Clark's strong terms, "bogus."[19] Even the modernist avant-garde, which we typically understand as profoundly antagonistic toward the past—reaching its apotheosis in the Russian Futurist desire to pitch Pushkin, Dostoevsky, and Tolstoy overboard from "the steamship of modernity"—reveals a simultaneous desire to repudiate the Russian Golden Age while valorizing the ages of stone and bronze.

That the past, "primitive" or not, proved to play such a role, further affirms the sense that such distinctions as the one between the "futurists" and "retrospectivists" collapse as the so-called "futurist" camps compete with previous generations precisely over who unleashed the full potential of a particular valorized

---

18 Nikolai Rerikh, "Radost' iskusstvu," in A. Mantel, *N. Rerikh* (Kazan: Izd-vo knig po iskusstvu, 1912), 15.

19 Katerina Clark, "The Avant-Garde and the Retrospectivists," in *Laboratory of Dreams: The Russian Avant-Garde and Cultural Experiment*, ed. John Bowlt and Olga Matich (Stanford, CA: Stanford University Press, 1996), 260.

past, and, moreover, how each would use archaeology. The future and the past did not comprise a rigid binary for the majority of Russian modernists, but were separated by a far more porous boundary. What these pages hope to show is that the past, whether deep or near, neoclassical or "primitive," formed an arena in which modernists distinguished themselves one from the other. As such, one basic goal of this book is to reveal both the inner distinctions between the various modes of retrospection manifested within nearly all the Russian modernist tendencies, and the ways in which they formulated their own projects as regards who would be the best inheritor, in spirit and in form, of the past.

***

Archaeological in theme, this book is primarily philological and cultural-historical in practice. Just as the modernist imagination sought to recuperate, for its own literary and artistic purposes, the archaeological remains found in the steppe, what emerges for us is a constellation of texts by which we can understand these artifacts as they were transformed in the modernist imagination. My task here is not to recount a steadfast march of the development and accumulating significance of two artifacts and one space from the early nineteenth century to the first three decades of the twentieth century, or a "tracing-back to the original precursors" to establish the philological history of these objects.[20] Instead, each chapter examines an exemplary case in which the statuary and the kurgan appear—sometimes together—in imaginative works of literature, the visual arts, or cinema. My selection has been guided by two primary concerns: the first is to focus on the interaction between archaeology and aesthetics in the Russian modernist period; and the second is to show how that interaction was elaborated in relation to artifacts found in the Eurasian steppe. The imaginative works examined in these chapters mark the conjuncture of these twin concerns, while also possessing an intensity of artistic attention

---

[20]   Michel Foucault, *Archaeology of Knowledge*, trans. Alan Sheridan (New York: Pantheon, 1972), 4.

and a complexity of thematic concerns and formal features that I believe reward sustained examination. They serve as a lens through which to view parallel intellectual and cultural tendencies within developments in Russian modernism. Hence, each chapter reconstructs a miniature literary and cultural history by focusing on an emblematic text in which a range of discourses, other literary texts, visions of Russian culture and history, and the concept of antiquity are contested.

Chapter One

The Archaeology of the Stone *Babas*
and the Modernist Inheritance

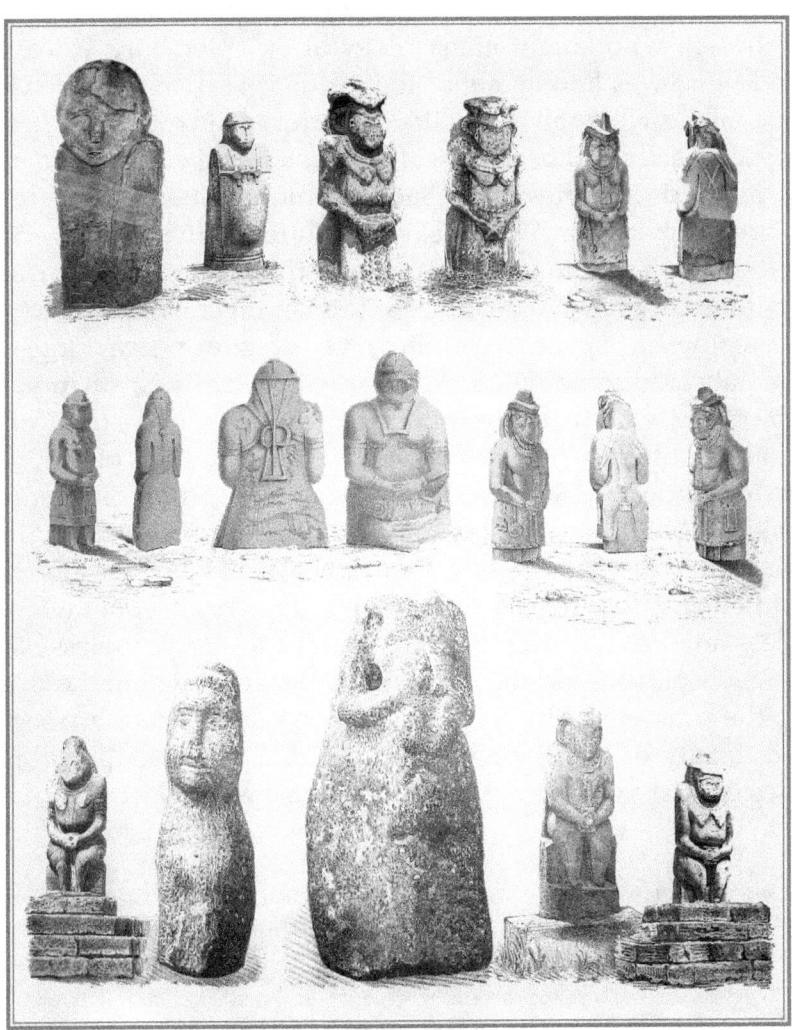

Figure 1.1.
Drawings illustrating Uvarov's "Knowledge about the Stone *Babas*" (1869)

In 1904, at the very dawn of the Russian modernist appropriation of the stone *babas*, the archaeologist Nikolai Veselovskii published an article that revealed both the allure and the problems involved in doing so. The article was entitled "Imaginary Stone *Babas*" ("Mnimye kamennye baby"), which the leading early modernist journal *Zolotoe runo* praised as "very interesting and detailed."[1] Veselovskii, who taught archaeology at St. Petersburg University, traced what was known about the statuary and, as the title of the article made clear, all the wild conjectures surrounding it.[2] Too many statuaries had been classified as "stone *babas*," and too many unsupported "theories" had been promoted about them. It was this predicament that Veselovskii sought to rectify: "It seemed that when the matter of the provenance and interpretation of the 'stone *babas*' arose, there were no limits to human inventiveness."[3]

Veselovskii spent the following decade researching—and ultimately repudiating as fictitious—the theories of previous archaeologists. In 1915, he published an expanded study of the statuary, entitled "The Current State of the Question of the 'Stone *Babas*' or '*Balbals*'" ("Sovremennoe sostoianie voprosa o 'kamennykh babakh' ili 'balbalakh'").[4] He begins with the observation that, "in the realm of Russian archaeology there hardly exists any question more muddled and obscure than that of the 'stone *babas*', about which an endless amount has been written, most of it utterly useless" (412). The whole alluring riddle of the statuary is indicated in these lines: first, the problem of its very designation—*kamennaia baba*; second, the difficulty of identifying what kind of statuary could properly be designated by the term; and, third, the endless speculation as to

---

1   *Zolotoe runo* (1906), no. 7-9: 179-80. Cf. Katherine Lahti, "On Living Statues and Pandora, *Kamennye baby*, and Futurist Aesthetics: The Female Body in *Vladimir Mayakovsky: A Tragedy*," *Russian Review* 58, no. 3 (July 1999): 452.

2   N. Veselovskii, "Mnimye kamennye baby" (offprint, St. Petersburg: Tip. P. P. Soikina, 1905); originally published in *Vestnik arkheologii i istorii* 17 (1904).

3   Ibid., 3.

4   N. I. Veselovksii, "Sovremennoe sostoianie voprosa o 'kamennykh babakh' ili 'balbalakh'," *Zapiski imperatorskogo odesskogo obshchestva istorii i drevnostei* 32 (1915): 412. All further citations will appear in the text.

its meaning and provenance. These were the intertwined dilemmas archaeologists faced as they tried to solve what Veselovskii calls "the unsolved riddle of these antiquities" (412). Intractable puzzles, the "stone *babas*" provoked interpretation and speculation. "Who hasn't touched upon the subject in print?," Veselovskii asks in his 1915 essay. "We can say that every literate person who has had the chance to see them has dwelt on the phenomenon: government officials, teachers, priests, doctors, even bankers, and, finally, women writers have written about them" (413).

The statuary opened up a space of fantasy and, as Veselovskii goes on to observe, started a competition over interpretation in which laymen, archaeologists, and writers participated. Many of them discarded previous hypotheses and gave themselves over to hermeneutic abandon when theorizing the meaning and origin of the statuary:

> Since no one knew anything reliable about these antiquities, anyone could write whatever he pleased; even though these were patent absurdities that found their way into print. In the total absence of any principle of restraint, there was a perfect space for fantasy. Each person resolved the question in his own way, as though intentionally trying to distinguish himself in some fashion from his predecessors by creating his own theory. (413-14)

The statues were mysterious and contested artifacts, inscrutable and, therefore, all the more susceptible to interpretation. They were, in this regard, at once a tabula rasa and a palimpsest; in the absence of reliable information, they were a blank slate upon which anyone could inscribe his or her own theory by wiping away previous theories. But those previous theories never went away, forming instead what one archaeologist referred to as a "labyrinth of conjectures" about the statuary,[5] which later generations would have to navigate, sorting through what was reliable and what could be discarded; or else try to escape by positing a new theory.

---

[5]   Andrei Fabr, "O pamiatnikakh nekotorykh narodov varvarskikh, drevne obitavshikh v nynesh-nem Novorossiiskom krae," *Zapiski imperatorskogo odesskogo obshchestva istorii i drevnostei* 2 (1848): 41.

It is not entirely clear when the statuary acquired the designation *kamennye baby*. In the eighteenth century, *baba* alone could designate a form of stone statuary, though *kamennaia baba* has also been attested.[6] Frequently the statues were also referred to as idols, with terms like *bolvan*, *istukan*, and *kumir*, used in such collocations as "stone idol" (*kamennyi istukan*). It was no less common to refer to the "so-called stone *babas*" (*tak nazyvaemmye kamennye baby*) or to place the term in quotation marks, as Veselovskii does, to indicate the conventional nature of the designation and the uncertainty about its propriety. There was another problem — gender designation. As Veselovskii reminded his audience in 1915, the feminine noun *baba* was a misnomer for the statuary, inasmuch as the idols typically classed as *kamennaia baba* included masculine forms. The terminological problem was due, Veselovskii surmised in 1915, to the Russification of the Turkic word *balbal* into *baba*, the former meaning "ancestor" or "warrior."

This being the case, to translate the term *kamennaia baba* poses no small difficulty for this book, just as it had for previous studies of the statuary. The art historian Alfred Salmony summarized the problem best, writing in 1952, "they are commonly known under the name given to them by the inhabitants of greater Russia who looked at these remnants of antiquity with awe, or turned to them for aid. They called them 'Kamennie Babi,' meaning stone women. Although the term refers definitely to the female sex only, it was and occasionally still is extended to all sculptural representations of humans encountered within and beyond the Eurasian steppes."[7] In the polyglot Salmony's essay, for example, we find them referred to as "Stone Women," *baba* and *babi*, *kamennaya baba*, "strange human sculptures," and "Eurasian cup-holders," and, when he wants to be precise about the statuary's gender, "stone men of the same provenance" (8). (Twenty years earlier, Salmony had also designated

6   *Slovar' russkogo iazyka XVIII veka*, s.v. "baba." The entry cites Zuev's *Putevye ocherki* as the source.

7   Alfred Salmony, "Notes on a 'Kamennaya baba,'" *Artibus Asiae* 13, no. 1/2 (1952): 6. All further references are cited in the text.

them as *la sculpture nègre inconnue de l'Est*, when he published an article on the statuary in the *Cahiers d'art* and associated it with "Negro Sculpture," which we will discuss in greater detail in chapter four.[8])

Various translations into French and German in the late nineteenth and early twentieth centuries also reveal art historians' and archaeologists' struggles with how to translate the term.[9] In German the statuary was referred to as *Mädchenfelsen, Steinbilder, Steinfiguren, Steinplastik, Becherstatuen, Steinmütterchen, Steinbaben*, or in one case, "Kaminza baba, die steinerne Frau."[10] In French, we find translations such as *les stèles à visage*, and a greater propensity to preserve the term *baba*, as in *une baba* or *les statues-babas*[11]; although one French report from the 1870s refers to it as *"kamennaya baba, ou les femmes de pierre"* —mostly, as we will see below, to compare it unfavorably to statues of Venus.

The various possible English translations, then, resolve certain problems and elide others: "Stone Woman" elides the issues of gender ambiguity and the origins of the term *baba*; "stone statuette" or "stone statuary" would resolve the confusion of the statuary's gender, but risks being so generic as to lose contact with the *babas* and the awareness in nineteenth- and twentieth-century texts of the conventionality of the term (e.g., *"tak nazyvaemye kamennye baby"*). The problem of translation is further compounded by the literary texts central to this book, which at times clearly consider the statuary feminine or masculine, and, at others, possibly play on

---

8   Alfred Salmony, "La Sculpture en pierre de l'est de la steppe eurasiatique," *Cahiers d'art* 12, no. 6-7 (1932): 45.

9   Joseph Castagné, "Étude historique et comparative des statues babas des steppes khirgizes et de Russie en général," *Bulletins et mémoires de la société d'anthropologie de Paris* I (1910): 375-407; Wladimir Demetrykiewirz, "Altertümliche steinerne Statuen, sog. 'Baby' Steinmütterchen, Becherstatuen in Asien und Europa und ihr Verhältnis zur slawischen Mythologie," *Bulletin de l'académie des sciences de Cracovie* (1910); August Hartmann, "Becherstatuen in Ostpreussen und die Literatur der Becherstatuen," *Archiv für Anthropologie* 21 (1892-93): 253-303; M. Wegel, "Bildwerke aus altslavischer Zeit," *Archiv für Anthropologie* 21 (1892-93): 41-72.

10   See Hartmann, "Becherstatuen in Ostpreussen," 255 and passim.

11   See Castagné, "Étude historique," 375 and passim.

its ambiguous gender. Some, moreover, refer to it as a proper name: Aleksei Remizov, as we discuss in chapter three, has his *kamennaia baba* say: "I'm no ordinary woman, but the Stone Woman" ("*Ia baba ne prostaia, a Kamennaia Baba*").[12] As the previous pages have indicated, I have opted to refer to them depending on the context as "the Stone *Baba(s),*" "stone *baba*(s)," "Stone Woman," or, for the most part, "the statuary," and to preserve the capitalization usage of the various writers whom I quote.

Just as the designation *kamennaia baba* or *kamennye baby* (plural form) tenaciously endured, so too did various hypotheses about which group made them linger on, despite mounting and contradictory archaeological evidence. Hypotheses ran from the time of the Scythians as they were known through Herodotus to the Sarmatians, Huns, Goths, Polovtsy and Pechenegs, Nogais, and Mongols, and to a lesser degree, to the Finns, ancient Bulgarians, Turks, and Celts. One theory even held that early Slavs were their creators. This diversity of views means that the age of the statuary and the identity of its makers could range over epochs and cultures separated by thousands of miles and several millennia. No less vast a range could be found in the conjectures as to what they represented or symbolized; depending on the people with whom they were affiliated, the statuary could signify anything from the divine to the quotidian: earth goddesses, nymphs, warriors, or important persons had all been suggested as models.

Indeed, as Veselovskii went on to note in the 1915 essay: "the appearance of such theories has not ceased even now that the question of the stone *babas'* provenance has been definitively solved" (414). The solution: the statuary was of Turkic origin (an assertion that has been repeatedly confirmed in contemporary archaeological scholarship[13])—and yet their murky cultural associations kept fueling more provenances obstinately enduring in the conceptions

---

12   Aleksei Remizov, "Kamennaia baba," in *Sobranie sochinenii*, ed. A. M. Gracheva (Moscow: Russkaia kniga, 2000), 2:142-44.

13   Iaroslav R. Dashkevich and Edward Tryjarski, *Kamennye baby prichernomorskikh stepei: Kollektsiia iz Askanii-Nova* (Wrocław: Zakład Narodowy im. Ossolińskich, 1982), 10, citing G. A. Fedorov-Davydov, *Kochevniki Vostochnoi Evropy pod vlast'iu zolotoordynskikh khanov: Arkheologicheskie*

about them (and indeed they continue to do so). Despite all this, the statuary remained culturally marginal in part because of the vastly different ways by which people assessed and valued them. They were less figures of ill repute than of origins so dubious that they could hardly lay claim to the prestige accorded to Johann Winckelmann's fragments in the eighteenth century or Heinrich Schliemann's in the nineteenth. Peasants were known to worship them; landowners to decapitate them; mid-nineteenth century museums collected them; and, in the final decades of the century, landowners were known to make "fake" versions of the statuary to adorn their estates.

Since Veselovskii made this assertion in 1915, right at the mid-point of my examination of the statuary's modernist career, one can hardly fault Russian modernists for thinking that the statuary possessed a specific origin—more often than not, Scythian—or for drawing upon the mythological lore that had accumulated around them.

While Veselovskii's aim was to repudiate the "patent absurdities" surrounding the statuary, the task of this chapter is to examine these "absurdities," conjectured provenances, and interpretations, taking them as significant in their own right. Products of human imagination and inventiveness, they reveal what went into affirming or denying the statuary's archaeological and aesthetic value. Not only do these previous works show the various interpretations asserted and discarded, they also display the methodologies invoked and superannuated in assessing the statuary. Indeed, the growing literature indicates the increase of the statuary's archaeological value—whatever the mystery of its origins—and the concomitant efforts to collect and preserve the statuary, which archaeologists were alarmed to find being destroyed or defaced, either by natural or human causes. These works, then, form the background against which we can compare the products of the Russian modernist imagination, and trace the associations, cultural values, and mythologies the modernists inherited.

pamiatniki (Moscow: Izd-vo Moskovskogo universiteta, 1966), 191; Fedorov-Davydov, "Idoly," in *Kurgany, idoly, monety*, 24-26.

i. "Rough Hewn Statues"

In eighteenth-century travelogues, we find references to stones carved into human form. Some were found atop kurgans, others standing alone in the vast fields of the steppe.[14] In the early 1780s, the academician and biologist Vasilii Zuev, traveling from St. Petersburg to Kherson, described what he termed a *bolvan* (idol) situated atop a "large kurgan," with a "round head like a sphere, upon which a quarter of its face had not been depicted, or had been erased by time" (501). On the left bank of the Abakan, which flows through the so-called Chinese Steppe, the German traveler Johann Falk, writing in 1785, described a statue known to locals as "Kurtask-Tash, or old-woman stone (*staroi-baby kamen'*)," which had "a human head carved into sandstone of a rosy hue." But the locals "had preserved not a single legend about these stones." Another idol (*istukan*), Falk noted, was located on the right bank of the Chernous and named "Kazan-kish-tash, or maiden stone (*devichii kamen'*)" (503). A decade later, the Baltic German traveler Johann Anton Güldenstädt documented an idol, standing on a hill near the banks of the Etak, near where it flows into the Kuma: "The lower half, almost up to the belt, consists of a four-sided column with figures and engravings, the letters being very similar to Greek and Slavic. The upper half presents a male figure, holding a horn in its hands. A multi-sided cross is engraved on the back of its head. Along the left side a saber and arrows are discernible, and along the right an arrow case" (503). Some twenty years later, in 1812, another traveler, Julius von Klaproth, saw one recorded by Güldenstädt, and noted that the male versions of the statuary wore hats that reminded him of those worn by the Chinese (503-4).

These were some of the accounts Count Aleksei Uvarov collected for an article he entitled "Knowledge about the Stone

---

[14] A. S. Uvarov, "Svedeniia o kamennykh babakh," *Trudy pervago arkheologicheskago s"ezda v Moskve* (Moscow: V Sinodal'noi tipografii, 1871), 501-20. All citations are to this edition and are cited in the text. I would like to thank Edward Kasinec, the former chief curator of the Slavic and Baltic Division of the New York Public Library, and the other curators for helping me obtain the images from Uvarov's article.

Babas" ("Svedeniia o kamennykh babakh") and presented to the 1869 Archaeological Congress held in Moscow. Uvarov, the son of the notorious ideologue of nationalism, was the head of the Imperial Russian Archaeological Society, and his various works marked a new stage of archaeological study in Russia.[15] His article surveyed all the extant material available to him on statuary designated "stone *babas*," summarizing some thirty works by writers of Russian, German, and French extraction, from the late eighteenth century onward. These testimonials belonged to various genres: travelogues, a mythology, archaeological articles on the statuary, and shorter dispatches and reports prepared for various archaeological societies. Taken together, they display all the controversies stirred up by the enigma of the statuary from the very beginning of their recorded history in modern Russia. They also indicate that it was an object constituted by a range of academic disciplines, from the anthropological to the archaeological and later the art historical, and those of laypeople.

It is difficult to say whether Uvarov's own views on the matter represent a significant watershed in the onward march of archaeological thought on the statuary and its aesthetic evaluation. On the one hand, his work reveals a greater effort at systematizing previous studies: it collects, sifts through, and organizes earlier reports and illustrations in order to delineate a framework for understanding the development of the statuary over time. On the other hand, later archaeologists—Veselovskii in particular—regarded Uvarov's work and that of others as a catalogue of persistent errors and enduring misconceptions, not reliable "knowledge" at all.

Indeed, the resplendent array of illustrations that accompanied Uvarov's report (figs. 1.1—1.2), drawn from the sources he gathered, reveals the astonishing variety and relative degrees of formal elaboration of the statuary that had been called "stone *babas*." The array makes clear how the term encompassed both masculine and feminine forms, since some examples have clearly marked

---

[15] For more on Uvarov's archaeological work, and the so-called Uvarov period of Russian archaeology, see Lebedev, *Istoriia otechestvennoi arkheologii*, esp. the section "Osnovnye dostizheniia 'Uvarovskogo perioda' (1846-1884)," 130-96.

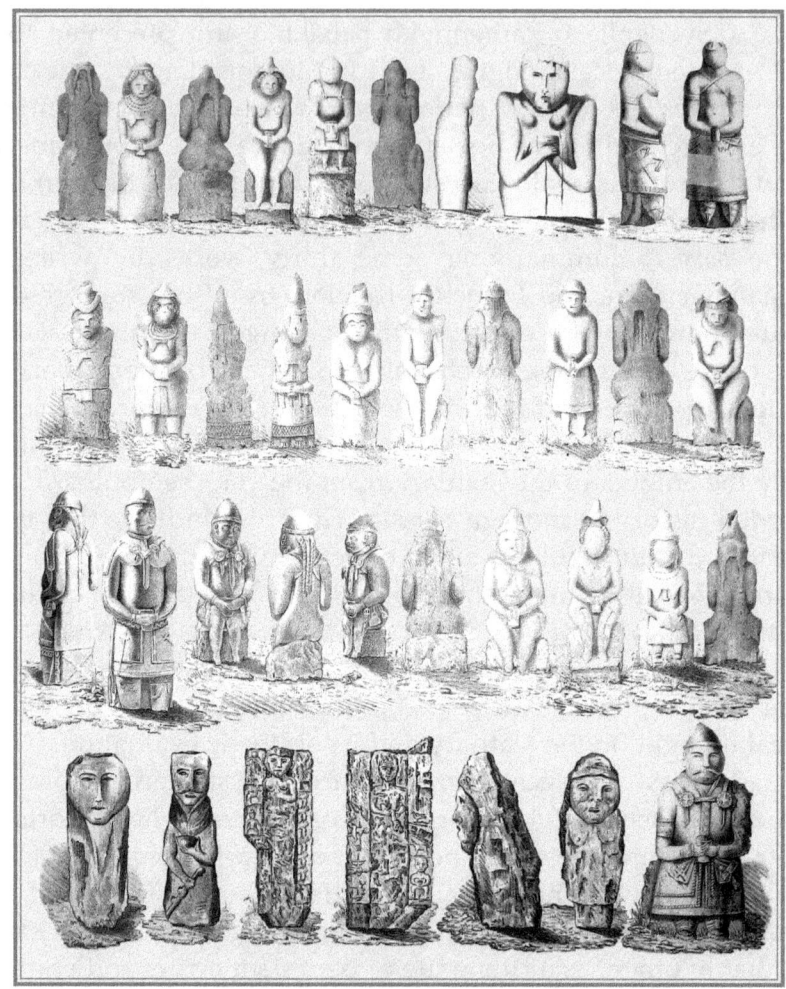

Figure 1.2.
Drawings illustrating Uvarov's "Knowledge about the Stone *Babas*" (1869).

mustaches and male genitalia. As we also see, some of the female
versions have bare breasts, with clearly delineated nipples; others
have earrings; and some have a necklace (*ozherel'e*), either flat or
beaded. Both male and female forms could have some type of head
covering: a cap (*shapka*), kalpak, or helmet (*shlem*), occasionally with
a fillet. The male versions were adorned with a neckband, caftans of

various lengths, and armor (*pantsyr'*), with belt or sash. Both male and female statues ranged in height from one foot to ten feet tall. A constant point of disagreement among archaeologists was the significance of the vessel carried by some of the statues, the reason why Salmony called them "Eurasian cup-holders." One theory that particularly galled Veselovskii was that the vessel was a box for tobacco (*tabakerka*), evidence that presumably supported a notion that the statuary was Mongolian; the author of this conjecture, Veselovskii notes, did not seem to know when tobacco came to the Old World. Veselovskii himself was far more circumspect in interpreting this feature, writing that he thought the vessel could signify the figure's position as a servant (*sluzhebnoe polozhenie*).[16]

One way to approach the "knowledge" produced on the statuary is to compare it with the discovery of Greek and Roman sculpture and their influence on the Renaissance imagination. Leonard Barkan has characterized it as follows: "When Renaissance artists look at works in the tradition of their own Christian civilization, whether religious or secular, they see a complex picture of the origins of their own society. Such art radiates meaning by reflecting the society's past. Excavated works seem by comparison almost nonrepresentational. Their alienness and the fragmentary nature of their exhumation create a new arena for art as independent from clear denotation, artistic conventions, conceptual significance, and sociological function."[17] There are several ways in which responses to the stone *babas* differ from Barkan's portrayal. The statuary was also "nonrepresentational" in the sense that no one could figure out what it meant or who made it. Solving those questions was the primary quest of many of the researchers and writers examined here. And while it clearly belonged to the past—how far back in the past remained unclear—it was uncertain whose past they reflected. Few were ready to assert that the figures "radiated meaning" as Russia's own past: while writers referred to the statuary as "our

---

16   Veselovskii, "Sovremennoe sostoianie," 416.

17   Leonard Barkan, *Unearthing the Past: Archaeology and Aesthetics in the Making of Renaissance Culture* (New Haven, CT: Yale University Press, 1999), xxxii.

stone *babas*," the statuary was property, but not patrimony; and
certainly not "our native antiquity." Still, it could serve as an arena
for exploring Russia's possible relationship to various antique
cultures and to the non-Russian portions of the empire; and it did
uphold archaeology's own role in asserting the presence of valuable
artifacts within the country.

We can thus read both Uvarov's catalogue and other reports
with the goal of identifying the strategies by which researchers
sought to assert the value of the statuary in both archaeological
and artistic terms. Threaded throughout these claims for the
statuary's value were other cultural and aesthetic values: long
deemed monstrous and crude, the formal qualities of the statuary

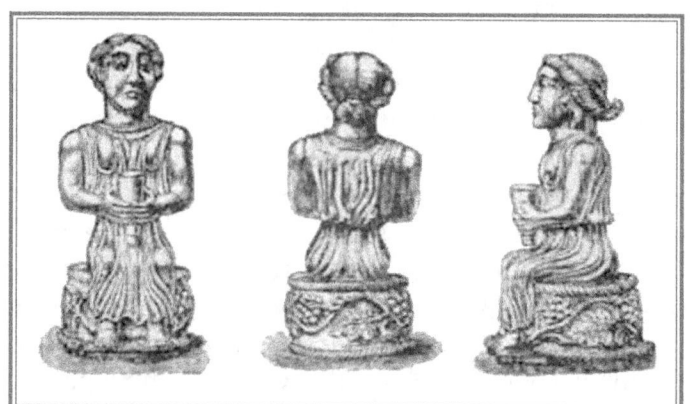

Figure 1.3.

Klad Petrossi,
as reproduced
in Veselovskii's
"Imaginary Stone
Babas" (1905).

were often compared unfavorably with the normative
proportions and aesthetic values enshrined by classicism. The
disproportion of the statuary was, for many, the measure of the
"barbarism" of the statuary and hence of its makers. Aesthetic
assessments were also employed in trying to resolve the puzzle
of the statuary and the question of its origins. To ask in whose
image the statuary was cast was to view it as representational.
And to ask what its various features meant was to interpret
it in representational and symbolic ways. Archaeology and
ethnography constructed their own field of value for the statuary,
and it would take a major shift in aesthetic values for the statuary's

formal qualities and accumulated cultural associations to undergo a wholesale transformation into modernist antiquities.

These strategies involved asserting family resemblances, linking the statuary to artifacts ascribed to other archaic groups, or else insisting upon its autochthonous development. What was often wrong with these assertions, as Veselovskii noted in 1915, was that "since the distant past, man has always been able to make human representations and statues for various purposes" (414). Indeed, in both of his studies, Veselovskii sought to exclude a range of statues he referred to as "Imaginary Stone *Babas*." As one sorted through that mass of "imaginary" statuary, it was just another error (in Veselovskii's view) to try to unify all of them into a line

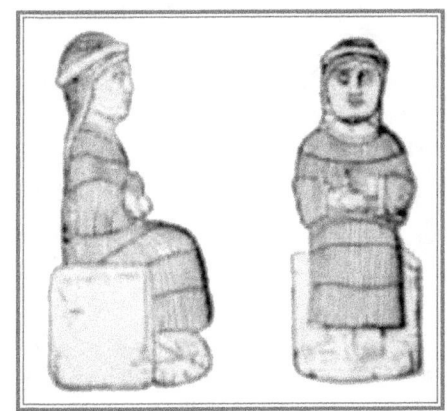

Figure 1.4.

Babylonian Statuette, as reproduced in Veselovskii's "Imaginary Stone *Babas*" (1905).

of development or a branch of an extended family tree. There had been many examples, including the Golden Woman (*Zlata baba*); the Klad Petrocci (fig. 1.3); the Babylonian Statuette (*Vavilonskaia statuetka*) (fig. 1.4); the Czech Statue, "Elizabeth" (*Cheshskaia statuia,* "Elizaveta") (fig. 1.5); Spanish and East Prussian stone statuary; and Caucasian stone statuary (fig. 1.7).

All these various interpretations of the statuary frequently oscillate between seeing the statuary as mimetic (cast in the image of its makers, whoever they might have been) or as allegorical or symbolic (leaving it open to even greater speculation about its significance). Claims for the mimetic understanding of the

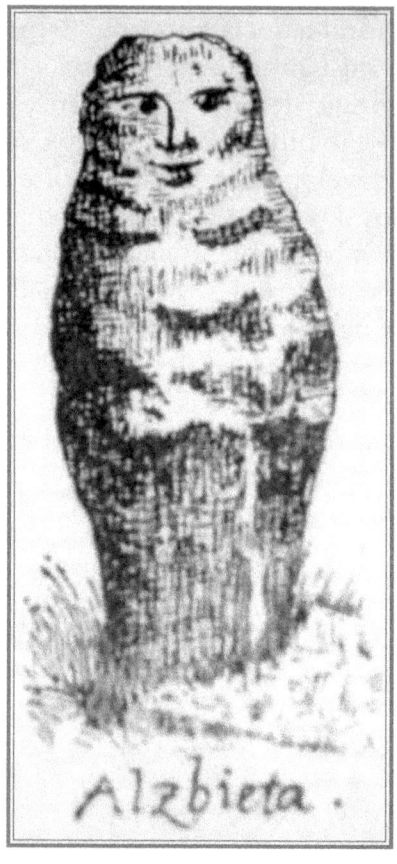

Figure 1.5.

The Czech Statue, Alzbieta,
as reproduced in Veselovskii's "Imaginary
Stone *Babas* (1905)."

statuary are evidenced in *Travels through the Southern Provinces of the Russian Empire, in the Years 1793 and 1794*, written by Peter Simon Pallas, the eighteenth-century polymath and intrepid German scholar living in Russia (fig. 1.6). His *Travels* furnished an account of "those rough hewn statues which are commonly placed on sepulchral hills [i.e., kurgans], in the steppes in the vicinity of the Yegorlyk, Kalaus, and Yei, as well as between the rivers Dniepr and Donetz."[18] Pallas highlights the statues' "broad, flat faces, resembling those of the present Mongolian race," and the "cup, or small pot, similar to that with which the idols of Tybet are represented" (459). Judging by these features, Pallas speculates that the statues were of Mongolian (or possibly even Hunnish) origin.

Pallas based his theory of the statues' origins and the criteria for their aesthetic evaluation on their ability to capture the physical features of their makers:

---

[18] Peter Simon Pallas, *Travels through the Southern Provinces of the Russian Empire, in the Years 1793 and 1794*, trans. Francis Blagdon, 2 vols. (London: T. N. Longman & O. Rees, 1802-3), 1:457. All further references are cited in the text.

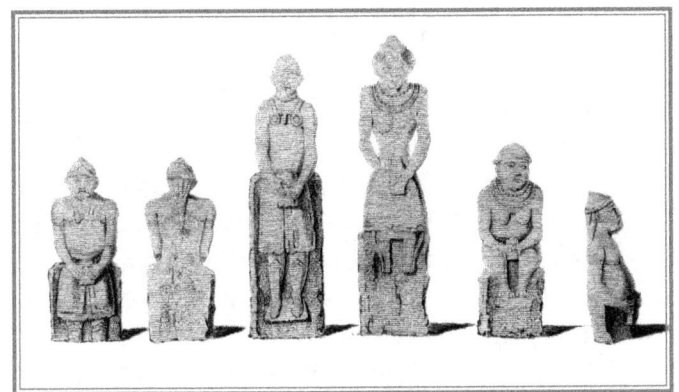

Figure 1.6.

Vignette illustrating Pallas's *Travels* (1802-3).

> It is farther remarkable that all the stone figures in the more eastern countries are hewn in a very rugged and shapeless manner, so that they frequently represent an uncouth mask; but in the plains around the Sea of Azof, especially in those situated to the North of that Sea, there are so many evident proofs of imitative talent, that the character of the face, the limbs and the costume of both sexes, together with their ornaments, may be distinctly traced. As such figures are frequently met with in those regions, it may be reasonably inferred, that the nation by which they were erected, must have lived there for a considerable space of time. (458)

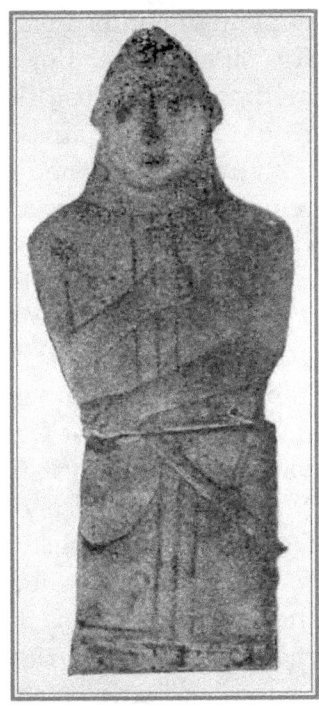

Figure 1.7.

Examples of Caucasian stone statuary, as reproduced in Veselovskii's "Imaginary Stone *Babas*" (1905).

Other archaeologists shared Pallas's mimetic approach, with the value it finds in "imitative talent." The German scholar Julius von Klaproth, for example, in his *Travels in the Caucasus*, ascribed the statuary to the Huns, because, like the *babas*, the Huns had "thick and strong limbs, thick necks and astonishing physiques."[19] This "mistaken opinion," Uvarov later lamented, had survived well into the nineteenth century (511). The Huns, in fact, were one of the groups that Russian archaeologists were utterly convinced could *not* have been the makers of the statuary. The statuary's countenance was thus a site of contestation: one writer argued that the statuary, which he claimed was made by Scythians, looked more like that archaic group rather than the Cumans (Polovtsy), the reason being that Scythians looked more European and Greek to him.[20]

Other accounts seek to move beyond claims that the statuary bears a likeness to its makers. Instead, they argued for an allegorical or symbolic interpretation as the only way to grasp the statuary's full significance. But viewing the statues as allegories of some mythological or historical event immediately ran into a problem that would bedevil many subsequent accounts: the statuary was shorn both from context and from discourse—as Pallas himself had earlier remarked, "the allegorical explanation of [the statuary] cannot be easily conjectured" (458). What researchers could not figure out was what the various symbols adorning the statuary signified.

Among the most fantastical accounts written from this view-point was an article by an amateur archaeologist, Andrei Fabr, "About the Monuments of Several Barbaric Peoples, Formerly Inhabiting Present-Day Novorossiisk" ("O pamiatnikakh neko-torykh narodov varvarskikh, drevne obitavshikh v nyneshnem Novorossiiskom krae"), which appeared in 1848.[21] As a member of the Odessa Society of History and Antiquity, Fabr was chiefly responsible for expanding its collection of the statuary.[22] He sought to refine those interpretations that had deemed the statues mere "sepulchral monuments" (*nadgrobnye pamiatniki*) and to think through the status of the "barbaric" statuary in relation to Greece. He argued that the statuary encompassed a far broader mythological worldview:

---

[19]   Cited in Uvarov, "Svedeniia," 511.

[20]   Ibid., 509.

[21]   Fabr, "O pamiatnikakh," 37.

[22]   Veselovskii, "Sovremennoe sostoianie," 441.

"these figures do not only represent the human form (*obraz chelovecheskii*); they incorporate history and mythology, and, possessing their own particular significance, take their place as sepulchral monuments in the form of allegorical representations."[23] Fabr distinguished between two kinds of monuments: "those that come to us from educated peoples" and "those left to us by uneducated peoples, that is, so-called barbarians." The latter, made by people without science or artistry, are "utterly simple, relating to the basic needs of a man who is still close to nature, and they stand in fields, kurgans, and on sacrificial altars."[24] "Educated peoples" were typified, perhaps unsurprisingly, by the Greeks. Notably, Fabr acknowledged that the Greeks, too, had developed over time, evidenced, in Fabr's view, by the fact that they had once created crude idols: "the primordial statues of Greek gods are monstrosities." However, by virtue of a progressive enlightenment the Greeks had advanced, whereas the works of the barbarians "remain forever in this primordial form."[25]

But why expend any effort to decipher the work of "barbarians"? "One of these kinds of monuments is distinguished by its mysteriousness," Fabr remarked. "I have in mind here our 'stone *babas*' which of course are also the work of barbarians" (38). What really interested Fabr was the possibility that this "barbaric" statuary could actually be linked to Greece. This was the fantastical part of his conjecture and the way to prove it, in his view, was "to search for the origins of our stone *babas*" (38) in Greek mythology. Fabr proceeded to do this by combining a theory of idolatry, the history of the movement of peoples through territories later incorporated into the Russian Empire, and a comparative mythology that equated

---

[23]   Fabr, "O pamiatnikakh," 37.

[24]   Ibid.

[25]   Ibid. All further citations will appear in the text. Fabr's views on the development of Greek art roughly coincide with the views established by Johann Joachim Winckelmann in his *Geschichte der Kunst des Altertums* (1764), which Fabr could have known either in the original or in French translation (1794). I rely here on Alex Potts's discussion of Winckelmann's conception of the development of Greek art in his introduction to Winckelmann, *History of the Art of Antiquity*, trans. Harry Mallgrave (Los Angeles: Getty Research Institute, 2006), 3.

the Greek and Slavic gods; Perun, for example, was the Slavic Zeus.
What Fabr needed for his argument to work was a plausible link
between the Greeks and the peoples who had inhabited the steppe:

> We now know that the idols of the Greeks arrived at our borders;
> that among the Greek idols were forest, lake, and river Nymphs
> (who resemble, in their essence, the portrayal of our stone *babas*);
> that the land where the latter can be found was once populated
> by the Celts; and finally, that on the other side of Europe, these
> people left representations closely resembling the stone *babas*, and
> that they worshipped the Greek gods. These considerations are
> extremely important; they reveal to us the probable provenance
> of the stone *babas* and lead us to conclude that these idols are
> all but Celtic divinities. So, at least, do the indications of science
> compel us to think. (44)

Later archaeological work laid waste to this hypothesis. Even so,
what remains notable in Fabr's method is that it sought to establish
the statuary's significance and provenance by searching for cultural
affiliations between it and artifacts from other ancient cultures. Such
a move could embed them all into a shared antiquity.[26]

Uvarov, by contrast, later argued that one could discern patterns of development within the statuary over time: "All the statues
(*izvaianiia*) known by the name of stone *babas* . . . should belong to
the same peoples, but at various stages of their development" (516).
As such, Uvarov's array (see figs. 1.1 and 1.2), despite its apparently
motley nature (for which Veselovskii would later criticize him[27]),
could be taken to form a continuum from an essentially "pri-

---

[26] It is important here to note that there is a complex history to the positive values ascribed to Greece in Russian culture; the authority of the Greek models Fabr cites could not be taken as axiomatic for the period. To cite here just one account of the reception of Greek antiquity: Monika Greenleaf observes that "the nineteenth-century revaluation of Greek antiquity was often synonymous with a relative upgrading of 'original,' 'barbarian' virtues, such as simplicity, crude strength, and directness of expression, over the decadent polish of the dominant civilization. The Greek enthusiast often claimed for himself sources of inspiration different from those of the reigning elite—nature, primitive directness of experience, 'untaught' expression, Dionysian fervor" (*Pushkin and Romantic Fashion: Fragment, Elegy, Orient, Irony* [Stanford, CA: Stanford University Press, 1994], 71).

[27] Veselovskii, "Sovremennoe sostoianie," 415.

mitive"—or crude—statuary to one that showed greater and greater signs of sculptural skill. This sign of development, too, could also indicate greater and more advanced cultural values; Uvarov surmised that the presence of both genders "evidences a degree of development of the peoples who erected them, in which both man and woman enjoy equal respect and an equal right to a monument" (515). What's more, he claimed that one could also discern the autochthonous development of their makers: it was a great achievement, and it was all their own:

> As for the artfulness with which these last *babas* are made, we see a great success in the development of the sculpture compared with the first. This success should strike us all the more for the distinctive qualities of all of these idols and the complete absence in them of the imitation of Greek sculpture, which indisputably demonstrates that the sculpture developed completely independently among these peoples and with the full preservation of their national character. (515)

Uvarov's views oppose Fabr's earlier argument at almost every turn, disclosing a second strategy for asserting the statuary's value; where Fabr sought to establish this value by affiliating it with Greece through Celtic intermediaries, Uvarov bases it on a development independent of external influence. In marrying the statuary's distinctive formal features to a narrative of its "successful" development, Uvarov appears to have been among the first archaeologists not only to assert that the statuary possesses aesthetic value, but also that it can challenge the cultural authority of Greece in the realm of aesthetics. The groundwork he lays for future generations—which makes recourse to "national character," perhaps under the influence of his father's triumvirate of Official Nationality (but now encompassing a pagan statuary)—blends together a story of artistry, national character, and the privileging of whomever made the statuary over the Greeks.

  To be sure, evaluating the statuary in terms of a normative aesthetics derived from the putative values of classical art hardly disappeared, and more often than not, led to radically disparaging the statuary and its makers. We have already seen how Pallas and Fabr were among the earliest to refer to the statues as "rude" or "rough hewn" or "monstrous," epithets repeated deep into the nineteenth century. In 1881, the Russian anthropologist Aleksandr Kel'siev could still observe:

> The stone *babas* strike one with their original, archaic, and monstrous style, with the astonishingly distorted taste of all the numerous sculptors of that time, who strove to depict, on an otherwise normal scale, the upper half of the human figure as significantly larger than it is in nature, and consequently, barbarically shortened the dimensions of the lower half.[28]

Kel'siev's account of crudeness modulates what we saw with Pallas, for whom the statuary represented its makers. Kel'siev, instead, operates with a universal model of the natural body, whose proportions are radically distorted by the taste of the "sculptors of that time." The stone *babas*, in his view, were made by artists—and their products could be considered art—but just in bad taste. Proper proportion, moreover, forms the parameters of civilization. Such views, however, did not mean that Kel'siev found no value in the statuary: it was just that those values were primarily archaeological; and while he could discern formal features in the statuary, they had no relevance (yet) for constructing a new aesthetic model (as they would later when radical foreshortening and disproportion became formal values that transformed the statuary into a precursor of Cubist aesthetics).

To my knowledge, nothing captures this disparagement of the statuary and the intricate story of its increasing visibility in archaeological circles better than a response to the statuary in France, by the critic Arthur Bordier. It is one of the pivotal markers of the growing significance ascribed to the statuary that it could be selected and exhibited abroad—not as Russian art, however, but as "anthropological" specimens. Thus, a Russian delegation, led by the anthropologist Dmitrii Anuchin, a member of the Imperial Society of Friends of the Natural, Anthropological, and Ethnographic Sciences

---

[28]   A. I. Kel'siev, "O kamennykh babakh," in *Trudy V-ogo arkheologicheskogo s"ezda v Tiflise, 1881* (Moscow: Tip. A. I. Mamontova, 1887), 77-78.

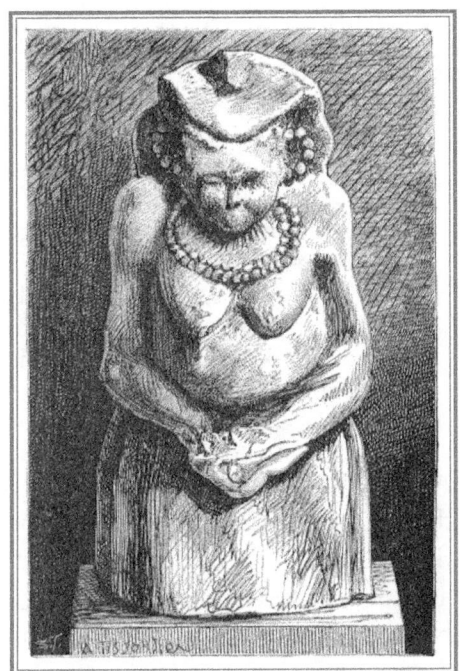

Figure 1.8.

Illustration for Arthur Bordier's review
in *La Nature* (1878).

in Moscow, contributed a display of artifacts drawn from various regions of the empire to the section on anthropology at the Paris International Exhibition of 1878. The delegation selected skeletons from the Sakhalin Islands, models of kurgans, and ancient stone implements. It also included eight facsimiles of the stone *babas*.[29] While the exhibits filling the main hall of the Trocadéro displayed artifacts from various European countries and objects brought from Mexico, Colombia, the Canary Islands, Oceania, and the Hawaiian Islands,[30] it was these eight stone statues that caught Bordier's eye.

[29] "Russie," in *Catalogue spécial de l'exposition des sciences anthropologiques* (Paris: Impr. nationale, 1878), 85-87. Anuchin went on to organize the "prehistory section" at the *Anthropology Exhibition* in Moscow in 1879. On this exhibition, see Ludwig Stieda, "Die anthropologische Ausstellung in Moskau 1879," *Archiv für Anthropologie* 14 (1883): 258-64.

[30] According to the art historian Robert Goldwater, the 1878 Exposition "gave the impulse for the foundation of an ethnographical museum," the Trocadéro, which subsequently became a crucial site where Western European modernists encountered their examples of "primitive" art. See Robert Goldwater, *Primitivism in Modern Art*, 2nd, exp. ed. (Cambridge, MA: Belknap Press, 1986), 7.

Writing in the French journal *La Nature*, Bordier offered "a word of explanation on some curious monuments, which doubtless struck visitors" (fig. 1.8):

> In the Russian exposition in the gallery of anthropological sciences, one's attention is drawn to some very curious statues. It is true that we possess little knowledge about them. . . . These statues, which represent women, and which have been found to the north of the Caucasus, near Piatigorsk, are known as *Kamennaya Baba*, or *femmes de pierre*. Are they divinities? Or important personages? We do not know. At the very least one sees how relative the ideal of beauty is for each people, and how far the *Kamennaya Baba* is from Venus, which Greece has left us.[31]

As the statuary had for many others, it puzzled Bordier—"Are they divinities? Or important personages?"—but since he could find no answers, he turned away from matters of interpretation to a brief on the disparities among cultures; Greece gave Venuses to France, while all Russia had to offer was these inexplicable *femmes de pierre*.

This aesthetic opposition between the classical and the pre-historic (or whatever category Bordier is operating with as he ruminates on the statuary) forms a continuing theme in archaeological writing on about the statuary from the nineteenth to the twentieth centuries. Indeed, such comparisons were drawn so frequently—either in the service of disparaging the statuary or in affiliating it with other cultures—that they became something of a basic reflex in accounts of the statues. Bordier's comment, for example, evinces the typical condescension toward various forms of folk art with which Russian modernists and art historians would later have to contend as they sought to recuperate their own artistic traditions as models for their art.[32] But Bordier's and Kel'siev's responses contain the kernel

---

[31]   A. Bordier, "Les Sciences anthropologiques à L'Exposition universelle," *La Nature: Revue des sciences et de leur applications aux arts et à l'industrie*, no. 285 (November 16, 1878): 409.

[32]   Comments like Bordier's address a range of styles that Russian writers and artists were seeking to recover for their own use around the turn of the century, while still remaining aware of (sometimes unhelpful) French opinion on these matters. Sergei Makovskii, the future editor of *Apollon*, cites the views of Gabriel Mourey's "L'Art populaire russe" (1903) on Russian art in his

of what modernists would later reevaluate in positive terms: the statuary strikes the eye; it commands attention, if not admiration, precisely because it violates normative aesthetic values. Modernists would subsequently advance the view that these very "violations" of classical (or neoclassical) proportions should better be read as the predecessors of altogether different aesthetic values—their own.

ii. Idols Destroyed, Idols Displaced, and the Steppe Denuded

In the opening paragraph of Vsevolod Garshin's short story "The Bears" ("Medvedi," 1883), there is a brief description of a kurgan and a stone *baba* that serves as an emblem of the destruction and dislocation of steppe artifacts. The story is set in the steppe, in the provincial town of Belsk, and its opening is overshadowed by absences apparent to the narrator:

> From here [the steppe] appears flat, and only the accustomed eye will discern within it the barely perceptible lines of gentle slopes, of unseen and deep hollows and ravines. Somewhere an old, plowed-over kurgan, grown into the earth, appears like a small hill, already without a stone *baba*, which perhaps now decorates the courtyard of Kharkov University as a Scythian monument or perhaps has been carried off by some *muzhik* and laid down into the wall of his cattle pen.[33]

Garshin is a marginal figure in the Russian literary canon; and this passage, too, is somewhat marginal to his text. The narrator does

---

"Talashkino": "This art is not refined. It only babbles, but the phrases that emerge from it are direct and open, like folk melodies in which the soul of the race resides . . . these are the works of artist-craftsmen, artists living in the atmosphere of cities, honing their skill through long hours of labor in museums and schools. And we must not demand of these artisans more than they can give. Let them remain just what we see: sincere and clumsy creators who find their inspiration only within and close to themselves and the nature that surrounds them, whose works reveal their imagination and the instincts of the tribe to which they belong" (Sergei Makovskii, "Talashkino" [1905], trans. Wendy Salmond, in *Experiment/Eksperiment: A Journal of Russian Culture* 7 [2001]: 291-92).

33   V. M. Garshin, "Medvedi," *Sochineniia* (Moscow and Leningrad: Khudozhestvennaia literatura, 1963), 133-34; first published in *Otechestvennye zapiski*, no. 11 (1883): 199-213.

not mention the statuary again, but the uncertainty surrounding its absence prefigures the story's plot, which involves a set of interlopers who cannot comprehend either the landscape or the ways of the region. They lack what the narrator calls an "accustomed eye," mistaking the steppe for an expanse without nuance; it's just flat, as the commonplace goes. By contrast, the narrator's awareness of the absent artifacts means that he can read the landscape in time, knowing the statuary had formerly stood atop a kurgan, and surmising its probable fate—either reduced to building material; or still preserved, but displaced and transferred to Kharkov University, where it had been transformed into a "Scythian monument" and thus become decor.

The landscape viewed by Garshin's narrator is similar to the one we find commonly described by archaeologists in their reports and travelogues, and likewise is the fate of the statuary and the kurgans. Archaeologists were as attuned to the presence of the kurgan and the statuary as they were increasingly aware of their conspicuous absence. Alarmed by the destruction and displacement of steppe artifacts, they aimed to recover and preserve the artifacts that remained. To read their reports, in other words, is to find a map taking shape, replete with the conspicuous presence, but also absence, of sites where the statuary had been found or was suspected to have stood in a steppe increasingly denuded.

Just two years before Garshin published "The Bears," for example, in a report to the Fifth Archaeological Congress held in Tiflis in 1881, the archaeologist Aleksandr Kel'siev gave an account notably similar, in both plot and lexicon, to that of Garshin's short story. The Imperial Russian Historical Museum had sent Kel'siev to collect the "most typical and best preserved statues," some of which, he noted as did Garshin, belonged to Kharkov University. [34] Even though we have already seen how Kel'siev disparaged the aesthetic qualities of the statuary, his belief in their archaeological value led him from fields into the villages, where he found dismaying scenes testifying to the "sad state" of many of "these curious monuments,"

---

[34]   Kel'siev, "O kamennykh babakh," 76.

which "together with the steppe kurgans . . . originate from an entirely shadowy period before the Tatars."[35] The peasants, Kel'siev noted, had turned the statuary into the "foundations of their houses and mills, placed [them] as the threshold stone at an entrance, thrown them into boggy areas to cross through the mud, and whimsically buried them head first in the ground."[36]

Whether Kel'siev is the source for Garshin's story is difficult to say—and what he observes here was commonly observed—but both were alerting their distinct readerships that stone *babas* were being used as construction material for cellars, churches, or even as road markers, which spurred archaeologists to seek support for collecting and preserving the statuary.[37] While such reports typically detail only the destruction of the statuary, they leave unremarked the issue of whether the statuary might actually have meant more to the peasantry than just building material. Archaeologists were also aware of the various ritual practices surrounding the statuary. One account, relayed in 1844 by Karl Desmet, a member of the Imperial Society of Agriculture of Southern Russia, again involves Russian peasants:

> On the property of Mme. Nekliuvaia there is a large kurgan, upon which stood a *"baba."* Since peasants had gotten it into their heads to offer her a form of worship, the manager of the estate ordered her toppled over. But during the famine of 1833-34, they put her back into place, maintaining that she would promote rain and the harvest, and they began to worship her even more zealously than before. At that point the manager ordered that the *"baba's"* head be cut off, and to this day it remains at the foot of the idol.[38]

---

[35] Ibid.

[36] Ibid., 77.

[37] On related practices of using archaeological artifacts as construction material, and their relationship with the ideologization of the space of the Crimea, see Andreas Schönle, "Garden of the Empire: Catherine's Appropriation of the Crimea," *Slavic Review* 60, no. 1 (Spring 2001): 1-23, esp. 10-11.

[38] "Korrespondentsiia," *Zapiski imperatorskago odesskago obshchestva istorii i drevnostei,* 1 (1844): 597.

Such an anecdote could be relevant to various aspects of Russian cultural life, from questions of folk belief to the persistence of paganism, or the so-called *dvoeverie* (dual faith).[39] Recorded practices of the Russian peasantry involving the statuary indicate forms of value beyond that of the archaeological or art historical, namely the religious and ritualistic, which also suggest the possibilities that peasants used the statuary for reasons beyond utilitarianism or destroyed them out of more than peasant whimsy. Perhaps using pagan statuary as the foundation for a church may have been linked to similar practices of situating a church on a formerly pagan site; or the mythological relationship of the statuary with fertility and harvest goddesses may have led to their selection for mills. Perhaps they were thought to bring good luck or a benign influence.

To be sure, these are speculations as to what the statuary could have meant to the peasantry. We do know, however, that Aleksandr Afanas'ev, the great folklorist and mythographer—whose work formed a common touchstone for later literary texts on the statuary and Russian mythology generally—records a variant of the peasant worship of the statuary in his *The Slavs' Poetic Views on Nature* (*Poeticheskie vozzreniia slavian na prirodu*), a comparative study of Slavic mythology published in the 1860s.[40] In a brief passage in that work, he describes ritual practices involving the statuary and a mythical account of where it came from:

> A woman was carrying buckets of water and turned to stone (an indication of those cups from which cloud maidens [*oblachnye devy*] pour rain upon the earth). Similar ideas are connected with

39 For a recent account of the relationship of paganism and Orthodoxy in Russia, see V. M. Zhivov, "Dvoeverie i osobyi kharakter russkoi kul'turnoi istorii," in *Razyskaniia v oblasti istorii* (Moscow: Iazyki slavianskoi kul'tury, 2002), 306-16.

40 A. N. Afanas'ev, *Poeticheskie vozzreniia slavian na prirodu: Opyt sravnitel'nogo izucheniia slavianskikh predanii i verovanii, v sviazi s mificheskimi skazaniiami drugikh rodstvennykh narodov*, 3 vols. (1865-69; reprint, The Hague: Mouton, 1969-70). To my knowledge, there is no comprehensive study of the influence of Afanas'ev's study on literary and artistic culture, which might approximate the parallel influence of James Frazer's *The Golden Bough*; see John B. Vickery, *The Literary Impact of* The Golden Bough (Princeton, NJ: Princeton University Press, 1973).

stone *babas* in the south of Russia. In times of drought, a settlement goes to the stone *baba*, places bread up to her shoulders, or sprinkles grain before her, and then bows before her, beseeching: "Save us, Babo-Babusen'ko! We shall bow still lower, only help us and save us from hardship" (*Pomilui nas, babo-babusen'ko! Budem klaniat'sia eshche nizhe, tol'ko pomozi nam i sokhrani ot bedy*).[41]

In treating the statues as pagan idols, these peasants may be something of the spiritual ancestors of the writers examined in coming chapters, in whose works we find the afterlife of this story of peasant idolatry. Notably, Afanas'ev's account of the ritual practices influenced modernist writers such as Remizov, and served as the source of one significant interpretation of the statuary rehearsed throughout the modernist period, which regarded the statuary as a benign intercessor, fertility goddess, or pagan idol, capable of commenting on the then-ongoing events of the Civil War (1918-22).

Other reasons for the destruction and displacement of the statuary were also recorded. However, the very efforts to preserve the statuary could also bring about its destruction. When, already in the 1850s, the Archaeological Commission had implored the Ministry of Internal Affairs to preserve the statuary, a sympathetic minister sent circulars from St. Petersburg instructing local officials to make every effort to do so. As Veselovskii reports, the circulars were sent throughout the empire, attesting to the vast geographical range over which the statuary was found: from Ekaterinoslav, Tauris, Kharkov, Kherson, Simbirsk, Saratov, Irkutsk. But, like the fate of so many official circulars swirling out from St. Petersburg (a process famously described by Andrei Bely in the prologue to his novel *Petersburg*), the fate of this one followed a Gogolian plotline:

> Local authorities, who were alarmed by the edict and who were afraid of being made responsible for the preservation of the statuary, hurried to reinstall the stone *babas* in their former sites, and understandably, they did not end up where they should have. In a few places, minor officials of the administration directed that

---

[41] Afanas'ev, *Poeticheskie vozzreniia*, 2:677, n. 1.

the statues be destroyed, in order to report to the authorities that such statues did not exist in their regions. (421)

While this effort to save the statuary gave rise to tragicomedy, the very process of collecting the statuary also led to its permanent displacement from the steppe, a result lamented by other archaeologists. Among the most poignant testaments to the dislocation of the statuary comes in an article by the archaeologist and historian Nikolai Brandenburg, written in the 1890s:

> A good many of the idols called stone *babas* have been preserved, although an incomparably larger quantity of them has already been destroyed. The greatest misfortune about this is that almost all of the specimens that remain intact have by now already been removed from their original locations, and have thus lost a significant part of their scientific archaeological significance.[42]

Notably, what Brandenburg considers the "greatest misfortune" is not the actual destruction of the statuary—which seems to go without saying—but rather its removal from where it allegedly originally stood facing east atop a specific kurgan. In this regard, archaeology, for Brandenburg, inheres not in objects alone, but in an object's relationship to its setting. Removing the statuary from its setting strips it of its "archaeological significance" and therefore of one possible way to resolve the question of its identity. According to Brandenburg, one could determine the provenance of the statues by determining who was buried within the kurgan.

Chief among those conjectured links between the statuary and the kurgans was that the statuary was of Scythian origin. Brandenburg was only the latest to link the statuary to the Scythians. As early as the 1830s, the historian Nikolai Vsevolozhskii wrote in his *Travelogue through South Russia to Crimea, Odessa, and Beyond* that "the monstrous stone idols, which had been situated upon nearly all kurgans, and where some have survived intact until now, show the features of Scythian nomadic peoples, or of those who descended

---

[42] N. E. Brandenburg, "K voprosu o kamennykh babakh," in *Trudy 8-ogo s"ezda v Moskve* (Moscow: Tip. Mamontova, 1897), 13.

from them, the Polovtsy or Pechenegs, despite the crude and ugly (*durnaia*) work."[43] This association was repeated throughout the nineteenth century by various archaeologists, albeit with varying degrees of assurance. Among the most important to advance this claim was the historian Ivan Zabelin, who reported in his article "Scythian Graves: The Chertomlyk Kurgan" ("Skifskie mogily: Chertomlykskii kurgan," 1865) that a stone *baba* had once stood on top of that kurgan, among the most celebrated excavations of a kurgan in the latter half of the nineteenth century.[44] Indeed, Zabelin notes that "in former times, such *babas* likely stood on many graves, for several of them are still called to this day *babovatye* [a kurgan with a *baba* placed atop it; MK], although no one remembers where a *baba* once stood upon them."[45] Following Zabelin, Brandenburg asserts that the statuary was Scythian based on the evidence that the earrings found in the kurgan bore a striking resemblance to those adorning the statuary.[46] Dmitrii Anuchin, too, in his 1898 Brokgauz-Efron encyclopedia entry on "Stone *Babas*," was ambiguous on the matter of the statuary's Scythian origins. He cites previous assertions of the link, leaving his readers to draw their own conclusions from Uvarov's observation that "stone *babas* stood upon kurgans, which, on the basis of excavations, turned out to be Scythian."[47]

In 1915 Veselovskii tried to completely dismantle this theory, taking both Uvarov and Anuchin, the writer of the encyclopedia entry, to task.[48] The statuary, he insisted, was not Scythian. Veselovskii

---

43 Cited in Veselovskii, "Sovremennoe sostoianiie," 415.

44 I. E. Zabelin, "Skifskie mogily: Chertomlytskii kurgan; Zapiska" (Moscow: Tip. Gracheva i Ko., 1865). See also, A. Iu. Alekseev et al. *Chertomlyk: Skifskii tsarskii kurgan IV v. do n.e.* (Kiev: Naukova dumka, 1991).

45 Zabelin, "Skifskie mogily," 5.

46 This was also reported at two other Scythian kurgans: the Aleksandrovskii Kurgan in the Ekaterinoslav district, which had been similarly adorned, and the Megulovskii Kurgan. See Brandenburg, "K voprosu," 16-18.

47 The entry drew on the work of Uvarov and on Hartmann's "Becherstatuen in Ostpreussen und die Literatur der Becherstatuen" (1892).

48 Veselovskii, "Sovremennoe sostoianie," 423.

drew support for his conclusion from reports by the Flemish traveler
Rubruquis, who observed in the thirteenth century that the people
he called the Cumans, whom Russians call Polovtsy, raised statuary
atop kurgans.[49] (Later archaeological studies, to underscore, have
ascribed the statuary to the Polovtsy, and have similarly invoked
the same evidence Veselovskii marshaled.[50]) Perhaps one reason
for the confusion—if not for the obdurate tenacity of affiliating
the statuary with the Scythians despite evidence to the contrary—
is that the Polovtsy, as we have just seen, were supposedly the
descendants of the Scythians; or, alternatively, that "Scythian,"
as the Byzantine sources used the word, could frequently serve
as an "archaic ethnonym" for a range of nomads,[51] the Polovtsy
included.

Veselovskii, in fact, offered his own account of why some
kurgans were found with the statuary located atop them, which
returns us to the theme of Garshin's narrator's sense of absences
in the steppe. Rebutting Brandenburg's claims about the Scythian
connection, Veselovskii instead argues that "stone *babas* were
transferred from small nomadic kurgans to the grandiose Scythian
[ones] for the sake of a strong effect" (413). He may not have
been entirely sure about this suggestion, since he relegates it to
a footnote. But it does indicate how archaeologists were discerning
a new range of aesthetic values beyond those inherent to the statuary itself: the nomads, too, it seems, were interested in various
forms of aesthetic display. Indeed, when they were found together,
the statuary and kurgan were said to have made for an extraordinary sight. As Veselovskii observed, "these statues, when they were
still found on kurgans . . . produced a strong impression upon

---

[49]   Ibid., 423-24. Among the first reports to include the account of Rubruquis was G. I. Spasskii,
       "Dneprovskie kurgany," in "Korrespondentsiia," *Zapiski imperatorskogo odesskogo obshchestva
       istorii i drevnosti* (1844): 593-96.

[50]   See the chapter "Idoly," in Fedorov-Davydov, *Kurgany, idoly, monety,*

[51]   The term is from István Vásáry, who has noted that Byzantine sources frequently used the "archaic
       ethnonym" of "Scythians" to refer to the Cumans (Polovtsy), which could indicate one source for
       the conflation of the two groups. See István Vásáry, *Cumans and Tatars: Oriental Military in the
       Pre-Ottoman Balkans, 1185-1365* (Cambridge: Cambridge University Press, 2005), 17.

travelers in the monotonous and limitless steppe" (413). But toward the end of the century, the statuary was disappearing from the very site in which its remarkable allure had first been noticed—the site that it, in turn, had filled with the nuances perceivable to an "accustomed eye."[52]

iii. The Modernist Peregrinations of the Stone *Babas*

In his *About Mayakovsky* (*O Maiakovskom*, 1940), Viktor Shklovsky relates the following anecdote about the peregrinations of a stone *baba*, which belonged to the family of David and Vladimir Burliuk, who were leading members of Russian Futurism, and friends and associates of Vladimir Mayakovsky. The Burliuks had found the statue around their residence in Chernianka a major site of early Futurist activity. Chernianka was located in "Hylaea," the archaic toponym from which the early Futurists took their name, Hylaeans, when they appeared on the modernist scene.[53] The Burliuks took the stone *baba*, carted it home, and installed it in the "family gallery." It was another of those many instances of displaced statuary lamented by archaeologists, but, like the story told by Garshin, this one, too, became the subject of art:

> David Burliuk grew up in the steppe, near Tauris, in the family of a manager of a large estate. There was little money in the family, but no lack of food. He, his brothers, and his sister, all of them drew. They even had their own sculpture gallery: a stone *baba*, which had been found on a kurgan. Later, they brought it to Moscow, when their father lost his job. Yet the further relocations of this family antiquity turned out to be beyond their means.

[52]   The historian Willard Sunderland has recently charted the various manifestations of this sense of the multiple threats facing the steppe among archaeologists, ethnographers, geographers, and literary artists. See the chapter "Correct Colonization" in his *Taming the Wild Field: Colonization and Empire on the Russian Steppe* (Ithaca, NY: Cornell University Press, 2004), 177-222.

[53]   For more on this period, see the chapter "Hylaea" in Vladimir Markov's *Russian Futurism: A History* (Berkeley and Los Angeles: University of California Press, 1968), 29-60, and the chapter "Hylaea" in Benedikt Livshits's memoir *Polutoraglazyi strelets: Stikhotvoreniia, perevody, vospominaniia* (Leningrad: Sovetksii pisatel', 1989), 310-47.

The stone *baba*, having mistakenly arrived in Moscow, got stuck at Nastasin's cross by a shed, in which students from an art academy would gather.[54]

Aleksei Kruchenykh tells the anecdote differently. In his *Our Arrival* (*Nash vykhod*, 1932), a memoir of his early Futurist years, Kruchenykh recounts a similar story about the statue's relocation from Chernianka to Moscow:

At dinner, David Davidovich [Burliuk] would talk a lot. By the way, I recall a story about a stone woman, they had unearthed not long ago from somewhere inside some kurgans (*otrytuiu im gde-to v kurganakh*). The hands of the woman were laid upon her stomach. David Davidovich joked:

—From this it's clear that higher emotions were not foreign to this goddess.

Something curious happened with this stone woman. When the father of the Burliuks retired, the Count permitted him to take with him some domestic items. . . . And here the stone woman completed a trip along the railroad from Tauris, to the Burliuks in Moscow, but there, unnecessary to anyone, she was thrown somewhere into a courtyard.[55]

As anecdotal accounts, both passages have their limits, of course; neither version of the anecdote indicates what the further peregrinations of this statue involved, nor do they delve deeper into what the students may have seen in it. Beyond speaking to the actuality of the modernist interest in archaeology, however, one notable value about both anecdotes is that they tell us about the distinct pathways along which the statuary entered into Russian modernism. Kruchenykh's version differs from Shklovsky's in that the journey of the *baba* ends in oblivion. Its movement to the capital marks its loss of value, since the statuary,

[54]   Viktor Shklovskii, *O Maiakovskom* (Moscow: Sovetskii pisatel', 1940), 23.

[55]   Aleksei Kruchenykh, *Our Arrival: From the History of Russian Futurism*, ed. V. Rakitin and A. Sarab'ianov, trans. Alan Myers (Moscow: RA, 1995), 40. I have adjusted the translation based on Aleksei Kruchenykh, *Nash vykhod* (Moscow: RA, 1996), 43-44; cf. Lahti, "On Living Statues," 452.

like some steppe ingénue, was once appreciated in the steppe, but ends up in the dump heap of the Moscow courtyard, where it is "unnecessary to anyone." The line recalls what Chekhov had once said of the steppe proper, when he spoke of steppe riches "sung by no one and necessary to no one." Shklovsky's version, by contrast, seems something like a classic parable of Russian Formalism's idea of literary evolution, with its emphasis on the movement of forms from the periphery to the center: the steppe *baba*, appreciated in its peripheral contexts by the Burliuks, who promote it to a "family antiquity," arrives in the capital, where, by dint of contingency and poverty, it finds its necessity and value in becoming the subject of art.

Despite their differences, both anecdotes present us with two themes with which we can conclude this chapter. The first is that they indicate the multiple venues in which modernists could have encountered the statuary, of which the steppe was only one site. And the second is the various ways in which necessity and aesthetics become interwoven in the evaluation and appropriation of the statuary. Indeed, these two themes are brought together again in the pages of Veselovskii's essays. As we learn from those pages, it is difficult to assess how rare it had become to see the statuary in situ, but Veselovskii remarks toward the end of his 1915 survey that one typically had to go to museums, both in the provinces and in the capitals, in order to view it. As we have seen, the quest to collect the statuary had begun in the 1830s, and by century's end, provincial museums in Ekaterinoslav, Simferopol, Novocherkassk, Ekaterinodar, Tiflis, Orenburg, and Tashkent all had their own collections. One of the best places to view the statuary was the Historical Museum in Moscow, whose collection was composed of exemplars from the Bakhmutskii district in the Ekaterinoslav province, located north of the Black Sea. Veselovskii had called this district the "kingdom of these statues" (*tsarstvo etikh statui*) —more accurately, though, the *former* kingdom, since many of the statues had been removed to the Historical Museum. The art historian Jane Sharp has singled out this museum as one of the central venues in which artists such as Natal'ia Goncharova and her husband, Mikhail Larionov, along with other Moscow art students, could have seen the statuary.[56] Country estates offered another opportunity to view it. As Katherine Lahti has discovered, major art dealers were also collecting the statues; one could find several examples of the statuary at Savva Mamontov's estate in Abramtsevo.[57] And, when there were no *babas* to be found, landowners ordered their peasants to sculpt new ones!

> The list of imaginary stone *babas* is relatively large, but in reality it turns out to be still larger if we say that amidst authentic stone *babas* there exist forged ones, manufactured not with the goal of deception but for the sake of satisfying aesthetic demands, however strange this might seem. It is known that many stone *babas* were taken from kurgans and distributed in city gardens as decoration. A particularly large number of stone *babas* were concentrated in the gardens of landowners. As a consequence of this fashion, several landowners who lacked authentic stone *babas*, have recently directed their peasants to manufacture statues for their gardens modeled on the stone *babas*.[58]

Just as Veselovskii had given us a way to consider the various acts of "human inventiveness" brought to bear upon the statuary—namely as a series of competitions among laymen and specialists each trying to outdo previous theories—he again points toward a central feature of the story of the stone *babas* in this passage. Whereas the statuary had formerly been evaluated (and often disparaged) for its aesthetic qualities, and its putative failure to correspond to neoclassical values of proportion, by the turn of the century, it was now able to accommodate a range of "aesthetic demands." Value and taste had shifted; and the statuary was now assessed in those terms. A fashion had emerged, which Veselovskii deems "strange," which not only enabled the statues' reevaluation, but also their reproduction. Such a change in aesthetic and cultural values reminds us again how the statuary—like Voloshin's archaic

---

[56]   Jane Sharp, *Russian Modernism between East and West: Natal'ia Goncharova and the Moscow Avant-Garde* (Cambridge: Cambridge University Press, 2006), 159.

[57]   Lahti, "On Living Statues," 450-51.

[58]   Veselovskii, *"Mnimye,"* 27.

mirrors—could both bring a range of associations in tow, or be made to reflect an array of present-day concerns.

What this, in turn, brings into focus is that a hermeneutics of writing about the statuary takes us beyond the question of provenance (who made the stone *babas*?) and into questions of the inventiveness and originality of the modernist artists themselves as they made the statuary responsive to their own "aesthetic demands." Clearly, any claim to be the first person to "see" the statuary is not literally true, but it was made time and again. As modernists looked into the past to discern an antiquity, they reconstituted an image of the statuary and of the steppe increasingly less available to them. As they imagined the statuary, they frequently staged encounters as though they were in the steppe, either standing in a field, or perched atop a kurgan. At times they did so to re-create a mythological past, at others to demonstrate their artistic perspicacity, or what we've seen Garshin call an "accustomed eye" that can perceive nuances in the steppe. They argued that it was hidden in plain view, waiting to garner its proper esteem from someone like them, even as previous generations had written about the statues, and by the first few years, landowners would reproduce them. The statuary was already disappearing from view in the steppe because these others had seen it and recognized its value, whether as construction material, beneficent idols, or collectible artifacts.

Chapter Two

A CULTURAL POETICS OF THE KURGAN

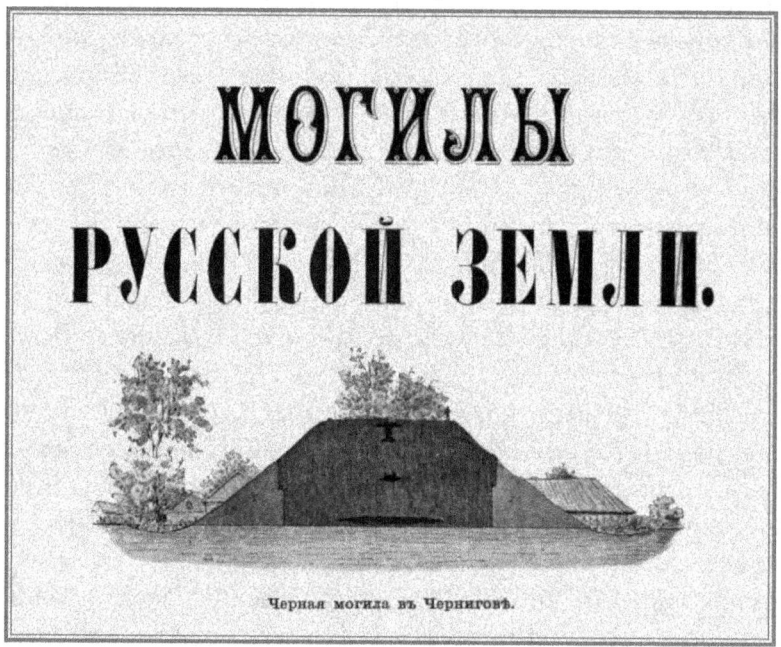

МОГИЛЫ
РУССКОЙ ЗЕМЛИ.

Черная могила въ Черниговѣ.

Figure 2.1.
Cover of Samokvasov's *Graves of the Russian Land* (1908),
depicting the Black Grave in Chernigov.

i. How to Excavate a Kurgan

In 1908, the eminent archaeologist Dmitrii Samokvasov published two studies on the various grave forms found in Russia. The first, *Graves of the Russian Land* (*Mogily russkoi zemli*) (fig. 2.1), begins with a reminiscence, as he looks back upon the three decades of his long career. Samokvasov's archaeological excavations had begun, he writes, when "the idea still held sway in historical and archaeological literature about the impossibility of distinguishing the pagan graves of the Russian land according to their historical epoch and nationality and, in particular, of distinguishing those graves that belonged to the Russian Slavic tribes of pagan times."[1] One reason the graves found throughout the vastness of Russia provoked such questions as to their origins was that so many peoples had piled up a mound of earth over an inner grave or crypt, albeit with different formal features and degrees of structural complexity and size. Who was interred within a mound? A Greek, a Slav, or a Polovets, or perhaps a Cossack or a Mongol? Or perhaps it belonged to a member of some other people, known or unknown? Such were the kinds of questions Samokvasov and others had sought to resolve and to provide some basic guide as they excavated the graves.

This burial form—known in English as *barrow, tumulus,* or *mound* and in Russian by such words as *kurgan, bugor,* or *nasyp'*— is thought to have arisen sometime in the fifth millennium BCE and then to have spread throughout the whole of the Eurasian landmass.[2] The large number of such burial forms and their puzzling origins gave rise to a vast range of studies in Russia.[3] Indeed, efforts to excavate the kurgans and to preserve the artifacts contained within them had already begun in the early eighteenth century, from the kurgans found in Siberia to those found north of the Black Sea, especially in the region between the Dnieper and the Don.[4] The study of these graves acquired greater systematicity over the course of the nineteenth century, during which one encounters the development of an archaeological practice known as "kurgan archaeology" emerging by mid-century.[5]

---

[1]   D. Samokvasov, *Mogily russkoi zemli: Opisanie arkheologicheskikh raskopok i sobraniia drevnostei* (Moscow: Sinodal'naia tip, 1908), ii.

[2]   Marija Gimbutas, "The Indo-Europeans: Archaeological Problems," *American Anthropologist* New series 65, no. 4 (August 1963): 815-36.

[3]   G. A. Tsvetaeva, *Sokrovishcha prichernomorskikh kurganov* (Moscow: Nauka, 1968), 5.

[4]   Formozov, *Ocherki po istorii russkoi arkheologii*, esp. the chapter "Arkheologiia v Rossii v pervoi polovine XIX veka."

[5]   Ibid.

Samokvasov was one of Russia's leading archaeologists in this area. In his other publication from 1908, *Excavations of Ancient Graves, and the Description, Preservation, and Publication of Grave Antiquities* (*Raskopki drevnykh mogil i opisanie, khranenie i izdanie mogil'nykh drevnostei*), he provided a detailed manual on excavation techniques.[6] The text begins with a description of the rules established by a committee at the Third Archaeological Congress in Kiev (1874), which had sought to codify new guidelines for "scientific excavations." The committee included other leading archaeologists and historians such as Nikolai Brandenburg and Count Aleksei Uvarov, whose works on the stone *babas* were discussed in the previous chapter, and Ivan Zabelin, whose writings on the kurgan will be a particular focus below.

"Each ancient earth mound," Samokvasov asserts, was a "material historical monument."[7] He compares the process of excavating the kurgans (a term he uses interchangeably with the word *nasyp'* or "mound") with the painstaking work that attends the publication of such literary monuments as medieval chronicles: "But where mistakes and inadequacies in the publication of a manuscript can be corrected by a second edition, the excavation of ancient earth mounds destroys the original."[8] Archaeology must aspire to philology in rigor, perhaps even more so since it destroys as its studies. Without a second chance, archaeologists must, according to Samokvasov, follow an ideal form of excavation practice that would investigate particular features of the kurgan.

The first tasks were to specify the location of the kurgan in relation to any nearby settlement, to ascertain whether a water source or ruins were in the vicinity, and to characterize the landscape in which it was found (for example, in a field or forest). Then, one should determine whether other kurgans were nearby, since the mounds were routinely found in groups. If so, one should note the

---

6   D. Samokvasov, *Raskopki drevnykh mogil i opisanie, khranenie i izdanie mogil'nykh drevnostei* (Moscow: Sinodal'naia tip., 1908).

7   Ibid., 5.

8   Ibid.

number of kurgans and whether any had been previously excavated, plundered, or destroyed. In the latter case, Samokvasov urged archaeologists to identify remnants of the destroyed kurgans in nearby structures. Both plunder and the use of kurgan materials for other building projects were commonly cited in the archaeological literature as reasons for their destruction. In this respect, one value commonly asserted for the kurgan beyond that of archaeology and aesthetics was that of treasure trove or archaic depot of construction material.

Samokvasov also want details on the nomenclature locals used for the grave form. Did they refer to the graves as *kurgans* or did they use other words such as *mogily, sopki, volotovki, mareny, roblenitsy, koptsy?*[9] There was another issue of naming in that many of the burial mounds had local toponyms: these included the Black, Old, Tsar (Tsareva), the Pointed (Ostraia), the Chertomlyk, Polovets, or Gold Kurgan; the Shepherd (Pastushka), the Twins (Bliznetsy), and the Magpie (Soroka). After gathering the local names for a given mound, a related task was to collect any local myths about its origins. If at all possible, he adds, one should ascertain how the myths might have arisen.

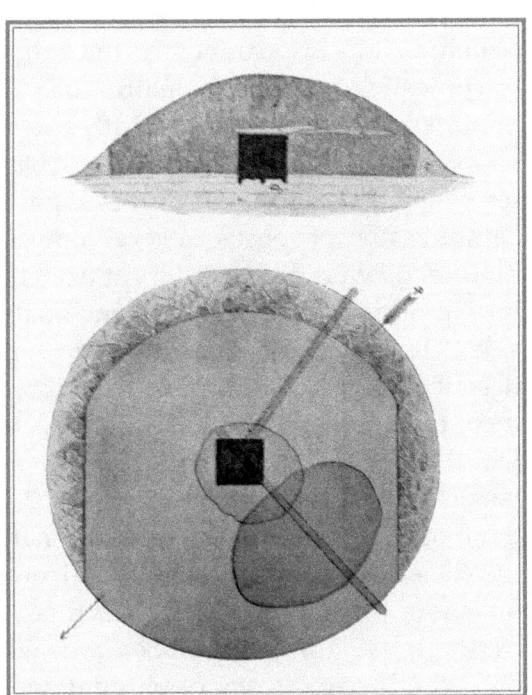

Figure 2.2.
Cross-section of a kurgan mound
in Samokvasov's *Excavations*
(1908).

9 Ibid., 8.

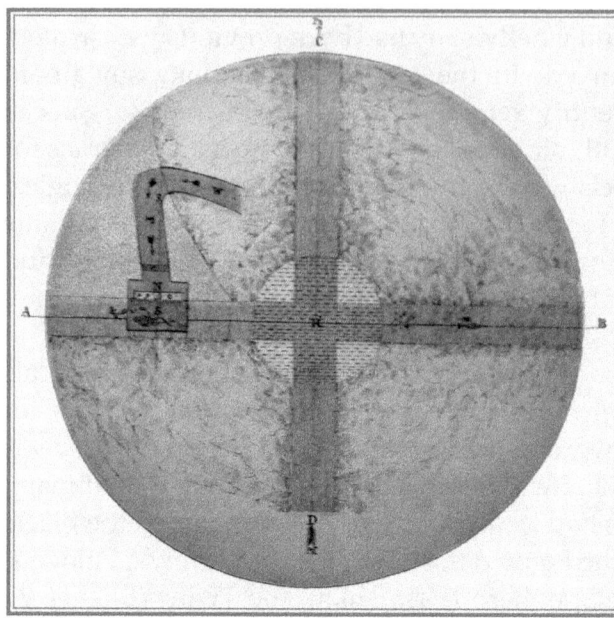

Figure 2.3.
Diagram depicting
overview of a kurgan
mound in Samokvasov's
*Graves of the Russian
Land* (1908).

Following this initial set of tasks, the next was to describe the structure and appearance of the kurgan. Was it "half a sphere" or conical? What was the nature of its peak? Was it "sharp, blunt, or sunken"? What was its width and its height? One should then proceed to dig, taking care in excavating the mounded earth to reach the inner crypt or crypts interred within it (figs. 2.2—2.3). Samokvasov proposes several options: one could remove the mounded layers above the crypt from top to base; one could burrow into it; or one could make a trench cutting directly into it from the side. Then, once inside the inner crypt, the archaeologist should describe its overall structure, describing how it was built and what it contained. How many skeletons were located in the inner crypt? Did the mound contain multiple graves, as had been the case with particularly spectacular kurgans (fig. 2.4)? What items accompanied the dead? Depending on the provenance, the items could include the skeletons of horses, vessels, and jewelry (fig. 2.5). Another major question, often posed about Scythian kurgans found around the northern bank of the Black Sea, was whether there was any gold— or, given the frequency of plunder, was any gold left? Such efforts

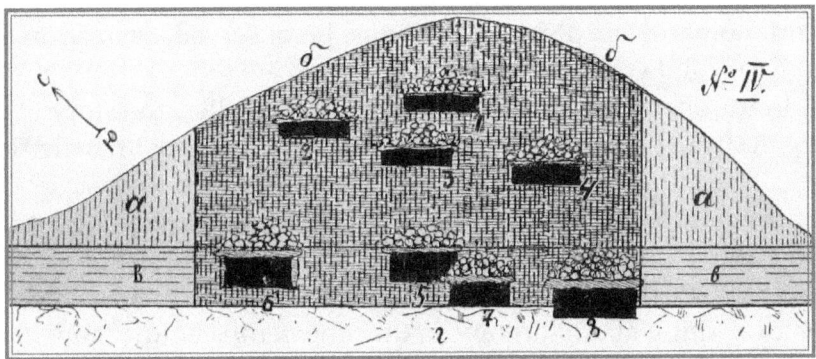

Figure 2.4.

Diagram depicting cross-section of a kurgan mound in Samokvasov's
Graves of the Russian Land (1908).

at systematizing the excavation of ancient graves faced various challenges.[10] Not all archaeologists followed the promulgated rules,[11] and the kurgans themselves had long been subject to an intensity of interest from professionals to laymen. So intense, in fact, that Ivan Linnichenko, a Russian historian, lamented the phenomenon of

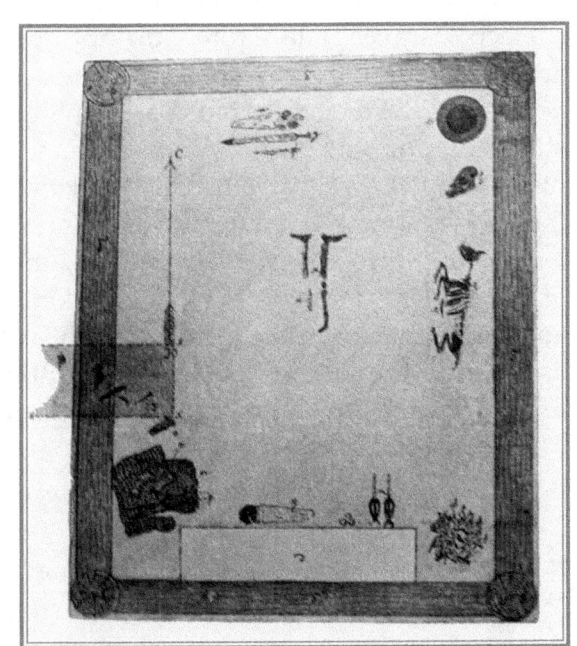

Figure 2.5.

Diagram depicting interior
of a grave in Samokvasov's
Graves of the Russian Land
(1908).

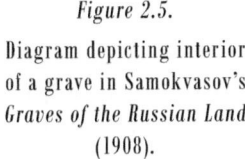

10 Formozov, *Ocherki*, 18.

11 Samokvasov, *Raskopki*,15

"kurganomania" in 1888: excavations, he observed, seemed barely distinguishable from grave robbing.[12]

In the sheer quantity of archaeological studies, the story of the kurgan dwarfs that of the stone *babas*. It is the same with belletristic texts. The kurgan's appearance in belles lettres is so vast, in fact, that it would be difficult to catalogue. One can survey the literary landscape of modern Russian letters to find writers as diverse as Alexander Pushkin, Mikhail Lermontov, Fedor Tiutchev, and Leo Tolstoy writing about kurgans in the nineteenth century, and, in the twentieth, Ivan Bunin, Konstantin Bal'mont, Velimir Khlebnikov, Sergei Tret'iakov, and Andrei Platonov. Not all can be given attention here (and we will turn to several in other chapters), nor, as far as I can tell, reward sustained attention. While no study has, to my knowledge, charted the kurgan's emergence and consolidation as a poetic site in belletristic texts, much less its place in Russian modernism, the totality of these writings, considered together, reveal that the kurgan formed a remarkable site within Russia's poetic topography.

It was during this period that Maksimilian Voloshin would author an apt comment that provides a guide to approaching the subject: "Graves," he wrote, "do not open by accident. Works of art arise from graves at those moments in history when they are necessary."[13] We can avoid Voloshin's providential tones, while still retaining his basic proposition regarding objects deemed historically necessary: Why did works of art, but also the graves themselves become valuable, even necessary, to aesthetics and culture for various periods in general, and for Russian modernism in particular? The coming pages take an episodic approach to answering that question, focusing on the values writers and thinkers ascribed to the kurgan, and on the shifting cultural and aesthetic forms through which they elaborated those values.

---

[12] Ivan Linnichenko, "Kurganomania" (1888), as cited in ibid., 15, n.1.

[13] Maksimilian Voloshin, "Chemu uchat ikony?" (1914) in *Liki tvorchestva* (Leningrad: Nauka: 1988), 295.

ii. Gnedich, *Iliada*

In Zelenetskii's *Epithets of Literary Russian Speech* (*Epitety literaturnoi russkoi rechi*) from 1913, we find a range of descriptors listed for the entry "kurgan": *bezmolvnyi* (silent, speechless), *besstrastnyi* (dispassionate), *mertvyi* (dead), *molchalivyi* (reticent), *nadmennyi* (haughty), and *odinokii* (solitary).[14] (There was no entry on *kamennaia baba*, whereas the entry on *step'* [the steppe] was enormous.) The epithets were taken from works from as early as the 1820s, and used by such figures as Aleksei Tolstoi, Afanasy Fet, Ivan Kozlov, and Ivan Bunin. While the entry is brief and does not include epithets affixed to the site in Russian letters, it indicates that by 1913 the word "kurgan" had sufficient literary currency in the Russian literary language to warrant inclusion in Zelenetskii's work. The entry further encourages us to ask when "kurgan," a word of Turkic origin, might have acquired that currency.[15]

Let me take as an exemplary possible case the celebrated translation of the *Iliad* into Russian by Nikolai Gnedich, who published the first installment of his work in 1809. Gnedich's translation revealed, according to one reviewer, Nikolai Polevoi, "a treasure house of language . . . [that] exposes the richness, power, and resources of our own language."[16] There had been previous attempts to translate the epic into both prose (by Petr Ekimov) and poetry (by Ermil Kostrov). Gnedich began his translation where Kostrov had left off, with Book VII. Given the themes of my book, one question Gnedich's translation provokes is: What did he use as the Russian equivalents for the Greek words for *graves* and *mounds*, for the *tumbos* and *sema* he encountered time and again in Homer?

---

14 *Epitety literaturnoi russkoi rechi* (1913), s.v. "kurgan."

15 Maks Fasmer, *Etimologicheskii slovar' russkogo iazyka* s.v. "kurgan."

16 V. V. Afanas'ev, ed., *N. Gnedich: Stikhotvoreniia i poemy* (Moscow: Sovetskaia Rossiia, 1984), 7; quoted in Frederick T. Griffiths and Stanley J. Rabinowitz, *Novel Epics: Gogol, Dostoevsky, and National Narrative* (Evanston, IL: Northwestern University Press, 1990), 7.

Пусть похоронят его кудреглавые мужи ахейцы
И на брегу Геллеспонта широкого холм да насыплют.
Некогда, видя его, кто-нибудь и от поздних потомков
Скажет, плывя в корабле многовеслом по черному понту:
—Вот ратоборца могила, умершего в древние веки:
В бранях его знаменитого свергнул божественный Гектор!—
Так нерожденные скажут, и слава моя не погибнет.

(VII: 85-91)[17]

Let the curly-haired Achaian men bury him
And heap up a mound upon the banks of the

wide Hellespont.
Some day, seeing it, one of [his] later generations.
Will say, sailing in a many-oared ship along the Black Sea,
"Here is the grave of a warrior, who died in ancient times:
In a battle, the divine Hector overthrew him, the

renowned one."
So those not yet born will say, and my glory will not perish.

(VII: 85-91)

The mere appearance of *kholm* (hill or mound) and the verb *nasypat'* (to pile) sparks no small degree of philological interest. When Gnedich uses *kholm* to translate *tumbos*, was "kurgan" available to him as a possible Russian equivalent?

As Gnedich worked on the complete translation over the next twenty years, he frequently faced the many depictions of burial scenes and burial mounds in the *Iliad*. And, during that time, "kurgan" apparently acquired enough currency that Gnedich used it for a burial mound outside Troy in Book II:

Есть перед градом троянским великий курган и высокий,
В поле особенный, круглый равно и отсель и оттоле.
Смертные, с древних времен, нарицают его Ватиеей,
Но бессмертные боги—могилою быстрой Мирины.

(II: 811-15)

---

[17]   Gomer, *Iliada*, trans. N. Gnedich (Moscow: Moskovskii rabochii, 1982). All citations are to this
edition, and are cited in the text.

There is before the city of Troy a great and tall kurgan,
By itself on the plane, equally round on one side and the other.
Mortals, since ancient times, call it the [Hill of the Thicket],
But the immortal gods [call it] the grave of the fleet Myrina.

(II: 811-15)

Again, for example, in Book XXIII, he uses "kurgan" to render Achilles's promise to raise a burial mound for the fallen Patroklos:

Гроба над другом моим не хочу я великого видеть,
Так, лишь пристойный курган; но широкий над ним
и высокий
Вы сотворите, ахеяне, вы, которые в Трое
После меня при судах мореходных останетесь живы.

(XXIII: 245-48)

And I do not want to see a great grave above my friend,
So only a proper kurgan; but above him a broad and tall one
You shall build, Achaeans, you who in Troy
Remain alive near the sea-roaming ships after I am gone.

(XXIII: 245-48)

And all these lexical items come together again at the end of the *Iliad*, with the burial of Hector:

Рано, едва розоперстая вестница утра явилась,
К срубу великого Гектора начал народ собираться.
И лишь собралися все (неисчетное множество было),
Сруб угасили, багряным вином оросивши пространство
Всё, где огонь разливался пылающий; после на пепле
Белые кости героя собрали и братья и други,
Горько рыдая, обильные слезы струя по ланитам.
Прах драгоценный собравши, в ковчег золотой положили,
Тонким обвивши покровом, блистающим пурпуром
свежим.
Так опустили в могилу глубокую и, заложивши,
Сверху огромными частыми камнями плотно устлали;
После курган насыпали; а около стражи сидели,
Смо́тря, дабы не ударила рать меднолатных данаев.
Скоро насыпав могилу, они разошлись; напоследок

Все собралися вновь и блистательный пир пировали
В доме великом Приама, любезного Зевсу владыки.
Так погребали они конеборного Гектора тело.

(XXIV: 788-804)

Early, scarcely had the rosy-fingered messenger
                            of morning appeared,
People began to gather around the pyre of illustrious Hector.
And only when all had assembled
                (there was an innumerable multitude of them),
They put out the pyre, having sprinkled
                            with crimson wine the space
Entire, where the blazing fire spilled forth; whereafter in the ash,
His brothers and companions gathered
                            the white bones of the hero,
Bitterly crying, abundant tears running along their cheeks.
Having gathered the precious ashes, they placed
                            [them] into a golden ark,
Wrapped with a fine cover, shining with a fresh purple.
So they laid [it] into a deep grave, and, having placed it [there],
They lay flat atop it many huge stones close together.
Afterward they piled up the kurgan,
                            and watchmen sat all around,
Lest a host of bronze-armored Trojans strike it.
Having quickly piled up the grave, they departed; and thereafter
All again gathered and feasted a glorious feast
In the great house of Priam, the master beloved by Zeus.
So they buried the body of Hector, breaker of horses.

(XXIV: 788-804)

Gnedich's rendition of Hector's burial is a veritable thesaurus entry on Russian words for graves—*mogila, grob, kholm, kurgan*. And we also find in these passages Gnedich affixing epithets that will accompany the kurgan over its long career in both archaeological writing and belles lettres: *velikii* (great), *vysokii* (tall, high), and *pristoinyi* (proper, seemly), which could be added to the entry in Zelenetskii's *Epithets*. So, too, in this passage, does Gnedich provide a condensed rendering of the Russian lexical equivalents for the whole process of constructing a kurgan: the conferring of the bones into a golden ark (*v kovcheg zolotoi polozhili*), which is laid to rest in a deep grave (*tak opustili v mogilu glubokuiu*), over which Hector's friends and brethren pile a "mound" or "kurgan" (*posle kurgan nasypali*). As established by the conclusion of the translation, then, the word "kurgan" was more firmly the Russian equivalent for these terms.

The story of the kurgan's place in the literary language is a complex one, however, since the word had been attested to in the eighteenth century. Did Gnedich—or his predecessors or contemporaries—understand "kurgan" to be a perfectly Russian word, or was it marked in some way as foreign? Among the earliest appearances of "kurgan" we find in the *National Corpus of the Russian Language* is in a passage from Mikhail Chulkov's *The Mocker, or Slavonic Tales* (*Peresmeshnik, ili slavenskie skazki*, ca. 1766-68), whereby Chulkov provides a whole typology of grave forms and descriptions as the customs and practices surrounding their construction and worship. In one case, Chulkov makes reference to the word "kurgan," when he notes to his readers the existence in certain parts of the country of a *"bugor, ili kurgan"* ("a mound, or *kurgan*").[18] The gloss betrays his doubt as to his readership's familiarity with the word, while also indicating what was perhaps his desire for greater terminological accuracy. The gloss suggests a moment in which the word "kurgan" emerged as a synonym of *bugor* and possessed linguistic circulation, but not sufficient familiarity among Chulkov's readers.

If, in the 1766 case of Chulkov the word "kurgan" retains an association with an unfamiliar register, and cannot stand as a self-sufficient term, then approximately fifty years later Gnedich would not need to supply such a gloss. To be sure, his selection of "kurgan" at any given moment of the translation might have rested less on the vagaries of stylistic change, than on the exigencies of metrics: the accent of *bugor* falls on the second syllable, and "kurgan" on the first. Gnedich may have required the latter to preserve the metrical scheme of the hexameter into which he translated the *Iliad*.

In either case, in promoting "kurgan" to the status of the Russian lexical equivalent of the Greek *tumbos*, Gnedich offered

---

[18] This is based on a search in *Natsional'nyi korpus russkogo iazyka*, with the search term "kurgan," accessed December 20, 2014.

a remarkable point of origin for the site's entrance into modern
Russian letters. His use of the word tells us as much about translation,
as it does of an act of philological and cultural appropriation.
Gnedich mines various verbal registers and sources to expand
the Russian literary language. In choosing "kurgan," he enabled
a Turkic word to become the Russian equivalent to the Greek. The
word finds its status consolidated within the literary language,
while also aiding in the broader project of demonstrating the
adequacy of the Russian language to Homer's Greek. Gnedich's use
of the word presents in miniature a confrontation not only between
the time of Gnedich's Russia and antique Greece, but also between
Russian and the lexical resources provided to the language through
its myriad contacts with other cultures, parts of whose languages
were Russified and their non-Slavic provenances possibly elided
through the act of translation.

The period when Gnedich took up his translation presents us
with a notable parallel between literary accounts of the kurgan and
the various archaeologies garnering the most attention in the first
several decades of the nineteenth century. As the archaeological
historian Aleksandr Formozov observes, during the 1810s and
1820s, various antiquities emerged from the ground, each vying
for, and enjoying the attention of Russian archaeologists. They had
an emergent interest in the archaeology of the Russian medieval
period (spurred on by the Napoleonic Wars) and in the archaeology
of Greek antiquity, the sites of which were located in the South of
Russia. In fact, as Formozov notes, what distinguished Russian
archaeologists such as Aleksei Olenin, Ivan Zabelin, and Aleksei
Uvarov from their Western European counterparts was that they
worked in both "antique and [Russian] medieval archaeology."[19]
This simultaneously held interest in various archaeologies mirrors
the place of the kurgan in Russian letters during the first half of
the nineteenth century. On the one hand, it is associated, through
Gnedich's translation, with Greek antiquity. On the other, it forms
a central site in the reinvigorated interest in the Russian medieval

[19]   Formozov, *Ocherki*, 42.

period, which we see elaborated by figures such as Pushkin, Anton Del'vig, and Aleksei Tolstoi. In short, the kurgans of Achilles and Hector as well as those of the *bogatyry* formed two principle provenances in poetic texts about the mounds.

Zelenetskii's entry on the kurgan, for example, drew several epithets from Sentimental and Romantic works, as expressed in such genres as the romance and the ballad. In these genres, we find the recuperation of the medieval figures of the *bogatyr'* (warrior-hero) and *vitiaz'* (knight).[20] Del'vig, for example, used the kurgan as a setting for a brief, twelve-line "Romance" ("Romans," 1822/29), in which we find a solitary knight standing on a kurgan:

> Одинок месяц плыл, зыбляся в тумане,
> Одинок воздыхал витязь на кургане.

> A solitary moon floated on, rippling in the fog,
> A solitary knight sighed upon the *kurgan*.[21]

We find similar examples of such scenes given extended treatment by other writers, as with Pushkin's ballad "Song of Oleg the Wise" ("Pesn' o veshchem Olege," 1822). In it, Pushkin recounts the tale of Oleg of Novgorod, whom a sorcerer warns that his horse would bring about his doom. After putting the horse down, Oleg feels remorse, goes to find the dead horse, whereupon a snake bites and kills him. The prophecy thus fulfilled, his friends perform a funeral rite, a *trizna*, which involves circling the kurgan:

> Пирует с дружиною вещий Олег
> При звоне веселом стакана.
> И кудри их белы, как утренний снег
> Над славной главою кургана . . .

> [. . .]

---

20   See Michael R. Katz, in "The Influence of Folk Ballads and the Ballad Revival on Russian Literary Ballads," *The Literary Ballad in Early Nineteenth-Century Russian Literature* (London: Oxford University Press, 1976).

21   A. A. Del'vig, "Romans," in *Polnoe sobranie stikhotvorenii* (Leningrad: Sovetskii pisatel', 1959), 160.

Ковши круговые, запенясь, шипят
На тризне плачевной Олега;
Князь Игорь и Ольга на холме сидят;
Дружина пирует у брега;
Бойцы поминают минувшие дни
И битвы, где вместе рубились они.

And vatic Oleg feasts with his retinue,
To the gay sound of the chalice.
Their curls are white, like morning snow,
Upon the glorious head of a kurgan

[…]

And the circular buckets, froth, and hiss
At the *trizna* of mournful Oleg
Prince Igor and Olga sit upon the mound
The retinue feasts at its base
The fighters recall former days,
And battles where together they fought.[22]

The image of the kurgan Pushkin conjures here marks martial glory and commemoration as acts belonging to the time of the kurgan's creation.[23] Such themes were common to Pushkin's poetic accounts of the kurgans. In his study *Pushkin and Archaeology*, Formozov singles out the kurgans as the archaeological monuments in the

[22]　A. S. Pushkin, *Polnoe sobranie sochinenii v desiati tomakh*, 10 vols. (Mosow: Nauka, 1960): 2: 108.

[23]　Pushkin possibly deploys the kurgan again in his poem "The Shield of Oleg" ("Olegov shchit," 1829), in which he refers to a *kholm* outside of Kiev. Where some scholars have taken *kholm* to refer to a "kurgan," Michael Wachtel points out the indeterminacy surrounding this term in the poem and notes instead that it could denote the hills outside of Kiev (*A Commentary to Pushkin's Lyric Poetry, 1826-1836* [Madison: University of Wisconsin Press, 2011], 137). For our purposes, the semantic range of *kholm* indicates the difficulty of reconstructing the story of the kurgan in Russian letters given the terminological range for burial mounds—as we saw above with Gnedich—and its recondite presence in such seemingly geological formations as *kholm*. Indeed, the archaeological historian A. A. Formozov observes that Pushkin also reveals various uses of the word "kurgan," sometimes using it in the sense of "burial mound" or as a geological formation (A. A. Formozov, *Pushkin i drevnosti: Nabliudeniia arkheologa* [Moscow: Nauka, 1979], 24-26).

Russian South that caught Pushkin's eye during his soujourn to the
region.[24]

Other treatments of the kurgan—such as the one we saw
in the introduction in Chekhov's "The Steppe"—mark a divide
between the time of a kurgan's creation and the time in which it is
encountered. In this case, the kurgan is perceived as a ruin or sign of
a forgotten past. Aleksei Tolstoi, for example, in his poem "Kurgan"
from the 1840s, extends the kurgan's association with the mourning
rite of the *trizna* one finds in Pushkin:

> В степи, на равнине открытой,
> Курган одинокий стоит;
> Под ним богатырь знаменитый
> В минувшие веки зарыт.
>
> В честь витязя тризну свершали,
> Дружина дралася три дня,
> Жрецы ему разом заклали
> Всех жен и любимца коня.
>
> In the steppe, on an open plain,
> A solitary kurgan stands.
> Beneath it a famous *bogatyr'*
> In past centuries was interred.
>
> In honor of the knight they performed a *trizna*,
> His friends fought for three days,
> At the same time the priests sacrificed for him
> All his wives and his beloved horse.

Tolstoi then links these themes directly to the story of the kurgan as
a monument to the glory of the knight:

> О витязь, делами твоими
> Гордится великий народ!
> Твое громоносное имя
> Столетия все перейдет!
> И если курган твой высокий
> Сровнялся бы с полем пустым,

---

24 Formozov, *Pushkin i drevnosti*, 24.

То слава, разлившись далеко,
Была бы курганом твоим!

O knight, of your deeds
A great people is proud!
Your thunder-bearing name
Shall traverse all the centuries!
And if your tall kurgan
Is ever leveled with the empty field,
Then fame, having spread far and wide,
Would be your kurgan.[25]

In such passages, Tolstoi might be seen as importing heroic themes and poetic immortality into a reimagined Slavic past; the song is accompanied by the sounds of the gusli, or psaltery, and the themes of the song—that glory will keep the knight safe in the afterlife—underpin the second stanza. In this regard, the earlier case of Gnedich's translation of Homer allows us to appreciate how Tolstoi reads the kurgan through similar questions of heroic immortality, fame, and monuments. Where Achilles had been promised *kleos aphthiton,* or "fame imperishable,"[26] however, the *bogatyr'* in Tolstoi's poem reawakens later to find that all he has left is the kurgan. Everything associated with the heroic past—from his confreres who had performed the *trizna,* to his very name—have all fallen into oblivion, and thus the promise of the first half of the poem goes unfulfilled:

И вот миновалися годы,
Столетия вслед протекли,
Народы сменили народы,
Лицо изменилось земли;
Курган же с высокой главою,
Где витязь могучий зарыт,
Еще не сровнялся с землею,
По-прежнему гордо стоит;

---

25   A. K. Tolstoi, "Kurgan," in *Polnoe sobranie stikhotvorenii i poem* (St. Petersburg: Akademicheskii proekt, 2006), 148-49.

26   Susanne Wofford, *The Choice of Achilles: The Ideology of Figure in the Epic* (Stanford, CA: Stanford University Press, 1992), 4.

А витязя славное имя
До наших времен не дошло.
Кто был он? Венцами какими
Свое он украсил чело?

And so the years passed,
The centuries flowed by,
Peoples replaced peoples,
The face of the earth had changed;
But the kurgan with its high head,
Where the mighty knight is interred,
Has still not drawn even with the earth,
Standing as proud as before;
Yet the glorious name of the knight
Has not come down to our age.
Who was he? With what wreaths of glory
Did he adorn his brow?

The kurgan signifies the sheer presence of the objects in the landscape, which testify to a forgotten past and an absent poetic tradition. The poet's questions therefore seem to circle around this absent historical and mythological knowledge, which leave him asking only the most general questions of the forgotten *bogatyr'*: How much blood did he spill? How many cities did he set aflame? Even though the "kurgan" in Tolstoi may ultimately testify to the absence of a literary tradition, in theme, genre, and the meter of amphibrachic tetrameter the text harkens back to Pushkin's earlier "Song of Oleg the Wise." As such, perhaps here we may be encountering the emergence of a poetic tradition whereby the kurgan forms a site of transhistorical dialogue between poets at the level of theme, genre, and meter, but one in which the image of the kurgan disavows that literary past even as it possibly recalls Pushkin's earlier ballad.[27] Indeed, many literary texts focusing upon the kurgan enshrine this commonplace of a "silent" kurgan standing in the steppe, attesting to a forgotten,

27   On the subject of poetic dialogues taking place at the kurgan, I suggest this in a reading of
      Fedor Tiutchev's poem "Ot zhizni toi, chto bushevala zdes'" (1871), in "A Remnant Poetics: The
      Chronotope of the Kurgan" in *The Persistence of Forms*, ed. Boris Maslov and Ilya Kliger (New York:
      Fordham University Press, forthcoming).

heroic past. In that guise, these works invert the structure of fame and immortality we find in the *Iliad*, indicating objects without poetic songs and the failure to secure immortality for a hero. The paradox of the kurgan as part of Russia's poetic topography is that so many works recapitulate the idea that the kurgan has no literary past, even as poets surely knew of other poems about it. At the very least, these oscillating themes of fame and oblivion are central facets of the literary career of the kurgan, and they parallel the kurgan's aesthetic function as either a mere landscape detail or as giving form to the steppe landscape itself, indeed, of giving the steppe a way to signify beyond just horizontal monotony.

iii. Vantage Points, ca. 1850

In 1848, around the same time as Tolstoi's "Kurgan," the poet Petr Viazemskii wrote a poem entitled "The Steppe" ("Step'"), describing that space as an "eternity upon the land," in which "the eye and ear go hungry":

> Бесконечная Россия
> Словно вечность на земле!
> Едешь, едешь, едешь, едешь,
> Дни и версты нипочем!
> Тонут время и пространство
> В необъятности твоей.
>
> [. . .]
>
> Пусто всё, однообразно,
> Словно замер жизни дух;
> Мысль и чувство дремлют праздно,
> Голодают взор и слух.

> Endless Russia,
> Is like an eternity on earth!
> You travel, travel, travel, travel
> For days and *versts* but for nothing!
> Time and space drown
> In your immensity.
>
> [. . .]

Everything is barren, monotonous
As though the breath of life has died
Thought and feeling idly doze
The eye and ear go hungry.[28]

In the face of this *spatial* eternity and *temporal* immensity of the steppe, such standard measures of time and space as "days and versts" fail to give the poet any bearing. Physically disoriented, the poet is nevertheless anchored poetically; in accounting for his experience of this confounding chronotope, he draws on various landscape topoi; the image of "Endless Russia" and the idea of "unbounded space" are both accompanied by the thumping trochees of "you travel, travel, travel, travel." Within this desolate landscape—which desolates both soul and sensorium—the poet briefly takes note of a group of kurgans:

Как разбитые палатки
На распутии племен
Вот курганы, вот загадки
Неразгаданных времен.

Like raised tents
At the crossroads of tribes
Here are the kurgans, here are the riddles
Of unsolved times.

Yet the kurgans do not occasion any prolonged meditation by the poet or spark a desire to resolve their riddle. This stanza, in fact, is framed by the two cited above, buttressing the sense that the kurgans cannot rupture the poet's experience of the "barren, monotonous" steppe.

Passages such as these abound in modern Russian literature; kurgans are mentioned, but to signify mere bumps in the landscape. Viazemskii, in fact, had observed kurgans at least once before, and on that occasion, they commanded even *less* attention when he described in his "Evening on the Volga" ("Vecher na Volge," 1816)

---

[28]   P. A. Viazemskii, "Step'," in *Stikhotvoreniia* (Moscow: Sovetskii pisatel', 1962), 286-87.

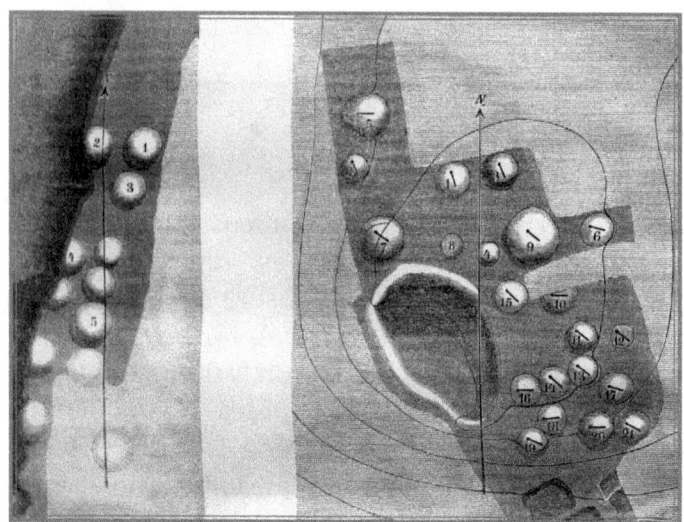

Figure 2.6.

Archaeological
diagrams
of the location
of kurgans, in
*Anthropological
Exhibition* (1878):
3:1: 56.

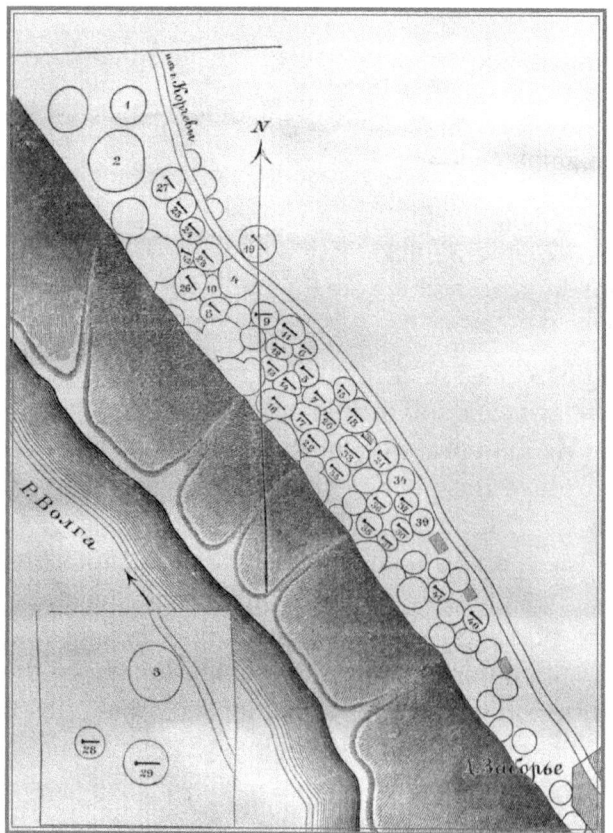

Figure 2.6a.

Archaeological diagrams
of the location
of kurgans along
the Volga, in
*Anthropological
Exhibition* (1878):
3:1: 56.

an "airy ridge of kurgans turning blue" (*griada vozdushnaia sineiushchikh kurganov*). While kurgans were certainly legible within the landscape—archaeological diagrams attest to as much (figs. 2.6 and 2.6a)—it is difficult to say why they mattered to some writers and not to others, and what prompted their becoming subjected to greater imaginative intensity. In Viazemskii's case, perhaps they did not mean more because the poet connected them to nomadic tribes; hence, the kurgans seem to be just markers of the passage of such peoples through space—just as he, too, is traveling—rather than potential elements enabling him to appreciate the landscape differently or to envision a heroic past, such as we saw above with Del'vig, Pushkin, and Tolstoi.

It was precisely as seen against this backdrop of spatial immensity, however, that the kurgan became significant for other writers, travelers, and archaeologists. To take one example, in 1844, just a few years before Viazemskii wrote his poem "Steppe," the traveler Grigorii Spasskii observed several encounters with kurgans in the Dnieper steppe. The "monuments of antiquity" (*pamiatniki drevnosti*), as Spasskii calls them, offers fixed points by which to orient oneself within the boundless landscape:

> The Dnieper kurgans. Monuments of antiquity known as kurgans, which begin in Southern Russia at the Samara river, stretch through the Dnieper steppe up to the Black and Azov seas, and are partially scattered over the Crimean Peninsula. Without these high mounds (*nasypei*) the traveler's gaze would often not find a thing upon which it could stop in the limitlessness of these plains: only they can sometimes break their sad monotony.[29]

In a landscape commonly perceived as a flat infinity, such writing on the kurgan as Spasskii's account points to its crucial aesthetic function: giving form to the landscape by puncturing the "sad monotony" of the steppe. Other travelers throughout the steppe commonly report this relationship between the kurgan and the

---

[29] G. I. Spasskii, "Dneprovskie kurgany," in "Korrespondentsiia," *Zapiski imperatorskogo odesskogo obshchestva istorii i drevnosti* (1844): 591.

landscape. Not only does Chekhov's narrator in "The Steppe" (1888) pause on what he called suspicious objects and the kurgans, but so, too, do foreigners traveling through other sections of the vast expanse. A certain E. Delmar Morgan, for example, writing in the *Scottish Geographical Magazine* about his travels through Volhynia (in the so-called Volhynia-Kholm forest steppe in present-day Ukraine), observed in 1888—the same year Chekhov published his story and Linnichenko noted "kurganomania" in archaeological studies—"were it not for these curious mounds the whole country I was travelling through would be one vast uninterrupted corn-field."[30]

Such ruptures in the landscape, Roland Barthes once observed, could be affiliated with a general aesthetic principle: "the picturesque," he remarked drolly, "is found anytime the ground is uneven."[31] Yet the kurgan does more than make the landscape "uneven" and thus picturesque; it is the very artifact that enables the steppe to have a form of signification other than sheer horizontality. In this regard, the kurgan is not just a sign of the past, but also an object that enters into a signifying order for the steppe. Indeed, it seems to create nothing less than the very conditions for steppe signification; it makes possible a set of contrasts, whether serving as a bench situated within spatial monotony upon which a traveler's gaze can find some way to measure and perhaps, even better, to perceive that monotony, or enabling a way to view the steppe, since it can serve as a rise in the ground from which to survey the steppe itself. In the latter capacity, the kurgan is no mere landscape detail, but alternately a focal point or vantage point that gives form and frame to spatial eternity.

***

[30]   E. Delmar Morgan, "Little Russia," *Scottish Geographical Magazine* 4: (1888): 538.

[31]   Roland Barthes, "The Blue Guide," in *Mythologies*, trans. Annette Lavers (New York: Hill & Wang, 1972), 74.

— Не беспокойтесь, —сказал Пьер. —Я пойду на
курган, можно?
—Да пойдите, оттуда все видно . . .

"Do not trouble yourself," said Pierre. "I will go to
the kurgan, if I may."
"Yes, do go; from there everything is visible . . ."
—Leo Tolstoy, *War and Peace*, 3:2:31

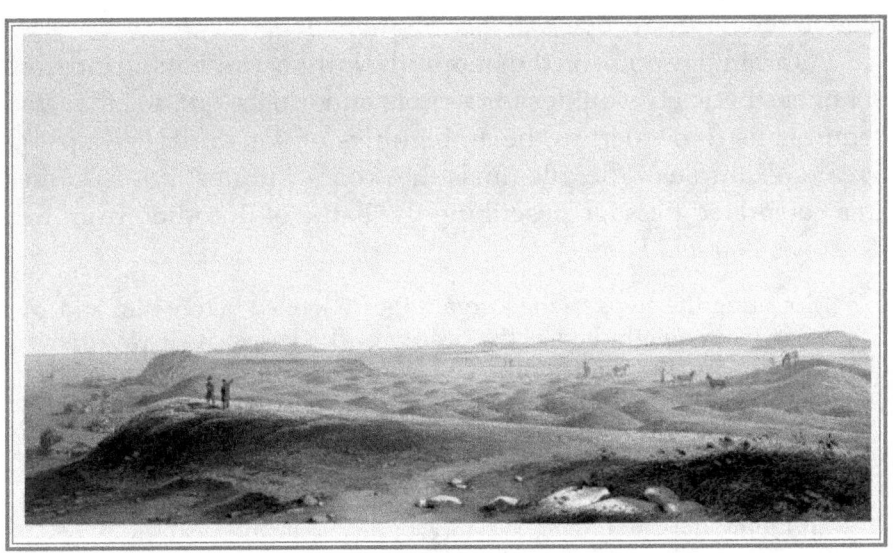

Figure 2.7.
"Temriuk: Kurgans near the Suvorov Fortification," plate IV
in *A Collection of Maps and Drawings toward the Study of the Antiquities
of Southern Russia and the Black Sea Coast* (1851).
Collection of the New York Public Library.

In the early 1850s, Aleksei Uvarov, whose work on the stone *babas*
was discussed in the previous chapter, traveled throughout the
Russian South, along the northern bank of the Black Sea—in particular
Crimea, where he visited Sevastopol and Simferopol and Kerch—

before heading to Temriuk on the southern shore of the Sea of Azof.[32]
Together with a talented draughtsman, a certain M. Vebel', Uvarov
assembled *A Collection of Maps and Sketches toward the Study of the
Antiquities of Southern Russia and the Banks of the Black Sea.* Since the
collection was being presented to the tsar, perhaps they were trying
to turn the imperial gaze upon the region in order to garner support
for further archaeological excavation. The gaze we find given more
prominence in the drawings, however, belongs to two "characters"—
perhaps Uvarov and Vebel—touring the region, researching and
recording the antiquities they find during their travels. In one, they
stand atop the peak of a kurgan, surveying the landscape in a manner
akin to what we saw Spasskii describe above (fig. 2.7).[33]

As a vantage point on the steppe, the kurgan presents an intricate
set of aesthetic possibilities for writers and artists, but one that also
requires us to be alert to the ambiguities of the word. Perhaps no
greater example of the dilemmas the word "kurgan" poses, comes
in a celebrated passage describing the Battle of Borodino from Leo
Tolstoy's *War and Peace*:

> Mounting the steps to the kurgan, Pierre looked before him and
> froze from delight before the beauty of the spectacle. It was the
> same panorama he had admired from that spot the day before,
> but now the whole place was full of troops and covered by smoke
> clouds from the guns, and the slanting rays of the bright sun,
> rising slightly to the left behind Pierre, cast upon it through the
> clear morning air penetrating streaks of rosy, golden-tinted light
> and long, dark shadows. The forest and the farthest extremity of
> the panorama seem carved in some precious stone. . . . All this
> was vivid, majestic, and unexpected, but what impressed Pierre
> most of all was the view of the battlefield itself.[34]

---

[32]   *A Collection of Maps and Drawings toward the Study of the Antiquities of Southern Russia and the
Black Sea Coast (Sobranie kart i risunkov k izledovaniam o drevnostiakh iuzhnoi Rossii i beregov
chernogo moria*, 1851. Collection of the New York Public Library.

[33]   A. D. Priakhin, *Istoriia otechestvennoi arkheologii* (Voronezh: Voronezhskii gosudarstvennyi
universitet, 2005), 89. See also Lebedev, *Istoriia otechestvennoi arkheologii*, esp. the section
"Osnovnye dostizheniia 'Uvarovskogo perioda' (1846-1884)," 130-96.

[34]   Leo Tolstoy, *War and Peace*, 2nd ed., trans. Louise and Aylmer Maude (New York: Norton, 1996), 703.
Translation adjusted.

The Battle at Borodino saw the most blood spilt on a single day both by the Russian army, led by General Kutuzov, and by Napoleon's Grande Armée in 1812 on their march toward Moscow. None of that carnage has yet occurred, and so Pierre exults in a landscape he perceives by turns as a "spectacle," a "panorama," and a heroic frieze. Given the emphasis in the passage on Pierre's aesthetic experience of the landscape, we might also wonder whether the object he deliberately ascends to furnish him with this vantage point might also carry any symbolic weight or aesthetic function.

If the kurgan in the passage were a burial mound, for example, it could serve as both vantage and portent; that is, to stand on a grave is to anticipate future graves. The problem, however, is that the kurgan Pierre ascends is not clearly a grave. As the passage continues, it becomes less clear what the kurgan at Borodino actually is:

> The kurgan upon which he ascended was the famous one known afterwards to the Russians as the Kurgan Battery or Raevskii's Battery, and to the French as *la grande redoute, la fatale redoute, la redoute du centre*, around which tens of thousands fell and which the French regarded as key to the whole position.
>
> The redoubt consisted of a kurgan, on three sides of which trenches had been dug. Within the entrenchment stood ten guns that were being fired through openings in the earthwork.[35]

The passage reveals some of the dilemmas of telling the story of the literary kurgan. With its wide semantic range, the word can denote either a mound located over a grave, or the entire complex of grave and mound. It can also, however, denote a geological formation, where its functional synonyms are "hill" (*kholm*), "small mound" (*nebol'shaia gorka*), or "embankment" (*nasyp'*); a military fortification, or "fortress" (*krepost'*); or a "redoubt" (*redut*), the latter being how Mikhail Lermontov refers to it twice in his poem "Borodino" (1837). It can also, in a combination of both the geological and martial senses of the term, denote a natural geological formation used for surveillance or in battle.

[35]   Ibid., 706. Translation adjusted.

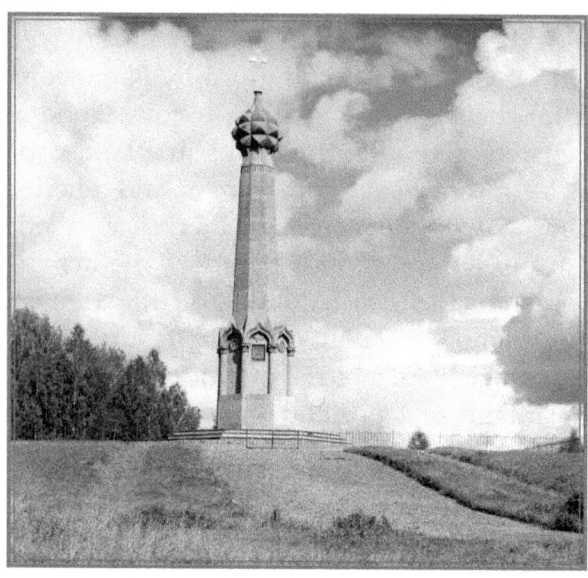

Figure 2.8.
Prokudin-Gorskii, photo of
the Raevskii Kurgan (1911).
Collection of the Library
of Congress.

Perhaps a natural formation is what Tolstoy had in mind with the kurgan at Borodino, even as he announces it as a mutable sign, whose designations shift from nation to nation, person to person. While his kurgan may lack a deep archaeological past, Tolstoy indicates here—by listing all those French and Russian names— that the kurgan is a *lieu de mémoire* and thus, despite the absence of archaeological relevance, nature becomes culture as the kurgan participates in the memorialization of war. In fact, Tolstoy already knew that kurgans could have this function before writing *War and Peace*, since he had described the so-called Malakhov Kurgan in his earlier "Sevastopol in August" ("Sevastopol' v Avguste," 1855). That site also witnessed extraordinary casualties during the Crimean War. Indeed, from the Napoleonic and Crimean wars all the way down to the Russian Civil War and World War II, such sites as the Raevskii Kurgan or Raevskii Redoubt, as it is called in a photo from 1911 by Sergei Prokudin-Gorskii (fig. 2.8); the Malakhov Kurgan; the extraordinary assemblage of the Mamaev Kurgan, which commemorates the Battle of Stalingrad (1942-43) (fig. 2.9); and the Kurgan of Glory (Kurgan Slavy), which was built in 1969 to commemorate Operation Bagration and the liberation of Belarus in 1944, have all marked the persistence of the kurgan, if not

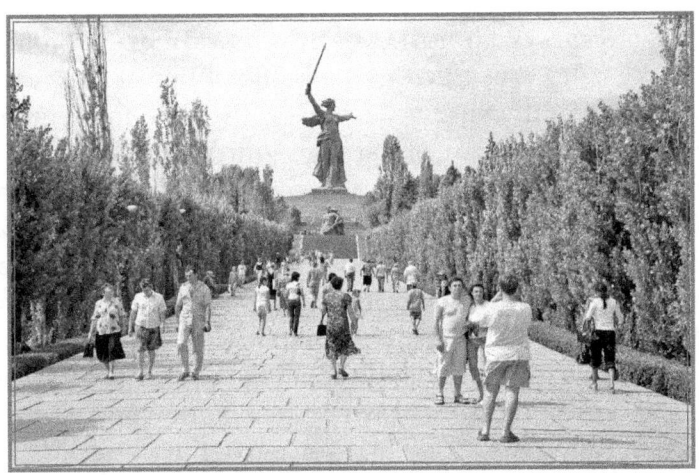

Figure 2.9.
Mamaev Kurgan. Lonely Planet Images. Photograph by Martin Moos. Getty Images.

as an actual burial mound, then as an archaic toponym central to Russia's and the Soviet Union's memorialization of war.

The remarkable symbolic flexibility of the kurgan as a grave form, and the vast geographic range over which it could be found, meant that it could be activated as a site to furnish contemporary events with a historical, even archaic precedent that verged on becoming a mythological paradigm. It is this function that we will focus on in coming chapters with Khlebnikov and Boris Pil'niak. But other examples could also be adduced here: in Isaac Babel's "Berestechko," a story from his *Red Cavalry Stories* (*Konarmiia*, 1926), the narrator observes: "We were advancing from Khotin to Berestechko. Our fighters were dozing in their saddles. A song rustled like a stream running dry. Horrifying corpses lay on thousand-year-old kurgans . . . We rode past the Cossack kurgans and the tomb of Bogdan Khmelnitsky. An old man with a mandolin came creeping out from behind a gravestone and with a child's voice sang of past Cossack glory."[36] These kurgans could either be

---

36 Isaac Babel, "Berestechko," in *The Collected Stories of Isaac Babel*, trans. Peter Constantine (New York: Norton, 2002), 270.

thousands of years old or just over three hundred—the reference to Khmelnitsky, who was killed in the Battle of Berestechko, indicates the mid-seventeenth century. However, the date matters less than does the tragic repetition of carnage within the region—perhaps Babel has in mind that the whole region is a burial ground—the signs of which are the kurgans upon which accumulates yet another layer of corpses. This image of a kurgan thus serves as an emblem for the overarching themes of the *Red Cavalry Stories*: the endless recurrence of violence and the profanation of nature. What both Tolstoy and Babel place into high relief in the story of the kurgan is that the site was an emblem of what the historian and archaeologist Ivan Zabelin called the "martial essence" of the steppe.

iv. 1876—The Grave Becomes a Cradle: Zabelin contra Chaadaev

In the opening pages of his unfinished *The History of Russian Life from the Most Ancient of Times* (*Istoriia russkoi zhizni s drevneishikh vremen,* 1876), the historian and archaeologist Ivan Zabelin devotes several extensive sections to the question of archaeology, and, in particular, kurgan archaeology. Zabelin was among the most prominent cultural figures to promote their study, undertaking numerous excavations of his own. In these opening pages, he focuses on the kurgans, and undertakes nothing less than the transformation of the archaic grave into a cradle: "The kurgan antiquities (*kurgannye drevnosti*), which are strewn upon our land, hide within themselves the true, genuine cradle of our national life."[37] It is a remarkable moment for the kurgan as a cultural site. With Zabelin, the kurgan is not only archaeological, but also historical. It marks a point of origin—a cradle—from which springs the history of the nation.[38]

[37] I. E. Zabelin, *Istoriia russkoi zhizni s drevneishikh vremen: Chast' 1* (1876–79; reprint, The Hague: Mouton, 1969), ix. All further references are cited in the text.

[38] Zabelin's metaphorical transformation of the kurgan into a cradle touches upon a curious etymology of the word *tumulus*: as David Summers observes, discerning the etymological link between "tomb," the Greek *tumbos* (which we've discussed above with the case of Gnedich), and *tumulus* and the Latin *tumere*, "the word *tumulus* is used by modern writers to refer to round

But there was a problem. Who was buried in the kurgan? And thus, whose inheritance was to be claimed in this grave turned cradle? The kurgan could be eminently valuable as an antiquity (as the term *kurgannye drevnosti* suggests), but at the same time a far from stable source given the uncertainty of its provenance: "With great zeal," Zabelin continues, "we have opened and continue to open the graves of the ancient inhabitants of our country, but nevertheless we do not reliably know whether these are our forefathers or whether they are foreign" (xii).

This desire to unearth a national past in the kurgans did not preclude Zabelin's interest in the archaeology of other peoples or in considerations of a universal story of humanity based on the archaeological record. Indeed, Zabelin draws on the work of two other academics—Karl Baer and Anton Shifner—in the introduction to his *History*, to assert that studying the past was a national responsibility: "If Russia does not study its own most ancient past, then it will not fulfill its task as an educated state. The matter has already ceased to be national: it has become a general concern of mankind" (viii-ix). But if Zabelin inflected the task of Russian archaeology with a universalist dimension, he also revealed a local polemic in which he was engaged:

> a researcher of the daily life of Russian antiquity is surprised in the first place by that circumstance in which a Russian, with respect to his culture, or to (his) historical and cultural products (*vyrabotky*), and in scholarly studies and in the consciousness of educated society, appears essentially as an empty place (*pustym mestom*), as a blank page (*chistym listom bumagi*), upon which— by virtue of historical, geographic, ethnographic, and other conditions—various nationalities (*narodnosti*) have inscribed their rules and regulations, customs and mores, trades and artistries, even national epic songs and so forth. (vi)

The images of an "empty place" and a "blank page"—commonplaces by Zabelin's time—are allusions to Petr Chaadaev, who had inscribed

burial mounds in general, but originally it was related to *tumeo, tumere* (to swell), which suggests pregnancy, inner energy, and life as well as death" (David Summers, *Real Spaces: World Art History and the Rise of Western Modernism* [London: Phaidon, 2003], 187).

them into "the Russian consciousness" in his "First Philosophical Letter" of 1837. Zabelin's historical mission, then, was something of a point-for-point rebuttal of Chaadaev. In positioning himself as a descendant of those *Slavons fanatiques* undertaking "diverse excavations" that Chaadaev dismissed in his "The Apologia of a Madman" (as we discussed in the introduction), Zabelin refuted the claim that all those excavations were in pursuit of mere *curiosités*. Repudiating these tropes, he installed the kurgan and his own archaeological work into a contest to decide whether anything from the past could be valuable to Russia at all.

To that end, Zabelin's works reveal a landscape far different than that of a tabula rasa, another commonplace that archaeology would prove most valuable in overturning. In his view, people simply did not know how to read the archaeological signs contained in the landscape. What Zabelin furnished was a way to read the steppe and other spaces of the Russian Empire through philology. He explains that the ancient Greeks, along with Roman and Byzantine writers, provide sources that "open our eyes, which are able with great attention to see and to value the silent monuments of our cradle" (ix). Chief among those ancients was Herodotus:

> the ancient rulers of our Land . . . could not but leave over the course of centuries some inheritance (*nasledstvo*). It is possible that in these hieroglyphs a particular chronicle is contained. It is necessary to read and to understand [the chronicle] since it says everything about our native land. This is why we think that no negative, doubting, and severe criticism of Shlözer [the historian with whom Zabelin is polemicizing] can take from Russian history its true treasure, its first chronicler, who is the Father of History, Herodotus . . . . The Father of History described our country 450 years before Christ. He traveled here, namely to the estuaries of the Dnieper, the Bug, and the Dniester. He saw much with his own eyes, and still more, he collected stories and rumors. . . . Unfortunately, Herodotus did not know our Far North at all. He recounts only the southern edges of the Russian land and says that, in his time, the entire country was inhabited by a people, who were called by the same name, the Scythians. (217)

Just as the *Iliad* famously served Heinrich Schliemann as a guide to Troy as he set out in the late 1860s,[39] Herodotus furnishes Zabelin with a similar map for Russia. With the aid of Herodotus, Zabelin played a leading role in excavating the various grave forms scattered throughout the Russian Empire, and in particular his excavation work in the Dnieper region. He drew upon "the Father of History" to further substantiate the notion that the Russian land, understood philologically, possessed archaic depth. Describing the Dnieper rapids, for example, he writes: "Here, Herodotus locates his Scythian [river] Heros, where they completed the burials of the Scythian Kings" (613).

It was in this region that Zabelin devoted much of his archaeological labor to excavating the Chertomlyk Kurgan beginning in 1859. He arrived there as a prominent historian, but, in the words of an archaeologist writing in the 1990s, as a "completely inexperienced archaeologist."[40] Zabelin undertook a number of excavations at the Chertomlyk Kurgan site in 1859–61, uncovering a remarkable cache of Scythian artifacts. He wrote up his findings in several works, among the most prominent being "The Scythian Graves: The Chertomlyk Kurgan" (1865),[41] reprinted in the appendix to *The History* as "The Ancient Scythians in Their Graves" ("Drevnie skify v svoikh mogilakh"). In the appendix, Zabelin notes that one could discern multiple provenances of the various kurgans found in the region north of the Black Sea: "We do not have the basis, however, to conclude that all these innumerable kurgans were built into mounds by the same tribe, for example, the Scythians. Here passed by, stopped, and lived many tribes and peoples who, doubtless, like the Scythians, left behind them a memory in the form of a grave mound, the sole structure that was possible on the naked steppe" (613).

---

[39]   For an account of Schliemann's discovery of Troy, and the debate it engendered between philology and archaeology, I rely on Suzanne L. Marchand, *Down from Olympus: Archaeology and Philhellenism in Germany, 1750-1970* (Princeton, NJ: Princeton University Press, 1996), 118-24.

[40]   A. Iu. Alekseev et al., *Chertomlyk: Skifskii tsarskii kurgan IV v do n.e.* (Kiev: Naukova dumka, 1991), 10.

[41]   I. E. Zabelin, *Skifskie mogily: Chertomlytskii kurgan* (Moscow: Tip. Gracheva, 1865).

Taken together, such lines as this from Zabelin's *History* and
his archaeological work provided an early example of the positive
valorization of the Scythians. To be sure, there were several powerful
currents against which we could measure the polemic of Zabelin's
work. The basic images prevalent in Chaadaev's account—the
void of Russian landscape, and the void of the soul, the absence
of objects testifying to a past—that we find challenged by Zabelin
were also extended and radicalized by Fedor Tiutchev. One of the
poet's enduring contributions to the Russian landscape tradition
was to codify the topos of "meager nature" (*skudnaia priroda*) in
his "These Poor Settlements" ("Eti bednie selen'ia," 1855), which
formed a capacious metaphor to encompass Russia's proverbial
boundlessness.[42] But this was a slightly less radical vision of
nature than we find in Tiutchev: in some of his bleakest visions
of the landscape, Tiutchev has Scythians and hordes and kurgans
in mind: In a letter from 1842, Tiutchev refers to the land beyond
Krakow as "a threatening plain, a Scythian plain" (*groznaia ravnina,
skifskaia ravnina*)."[43] This vision of nature as a limitless expanse of
threat extends deep into the poet's career; we find, for example,
Tiutchev remarking upon a set of kurgans in one of the finest of
his late lyrics, published roughly around Zabelin's *History*, which
is referred to as "From That Life That Raged Here" ("Ot zhizni toi,
chto bushevala zdes'," 1871), and also known by the title "Along
the Road to Vshchizh" ("Po doroge vo Vshchizh"), which takes its
title from the village Tiutchev frequently visited:

> От жизни той, что бушевала здесь,
> От крови той, что здесь рекой лилась,
> Что уцелело, что дошло до нас?
> Два-три кургана, видимых поднесь . . .
>
> Да два-три дуба выросли на них,
> Раскинувшись и широко и смело.

[42] See, for example, Christopher Ely, *This Meager Nature: Landscape and Identity in Imperial Russia* (DeKalb, IL: Northern Illinois University Press, 2002).

[43] Cited in Yuri Lotman, "Poeticheskii mir Tiutcheva," in *F. I. Tiutchev: Pro et contra* (St. Petersburg: RKhGI, 2005), 843.

Красуются, шумят,- и нет им дела,
Чей прах, чью память роют корни их.[44]

Of that life, which raged here,
Of that blood, which here streamed forth,
What has survived, what has come down to us?
Two or three kurgans, visible to this day . . .

And two or three oaks have grown upon them,
Having stretched out broadly and daringly.
They stand out, rustling—and are unconcerned
About whose dust, whose memory their roots dig into.

This opening landscape description is then drawn into what is his supreme, and, some critics have argued, his nihilistic vision of natural oblivion, as nature consumes the "memory" contained with the kurgans, which are themselves testaments to a bloody past.

It was within this landscape where Zabelin would locate his own story of perpetual violence, as he makes a comment about the Scythians that serves as a harbinger of the range of associations surrounding Scythian archaeology during the modernist period. He writes: "The southern border extended as the boundless steppe, in which lived the Scythians, a renowned people, wise, invincible, and possessing a miraculous art of warfare, for it was impossible to catch or to find them in the steppe, just as it was impossible to escape them" (2). For Zabelin, the Scythians were at the origin of an enduring quality of the steppe landscape; he observes that Scythian warfare

fully and very clearly expressed, so to speak, the martial essence (*voennoe sushchestvo*) of our steppes, indeed of our entire country, from which neither Darius the Persian, who went to battle with the Scythians, nor Napoleon, the leader of the Gauls, battling with the Russians, was able to escape with glory. (2)

---

[44] F. I. Tiutchev, *Stikhotvoreniia. Pis'ma* (Moscow: Sovetskii pisatel', 1957), 291. The poem was not published until 1886. An earlier variant of the poem explicitly connects the kurgans to "a long-forgotten past (*starina*)": "As though from out of a fog of / An antiquity forgotten long ago / Come two or three kurgans (Лишь кое-где, как из тумана / Давно забытой старины, / Два-три выходят здесь кургана)."

This analogy between Darius and Napoleon establishes the basic framework for a powerful paradigm whereby this archaic people is transformed into a model for the perception of later historical events. As it turns out, Russians and Scythians are not so far apart when it comes to their shared capacity to defend themselves: the Scythians defeated an outside invader, Darius; those who defeat an outside invader are Scythians; the Russians defeated an outside invader: Could that mean the Russians are Scythians? With Zabelin, the link of Russia with the Scythians remains an analogy, but several decades later, during the modernist period, it will become an essential, mythological paradigm for figures such as Aleksandr Blok and Benedikt Livshits. What's more, Zabelin's encoding here of the steppe's "martial essence" provides an apt template for modernist writing during the Russian Civil War, when literary accounts of that experience—such as the kind we saw above with Babel—are situated precisely at this conjunction of the archaeological remnants of the kurgan and the seemingly endless repetition of steppe warfare.

v. Archaeological Defamiliarization

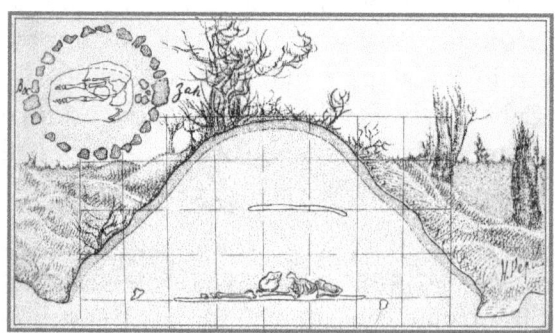

Figure 2.10.
Roerich, Archaeological sketch (1898).

Before Nicholas Roerich became a famous artist, he was an aspiring archaeologist, sketching kurgans (fig. 2.10) and other archaeological sites, as well as writing on a range of archaeological themes. In 1898 he wrote an essay in dialogue form entitled "On the Kurgan" ("Na kurgane"). In it, Roerich argues that the breadth of archaeological objects possessing cultural value should be expanded both chronologically and geographically.

One of Roerich's primary goals in this essay was to take up the cause for the Russian North, a region that would prove central to his own archaism and his celebration of such ancient peoples as the Varangians. Roerich's interlocutor is incredulous about his claims for the North: "It's all fine and good to talk about archaeology in Greece, in Italy, and finally, in our South and East, but the local Melanchlaeni and Hyperboreans could hardly have left behind anything interesting."[45] The only things of archaeological value in the region, the interlocutor facetiously remarks, are some Swedish buttons from the Petrine period.

Still, whether the focus was on the archaeology of the Russian South or the North, the aim of Roerich's essay was no less a case for archaeology in modern life. He pleads this case to his imaginary interlocutor, who views archaeology as nothing more than the "dusty science" of "dead things" (mertvechina) practiced by "Gravediggers! Vampires! Prosaists!" (1). Instead, the primary force of archaeology in Roerich's view is its capacity to free us from our ingrained habits of perception:

> If there exists an order of objects that allows us to break out of the maelstrom of everyday custom and through to the surface, even if only for a moment, or to glimpse further than palaces and higher than gigantic factory stacks, then archaeology cannot but have a place within such an order. (26)

Digging into the ground, rather than looking from the heights, would reveal the world of the deep past. In valorizing archaeology as a practice that can help one escape from "the maelstrom of everyday custom," Roerich anticipates one of Russian modernism's seminal ideas concerning the nature and function of art: ostranenie, or defamiliarization. In its classic formulation by Viktor Shklovsky, this notion proposes that art's essential purpose and effect is to restore to our blunted senses the strange palpability of objects that have become so familiar as to be unnoticeable—to make the stone

---

[45] Nikolai Rerikh, "Na kurgane" (1898), in *Sobranie sochinenii: Kniga pervaia* (Moscow: Izd-vo I. D. Sytina, 1914), 1. All further citations are to this edition and are cited in the text.

stony, as Shklovsky famously had it. To be sure, there are notable differences between Roerich's view of archaeology and Shklovsky's view of art. While both aim at breaking down our deleterious habits of perception, they differ as to the status ultimately accorded to the object. Whereas Shklovsky negates the object ("Art is a way of experiencing the making of an object, the object itself is not important"[46]), Roerich suggests that the archaeological artifact, once discovered, possesses an inherent capacity to defamiliarize. What they shared, however, was that both thought through the role of defamiliarization in relation to the processes of modernity: the economy of factory labor for Shklovsky, and the vantage points of modern life for Roerich.

When Roerich's "On the Kurgan" was reprinted in his collected works in 1914, the case for archaeology's value—and the case for that of *starina* generally—had been well established as a central facet common throughout modernist tendencies and among the public at large. The introduction to the volume begins with the observation: "These days many speak about the past (*starina*). In it they search for new paths for art. And the prophecies of those few who love our ancient beauty, who uniformly believe that by means of the past we shall grow younger, are coming true."[47] In these lines, the editor of the volume essentially recapitulates claims Roerich had made in his 1908 essay "Joy in Art," where he announced his investigation into the deep past as a "search for the sources of art," for "primordial beauty (*pervobytnaia krasota*)," and for "the joy in art."[48] This view, as Aleksandr Formozov observes, represents the Russian equivalent of the link between archaeology and aesthetics typically associated with Winckelmann in the West.[49]

But the kind of revivalism of the past central to Roerich's idea was actually a point of contention over various pasts, the selection of

[46] Viktor Shklovskii, "Iskusstvo kak priem" (1917/19), in *Poetika: Sbornik po teorii poeticheskogo iazyka* (Petrograd, 1919), 3:101-14.

[47] Rerikh, "Ot izdatelia," in *Sobranie sochinenii*, vii.

[48] Rerikh, "Radost' iskusstvu," in Mantel, *N. Rerikh*, 15.

[49] Formozov, *Ocherki*, 9.

which served as a way for Russian modernist camps to distinguish themselves from one another. One reason we know this is that avant-gardists like Benedikt Livshits, to take one example, writes in his memoir of Russian Futurism, *The One and a Half-Eyed Archer* (*Polutoraglazyi strelets*, 1933) that previous generations, though they may have shown an interest in the "primordial" or "primitive," did not understand its radical power:

> A penchant for the primitive, particularly for the everyday icon paintings hung in laundries, hairdressing parlors, and other provincial establishments and trades, which had proven to have such an influence on the art of Larionov, Goncharova, and Chagall, spurred Burliuk to buy up the signboards of handicraft works with his last dime at a time when Benois and Grabar' regarded them with disdainful indifference. The love of folk art, the attraction toward the primitive in all its forms, to the art of Polynesia or ancient Mexico, was not for Burliuk the whimsy of a satiated taste nor the connoisseurship of people like Sergei Makovskii. No, this passion had beneath it a far deeper ground.[50]

As Livshits indicates here, various modernist camps could evince an interest in a specifically "primitive" past. As such, what is significant is not that any one group of modernists was "original" in claiming a particular patrimony from the past. What mattered was both the "rhetoric" of originality and its accompanying challenge of who was the better inheritor of the past.

Despite the debate over the past Livshits records in these lines, they reveal how the common division of Russian modernists into future-oriented technophiles or retrospectivists fails to account for the deep urgency assigned to the past throughout the modernist factions. When the early Russian Futurists proclaimed "from the heights of skyscrapers" that the literary work of their predecessors amounted to "nothingness," it was a polemical gesture that

---

[50] Benedikt Livshits, *Polutoraglazyi strelets*, in *Polutoraglazyi strelets: stikhotvoreniia, perevody, vospominaniia* (Leningrad: Sovetskii pisatel', 1989), 333. Translated as *The One and a Half-Eyed Archer*, trans. and ed. John Bowlt (Newtonville, MA: Oriental Research Partners, 1977), 53. Page numbers refer to each volume respectively. The translations have been occasionally adjusted.

consigned the luminaries of the past to oblivion, and seemed to harness their own work to urban modernity. But we might also remember how in 1912 a central site of early Russian Futurism was Hylaea, a region deep in the Pontic steppe, where Livshits, Khlebnikov, and the Burliuk brothers followed up on their amateur interest in archaeology, and, as we saw in the previous chapter, formed family galleries in which they included stone *babas*. They could ascend skyscrapers or descend into kurgans and neither pursuit seemed a contradiction of the other.

vi. Steppe Archaism and the Stratification of Time

Perhaps one reason for the absence of a contradiction between these orientations toward archaeology and industrialization was that early Russian Futurists found archaeology to yield models of time and space commensurate with their own aesthetic values. It was at Hylaea, for example, where archaeology and modernist aesthetics found one of their most remarkable conjunctions. There, early Russian Futurists, who took the name "Hylaeans," located a quintessential borderland between the Greek and Scythian worlds on the northern bank of the Black Sea, once the limit of the world known to the Greeks and incorporated millennia later into the Russian Empire. In a passage from Livshits's *The One and a Half-Eyed Archer,* he describes his experience of this landscape as more mythological than real:

> Instead of a real landscape, detailed by all kinds of things that are signified by words found in Dal''s dictionary, there arises before me an immense valley which strikes the eye like a phosphorescent whiteness. There, beyond the point of the horizon, is the lice-ridden, black-fleeced belt of Aphrodite of Tauris—did it really exist?—and the swarming of innumerable herds of sheep. Well, not really: this is the cloak of Nessus that Heracles let fall in the Hylaean steppe (contrary to the myth). Returning to its sources, history is created anew. The wind from the Euxine Pont swoops in with a snowstorm, repudiating the mythology of Lubker, denudes the kurgans that have been covered by lethargic snow, and throws up a swarm of Hesiodic shadows, reshuffling them

while still in the air, before coming to rest there beyond the barely
visible expanse in the form of a mytheme that gives wing to our
will.[51]

Matter is here apparently given over to myth, reality incarnates
mythology, and the details of the scene are not particulars "of
a real landscape" but iterations of mythological paradigms. Indeed,
Livshits's view of time suspends historical progress, so that even
when he writes, "returning to its sources, history is created anew,"
the view is one of endless circulation rather than linearity.

It was this repudiation of history and the privileging of myth,
which, according to Boris Gasparov, we find throughout Russian
modernist culture. Myth was the period's "prevailing mode":
"Those who strive for total transcendence of previous cultural
experience must necessarily eschew historically oriented thought;
by its very nature their aspiration is both panchronic and atemporal.
The flow of historical time is brought to a halt by a messianic act
of total renewal, and all previous epochs merge in a new ideal
synthesis."[52] If Russian modernist culture elevated mythology to its
dominant structural and metaphysical principle, this gave rise as
well to several related antinomies that structured the basic typology
of the period: the paradigmatic prevails against the syntagmatic,
the synchronic displaces the diachronic, and simultaneity abolishes
temporal succession. The distinctiveness of phenomena, whether in
time or space, is annulled, and events and things are but "iterations
of some mythological paradigm or archetype."[53] The landscape

---

[51] Ibid., 321/44.

[52] Boris Gasparov, introduction to *Cultural Mythologies of Russian Modernism: From the Golden Age to the Silver Age*, ed. Boris Gasparov, Robert P. Hughes, and Irina Paperno (Berkeley and Los Angeles: University of California Press, 1992), 2-3.

[53] Gasparov's views point to the shared values of Russian modernist culture and modernism generally, as, for example, elaborated by Joseph Frank and his concept of "spatial form." In Frank's words: "What has occurred, at least so far as literature is concerned, may be described as the transformation of the historical imagination into myth—an imagination for which historical time does not exist, and which sees the actions and events of a particular time only as the bodying forth of eternal prototypes" ("Spatial Form in Modern Literature," in *The Widening Gyre: Crisis and*

Livshits describes above, then, typifies this prevailing mode; history, as he understands it, is hardly linear or progressive, but circular. History returns to its sources, and through that return, it is revitalized.

But we also find in the same chapter by Livshits another version of panchronism based not entirely on mythology, but on archaeology:

> Hylaea, Ancient Hylaea, trodden by our feet, was acquiring the meaning of a symbol; it was to become a sign.
>
> Even later strata were exposed. Behind Hesiod, there was Homer.
>
> Once, going through the servants' quarters, I noticed a strange commotion. In a merry ring, the inhabitants of the house had circled around a figure in a sheepskin coat. This was a shepherd who had spent a whole year in the steppe, miles from human habitation. Hundreds of these shepherds wandered around the edges of the Mordonov estate driving their flocks from place to place—the direct descendants of Odysseus's rams and sheep. These people had gone wild and had almost forgotten how to speak. Not seeing women for years on end, they satisfied their sexual needs through bestiality.
>
> In the summer months Vladimir used to devote himself passionately to excavating the less-ancient kurgans, finding Scythian bows and crowns with which he armed his one-and-a-half-eyed archers for mortal combat with the Parisian women he had fragmented into their basic planes.
>
> Time, losing its borders, stratified (*rasslaivalos'*) in all directions in Chernianka.[54]

Mastery in Modern Literature ([Bloomington: Indiana University Press, 1968], 60). Frank's concept of "spatial form" has been the subject of wide-ranging debate, with subsequent literary critics frequently doing less to repudiate his initial claim of the elevation of myth over history, than to critique its ethical implications, or fault it for not going far enough, since space is proposed as a constitutive element of nearly all literary texts. For a summary of the debate, see W. J. T. Mitchell, "Space and Time: Lessing's *Laocoon* and the Politics of Genre," in *Iconology: Image, Text, Ideology* (Chicago: University of Chicago Press, 1986), 95-115; and Frank's response to his critics, "Spatial Form: Thirty Years After," in *Spatial Form in Narrative*, ed. Jeffrey R. Smitten and Ann Daghistany (Ithaca, NY: Cornell University Press, 1981), 202-44.

[54] Livshits, *Polutoraglazyi strelets*, 321-22/45.

The stratification of time in Hylaea confronts us with a form of simultaneity that perceives archaeological vestiges in the landscape in tandem with mythology, where the hard matter of the past is presented to the viewer. In its immediate context of the chapter, the stratification of time corresponds to many of the values Livshits finds in the Futurist grappling with the aesthetics of Cubism, which we already see in the passage as the "fragmentation" of the Parisian women into "basic planes." For Livshits, this is Cubism armed with Scythianism, the deep past conjoined with a new aesthetic tendency to level a challenge to other representational systems or conventional depictions of landscape, and, indeed, even to the sources of Cubism—namely France—that the Futurists would undertake as they made Cubism their own.

We know that in 1911, Livshits and the other Hylaeans were deeply preoccupied with studying Cubism, the new aesthetic import from Paris, and translating it into other media, in particular, poetry. Livshits, for example, wrote a poem in prose entitled "People in Landscape" ("Liudi v peizazhe," 1911), first published in *A Slap in the Face of Public Taste* (*Poshchechina obshchestvennomu vkusu*, 1912)—a poem that he describes in the chapter as an "attempt at an authentic Cubist construction of a verbal mass."[55] The poem's title derives from the Hylaeans' interest in landscape as a major subject of Cubist experimentation: as Livshits informs us, it was David Burliuk who pursued "landscapes from several points of view."[56]

This was not only a painterly pursuit. On one level, it has a cultural program. As Livshits later writes in the memoir, what they find in Hylaea are "atavistic strata, diluvian rhythms, confronting the West and sustained by the East, approached in a relentless cataclysm, flooded by the light of prehistory, dreaming in a cloud of a savage horseman, a Scythian warrior, turning his face backward and with only a half-eye on the West—the one and a half-eyed archer!" (373/92). This split vision, in a sense, is a form of defamiliarization, again borne out of archaeology, that aims at nothing less than

---

[55]   Ibid., 329/58. The work can be found on p. 547 of this volume.

[56]   Ibid. All further references cited in the text.

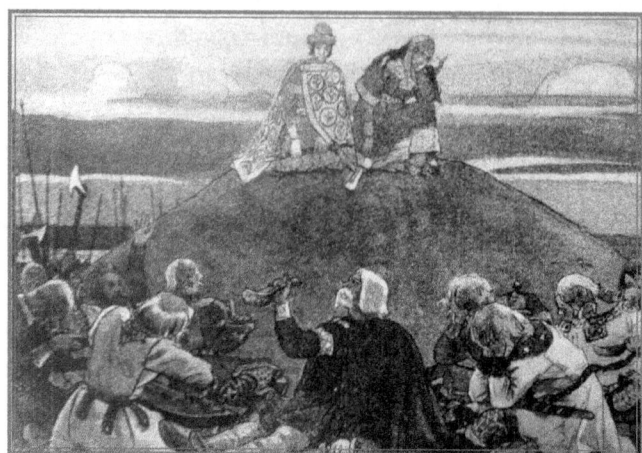

Figure 2.11.
Vasnetsov, illustration
of Pushkin's
"Oleg the Wise,"
in *The Library
of Great Russian
Writers* (1909).

offering a new way of seeing that takes into account the deep past, while aiming at the West: "Everything will assist in this renewed perception of the world: displaced construction, a multiplicity of perspectives, seas of the color black (which had been rejected by the Impressionists), pandemonium of planes and an unprecedented treatment of texture" (330/51).

We can extrapolate from the passage a primary relationship between archaeology and modernism that informs so much of the modernist effort, which, as we will see, gives aesthetic form to the multiple temporalities it locates within the steppe. It did not discover these temporalities; thanks to figures such as Zabelin they were already known, and the poets and archaeologists surveyed above testify to the fact that the kurgan was highly legible within the landscape. Instead, what modernist texts seem to foreground are those strata that reveal how the prevailing mode of mythological simultaneity had a distinctly archaeological cast.

The form of engagement with the archaeological that I am privileging here also has some inner distinctions. Other artists, by contrast, reimagined these works during the time of their creation. We could, for example, turn back toward Pushkin's "Song of the Oleg the Wise," which we discussed above, and recall that it was illustrated by Viktor Vasnetsov. The illustration reimagines the time and setting of Oleg (fig. 2.11), evincing one archaizing mode in which ancient content seems to predominate, while being elaborated within a prevailing period style, such as painterly realism, which also structures Vasnetsov's panel frieze *The Stone Age* (*Kamennyi vek*, 1883-85) for the Historical Museum in Moscow. Such attempts to re-create the past in the painterly idiom of the present did not fare well in the most radical modernist experiment of the time — Stravinsky and Roerich's *The Rite of Spring*, which generated not only outrage at the formal radicalism of the score, but also criticism among its supporters that Roerich's sets did not offer visual equivalents to the more innovative aspects of the score. The critic Roger Fry, to take one example, deemed Roerich's stage designs "rather fusty romanticism."[57]

If an archaism of content but not form was one path, archaic content married to radical innovations of form was another, driving parallel artistic experiments in Russian and in modernism internationally. As Hugh Kenner observes, "The young Ezra Pound had been susceptible to the magic of time, and had archaized accordingly. This only meant, as he came to see, a bad style, which he worked to discard. When it was gone, all times could lie on the same plane, 'in the timeless air.'"[58] That is to say that alongside a mode of archaic reconstruction typified by figures such as Vasnetsov, another way to grapple with the artifacts of the past such as the kurgan was to continually register them as archaeological, in other words, interwoven into the fabric of the present. Even as writers and artists may have focused on the kurgan or the stone *baba* as objects of the deep past, they wrote from the perspective of the present. That present could, to be sure, dilate into panchronism, but it held firm to a vision in which the signs of the past intermingle in various ways with the events of the present.

That such complex temporal experiences take place by and large in the steppe (though, in fact, the kurgan appears throughout the Eurasian continent), upended some of the standard topoi of steppe monotony. Modernist texts not only radically defamiliarize those commonplaces, but also throw them overboard. As Mikhail

57   Cited in Lynn Garafola, *Diaghilev's Ballets Russes* (New York: Da Capo Press, 1998), 68.

58   Hugh Kenner, *The Pound Era* (Berkeley and Los Angeles: University of California Press, 1971), 30.

Epstein describes it, extending Bakhtin's concept of the chronotope: "In attempting to apply the Bakhtinian concept of the chronotope to Soviet civilization, one discovers a curious pattern: *chronos* is consistently displaced and swallowed up by *topos*. Chronos tends toward zero, toward the suddenness of miracle, toward the instantaneousness of revolutionary or eschatological trans-formation. Topos, correspondingly, tends toward infinity, striving to encompass an enormous land mass and even the earth itself."[59]

As Epstein makes clear in other passages of his essay, the leitmotif of a steppe without time was hardly less central to Russian writers in the nineteenth century, as we have seen in the case of Viazemskii. Steppe artifacts like the stone *baba*, but more emphatically the kurgan, were a counter-model to prevailing ideas of steppe signification.[60] On the one hand, the kurgan could offer a vertical axis, however stunted, allowing a given writer to survey the land or ponder what was interred within. The kurgan stratifies the steppe, opening up temporal and archaeological layers that had not been sensed before and that challenged notions of sheer, timeless horizontality. On the other hand, the kurgan offers a mode of signification based on networks rather than strata, forming a kind of node within a vast space and testifying to the traces of former peoples. To a discerning eye, that vast space revealed the traces of time.

[59] Mikhail Epstein, "Russo-Soviet Topoi," trans. Jeffrey Karlsen, in *The Landscape of Stalinism: The Art and Ideology of Soviet Space*, ed. Evgenii Dobrenko and Eric Naiman (Seattle: University of Washington Press, 2003), 277.

[60] I am indebted to Anne Lounsbery's "Saussurean Steppe: Meaning in a Flat Landscape," *North American Chekhov Review* (Summer 2012): 12-22, for helping me to think through the idea of steppe signification as a particular problematic of Russsian cultural history and Russia's symbolic geography.

Chapter Three

Ancient Statues, Ancient Terrors

In 1906, *Znanie*, the miscellany edited by Maxim Gorky, published a selection of thirteen poems by a relatively new voice on the Russian literary scene, Ivan Bunin.[1] The subjects of the poems ranged geographically and chronologically: one finds the poet speaking as a "simple maiden" in a poem set near the Bosphorus; another took the mosque of Hagia Sophia as its subject; while another, on the "kingdom of the Amazons," was set on the banks of Asia Minor. There were two poems in the selection, placed one after the other, prompted by encounters with archaic statuary. The first poem was entitled "Aeschylus" ("Eskhil"):

> Я содрогаюсь, глядя на твои
> Черты немые, полные могучей
> И строгой мысли. С древней простотой
> Изваян ты, о старец. Бесконечно
> Далеки дни, когда ты жил, и мифом
> Теперь те дни нам кажутся. Ты страшен
> Их древностью. Ты страшен тем, что ты,
> Незримый в мире двадцать пять столетий,
> Незримо в нем присутствуешь доныне,
> И пред твоею славой легендарной
> Бессильно Время. — Рок неотвратим,
> Все в мире предначертано Судьбой,
> И благо поклоняющимся ей,
> Всесильной, осудившей на забвенье
> Дела всех дел. Но ты пред Адрастеей
> Склонил чело суровое с таким
> Величием, с такою мощью духа,

---

[1]   The poems appeared in *Sbornik tovarishchestva 'Znanie' za 1906 god: Kniga deviataia* (St. Petersburg: Znanie, 1906), 203-4.

Какая подобает лишь богам
Да смертному, дерзнувшему впервые
Восславить дух и дерзновенье смертных.

I shudder, looking upon your
Silent features, full of a powerful
And severe thought. With ancient simplicity
You are carved, O Ancient One. Endlessly
Distant are the days, when you lived, and like a myth
Those days now seem to us. You are terrifying
                                        by their antiquity.
You are terrifying since you,
Unseen in the world for twenty-five centuries,
Have been present in it unseen up till now,
And before your legendary glory
Time is impotent.—Fate is inevitable,
Everything in the world is foreordained by Destiny,
And blessed are those who bow down before her,
The Omnipotent one, who has condemned to oblivion
The doings of all deeds. But before Adrasteia you
Bowed your fierce brow with that
Grandeur, with that might of the spirit,
Which is proper only to the gods
And to the mortal, who dared for the first time
To glorify the spirit and daring of mortals.

The poem following "Aeschylus" was entitled "The Stone *Baba*" ("Kamennaia Baba"):

От зноя травы сухи и мертвы.
Степь—без границ, но даль синеет слабо.
Вот остов лошадиной головы.
Вот снова—Каменная Баба.

Как сонны эти плоские черты!
Как первобытно-грубо это тело!
Но я стою, боюсь тебя . . . А ты
Мне улыбаешься несмело.

О, дикое исчадье древней тьмы!
Не ты ль когда-то было громовержцем?
—О, да, не Бог нас создал. Это мы
Богов творили скотским сердцем.

From the intense heat the grasses are dry and dead.
The steppe is without borders, yet the distance appears
                                        weakly blue.
Here is the skull of a horse's head.
Here again is the Stone *Baba*.

How drowsy are these flat features!
How primitively rude is this body!
But I stand in fear of you . . . Yet you
Smile at me timidly.

O savage progeny of ancient darkness!
Were you not once the Thunderer?
—Yes, it was not God who created us. It was we
[Who] created the gods with our bestial heart.

That Bunin placed the two poems side by side readily presents us with a set of juxtapositions. Both are about statues, and both about the poet's sense of terror or awe in the face of them, one poem involving the aesthetic of "archaic simplicity" and human daring, and the other "primitive rudeness" and human bondage. Bunin sharpened the contrast between the two poems when he revised "The Stone *Baba*," and made more explicit the theme of enslavement by changing the adjective "bestial" (*skotskim*) into "slavish" (*rabskim*) in the poem's last line:

—Не бог, не бог нас создал. Это мы
Богов творили рабским сердцем.

Not God, not God created us. It was we
[Who] created the Gods with our slavish heart.[2]

In these encounters with archaic statuary, Bunin found an occasion to consider the relationship of aesthetics to culture and

2   As far as I have been able to ascertain, the change from *skotskim* to *rabskim* occurred that same year when the poem was republished in Bunin's *Stikhotvoreniia, 1903-06* (St. Petersburg: Tipografiia Montvida, 1906). In that edition, Bunin also changed the sequence of the poems, and so "Kamennaia baba" does not follow "Eskhil." The sequence was restored as early as his *Stikhotvoreniia, 1903-06: Manfred Bairona*, 2nd, exp. ed. (Moscow: Knigoizdatel'stvo pisatelei, 1912), 121. The sequence remains the same in his *Sobranie sochinenii v deviati tomakh*, 9 vols. (Moscow: Khudozhestvennaia literatura, 1965–67), 1:247-48. All references to Bunin's works are to this edition and are cited in the text.

philosophy, and to conceive a philosophical anthropology on the basis of artifacts from the deep past. What his poems offer us, in turn, is an occasion to consider several poetic accounts of the stone *babas*, since the themes of simplicity and rudeness, of terror and enslavement, impinge upon broader debates animating the early modernist period. On the one hand, these debates concern the values ascribed to archaic statuary, along with the different sites in which writers such as Valery Briusov, Sergei Gorodetskii, and Aleksei Remizov located them, whether in their own works on the stone *babas* or in those on archaic statuary. On the other hand, Bunin's poems point toward debates circulating on the archaic generally, which track nothing less than the relationship of the human to the divine, and disclose the predicament of modern culture and its unsteady relationship to the deep past.

To follow the various trajectories converging in Bunin's poems and extending outward from them is to find thematic parallels—not only with the aforementioned writers, but also with the philosophical and archaeological speculations of figures such as Viacheslav Ivanov and Pavel Florenskii, whose work on both the statuary and archaic artifacts form a parallel story to that of Bunin's in the coming pages. Considered in these terms, Bunin's poems reveal a constellation of comparable concerns and themes that reveal how this episode in the career of the *babas* finds the statuary poised at a central moment in the trajectories of Russian modernism, caught between a renewed interest in Greek antiquity and an emergent, but still ambivalent interest in the aesthetics and cultural value of the "primitive."

i. Archaic Simplicity

A year after Bunin published the two poems, he set off on an extended journey to various ancient sites.[3] He and his common-law wife, Vera Muromtseva, traveled from the Russian South to

---

[3]   A. Boboreko, *I. A. Bunin: Materialy dlia biografii (s 1870 do 1917)* (Moscow: Khudozhestvennaia literatura, 1967), 107.

Europe, the Levant, and Egypt. In May 1907, he wrote to a friend: "We have been in Tsargrad, Athens, Alexandria, Haifa, Jerusalem, Jericho, Hebron, and by the Dead Sea! I am now writing to you from Syria, from Beirut. Tomorrow we are going to Damascus and then to Nazareth, Port Said, Cairo; and after we have seen the Pyramids, we are coming home, again through Athens!"[4] The following day, he and Muromtseva sent another missive, this time to her family: "Greetings from Syria, from Baalbek. We have been to the ruins of the ancient Temple of the Sun! We are alive and well!"[5]

The sites Bunin visited belonged to something like an expanded Grand Tour, taking travelers beyond the antiquities of Greece and Rome to those of other ancient civilizations and epochs. The Baedeker guide for Palestine and Syria, for example, recommends itineraries similar to those Bunin reports; the seven-day trip from Beirut to Damascus, features the ruins at Baalbek.[6] "All my most cherished journeys," Bunin wrote, long after he had emigrated to Europe after the Revolution, "took place in those lost kingdoms of the East and South, in the dead and forgotten lands, among their ruins and cemeteries."[7] Or, in another telling recollection of these travels in an interview: "How strange," his interlocutor said to him, "that you chose to travel to all those savage places at the ends of the earth," to which Bunin responded: "Savage indeed. Note how all the necropolises and graves of the world attracted me. It's necessary to note this and puzzle it out (*rasputat'*)!"[8]

There would have been much material to draw upon in trying to answer what caused this attraction in his work. The themes

---

4   Letter to Nikolai Teleshov [May 4, 1907], cited in Thomas Gaiton Marullo, *Ivan Bunin: Russian Requiem, 1885-1920: A Portrait from Letters, Diaries,* and *Fiction* (Chicago: Ivan R. Dee, 1993), 106.

5   Letter to the Muromtsevs [May 5, 1907], cited in ibid., 106.

6   *Palestine and Syria with the Chief Routes through Mesopotamia and Babylonia: Handbook for Travellers* (Leipzig: K. Baedeker; New York: C. Scribner's Sons, 1906), 318-36.

7   Cited in D. J. Richards, "Comprehending the Beauty of the World: Bunin's Philosophy of Travel," *Slavonic and East European Review* 52, no. 129 (1974): 521.

8   Cited in Boboreko, *I. A. Bunin*, 107. For more on Bunin's attraction to antiquity, see Serge Kryzytski, *The Works of Ivan Bunin* (The Hague: Mouton, 1971), 64.

we find in Bunin's two poems that primarily concern us here
had preoccupied him since at least the previous decade. And the
attraction took many forms. Nearly a decade before he had published
the poems, Bunin had written Briusov in May 1899: "Life is terribly
solitary and incomprehensible. . . . I'm going to the country. . . . I'm
going to think thoughts upon steppe graves (*Budu dumat' dumy na
stepnykh mogilakh*)."[9] Bunin evidently found solace in the meditative
possibilities of lying upon those "steppe graves" (that is, kurgans)
to contemplate time and the deep past. And he seems to have been
associated with doing so since Konstantin Bal'mont dedicated
a four-stanza poem to him entitled "Feather Grass" ("Kovyl'," 1895),
in which he included the stanza:

> И мерцание мелькнувшее
> Исчезает за туманами,
> Утонувшее минувшее
> Возникает над курганами.

> And the flashing twinkling
> Disappears behind the mists,
> The drowning past
> Arises above the kurgans.[10]

This association of Bunin with steppe artifacts may have arisen
because he had published in 1895, "On the Donets" ("Na Dontse"),
in which he describes a situation and mood similar to those in his
letter to Briusov and to the themes and concerns that also inform his
encounters with Aeschylus and the stone *baba*:

> The kurgan was wild, and still untouched by the plow. It had
> spread into two hills, and, like a withered tablecloth of faded
> green velvet, it was covered with a year-old grass. The gray
> feather grass silently swayed a bit upon its side—pitiful remnants
> of feather grass. Time—I thought—forever passes it by; in age-old
> oblivion it only remembers that far-off past, former steppes and

9   Letter to Briusov, May 25, 1899, cited in ibid., 75.

10   K. Bal'mont, "Kovyl'," in *Izbrannoe: Stikhotvoreniia, perevody, stat'i* (Moskva: Khudozhestvennaia
     literatura, 1980), 46.

former peoples, whose souls were nearer and dearer to it, who were able to understand, better than we could, its whisper, one full of the age of the desert's pensiveness, speaking wordlessly of the insignificance of earthly existence. (2:108)[11]

The kurgan is both a sign of time passing, and an index of the narrator's belatedness. He knows the site has endured "untouched" into the present, even as it faces the common threat of agricultural cultivation. Aware of the future destruction of the kurgan, the narrator is no less aware of accumulating loss. He imagines a time when the kurgan enjoyed greater concord with a former steppe, and a former people. An implicit question posed in the passage is, how one might one overcome this temporal divide between oneself and the kurgan? One way to bridge this divide emerges when the narrator recognizes how the steppe is imbued with a literary past: "In the southern steppe," he remarks, "each kurgan seems to be a silent monument of some kind of poetic true tale (*mol'chalivym pamiatnikom kakoi-nibud' poeticheskoi byli*). To stay for a time on the Donets, at Small Tanais, of which *The Lay of Igor's Campaign* sang — this had been a dream of mine for a long time" (2:108). Poetry, and the lyricized historical narrative the *Lay* represents, mediates the relationship between the kurgan and the narrator, enabling him to conceive the archaeology of the steppe through literature.

Literature also serves to mediate the relationship between the poet and the artifacts of the past in "Aeschylus," but not, as we will later see, with the stone *baba*. The tragedian's likeness, carved with "ancient simplicity," is both an object of description and a conduit for dialogue. The poet directly addresses the likeness — without specifying whether it is a statue or a bust — and shudders at the "powerful and severe thought" expressed through its "silent features," which anticipates the revelation at the end of the poem of Aeschylus's daring before the gods. The mute object is one gap in

---

[11]   Bunin's "Na Dontse" was later titled "Sviatye gory." Its first publication date has yet to be established, although the commentators of his collected works believe it to have been around 1895, when Bunin visited the monastery described in the work. "Na Dontse" was published in Bunin's 1897 collection, *To the Edge of the Earth (Na krai sveta)*.

the relations between the poet and "Aeschylus"; another is a temporal gap that separates the poet from the time of the tragedian:

> Далеки дни, когда ты жил, и мифом
> Теперь те дни нам кажутся. Ты страшен
> Их древностью . . .

> Endlessly distant are the days, when you lived, and like a myth
> Those days now seem to us. You are terrifying
> By their antiquity . . .

The feeling of terror and awe is generated by the association of Aeschylus with an inaccessible antiquity on the one hand, and, on the other, his ability to endure to the present day:

> Ты страшен тем, что ты,
> Незримый в мире двадцать пять столетий,
> Незримо в нем присутствуешь доныне,

> You are terrifying since you,
> Unseen in the world for twenty-five centuries,
> Have been present in it unseen up till now,

The portrayal of Aeschylus developed throughout the remainder of the poem conflates the tragedian with his hero, Prometheus. As the Brokgauz-Efron encyclopedia entry tells us, the image of Prometheus could signify the subordination of all things, including the gods, to Fate—or, in a Byronic mode, the "incarnation of the highest strivings of man for freedom."[12] For Bunin, Aeschylus embodies that daring, his "legendary glory" that enables him to overcome Fate, which takes various forms throughout the latter half of the poem: whether in its divine embodiment in the goddess Adrasteia; in the synonyms of *Rok* and *Sud'ba*; or in the epithet

---

12 *Entsiklopedicheskii slovar' F. A. Brokgauza i I. A. Efrona*, s.v. "Prometei." The entry provides an assessment of the values various writers ascribed to Prometheus, focusing in particular on the work of Goethe, Schlegel, Byron, and Shelley. Bunin apparently found in Aeschylus a precursor for his own artistic endeavors, of which he once said: "All my life I have striven, consciously or unconsciously, to overcome and destroy time and space and form" (cited in Richards, "Comprehending the Beauty of the World," 521).

neotvratim (inexorable, unavoidable), applied to Fate (*Rok—neotvratim*)—one of two monikers commonly applied to Adrasteia in Russian (the other being *neizbezhnaia*).

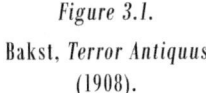

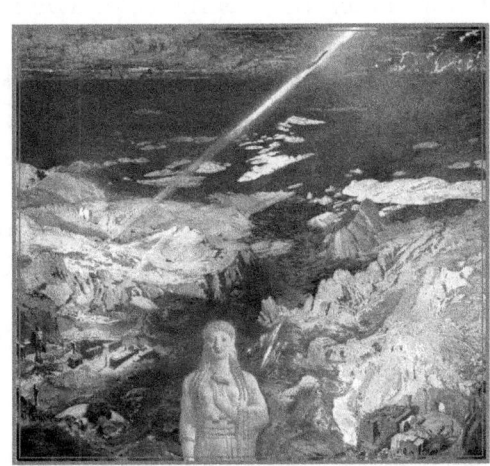

Figure 3.1.
Bakst, *Terror Antiquus*
(1908).

The themes and aesthetic experiences constellated in Bunin's poem are curious because they likely readily call to mind a far-better-known example of "ancient terror" caused by archaic statuary from the period—Leon Bakst's painting *Terror Antiquus* (fig. 3.1)—and the eponymous essay by Viacheslav Ivanov that it inspired. Ivanov writes: "'Terror Antiquus': that is how the artist named his painting. By ancient terror he meant the terror of fate. *Terror antiquus* is *terror fati*. He wanted to show that the ancients viewed as relative and transient not only all that is human but also all that was revered as divine. Only Fate (*Eimarménē*), or universal necessity (*Anánke*), the inevitable 'Adrasteia,' the faceless countenance and hollow sound of unknown Destiny, was absolute."[13] Whereas in the face of Adresteia, Bunin could find a story of freedom and daring in

13 Ivanov's "Drevnii uzhas: Po povodu kartiny L. Baksta 'Terror Antiquus' was first published in *Zolotoe runo*, no. 4 (1909): 51-65. The translation is from Viacheslav Ivanov, "Ancient Terror: On Leon Bakst's Painting *Terror Antiquus*," in *Selected Essays*, ed. Michael Wachtel, trans. Robert Bird (Evanston, IL: Northwestern University Press, 2001), 154. All citations are to this translation and are cited in the text.

"Aeschylus," Bakst, as Ivanov went on to note, "showed masculine daring and warring to be powerless before the will of Destiny" (154).

The appearance of Adrasteia, the theme of human daring before Fate, the experience of awe and terror, and the role played by archaic statuary: each work shares these features. It is difficult, however, to ascertain what might link Bunin with Bakst and Ivanov, or why they all took up these subjects around the same time. Bunin's poem precedes Bakst's painting, and Ivanov published his essay on the painting in *Zolotoe runo* in May 1909. Perhaps Bunin influenced the latter, or, alternatively, as they thought through the relationship of man to the divine as it was symbolized in archaic statuary, perhaps they recalled passages on "Prometheus" from *The Birth of Tragedy*, in which Nietzsche asserts that the "innermost kernel of the Prometheus story [is] the necessity of sacrilege imposed upon the titanically striving individual."[14] Indeed, during the period, the words "daring" and "slavish," which inform Bunin's two poems, possessed a Nietzschean "surcharge," along with such other terms as "Promethean."[15]

While looking back to find a common source, say in Nietzsche, presents one way to consider their shared thematic concerns— we will return to Nietzsche at the conclusion of the chapter— I want instead to consider a later text in which we find a notable convergence of the elements unifying these three works and a thematic bridge to the stone *babas*: Pavel Florenskii's lecture "The Stratification of Aegean Culture" ("Naplastovaniia egeiskoi kul'tury"), from 1913.[16] In this essay, Florenskii draws on both Ivanov's "Ancient Terror" and Voloshin's "Archaism in Russian Painting" (discussed in the introduction to this book), which he

---

[14]   Friedrich Nietzsche, *The Birth of Tragedy: Out of the Spirit of Music*, in *Basic Writings of Nietzsche*, trans. Walter Kaufmann (New York: Modern Library, 1992), 72.

[15]   Bernice Glatzer Rosenthal, *New Myth, New World: From Nietzsche to Stalinism* (University Park, PA: Penn State Press, 2002), 29-30.

[16]   P. A. Florenskii, "Naplastovaniia egeiskoi kul'tury," *Bogoslovskii vestnik* 11, no. 6 (1913): 346-89. The translations are from "The Stratification of Aegean Culture," in *Beyond Vision: Essays on the Perception of Art*, ed. Nicoletta Misler, trans. Wendy Salmond (London: Reaktion Books, 2002), 141-73.

interweaves into an extraordinary account of the stone *babas* and other archaic artifacts. In this regard, what we see in these various conceptions of "ancient terrors" are the multiple paths running through early Russian modernism, at times in parallel, at times converging. Rather than offering a story of influence, they reveal a pattern of shared concerns in these works, circulating around archaic statuary in general, and the stone *babas* in particular.

Two chapters ago, we saw how archaeological thinking on the statuary oscillated between expanding the network of relations into which the stone *babas* were embedded, and winnowing down what the archaeologist Veselovskii called "imaginary" relations. Florenskii's discussion of the statuary certainly followed the first path. His philosophical ambition and the purview of his speculations— which combined archaeology, comparative mythography, theology, and philosophical anthropology—reveal a broad awareness and eager reception of archaeological developments from the late nineteenth century onward in Russian culture during the period. His reference points throughout the work range from Voloshin's essay on archaism to a host of European and Russian archaeological and mythological studies. As he makes clear at the conclusion of "Stratification," his scope was far greater than the essay's title announced: "Such is the most ancient understanding of the primordial origins of all being. It forms a substratum in the thickness of stratifications on which Greek philosophy was later to emerge" (173). Florenskii extended his considerations both geographically—beyond Aegean culture and even the discoveries on Crete by archaeologists such as Sir Arthur Evans—pointing toward artifacts from all corners of the Eurasian continent, and chronologically, pursuing the traces of the deepest of pasts. He did so, he remarks, to understand what he terms the replacement of "matriarchal power" by "the universal primal power of the male" (173).

It was within this broadly configured mythological and archaeological framework that Florenskii approached the statuary. In the extensive section he devotes to them, he reveals his awareness of the archaeological debates surrounding the *baba*'s age and provenance. He surveys many of the hypotheses we discussed previously, into which Florenskii insinuates his own speculation on the statuary's symbolic meaning. The statuary, he notes, was often placed "on burial kurgans by the populations of the south Russian steppes and was obviously a religious symbol connected in the closest and most intimate way with the idea of death. Where we erect a cross on a grave, these prior inhabitants of our land, who were also perhaps our ancestors, placed these 'women' on their graves" (157). Given the themes of this book, what might first strike us in these lines is Florenskii's tentative and intriguing suggestion that the makers of the statuary could possibly be "our ancestors"— which his contemporaries in the avant-garde would later assert with greater polemical force. But it is ultimately his greater concern with locating "the primordial origin of all Being" that dwarfs even that suggestion. To that end, Florenskii crafts a speculative archaeology, embedding the statuary into a network of relations that transcends nations and ethnicities by unearthing universal ties in the deep past.

Within that framework, the statuary enables Florenskii to bring the archaeological past found in Russia not only into line with broader developments of early-twentieth-century archaeology, but also into a universal human narrative. He considers the statuary a representative on Russian soil of a universal cult of "Mother Earth": "Whether in the Scythian steppes, in sultry India or the tragic *Iliad*, the cult of chthonic divinities, no matter what they are called, always 'combines the idea of the blessed birth of Mother Earth with the idea of the horror of death, whose place is likewise in the depths of the earth'" (158). Florenskii drew this citation on the combination of life and death in specific symbolic forms from the Austrian paleontologist Moritz Hörnes. The primary symbol in the case of the *babas*, Florenskii argues, is the vessel they were often found holding: "Squeezing the breasts and holding a bird to the bosom are even more widespread motifs, even more canonical, so to speak, for Mother Earth. She is Death and she is also Birth. She is genitrix and also destroyer" (158). Florenskii also took these last two terms—"genitrix" and "destroyer"— from Hörnes, which he then coupled together with Ivanov's "Ancient Terror" and, in particular, Ivanov's thoughts on female deities:

But whether this concept of the One World Goddess emerges from a form of human life or from something else, one fact at least is certain: "Any investigation of the history of female deities, by whatever name the Many-named is called, whether Artemis or Aphrodite or Athena or Astarte or Isis, puts us on the trail of the original thelymonotheism, a female monotheism. All female divinities are in essence facets of the one goddess and she is the female principle of the world, one sex elevated to the absolute" . . . *In their essence, our stone women are that same all-victorious Aphrodite.* (159; italics mine)

The citation in the passage from "Ancient Terror" furnishes Florenskii with the mythological support to link the statuary to Aphrodite, but also ultimately to Fate. Florenskii combines what he borrows from Ivanov with the lesson of another ancient artifact, the so-called Nautilus Ornament, one of the central discoveries at Minos, which Florenskii understands as "further proof of the widespread cult of Aphrodite-Astarte, Fate or Time" (173). Such linkages among an array of artifacts—from the stone *babas* to the Nautilus Ornament—and their mythological significance, reveals how Florenskii reads the archaeological record as an emanation of primordial origins he also found delineated in Ivanov's "Ancient Terror"; in Florenskii's recapitulation of the essay, the "future task will be to understand the next layer, to move from the universal proto-environment of the female to the universal primal power of the male" (173).

It is this concern with tracing how male power supplanted that of female power that forms a notable parallel with Bunin's "Aeschylus" and "The Stone *Baba*." Ivanov had speculated that "the grandiosity and monstrosity of the forms in which the dominion of women and female monotheism were affirmed, can be judged by the energy of the male reaction against female despotism and the destruction of men by women" (157). According to Ivanov, the author who "vividly remembered" this sense of formal monstrosity was none other than Aeschylus, in whose *Oresteia* Ivanov finds that "Orestes's emotional conflict is largely a matter of choosing between his mother and his father" (157-58). The compulsion toward matricide, in turn, was a desire for "harmony and order against

orgiasm" (158). Ivanov goes on to elaborate a complex range of
consequences from this desire for matricide and the establishment
of order that are too broad to rehearse here. Two, however, are
germane to Bunin: Ivanov likewise considers archaic statuary to
embody a distinct relationship between man and god, as evidenced
in his reading of Bakst's painting; and both writers link their
contemplation of statuary to what Ivanov understood as a story
of "spiritual freedom, the energy of his willful, creative, godlike
self-determination" (159). For Bunin, however, freedom is linked
to Aeschylus, while in the "The Stone *Baba*" he largely leaves out
the entire edifice of Ivanov's and Florenskii's gendered mythology,
while retaining the story of primordial enslavement and human
bondage.

ii. Primitive Rudeness

For all their differences in cultural orientation and in the prestige
of their central figures, "Aeschylus" and "The Stone *Baba*" share
two themes: how to overcome the gap between past and present,
and how encounters with archaic statuary reflect conceptions of
the human and the divine. The problem of "The Stone *Baba*" is
that this gap *cannot* be overcome. The statue, as Bunin imagines it,
obstinately refuses to divulge the story of its origins, and no works
on a par with those of Aeschylus exist to challenge that temporal
divide or to elaborate a tale of human daring.

    The first stanza locates the poet in an arid steppe, with signs of
death all around. He, curiously, has seen the statuary before: "Here
again is the Stone Baba" (*Vot snova—Kamennaia Baba*). We do not
know how many times, nor why this particular encounter occasions
the lyric nor why he sees it not only "again" but "anew," as the
word *snova* suggests. Still, the statuary possesses enough currency
that he refers to it as a proper noun. Indeed, the poet reveals even
more of his knowledge of the statuary in the second stanza, when
he moves from the description of the landscape to that of the
statuary's physical attributes; its "primitively rude" body and the
"drowsy," "flat features" of its countenance are the topoi we have
seen typically associated with the statuary.

That these features inspire fear in the poet links the poem to "Aeschylus," but fear represents something of the puzzle of the poem. Indeed, that the poet fears the statue in stanza two appears to run counter to the story told by the rhymes in the first and second stanzas—*baba/slabo* (*baba/weakly*) and *telo/nesmelo* (*body/timidly*). Such features hardly seem capable of generating fear. Indeed, much of the poem turns upon this disjunction between the poet's expectation and the reality of the *baba*, coupled with his frustrated desire that the statuary tells its story. That frustration intensifies in the last stanza, when the poet directly addresses the *baba*, referring to it as a "savage spawn" (*dikoe ischad'e*), and associates it with a male divinity akin to Zeus (two reasons for retaining *baba* as the translation rather than "stone woman"). This apostrophe to the statue asks that the *baba* confirm the poet's speculation that it belongs to some chthonic past, and that it once held some vaunted status as a god.

Here, we might recall that the relationship between poets and statuary generally involves frustrating various forms of desire (in particular, male desire for feminine statuary)—be it the desire for communication, or intimacy (even carnal, as in the case of Pygmalion), or power.[17] Indeed, the figure of apostrophe that Bunin deploys at the end of stanza two belongs to a common repertoire structuring literary encounters with statuary.[18] It is closely related to the figure of *prosopopeia,* which Paul de Man defines as "the fiction of an apostrophe to an absent, deceased, or voiceless entity, which

---

[17]   See W. J. T. Mitchell, "Ekphrasis and the Other," in *Picture Theory: Essays on Verbal and Visual Representation* (Chicago: University of Chicago Press, 1994), 151-81; Victor Stoichita, *The Pygmalion Effect: From Ovid to Hitchcock*, trans. Alison Anderson (Chicago: University of Chicago Press, 2008), 3.

[18]   Paul de Man, "Autobiography as De-Facement," in *The Rhetoric of Romanticism* (New York: Columbia University Press, 1984), 65-81. Leonard Barkan, in turn, puts the trope to spectacular use in his study on Renaissance archaeology, where the objects with which he deals are not metaphorical, but real pieces of exhumed (and disfigured) sculpture, "whose literal possession of mouth, eye, and face may be quite problematic. . . . The result is a more complex interplay of tropes and realities, of rhetoric and history. The voices that reconstruct ancient art objects will turn into dialogues; whoever is speaking, the conversation will be both historical and transhistorical" (*Unearthing the Past: Archaeology and Aesthetics in the Making of Renaissance Culture* [New Haven, CT: Yale University Press, 1999], 211).

posits the possibility of the latter's reply and confers upon it the power of speech."[19] From this perspective, the rhetoric of the poem could be seen to reach its greatest intensity in the last two lines, when Bunin resolves the encounter with the statuary by introducing the themes of herd-like timidity (in the first version of the poem) and slavish servility (in the later version):

> —О, да, не Бог нас создал. Это мы
> Богов творили скотским сердцем.

> —Not God, not God created us. It was we
> [Who] with bestial hearts created the gods.

One question we might briefly explore is the slight ambiguity of who speaks these two lines: Is it the poet or possibly even the *baba* itself? The dash, for example, could suggest reported speech, and, if so, the stunning rhetorical possibility that the statuary emerges to announce itself as the very progenitor of the gods of that shadowy world. If the statuary speaks these lines, then the *baba* fulfills the poet's desire for it to disclose the secret of its provenance.

Bunin's contemporaries would have had some reason to think that the *baba* could have emerged as the speaker. Since his abiding interest in antiquity did not mean a unified style or poetics, he had written numerous poems in which he adopts various personae, from divinities to historical figures, and, even on one occasion, a ruin. In the poem "Agni," for example, the first-person speaker is the Vedic god of fire:

> Лежу во тьме, сраженный злою силой.
> Лежу и жду, недвижный и немой:
> Идут, поют над вырытой могилой,
> Несут огни, — вещают жребий мой.

> I lie in the darkness, slain by an evil force.
> I lie and wait, motionless and silent:
> They come, and sing above the dug-up grave,
> [They] bear fires, —and prophesy my fate. (1: 249)

---

19   De Man, "Autobiography," 76.

Another poem from 1905 stages a *Titanomachia* between the Egyptian gods Set and Ra-Osiris—who are the symbols, or mythological principles, of light and darkness, creation and destruction. The speaker here is Set, who addresses his rival:

> Ра-Озирис, владыка дня и света,
> Хвала тебе! Я, бог пустыни, Сет,
> Горжусь врагом: ты, побеждая Сета,
> В его стране царил пять тысяч лет.

> Ra-Osiris, master of the day and of light,
> Praise be to you! I, the god of the desert, Set,
> Am proud of my enemy: you, vanquishing Set,
> Reigned in his country for five thousand years. (1:217)

But just two years after "The Stone *Baba*," Bunin published a four-stanza lyric, "In the Archipelago" ("V arkhipelage," 1908), which concludes with the lines:

> Дым облаков курился по горам,
> Пустынный мыс был схож с ковригой хлеба.
> Я жил во сне. Богов творил я сам.

> The wisp of clouds smoked along the mountains,
> The barren cape was like a loaf of bread.
> I lived in a dream. I myself created the gods. (1:302)

Clearly identifying the lyric poet as the speaker, these lines indicate the extent to which "The Stone *Baba*" contains themes that had preoccupied the poet during those years, while helping to clarify how the last two lines of the earlier poem resolve into a theogony that finds its origins in man. In this, Bunin seems to be drawing on such views as those of Ludwig Feuerbach, whose proposition that "theology is anthropology and physiology" echoes in the poet's assertion that men are progenitors of the gods.[20] Bunin records in the last lines of "The Stone *Baba*" a miniature history

---

[20]   Ludwig Feuerbach's influential views on the relationship of man to the divine, as elaborated in *The Essence of Christianity*, were perhaps at the fore here, since the book had just been republished in Russian in 1906 as *Sushchnost' khristianstva* by the publishing house Mysl'.

of man for which the stone *baba* emerges as an enduring sign of a bestial, slavish stage of human development. They present a counter-image to that of "Aeschylus." While the statue's reticence frustrates and thus intensifies the desire for it to disclose its origins, the statue is not Galatea—neither clearly in gender, nor in aesthetic value. But rather than seeing this as a moment of apostrophe and a consideration of muteness, we might see it as a moment of the poet's surprise. That is, the question Bunin poses as to whether the *baba* was once a Zeus figure could indeed be rhetorical, that is, expressing not so much the desire for communication, but rather the poet's surprise that this very object could have once been associated with a divinity. In that sense, what terrorizes the poet is his recognition that the statuary belongs to an early, primitive stage of man.

The themes Bunin brings together in his account of the *baba* have a notable precursor in a poem by Valery Briusov, which also helps to flesh out these various relations of the divine and the anthropological taking shape around archaic statuary. Like Bunin, Briusov displayed an interest in the archaic and in archaeology, which is perhaps why the former had written the latter about meditating upon kurgans. Indeed, Bunin likely knew Briusov's poem "On Easter Island" ("Na ostrove Paskhi"), which had appeared in his 1895 collection *Chefs d'oeuvre*, in which Briusov, too, invokes the category of "rudeness" in his commentary to the poem:

> Upon the island one meets gigantic statues (or, more accurately, busts), carved out of whole stones, which are, by the way, rather rude (*grubyi*). Judging by everything, they could not have been erected by those impotent savages whom Roggeveen [the Dutch explorer who "discovered" Easter Island in 1722; MK] encountered on the island. It remains to suggest that these are the monuments of a people who have completely disappeared. [21]

---

[21] Valery Briusov, *Polnoe sobranie sochinenii v semi tomakh* (Moscow: Khudozhestvennaia literatura, 1973), 1:576. All further references are to this edition and are cited in the text. It falls outside of the purview of this book to consider the status of archaeology in Briusov's work, in particular his extraordinary lectures on, for example, Aegean and Egyptian art, collected in *Uchiteli uchitelei* (1917), and the poems he wrote on archaic and archaeological themes such as "The Golden Reindeer" ("Zolotoi olen'," 1917), collected into *Between Past and Future* (*Mezh proshlim*

Besides their interest in the primitive and the rude, Briusov's and Bunin's poems also share several thematic and rhetorical forms — indeed, so much so that the latter seems in dialogue with the former. Among the primary differences between the two are the geographical coordinates in which their encounters with primitive statuary take place, and the relationship between the human and the divine they articulate.[22]

The subtitle of Briusov's poem, "The Meditation of a Sorcerer-Enchanter" ("Razdum'e znakharia-zaklinatelia") (1:68-69), recalls the Russian Symbolist association of poetry with magic. Elaborated in various works throughout the early years of the twentieth century, the theme links such texts as Bal'mont's essay "Poetry as Magic" ("Poeziia kak volshebstvo,"1915) and Khlebnikov's poem "Incantation by Laughter" ("Zakliatie smekhom," 1908). At the outset of Briusov's poem, the sorcerer-enchanter wanders amidst the jagged cliffs on Easter Island when he encounters the immobile and silent statues — "mute, giant people" (*Nemye, gromadnye liudi*). As in Bunin, terror, too, is present here:

> Лица мне не видно в тумане,
> Но знаю, что страшно и строго.
> Шепчу я слова заклинаний,
> Молю неизвестного бога.

> In the mist, the face is invisible to me,
> But I know it's terrifying and severe.

i budushchim). The subject of that poem is an archaeological artifact held in the collection of I.S. Ostroukhov. One likely source of Briusov's interest in the topic and discipline was his younger brother, A. Ia. Briusov (1885-1966), an archaeologist.

22   Easter Island statuary has a particularly notable history in the consideration of primitive art by Russian avant-gardists. In 1914, the Union of Youth (Soiuz molodezhi) published a long essay by the artist, art critic, and theorist Vladimir Markov (Voldemārs Matvejs), "The Art of Easter Island" ("Iskusstvo ostrova Paskhi"), which offered a reassessment of the statuary. Markov's contribution to the period's conceptualization of primitive art is a fascinating case in its own right. Along with his work on Easter Island statuary, Markov wrote *Negro Art (Iskusstvo negrov)* in 1913; it was published in 1919, again by the Union of Youth. According to the art historian Jack Flam, Markov's work represents "one of the first in-depth examinations of aesthetics and symbolism in African art." See Flam's discussion of Markov's text in his anthology *Primitivism and Twentieth-Century Art: A Documentary History* (Berkeley and Los Angeles: University of California Press, 2003), 61-66.

I whisper words of incantation
I entreat an unknown god.

The incantation and the entreaties are to no avail; the statuary will
not respond. And the sorcerer-enchanter grows alarmed by the
impossibility of knowing the origins of the statuary:

И много тревожит вопросов:
Кто создал семью великанов?
Кто высек людей из утесов,
Поставил их стражей туманов?

And many questions disturb:
Who created this family of giants?
Who carved the people out of the crags
[Who] put them [here] as guardians of the mists?

The impossibility of answering the question of origins leads the
sorcerer-enchanter to question both himself and the "pitiful race" to
which he belongs, and why, ultimately, they are unworthy of such
awesome forms:

Мы кто? — Жалкий род без названья!
Добыча нам — малые рыбы!
Не нам превращать в изваянья
Камней твердогрудые глыбы!

Иное — могучее племя
Здесь грозно когда-то царило,
Но скрыло бегучее время
Все то, что свершилось, что было.

Who are we?—A pitiful race without a name!
Our catch—small fish!
It is not for us to transform hard-hearted
Blocks of stone into statuary!

It was another powerful tribe
[Who] once terrifyingly ruled here,
But fleeting time has hidden
All that was accomplished, all that was.

While Briusov here touches upon the commonplace of time as the force holding sway over everything, erasing the name of the powerful tribe, the greater terror here is the confrontation with a monumental past that leads to the recognition of a diminished present. The divide separating past and present, then, is measured in terms of knowledge and power, and neither can be overcome:

О прошлом никто не споет нам.
Но грозно, на каменной груде,
Стоите, в молчаньи дремотном,
Вы, страшные, древние люди!
[. . .]
О, если б на наши вопросы
Вы дали ответ хоть единый!

No one shall sing to us of the past.
But threateningly, upon the stone heap,
You stand, in drowsy silence,
You, terrible, ancient people!
[. . .]
O, if only you would give but one answer
to our questions!

Many of these lines presage the basic dynamics underpinning Bunin's encounter in "The Stone *Baba*." They share themes of obstinate reticence; the inaccessibility of and desire for communion with the past; and the experience of terror. Briusov also combines "rudeness" with "terror," but what he charts here is a story of decline in the face of the monumentality of the past; the current race is no longer adequate to the monumental past. What Bunin charts, by contrast, is the story of diminishment of the primitive past, no longer capable of exercising command over the present. Whether the differences between the two poets and their encounters with "rude" statues are due to their philosophical predispositions or to the differences in the statuary is difficult to say. But it does help to underscore how fear when confronting the *baba* seems generated by the incommensurability between the statue Bunin encounters and the provenance he imagines for it. The story of enslavement is thus all the more terrifying now that this "god" made of stone timidly smiles in a moribund steppe, and the poet recognizes that "we" were once terrified of such things. The encounter with the primitive past tells him only how far man has come: Can this really be a god that once inspired worship?

iii. "No Ordinary Stone Woman"

While Bunin's poem refers us to Nietzsche and Feuerbach, and, by extension, to parallel considerations of archaic terrors and statuaries by Florenskii, Ivanov, and Briusov, the epithet Bunin attaches to the body of the stone *baba*—primitively rude (*pervobytno-grubo*)—also signals to us aesthetic developments running in parallel with the poem. While variations of the locution had been commonly used in writing on the statuary, it acquired new currency during the period through the reevaluation of "primitive" objects and styles. The critic and poet Boris Sadovskoi, for example, reviewed a book of poetry by Sergei Gorodetskii, entitled *Bright Green (Iar')*, in 1907— a year after the appearance of Bunin's "The Stone *Baba*"—in which he used a similar collocation to designate a trend he lamented in recent poetry:

> The poetry of Mr. Gorodetskii is notable for that turn, characteristic of these past years, from refined culture toward the rudely primitive (*k gruboi pervobytnosti*). S. Gorodetskii is not just a "singer of nature"; he isn't a landscapist (*peizazhist*), as is, for example, I. Bunin: he is an enemy of "Cities," a poet of the savage, standing beyond the borders of culture, of the world.[23]

Whether Sadovskoi knew of Bunin's "The Stone *Baba*" when he deemed him a "landscapist" is uncertain, but Bunin certainly did not manifest the formal and thematic elements of the rudely primitive Sadovskoi noted in Gorodetskii: blood sacrifices, the blows of a flint axe on a living body, wood goblins, and the like. Nor was Bunin inclined to embrace the rough, rhythmical innovations Sadovskoi also associated with the style.

---

[23] Boris Sadovskoi, "Sergei Gorodetskii: Iar'; Stikhi liricheskie i liro-epicheskie. Spb., 1907 g.," *Russkaia mysl'* 5 (May 1907): 85.

We can discern some of the basic gestures of that aesthetic of the "primitive"—and the matrix of cultural values in which it operated—if we consider a later poem by Gorodetskii, his own version of "Kamennaia baba," published in the journal *Galchonok* in 1911:

Про каменную бабу
Старуха говорит,
И в поле голос слабый
Торжественно звучит:
Подумайте-ка дети,
Какая старина!
Века стоят на свете
Такие как она.
Им жертвы приносили,
Молились прежде им,
Обмазывать любили
Их медом золотым.
Языческое пенье
На праздниках весны,
Походы и сраженья
Им помнятся, как сны.
И только солнце знает,
О чем они молчат,
Когда на них бросает
Вечерний алый взгляд.

About the stone woman
An old woman speaks,
And in the field [her] weak voice
Solemnly resounds:
Think about it, children,
Such an antiquity!
In the world they stood for centuries
Such things like her.
They brought sacrifices to them,
They used to pray to them,
They loved to anoint
Them with golden honey.
A pagan song
On springtime holidays,
The hunts and the battles,
They remember, like dreams.

And only the sun knows
About what they keep silent,
When it throws upon them
The evening's crimson glance.[24]

Written in iambic trimeter—perhaps most significantly used by
Nikolai Nekrasov in his "Who Lives Well in Rus'?" ("Komu na Rusi
zhit' khorosho?," 1877)— the meter does not evince the more radical
innovations Sadovskoi diagnosed as typifying the turn toward the
"primitive." Still, it underpins the folkloric motifs of the poem,
which, like Chekhov's "The Steppe," consolidates the role of nurses
and old women from the steppe as the custodians of stories about
the landscape. They bind the stone *baba* to a celebrated pagan past
of springtime holidays and sacrifice: "What an antiquity!" (*Kakaia
starina!*).

By contrast, Bunin's own turn toward the "rudely primitive"
incarnated in the *baba* reveals a shared interest in theme, but not in
style. Indeed, Sadovskoi's views remind us that Bunin's "The Stone
Baba" is a poem *about* the "primitive," not a folkish account of it as
in Gorodetskii. The iambic pentameter and alternating rhymes of
Bunin's poem constitute something like a formal bulwark against
the primitive—or at least one in which a philosophical meditation
on the primitive can be conducted—rather than a formal approxi-
mation of the values associated with it. One reason that formal
bulwark matters is that this move toward the archaic and the
primitive throughout a range of modernist camps became the subject
of a range of cultural and philosophical debates in the period. It
was precisely this kind of celebration of the pagan past lamented
by Sadovskoi, which took off within modernist circles in parallel
with Bunin's and Gorodetskii's accounts of the statuary.

There is, in fact, another work that we will now consider,
because it provides a notable summary of such themes as statuesque
reticence and paganism, while also providing us a circuitous
route that takes us back to the story of ancient terror in Bunin and

---

[24] Sergei Gorodetskii, "Pro kamennuiu babu," *Galchonok* 12 (1911): 43. I want to express my
gratitude to Boris Maslov, and especially to Dmitrii Kalugin, for helping me obtain this poem.

Ivanov. In 1908, two years after Bunin published his poems, Aleksei Remizov took up the subject of the statuary in his own version of the "The Stone Woman" (yet another "Kamennaia baba"), one of a cycle of tales included in his *Toward the Ocean-Sea* (*K moriu-okeanu*).[25] The protagonists Alalei and Leila, who have been walking "from kurgan to kurgan," come upon a stone woman and decide to spend the night near her:

> The Woman looks into the night. They look upon the Woman.
> —What are you, Woman?—What do you see?—What do you know?
> —I'm no ordinary woman, I'm the Stone Woman,—the Woman intoned like an oracle,—for many centuries I have stood in the free steppe (*v vol'noi stepi*). And before God had the sun in heaven, there was only darkness, and we all lived in the dark. (144)

In Remizov's hands, the statuary has now acquired voice and a rudimentary sentience that she had not possessed in earlier literary representations. As with Bunin, the statuary has enough currency that Remizov capitalized the name, while also more clearly identifying it as feminine (hence the translation of *baba* here as "Woman"). The Stone Woman reveals her knowledge of that tenebrous time before the creation of the sun, which identifies her as belonging to a pagan Slavic past in its earliest beginnings. Remizov presents a curious admixture here of the pagan and the Eastern Orthodox Christian; the movement from darkness to light is told by a statue that seems like the idol of some chthonic deity.

That the statue speaks at all should not be overlooked, since that was something inaccessible not only to Bunin's and Briusov's lyric personae, but also to most poetic accounts of sculpture. To be sure, we find other examples in the Russian literary tradition of statues that speak: Pushkin's "The Stone Guest" ("Kamennyi gost'," 1830) and Andrei Bely's version of the Bronze Horseman in his novel *Petersburg* (*Peterburg*, 1916) are two notable examples. The

---

25   Aleksei Remizov, "Kamennaia baba," in *Sobranie sochinenii*, ed. A. M. Gracheva (Moscow: Russkaia kniga, 2000), 2:142-44. The work was dated 1908, and published in 1909. All further references are to this edition and are cited in the text.

Horseman, to recall, speaks the inscription at its base in *Petersburg*: "Petro Primo, Ekaterina Secunda,"[26] when it acquires voice in the delirium of the novel's character Dudkin. As François Rigolot has observed on the generic forms in which statuary acquires voice, "in a fantastic tale, every descriptive detail in a text points to the unreal, except for the materiality of the inscription."[27] Whereas the Bronze Horseman, in speaking its own inscription, tells the story of its autocratic provenance, for Remizov's Stone Woman no such inscription is present, but it, too, speaks a story of origins.

What enables Remizov's version of the Stone Woman to do so is mostly generic: unlike the more metaphysical tenor of Bunin's poem, whose lyrical transports are ultimately restrained by a reality principle, Remizov's is a folkloric world in which such fantastic colloquies between human beings and their reticent others (i.e., statues, animals) are possible. Either they happen naturally, or there are rituals to undergo; we are told in another story from the collection that the protagonists "ate snake porridge in order to know and to understand the language of beasts, birds, and flowers, and sipped a fragrant brew of magical grasses" (2:97). As Henryk Baran has observed, "the 'stone woman' is witness to the deepest past; the product of divine punishment for sin, she warns the two travelers against misconduct. The imaginative product of myth, she fully participates in the world of the marvelous brought into being by the author."[28]

Remizov created his marvelous world out of the tales recorded by nineteenth-century folklorists and archaeologists. Indeed, he even alerted his readers to these sources in the annotations he appended to a later edition of *Toward the Ocean-Sea*.[29] Harkening back

---

26   Andrei Bely, *Petersburg*, trans. Robert A. Maguire and John E. Malmstad (Bloomington: Indiana University Press, 1978), 214.

27   François Rigolot, "Ekphrasis and the Fantastic: Genesis of an Aberration," *Comparative Literature* 49 (Spring 1997): 106.

28   Henryk Baran, "Towards a Typology of Russian Modernism: Ivanov, Remizov, Khlebnikov," in *Aleksej Remizov: Approaches to a Protean Writer*, ed. Greta Slobin (Columbus, OH: Slavica, 1986), 188.

29   Baran notes that Remizov added the annotations in the second edition of *Posolon'*, in part because of charges that he had plagiarized folkloric texts (ibid., 177-82).

to the use of annotations—by Pushkin, Nikolai Gogol, and Nikolai Leskov—to explain ethnographic detail or literary precedent, Remizov referred his readers to Afanas'ev's *Slavs' Poetic Views on Nature*,[30] which we discussed in chapter one. Remizov did not cite what passage from Afanas'ev he drew upon in fashioning his own "Stone Woman," but he seems to have focused on Afanas'ev's image of the statues as women who were turned into stone and on the ritual practices surrounding the *baba* during times of drought. As the Stone Woman tells her story, her petrifaction is due to an infraction against the sun:

> We brought along sieves: let's gather the light into the sieve, and bring it into the pits. Our earthen pits had no windows. We raised a sieve to the sun, and got it full of light, and it spilt over the edge, but as soon as we tossed it into the pit—there was nothing. And God's sun went higher and higher, and had already begun to beat down. . . . And here's what came of it: we began to spit at the sun. And suddenly we turned into stone. (2:144)

While Bunin sees the statuary as an aesthetically crude form, Remizov locates crudeness in its behavior. The Stone Woman is punished for daring to challenge the sun: she is, in a sense, defiant like Prometheus, but without an Aeschylus to transform that tale into a story of human daring. However, she redeems herself by turning the story of her punitive metamorphosis into a morality tale for the two heroes. After these lines, the Stone Woman goes on to admonish Alalei and Leila to "kiss our Mother Earth" (*potseluite mat' nashu zemliu*) (2:144).

Just as the locution "primitively rude" alerted us to an associated discourse of the "primitive" in poetry criticism around Bunin's time, so, too, does Remizov's admonition "kiss our Mother Earth." The phrase points us to another path in which we can see how the primitive takes off in modernist circles in the years after Bunin published his poem, and Remizov his tales. As the scholar Igor Popov has uncovered, the Stone Woman's admonition is significant

---

[30] Afanas'ev, *Poeticheskie vozzreniia slavian na prirodu*, 2:677.

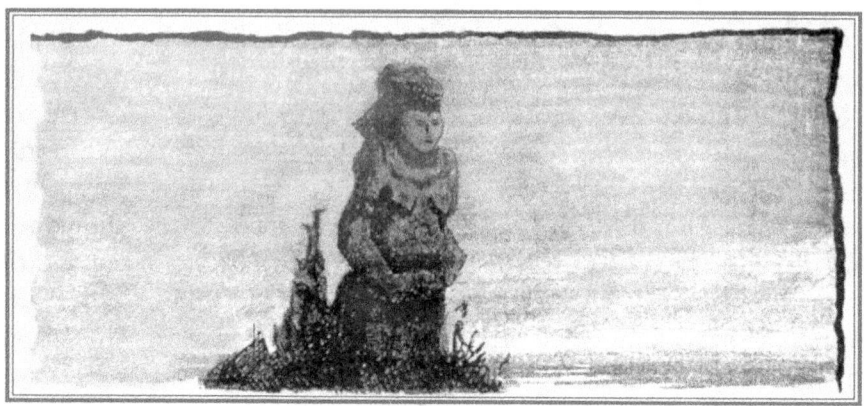

Figure 3.2.
Roerich, Sketch of the Stone Woman,
in the *Literary Anthology of Works by Students of St. Petersburg University* (1896).

because Remizov had sent Nicholas Roerich a manuscript copy of "The Stone Woman." The story, Popov suggests, inspired Roerich as he and Igor Stravinsky were preparing the libretto of *The Rite of Spring*.[31] According to Popov, the "parting words" of Remizov's Stone Woman—"Kiss her, our Mother Earth, praise her" (*potseluite mat' nashu zemliu, pozdrav'te*)—find their way into Roerich's libretto at the end of part one, which he entitled "The Kiss to the Earth." It is a central moment in *The Rite*, and it turns out that the Stone Woman, whose obstinate silence so frustrated Bunin, was its point of origin.

We can expand Popov's account to note that Remizov's "The Stone Woman" must have also struck Roerich as both familiar and innovative. According to Maksimilian Voloshin, the stones that primarily interested Roerich were those in the Russian North: "In Roerich's world, there are so many stones and so little soil that trees have nowhere to grow. He is, in reality, an artist of the Stone Age: not because he occasionally tries to represent the people and the buildings of that time, but because of the world's four elements he

---

31 Aleksei Remizov, *Storona nebyvalaia*, ed. Igor Popov (Moscow: Russkii put', 2004), 465. My thanks to Robert Hughes for bringing this work to my attention.

knows only earth, and in earth only its bony foundation—stone."[32]
Roerich's archaeological work, in fact, extended far beyond the
North. He had known of the statuary at least since his student days
at St. Petersburg University, where, in the late 1890s, he attended
lectures by Nikolai Veselovskii, the author of "Imaginary Stone
Babas." But even earlier, in 1896, he was the principal illustrator for
the *Literary Anthology of Works by Students of Petersburg University*
(*Literaturnyi sbornik proizvedenii studentov Peterburgskogo universiteta*).
Among the various illustrations he furnished the collection was
one of the stone women (fig. 3.2).[33] Roerich would later refine this
interest in stones and the Stone Age into a general aesthetic and
philosophical stance, when he argued in "Joy in Art," that only the
"ill-informed" continued to link the Stone Age with savagery, and
that one must instead seek to understand the culture it represents.[34]
It was that culture, in a sense, which he sought to re-create when he
and Stravinsky undertook *The Rite.*

Lodged within this connection between Remizov, Roerich, and
The Rite is another dimension that gets us back to the story of Bunin
and Ivanov. What Bunin staged in his pairing of "Aeschylus" and
"The Stone *Baba*" was a central divide, radiating into various seg-
ments of Russian modernist culture, concerning the different modes
and values of simplicity. As the musicologist Richard Taruskin reminds us, the locus classicus of this debate on simplicity and the
pursuit of it was Mikhail Gershenzon and Viacheslav Ivanov's
"A Corner-to-Corner Correspondence" ("Perepiska iz dvukh uglov")
of 1921. In the penultimate letter of their correspondence, Ivanov
touches upon the philosophical and cultural ramifications of two
distinct modes of simplification: *oproshchenie* and *uproshchenie*, both

---

32 Voloshin, "Arkhaizm v russkoi zhivopisi," 279. For full cite, see note 4 of introduction.

33 For more on Rerikh's participation in the anthology, see A. N. Bondarenko, "Slovo k 100-letiiu
    okonchaniia N. K. Rerikhom St. Peterburgskogo universiteta," *Peterburgskii rerikhovskii sbornik*,
    1 (1998), http://www.roerich-museum.org/PRS/catalog.php?id=1&pn=2. Rerikh would later
    return to the statuary in 1937, in the painting *The Stone Woman: Mongolia (Kamennaia baba:
    Mongolia)*. See E. P. Matochkin, "Arkheologicheskie motivy v iskusstve N. K. Rerikha," *Peterburgskii
    rerikhovskii sbornik*, 2-3 (1999), http://www.roerichmuseum.org/PRS/catalog.php?id=2&pn=1.

34 Rerikh, "Radost' iskusstvu," in Mantel, *N. Rerikh*, 37.

built upon the word *prostota* (simplicity). The first connotes a sense of "going wild," and the second the transformation of complexity into simplicity:

> The magic formula, to our intelligentsia, is *oproshchenie*; this shows to what extent they are severed from their roots. They think that by "becoming simple" they will put down roots, be able to feel that they have roots. . . . *Oproshchenie* is betrayal, oblivion, defection—a cowardly listless reaction. The idea makes as little sense in relation to culture as it would in mathematics, which recognizes only *uproshchenie*, that is, the reduction of complexity to a simpler, perfected unified form. . . . The savage finds no joy in his pointless freedom, nor does the man who succumbs to the lure of oblivion and "simplifies" himself into the likeness of a savage; he is dejected and sad.[35]

This opposition, as Taruskin observes, animated the reception and debate on a range of works, the foremost of which was *The Rite of Spring*.[36] Roerich and Stravinsky's collaboration raised the question of whether this central achievement of Russian modernism in its primitivist disposition constituted an *oproshchenie* or an *uproshchenie*; was it, in Taruskin's words, "an *uproshcheniye*, a breakthrough to the simplicity of a higher truth, or merely an *oproshcheniye*, the reductive renunciation of all refinement of thought and feeling in favor of the crude simplicity of the barbarian?"[37] The appeal of either forms of simplification, as Ivanov made clear, could be registered in aesthetic and cultural terms and associated with such figures as Leo Tolstoy (whom Ivanov saw as committed to *oproshchenie*). In his criticism of this form of simplification, Ivanov was echoing a line from Nietzsche's *The Birth of Tragedy*, a central touchstone for the *Correspondence*, in which Nietzsche diagnosed the symptoms of the "tremendous historical need of our unsatisfied modern culture"

---

[35] Mikhail Gershenzon and Viacheslav Ivanov, "A Corner-to-Corner Correspondence," in *Russian Intellectual History: An Anthology*, ed. Marc Raeff (Atlantic Highlands, NJ: Humanities Press, 1966), 398.

[36] Richard Taruskin, *Stravinsky and the Russian Traditions: A Biography of the Works Through "Mavra,"* 2 vols. (Berkeley and Los Angeles: University of California Press, 1996), 1:854-55.

[37] Ibid., 1:951.

that are also germane to this chapter: "And now the mythless man stands eternally hungry, surrounded by all past ages, and digs and grubs for roots, even if he has to dig for them among the remotest antiquities."[38]

Bunin's poems, to be sure, never acquired the prestige of *The Rite*, but they partake in this general theme of the opposition through their own effective antonyms of simplicity (*prostota*) and crudeness (*grubost'*). They turn on the same opposition as *uproshchenie* and *oproshchenie*, and they form two of the categories associated with the turn toward different kinds of antiquity, remote or near, that were invoked to satiate this hunger for a past in modern man. Bunin, like Ivanov, ultimately preferred the category of simplification to "going wild." He makes this emphatically clear in a meditation on "antiquity" that we find in his "Sea of Gods" ("More bogov," 1908), one of several travel sketches he wrote during the period, in which he describes viewing the Acropolis:

> Taking their cue from the deathly white, ox-eyed statues, from thousand-year-old understandings about Bacchae and dryads, about gods and festivals with flowers and choruses—as if in ancient Greece all they did was celebrate—thousands and thousands of people have pictured for themselves some kind of vulgar Elysium instead of this stony, arid country. What was the Acropolis like? All binoculars searched it out, the Greeks from the quarterdeck eagerly pointed into the distance. And finally I found it: something vaguely yellowed upon a stony hill, standing all alone beyond a sea of roofs in the valley, something akin to a small, savage fortress. And, having looked upon this naked mount of the Pelasgians, for the first time in my life and with all my being, I felt *antiquity* (*drevnost'*). (3:336)

The italics are Bunin's. His experience of the arid matter of antiquity distinguishes him from all those travelers conjuring up "vulgar Elysiums," their hungering, touristic eyes searching out a fantasy of the past. What Bunin insists upon instead, as he relates shortly after this passage, is that the antiquity he encounters evinces the value

---

[38] Nietzsche, *The Birth of Tragedy*, 136.

of simplicity: "God, how all of this is simple, old, and beautiful" (*Bozhe, kak vse eto prosto, staro, i prekrasno*) (3:337). Bunin could say this of the Acropolis. He could not, with Gorodetskii, say of the stone *baba:* "What an antiquity!" (*Kakaia starina!*). What we will see in the next chapter, however, is what happens when the stone *babas* are taken up by the avant-garde, who shared with figures such as Remizov and Gorodetskii the project of valorizing Russia's own indigenous antiquity.

Chapter Four

HOW A MODERNIST ARTIFACT IS MADE: THE "NATIVE ANTIQUITY" OF THE STONE *BABAS* AND THE INDIGENIZATION OF CUBISM

In December 1911, the poet Sergei Bobrov, representing the avant-garde group the Donkey's Tail, delivered a speech entitled "The Foundations of the New Russian Painting" ("Osnovy novoi russkoi zhivopisi") to the All-Russian Congress of Artists assembled in St. Petersburg.[1] The Donkey's Tail (whose members included Natal'ia Goncharova and Mikhail Larionov) was but one of the many tendencies of Russian art, from the venerable to the nascent, represented at the congress.[2] Among the attendees and organizers were such luminaries of the Russian art world as the artist and art historian Alexandre Benois; the painters associated with archaism, Viktor Vasnetsov and Nicholas Roerich; the collector Sergei Shchukin; and the arch-realist and Wanderer (*Peredvizhnik*) Ilya Repin.

The conveners of the congress had hoped that the attendees would engage in "friendly work on the defined program," while exchanging views on the past and future of Russian art. But comity proved too much to expect. When, for example, the proceedings of the congress were reviewed several years later in the art journal *Apollon*, the reviewer noted that those in attendance had "only

---

[1]   S. P. Bobrov, "Osnovy novoi russkoi zhivopisi," in *Trudy vserossiiskogo s"ezda khudozhnikov: Dekabr' 1911-Ianvar' 1912*, 3 vols. (Petrograd: T-vo R. Golike i A. Vil'borg, 1912), 1:43. Other articles from the congress will be cited by the author's last name, article title, followed by *Trudy* and the volume number.

[2]   "Kratkii obzor deiatel'nosti ustroitel'nogo komiteta vserossiiskogo s"ezda khudozhnikov," *Trudy*, 1:iv.

irritated recollections of useless debate, where a few voices shouted at once without hearing each other."[3]

What proved particularly contentious was the session that included Bobrov. His speech was part of the section "Questions on the Aesthetics and History of Art," which included the artist and publisher Nikolai Kul'bin and Wassily Kandinsky, who did not attend, but whose "On the Spiritual in Art" ("O dukhovnom v iskusstve") Kul'bin delivered in his stead.[4] As the official proceedings of the congress noted: "It goes without saying that particular attention was devoted to the newest tendencies in art, to those tendencies that so strongly excite contemporary society, provoking heated debates for or against. Their speeches, which were distinguished by the fervor and contemporary relevance of the questions broached, naturally provoked a lively exchange of opinion."[5]

In fact, Bobrov's speech overshadowed those of Kul'bin and Kandinsky (although the latter's contribution is the principal reason for the enduring place of the congress in art history[6]); "still more interesting [than Kandinsky's 'On the Spiritual in Art'] was the discussion concerning the credo of the Donkey's Tail, many theses of which were met with serious irritation."[7] Particularly irritating in Bobrov's speech were his views on the development of art and the array of objects he promoted as models for a new art:

> . . . Russian *purists* at the present time have stopped studying in France. Having overcome the French, Russian *purists* saw that so

[3] "Trudy vserossiiskogo s"ezda khudozhnikov v Petrograde Dekabr' 1911–Ianvar' 1912," *Apollon* (January 1916), no. 1:55-56.

[4] Kul'bin and Kandinsky would later collaborate again on the seminal publication *Der Blaue Reiter Almanach*, published in 1912. See *The Blaue Reiter Almanac*, new documentary edition, ed. Klaus Lankheit (New York: Viking Press, 1974).

[5] "Voprosy estetiki i istorii iskusstv," *Trudy*, 1:2.

[6] John E. Bowlt and Rose-Carol Washton Long, eds., *The Life of Vasilii Kandinsky in Russian Art: A Study of "On the Spiritual in Art"*, trans. John E. Bowlt (Newtonville, MA: Oriental Research Partners, 1980), 22-23; Sharp, *Russian Modernism between East and West*, 149.

[7] "Voprosy estetiki i istorii iskusstv," *Trudy*, 1:2.

much remained untouched and undeveloped in their motherland: our astounding icons, those premier crowns of Christian art, our old *lubki*, Northern embroideries, stone *babas*, the *bas-reliefs* made on communion bread, or on crosses, and our old signboards. Here there is so much novelty, untouched by anyone. . . . Henceforth, our native antiquity (*nasha rodnaia starina*), our archaism (*nash arkhaizm*) shall lead us into unexplored areas. (43)

"Our native antiquity, our archaism"—these two terms mark this episode of the statuary's career in Russian modernism as evincing the most polemical and programmatic force.[8] To nest the stone *baba* into this discourse of a "native antiquity" means that the statues were now operating within a matrix of aesthetic and cultural values that did not discriminate in terms of chronological or cultural distinctions. Instead, the statuary took its place among a group of objects in which the Christian is found side by side with the pagan; the sacred with the mundane; objects of worship with objects of cottage manufacture. What mattered instead was form; each object was evaluated for its potential to serve as a model for a future art, but one whose realization would trace a circuitous route through an unclaimed past.

Few at the congress or elsewhere would have disagreed with Bobrov's argument that the past was relevant to future art. Those who convened the congress set forth as one of its guiding principles the notion that "a strong country does not sever ties to its past, but the past [of Russia] is insufficiently studied, and its artistic monuments disappear daily. While it is not too late, and while time has not wiped clean all its traces, the responsibility of those who look into the future is to tend to the Russian national artistic achievement and to direct our artistic forces toward it."[9] For the conveners, the path to the future also lay through the past, and the art of the future

---

8   For more on "archaism" in Russian modernism, see Shevelenko, "Modernizm kak arkhaizm," 141-83. The concept is also the subject of her work in progress, "Modernism as Archaism: Nationalism and the Quest for a Modernist Aesthetic in Russia." I thank her for sharing parts of her manuscript with me.

9   "Kratkii obzor," iv.

would emerge in tandem with the study and preservation of past monuments.

While many at the congress focused upon artifacts and sites in which they discerned sources of "Russian national artistic achievement," others, such as Bobrov, addressed subjects that were less readily assimilated into prevailing views on national art, eager instead to push their search deeper into the past or the hinterland.[10] Although the conference program included themes such as Old Russian art, Russian icons, or the wooden edifice of Tsar Aleksei Mikhailovich's Kolomensky Palace, we also find topics on Siberian art and the art of "primitive" peoples. The problem, time and again, was *which* past should be promoted. As the art historian Dmitrii Ainalov observed in his speech to the congress, one reason for the intensity of the debates was that "in the world of artists, a differentiation and stratification has occurred that is incredible in terms of its variety, which has been incorrectly explained as the complete absence of discipline." What had been lost, Ainalov argued, was "a common path and tempo in the forward movement of Russian art."[11] This lack of a common path toward the future meant the discovery and valorization of a range of pasts.

Indeed, the objects Bobrov included in his menagerie of native antiquities immediately provoked the resistance of those attending his speech. In the official account of the congress, one audience member, the painter Aleksei Afanas'ev, objected to Bobrov's claims.

---

10   Many of the objects Bobrov includes in his avant-garde menagerie have been extensively ana-lyzed for their role in avant-garde art: the icon, the broadsheet, and the *lubok*, in particular, served as extraordinary resources for various modernist camps and the latter's exploration of the deep past, urban street culture, and folk forms in their search for models for their art. On painted shop signs, see A. V. Povelikhina, *Russkaia zhivopisnaia vyveska i khudozhniki avangarda* (Leningrad: Avrora, 1991); on *lubki*, see Anthony Parton, "Russian Folk Art and the Sources of Neo-Primitivism," in *Mikhail Larionov and the Russian Avant-Garde* (Princeton, NJ: Princeton University Press, 1993), 77-95; Sharp, "Nationality on Display: Official Exhibitions, Avant-Garde Interventions," in *Russian Modernism*, 143-73. For recent scholarship on icons and Russian modernism, see Jefferson J. A. Gatrall and Douglas M. Greenfield, eds., *Alter Icons: The Russian Icon and Modernity* (University Park: Penn State Press, 2010).

11   Ainalov, "O nekotorykh sovremennykh techeniiakh v russkoi zhivopisi," *Trudy*, 1:6, cited in the *Apollon* review, "Trudy vserossiiskogo s"ezda," 58.

Afanas'ev agreed that the Donkey's Tail "has brought in new trends," but he found that it "also aims to preserve these *primitive artifacts* (*primitivy*), which exist in the present. These things, which I have seen," he went on to remark, "are terrible and horrible. They demonstrate that their creators were profoundly unhappy. . . One should pity them."[12] Rude, uncouth, barbaric, savage, and now *unhappy* to boot: such were the epithets—old and new—employed in assessing the statuary and marshaled into the service of the opposition, which sought to bar promoting them to the stature of art, to the rank of "our native antiquity."

For his part, Bobrov dismissed this view as a subjective matter of taste. The official account does not record him making any further comment beyond that. But he had more to say in a different genre a couple of years later. His statements at the congress proved more than just programmatic and they applied to more than just Russian painting. Returning to the subject of the stone *babas*, Bobrov published a poem entitled "Kamennaia baba" in his poetry collection *Gardeners over the Vines* (*Vertogradari nad lozami*, 1913):

КАМЕННАЯ БАБА

Б. Н. Бугаеву

В степи седеющей курган
Ты издали заметишь темный,
На нем — горбатый истукан,
Он серожелтый и огромный.

На степи он и на закат
Бросает неживые взоры, —
На дымы отдаленных хат,
На возмущенные просторы.

Ты издали к нему взирай
В гигантскую обрубка муку.
Поднимет на печальный край
Он неослабнувшую руку;

Он издали кивнет — и нет:
Стоит как встарь окаменелый, —
Он — непостигнутый, поэт —
Подъемлет каменное тело.

Он разобьет, загрохотав,
Твои лукавые реченья
И опрокинет в зыби трав
Жизни отвергнутой мгновенья.

Встречай же жизнь! остановись
Перед восторженным полетом;
Разверзнет трепетная высь
Облак — пустеющим киотом.

Следи, прикованный к земле,
Как он несется величавый
И тонет в тучи ярой мгле,
В блистаниях закатной славы. —

Мгновенный сон! земной обман!
И не было его нелепей! —
И на кургане истукан
Сурово озирает степи.[13]

In the graying steppe
You will note from afar a dark kurgan,
Upon it, a hunchbacked idol,
It's grayish-yellow and huge.

Upon the steppes and at dawn
It casts lifeless glances
Upon the smoke of distant peasants' huts,
Upon indignant expanses.

Gaze, you, toward it from afar,
Upon the gigantic torment of the stump.
[How] it will raise to the sad land
Its untiring arm.

---

13   Sergei Bobrov, "Kamennaia baba," in *Vertogradari nad lozami* (Moscow: Lirika, 1913), 111-12. All of the titles in Bobrov's collection are capitalized, so it is unclear whether he is referring to the statuary by a proper name as did other poets.

From afar it will nod — but no:
It stands, as of old, petrified,
It is not yet comprehended, a poet
Who will raise its stone body.

Roaring, it will shatter
Your cunning locutions,
And topple over into the ripple of grass
Moments of rejected life.

Encounter life! Stop
Before the rapturous flight
The trembling height shall open wide
A cloud, like an empty icon-case

Follow, [you who are] riveted to the ground,
How it, majestic, rushes along,
And drowns in the furious darkness of the storm cloud,
In the shimmering of twilight grandeur.

A momentary dream! An earthly deception!
Nothing more absurd than it! —
And upon the kurgan, the idol
Severely surveys the steppes.

These eight stanzas of Bobrov's poem contain the multiple currents circulating in Russian modernism circa 1913; they are inscribed into the formal features of the poem and its accompanying paratexts. There is, as well, the poem's notable allusion to Pushkin's "The Bronze Horseman" ("Mednyi vsadnik," 1837), established both lexically and gesturally; this marks the confrontation between the steppe statuary and Petersburg's genius loci, which lords not only over the capital but also over the tradition of Russian literary statuary.[14]

---

[14] The assertion of the Bronze Horseman as St. Petersburg's genius loci is from N. Antsiferov, *Dusha Peterburga* (St. Petersburg: Brokgauz-Efron, 1922), 27. For further extensions of Antsiferov's view of the Bronze Horseman, see Katerina Clark, *Petersburg: Crucible of Cultural Revolution* (Cambridge, MA: Harvard University Press, 1995), 3-16; and Olga Matich, introduction to Petersburg/*Petersburg: Novel and City, 1901-1921*, ed. Olga Matich (Madison: University of Wisconsin Press, 2010), 10-16.

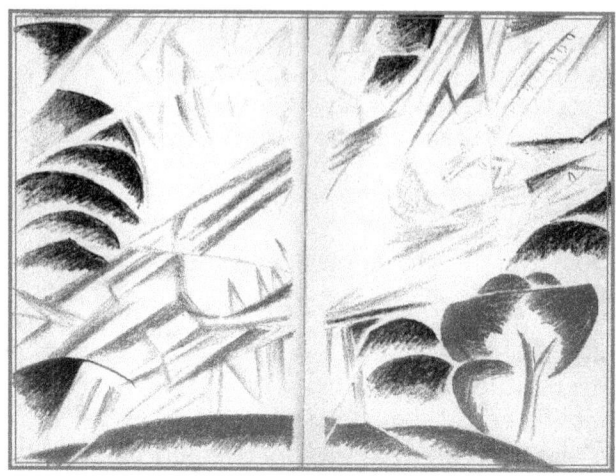

Figure 4.1.
Goncharova,
Lithograph of the stone
women in Bobrov's
Gardeners over the Vines
(1913).

Bobrov's poem is doubly retrospective. It surveys both the Russian literary tradition in the form of "The Bronze Horseman," as well as the objects from the past that had been excluded from that tradition as represented by the stone *baba*, perhaps the best translation here given the masculine pronouns used in references to it in the poem. This retrospection is accompanied by two explicit sideways glances, found in the poem's paratexts, which gesture to Bobrov's contemporaries and the aesthetic tendencies with which they were associated. The poem was dedicated to B. N. Bugaev, better known as Andrei Bely, and with whom Bobrov had studied metrics. And the volume in which it was published included ten lithographs by Natal'ia Goncharova, Bobrov's contemporary in the Donkey's Tail, whose paintings and statements on the statuary he surely knew. One lithograph (fig. 4.1), entitled *Kamennaia baba*, depicts the statuary in a Cubist idiom and marked another occasion for Goncharova to return to the subject of the statuary.

That both Bely and Goncharova are connected by Bobrov indicates that his poem is a matrix within which different modernist tendencies can be considered together: specifically, those of Symbolism and avant-garde Neo-Primitivism. The former supplies the poem with the phantasmic structure of the statuary's movement and the insistence on the dilemmas of sense perception. The latter enables the poem's valorization of the statuary, its formal values of mass and disproportion, and its still-unrecognized status as an antiquity capable of challenging the status of the Bronze Horseman.

The coming pages seek to account for how both the artifact and the artists represented two marginal positions—the statue as an unacknowledged antiquity, and Bobrov and Goncharova as outsiders in the cultural sphere. As the art historian Jane Sharp has written of the artists of the Donkey's Tail: "by creating their own collections they sought to overcome critical prejudices that excluded the Russian modernists from the national cultural paradigm—whether as part of a European or indigenous Russian tradition. . . . As Russian artists, they were perceived as primitives themselves, incapable of fully realizing the priorities of European art that occupied the center of art criticism and historiography."[15] If the 1911 congress had raised the question of how the past could be relevant to a future art, then formally encoded within Bobrov's poem was, if not a solution, then an attempt to work through that question. One reason to pay such close attention to the poem is that we can thereby see how it conducts a negotiation among the Russian literary tradition, the influence of Western modernism, and the internal debates within Russian modernism about the future of Russian arts and letters. That the poem seeks to negotiate among them—rather than, for example, opting to jettison one past in favor of another or to favor one modernist mode over another—seems to reflect Bobrov's goal of making "our native antiquity" responsive to what Ainalov called the unprecedented "stratification" in the art of the period. These poetic strata disclose Bobrov's overall sense of the multiplicity of antiquities present in Russia, and the ways in which they enter into juxtaposition one with another.

i. The Stone *Baba* and the Bronze Horseman

When Bobrov's *Gardeners* appeared in early 1913, one uncharitable reviewer quipped that the book was "a mixture of Pushkin, Tiutchev, and French poets sprinkled with the cologne of futurism

---

[15]   Sharp, *Russian Modernism between East and West*, 157-58.

and strewn with the pepper of the 'Donkey's-tail-ism.'"[16] Bobrov, to be sure, had invited such a response. Over the course of the book's seventy poems of varying lengths and genres, *Gardeners* was dedicated to the memory of Charles van Leberghe, and contained epigraphs not only from Leberghe's poetry, but also from Mikhail Kuzmin and Aloysius Bertrand, Novalis, Afanasy Fet, Viacheslav Ivanov, E. T. A. Hoffmann, Evgenii Baratynskii, Mikhail Lermontov, Ivan Konevskoi, Stéphane Mallarmé, Gérard de Nerval, Arthur Rimbaud, Vladimir Solov'ev, François Villon, and Nikolai Iazykov. These were just the epigraphs. The range of dedications was no less vast and varied: they included Nikolai Aseev, Sergei Raevskii, Grigorii Rachinskii, Boris Sadovskoi, and Igor Severianin. Goncharova not only supplied the lithographs, but was also the dedicatee of one poem. With all these references, epigraphs, and dedications, *Gardeners* was Western European and Russian literary and artistic culture writ large. While the reviewer found in this range of references Bobrov's flagrant attempt to insinuate his work into an array of traditions and trends, one reason that the scope of Bobrov's ambition captures our interest is that it also indicates the range of sources with which he frequently dealt. His treatment of the statuary thus typified his broader attempt to reconfigure various literary and artistic cultures throughout the collection.

This reconfiguration of tradition animates his use of the Bronze Horseman. In the opening stanzas, Bobrov elevates the stone *baba*—that curious representative of an archaic, primitive past—to the rank and the iconological and associative realm of the Bronze Horseman:

> В степи седеющей курган
> Ты издали заметишь темный,
> На нем—горбатый истукан,
> Он серожелтый и огромный.
>
> На степи он и на закат
> Бросает неживые взоры,—

---

[16]   Cited in Markov, *Russian Futurism*, 406, n. 5. Markov, by contrast, notes how "Bobrov stuns the reader with his amazing literary erudition, which he generously displays in numerous epigraphs" (232).

На дымы отдаленных хат,
На возмущенные просторы.

In the graying steppe
You will note from afar a dark kurgan,
Upon it, a hunchbacked idol,
It's grayish-yellow and huge.

Upon the steppes and at dawn
It casts lifeless glances,
Upon the smoke of distant peasants' huts,
Upon indignant expanses.

In these lines, Bobrov alludes to Pushkin's work and the central encounter between the statue and Evgenii, who will soon be driven both mad and to his death:

И он, как будто околдован,
Как будто к мрамору прикован,
Сойти не может! Вкруг него
Вода—и больше ничего!
И, обращен к нему спиною,
В неколебимой вышине,
Над возмущенною Невою
Стоит с простертою рукою
Кумир на бронзовом коне. (4:389)

[. . .]

Он мрачен стал
Пред горделивым истуканом
И, зубы стиснув, пальцы сжав,
Как обуянный силой черной,
«Добро, строитель, чудотворный! —
Шепнул он, злобно задрожав, —
Ужо тебе!» (4:395)

And he, as though bewitched,
As though onto marble riveted,
Cannot get down! About him
Is water and nothing more!
And with (his) back turned to him,
In unshakeable eminence,
Over the indignant Neva

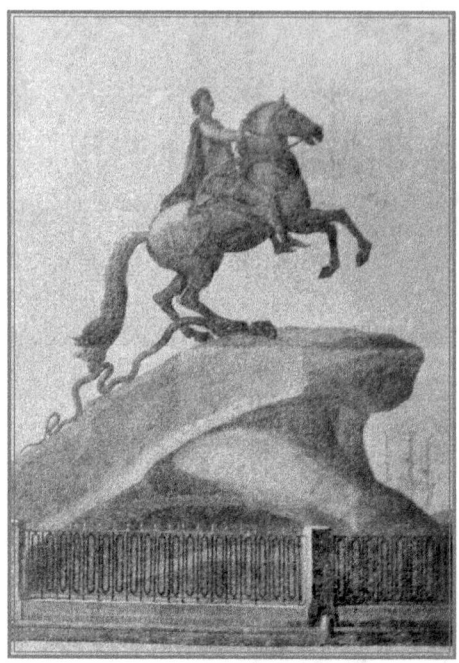

Figure 4.2.

Skorodumov, Gravure of the Bronze
Horseman in the Brokgauz-Efron
edition of "The Bronze Horseman"
(1907-15).

> Stands with outstretched hand
> The Idol on (his) bronze steed. (413-15)
>
> [. . .]
> He grew somber
> Before the prideful idol
> And, teeth clenched, fingers tightened into fists,
> As though possessed by (some) black power,
> "Fine, wonder-working builder!" —
> He whispered with a shudder of spite —
> "I'll (show) you."[17] (423)

By juxtaposing the statuaries that dominate the steppe and St. Petersburg—and, by extension, his poem with that of Pushkin's—Bobrov
generates much of the force of the poem, collapsing the symbolic
difference (and distance) that divides them. The allusions to "The

---

[17]   A. S. Pushkin, "Mednyi vsadnik," in *Polnoe sobranie sochinenii v desiati tomakh*, 3rd ed. (Moscow:
Nauka, 1963), 4:376-98, as translated in Alexander Pushkin, *Pushkin Threefold*, trans. Walter
Arndt (Ann Arbor, MI: Ardis, 1993), 400-27. Translation adjusted. All references are to these
editions and are cited in the text.

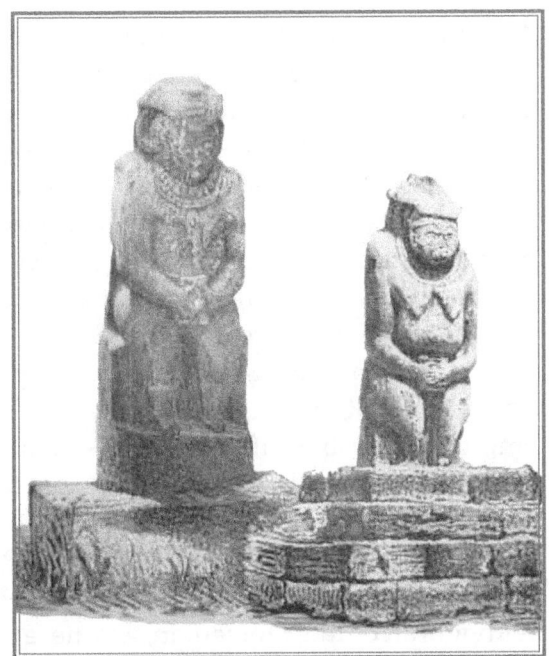

Figure 4.3.

Drawings illustrating
Uvarov's "Knowledge about
the Stone Women" (1869).

Bronze Horseman" are both lexical and iconological: the stone *baba* "casts lifeless glances / Upon indignant expanses" (*brosaet nezhivye vzory . . . na vozmushchennye prostory*), while the Bronze Horseman stands "above the indignant Neva" (*nad vozmushchennoiu Nevoiu*). Both are referred to as an "idol" (*istukan*): the statuary as "a hunchbacked idol" (*gorbatyi istukan*) in stanza one, and the Horseman as "the prideful idol" (*pred gordelivym istukanom*). These lexical parallels are accompanied by a forceful, gestural parallel: the statuary, Bobrov indicates, "will raise its untiring arm" (*podnimet . . . / On neoslabnuvshuiu ruku*), just as the Horseman gestures with its "outstretched arm" (*s prostertoiu rukoiu*) (figs. 4.2 and 4.3).

At first blush, the juxtaposition seems like a classic instance of brash avant-gardism. It dismantles the structure of prestige that underpins the predominant mythologemes of Russian cultural history, collapsing the symbolic antinomies of East and West: the putative wastelands of the steppe and the window opened to the West by St. Petersburg; the marginal statue and Petersburg's genius loci. The juxtaposition calls to mind the avant-garde's promotion of collage to a central organizing principle. In Katerina Clark's words, "whichever way the paradigmatic gesture is defined—collage, montage, breaking or confusing the frame, and so on—it involves placement or juxtaposition with the aim of confounding borders and hierarchies. One has to place the like against the unlike in order to 'see' anew."[18] In this regard, a whole range of oppositions emerge: one statue is primitive, the other the supreme symbol of Russian modernity and empire, straddling neoclassical and baroque styles.[19] One is of unknown origin and provenance, the other commissioned by Catherine the Great and sculpted by Étienne Falconet; one is situated upon a kurgan, the other perched upon the so-called Thunder Rock, where it symbolizes Petersburg's, if not the entire empire's, veritable—if precarious—center of gravity. The stone *baba* may once have induced a sense of mystery, even a sense of fear, in earlier poets, but never before had it evoked the whole empire.

It is through this allusion to Pushkin that Bobrov charts his oblique entry into the company of Russian modernists who reinvigorated the Horseman, statue and text, for their time. As N. V. Izmailov notes, "at the beginning of the twentieth century, Pushkin's *poèma* found ever more frequent reflection in the work of the Symbolists, poets and prosaists."[20] Those figures for whom "The Bronze Horseman" served as a touchstone for such themes as urbanism, world-historical revolution, and apocalyptic fervor included leading modernists from Innokentii Annenskii to Blok to Anna Akhmatova, as well as Bely, whose *Petersburg* began its serial publication the year Bobrov published the poem. This association with Bely is particularly crucial given the poem's

---

18   Clark, *Petersburg*, 34. The reference to "paradigmatic gesture" extends Marjorie Perloff's focus on collage in *The Futurist Moment: Avant-Garde, Avant Guerre, and the Language of Rupture* (Chicago: University of Chicago Press, 1986), esp. chapter 2.

19   As Alexander M. Schenker writes, "In the *Peter the Great*, Falconet's last and greatest work, the dignified Neoclassical posture of the tsar coexists with the Baroque restlessness of the rearing horse and the fluid, wave-like shape of the pedestal" (*The Bronze Horseman: Falconet's Monument to Peter the Great* [New Haven, CT: Yale University Press, 2003], 265). See also Julie A. Buckler's discussion of the statue as embodying "monumental eclecticism" in *Mapping St. Petersburg: Imperial Text and Cityshape* (Princeton, NJ: Princeton University Press, 2003), 73-78.

20   N. V. Izmailov, "'Mednyi vsadnik' A. S. Pushkina" in A. S. Pushkin, *Mednyi vsadnik: Poèma*. Literaturnye pamiatniki (Leningrad: Nauka, 1978), 248.

dedication to him. It indicates that Bobrov's poem is as much in dialogue with Bely as it is about gesturing toward Pushkin. I want to coordinate a reading of the poem from these two angles—returning to the Goncharova lithograph in the next section—and pursue the allusion to Pushkin alongside Bobrov's admonishment to his addressee not to mistake fantasy for reality. In other words, the addressee should not think, as Evgenii did, that statues can come to life.

Pushkin scholars would remind us that the link between "The Bronze Horseman" and idolatry—one of the central terms for the allusion in Bobrov—has a complex textual history. This history and its reception, in fact, help to flesh out some of Bobrov's potential sources as he fashioned his image of the *baba* and the Bronze Horseman. Pushkin's personal censor, Nicholas I, objected precisely to this affiliation of the Bronze Horseman with idols, and thus to the words *istukan* and *kumir* in the original drafts of the work. Both *istukan* and *kumir* (*kumir na bronzovom kone*) were replaced by *gigant* (giant) in the expurgated edition prepared by Zhukovskii that held sway for the remainder of the nineteenth century.[21] These words, however, reacquired particular currency—and relevance for Bobrov—when they were restored in the 1904 version prepared by Petr Morozov. This currency was appreciated in 1909, when "The Bronze Horseman" appeared in the third volume of Pushkin's *Collected Works* in the series The Library of Great Authors (*Biblioteka velikikh pisatelei*). This text was accompanied by an essay by Valery Briusov; illustrations by Alexandre Benois, one of which depicts the statue in pursuit of Evgenii; and a gravure by G. I. Skorodumov.[22]

---

[21]   As Andrew Kahn notes, "popular editions of Pushkin's works, such as the 1880 text of Maikov, restored all or part of the crucial confrontation between the statue and Evgenii while retaining certain euphemisms that Zhukovskii had introduced to dodge the censor; hence, for instance, 'gigant' (instead of 'kumir') was fossilised in the text . . . for the more controversial 'istukan'." (*Pushkin's* The Bronze Horseman [London: Bristol Classical Press, 1998], 8).

[22]   A. S. Pushkin, "Mednyi vsadnik," in *Pushkin: Biblioteka velikikh pisatelei* (St. Petersburg: Brokgauz-Efron, 1907-15), 3:456-82.

Briusov, in fact, called attention specifically to the restoration of both offending words in his commentary to the poem, when he emphasized how the epithets *kumir, gordelivyi istukan*, and *stroitel' chudotvornyi*, were central to an understanding of the work. Namely, the terms indicated that the "hero of the story (*povest'*) is not Peter, . . . but 'The Bronze Horseman,' the 'proud idol' (*istukan*), and above all, the 'idol' (*kumir*). It is precisely as an 'idol' ('*kumir*'), that is, as something deified, that Pushkin himself names the monument to Peter." Briusov then reminded his readers of the textual differences between these various editions when he added the separate note: "The expression '*gigant*' does not belong to Pushkin; it was a correction by Zhukovskii."[23]

Bobrov probably knew Briusov's commentary with its reminder that Pushkin emphasized the status of the Bronze Horseman precisely as an *idol*, rather than simply a statue—even a "giant" one—of Peter the Great as a historical personage. The poem even seems to refer to this fraught textual history of "The Bronze Horseman," when Bobrov uses both *istukan* (twice, at the beginning and end) and a form of *gigant* (in line ten: *gigantsksuiu obrubka muku*). These lexical and iconological parallels attest to the care he took in constructing the juxtaposition between the two statues, the neoclassical and the primitive. The poem was anything but a piece of clumsy iconoclasm.

Indeed, it may be too easy (and misleading) to align Bobrov's juxtaposition of the Bronze Horseman and the statuary with other currents of Russian Futurism (which he had not yet fully joined) in 1913—that is, to interpret what he is doing in the poem as typifying the brash posturing against the traditions of the Golden Age that had reached its apotheosis the year before with the publication of the manifesto *A Slap in the Face of Public Taste* (*Poshchechina obshchestvennomu vkusu*, 1912).[24] Bobrov, in fact, was antagonistic toward the Hylaea group, the authors of *A Slap*, who included David Burliuk, Aleksandr Kruchenykh, Vladimir Mayakovsky, and

---

[23]   V. Briusov, "Mednyi vsadnik," in *Pushkin: Biblioteka velikikh pisatelei*, 3:471-72.

[24]   *Manifesty i programmy russkikh futuristov* (Munich: Wilhelm Fink Verlag, 1967), 50-51.

Velimir Khlebnikov (who signed as "Viktor Khlebnikov"), and far less opposed to the old idols; indeed, the range of his epigraphs and dedications suggest his determination to locate his work within the poetic and artistic cultures of both past and present. In this, however, Bobrov was joined by other members of the Futurist camp such as Benedikt Livshits, a close associate of the signatories of *A Slap*, who nevertheless sought to negotiate freely among the various tendencies active in Russian modernism. What I. V. Koretskaia has argued in the case of Livshits could well be applied to Bobrov: "the poetry of Livshits, a refined Westernizer, who connected his creative fate with the primitivists of Hylaea, revealed his own boundary case between the neoclassical, which was oriented in its form and content toward the values of the cultural tradition, and Futurism, which was rushing to destroy those values."[25] (We saw this feature of Livshits in chapter two, and the multiple mythological references he makes in perceiving the landscape of Hylaea.) Indeed, not only *Gardeners* evinces a similar straddling of the boundaries between various poetic tendencies, but Bobrov's later work also testifies to his firm commitment to the poetic achievement of past generations, in particular that of Pushkin, who was the subject of Bobrov's essay "Love for Pushkin" ("Liubov' k Pushkinu," 1914), which he included in his volume *Notes of a Versifier* (*Zapiski stikhotvortsa*, 1916).[26]

At various levels of "The Stone *Baba*," then, we find a similar negotiation between the cultural tradition and the primitive, each of which is respectively represented by the two statues. To see the poem this way means that other elements of the poem can be read as deepening the poem's link to Pushkin or adumbrating its primary archaistic theme. Consider, for example, the crucial fourth stanza in which we find, economically compressed, the theme of the oscillation between illusion and reality: the dramatic metamorphosis of the statue into both a mobile object and a poet:

---

[25] I. V. Koretskaia, "Literatura v krugu iskusstv," in *Russkaia literatura rubezha vekov (1890-e–nachalo 1920-x godov)* (Moscow: IMLI RAN, 2001), 178.

[26] Sergei Bobrov, "Liubov k Pushkinu," in *Zapiski stikhotvortsa* (1916; reprint, Letchworth, England Prideaux Press, 1973), 21-29.

Он издали кивнет—и нет:
Стоит как встарь окаменелый,—
Он—непостигнутый, поэт—
Подъемлет каменное тело.

From afar it will nod—but no:
It stands, as of old, petrified
It is not yet comprehensible, a poet—
Will raise its stone body.

These quick fluctuations between affirming the statue's stasis while portending its mobility are conducted with exacting speed. The first line of the stanza raises the possibility of movement only to dismiss it in the very same line, and then raise it again at the end of the stanza. These fluctuations are tied to the theme of vision throughout the poem, and the chimerical movement of the statue anticipates the announcement that what happens in the poem is ultimately an "earthly deception": a mirage of movement shimmering in the steppe heat, there one moment, gone the next.

One feature of the stanza that gives us pause is the pairing *okamenelyi* (petrified)/*telo* (body)—an approximate or poor rhyme.[27] This rhyme could also allude to Pushkin, via Briusov's commentary. In his essay on "The Bronze Horseman," Briusov had remarked on various facets of the rhyme schemes Pushkin used, singling out the same approximate rhyme when he noted that "Pushkin, according to pronunciation, freely rhymes adjectives ending in *ый* (yi) with adverbs ending in *о*."[28] If the allusion to Pushkin (via Briusov) on the basis of this rhyme has any purchase, then it suggests the various layers of poetic form upon which Bobrov establishes the relationship between his poem and Pushkin's.

But another question posed by the stone body of the statuary is: What has this to do with its status as a poet? We do get some sense of the kind of poetry the statue would produce in the next stanza,

---

[27] See Barry P. Scherr, *Russian Poetry: Meter, Rhythm, and Rhyme* (Berkeley and Los Angeles: University of California Press, 1986), 200.

[28] Briusov, "Mednyi vsadnik," 3:470.

when Bobrov imagines that the statue will emit a crashing roar that will destroy the "cunning locutions" of the poet's addressee:

> Он разобьет, загрохотав,
> Твои лукавые реченья
> И опрокинет в зыби трав
> Жизни отвергнутой мгновенья.

> Roaring, it will shatter
> Your cunning locutions,
> And topple over into the ripple of grass
> Moments of rejected life.

On one level, several lexical and thematic aspects of the stanza again bring us back to Pushkin, in particular the moment shortly after Evgenii's defiant threat to the statue, when the Bronze Horseman, too, begins to rush through the square, "as if it were the roaring of thunder" (*groma grokhotan'e*):

> "Добро, строитель чудотворный! —
> Шепнул он, злобно задрожав, —
> Ужо тебе! . . ." И вдруг стремглав
> Бежать пустился. Показалось
> Ему, что грозного царя,
> Мгновенно гневом возгоря,
> Лицо тихонько обращалось . . .
> И он по площади пустой
> Бежит и слышит за собой—
> Как будто грома грохотанье—
> Тяжело-звонкое скаканье
> По потрясенной мостовой.
> И, озарен луною бледной,
> Простерши руку в вышине,
> За ним несется Всадник Медный
> На звонко-скачущем коне. (4:395-96)

> "Fine, wonder-working builder!"—
> He whispered with a shudder of spite—
> "I'll show you." And suddenly full tilt
> He set off running. It seemed
> To him the dread tsar's face, instantly aflame with wrath,
> Was slowly turning . . .

And he runs down the empty square
And hears behind him,
As if it were the roaring of thunder,
A heavily ringing gallop
Over the quaking pavement.
And twilit by the pallid moon,
Arm reaching forth on high,
There speeds after him the Bronze Horseman
Upon the clangorously galloping steed. (425)

If the lexical parallels (*zagrokhotav/groma grokhotan'e*) link the two works, then they also suggest that the thunderous noise of the Bronze Horseman is now met by that of the stone *baba*. Its "roar" is here pitched to a primitivist aesthetic challenge leveled against the addressee's "cunning locutions."

The poem's primitivist challenge, its allusive structure, and the themes of mobile statuary, come together in the subsequent stanzas in which the poet invites his addressee to bear witness to various flights of fancy:

Встречай же жизнь! остановись
Перед восторженным полетом;
Разверзнет трепетная высь
Облак—пустеющим киотом.

Следи, прикованный к земле,
Как он несется величавый
И тонет в тучи ярой мгле,
В блистаниях закатной славы.

Encounter life! Stop
before the rapturous flight;
the trembling height shall open wide
A cloud—like an empty icon case.

Follow, you who are riveted to the ground,
how it, majestic, rushes along,
and drowns in the furious darkness of the storm,
In the shimmering of twilight grandeur.

These stanzas are notable for both the metrical instabilities we find Bobrov deploying in them, and for their intertextual gestures toward Pushkin's poem. As Mikhail Gasparov has observed, we also find in these two passages several curious metrical and rhythmical features. Gasparov notes that the word *oblak* (cloud) is an archaic singular form, which "sharply break[s] from the traditional rhythm of the iambic tetrameter," the poem's dominant metrical structure. The break achieves what Gasparov calls a "rhythmical italicization" within the stanza and should not be read as a mistake.[29] On one level, we could add that *oblak* amplifies the archaic lexical registers Bobrov uses in the poem since *istukan*, too, by Bobrov's time, possessed an archaic resonance. One could add to Gasparov's account that the break caused by *oblak* extends the theme of the statuary's disruptive force onto the metrical level, shattering both the "cunning locutions" of the addressee and the metrical stability of the poem. What might seem a metrical mistake turns out instead to be a metrical shock of the archaic.

These stanzas also return us to Pushkin insofar as the re-markable movement of the statuary in Bobrov echoes not only the Bronze Horseman's thunderous rushing through the square, but also gestures to Evgenii's being "riveted to the marble" during the flood:

> И он, как будто околдован,
> Как будто к мрамору прикован,
> Сойти не может! Вкруг него
> Вода—и больше ничего! (4:389)

> And he, as though bewitched,
> As though onto marble riveted,
> Cannot get down! About him
> Is water and nothing more! (413)

This parallel between Evgenii and the poem's addressee—the first riveted to the marble, the other to the earth, and both surrounded

---

29   M. L. Gasparov, *Russkie stikhi 1890-kh–1925-go godov v kommentariiakh* (Moscow: Vysshaia shkola, 1993), 101.

by "seas" of water and steppe grass—seems to warn the addressee
not to will himself into madness (one sign of which is the idea that
statues come to life), but rather to stay rooted to the earth. The
fantasy, in short, collapses by the end of the poem with this final
image of the statue, just as "you" first saw it:

> Мгновенный сон! земной обман!
> И не было его нелепей! —
> И на кургане истукан
> Сурово озирает степи.

> A fleeting dream! An earthly deception!
> There was nothing more absurd than it! —
> And upon the kurgan, the idol
> Severely surveys the steppes.

The admonition to stay rooted in the earth reveals, in part,
Bobrov's complex working through of the legacy of Symbolism,
indeed, one that is taking place throughout the pages of *Gardeners*.
He showed some of his debts to the movement in his poem "Legacy"
(*Zavet*), which appears in book one of *Gardeners*. This frequently
cited poem is often singled out as his most programmatic work,
in which he announced: "Blessed Symbolism / Has revealed to
us shores and forests" (*Otkryl nam berega i pushchi /Blagoslovennyi
simvolizm*).[30] But those revelations could no longer suffice, inasmuch
as Bobrov, in Vladimir Markov's words, "refus[es] to follow the
example of the famous symbolist leaders, refus[es] to fall victim
to an old-fashioned aestheticism (Bryusov), or to equate poetry
with religion (V. Ivanov), or to become mired in the swamps of
preliminary metaphysical consideration (Biely)."[31]

Indeed, in his speech at the 1911 congress, Bobrov had insisted
that the *babas* and other primitive artifacts lacked guile, which he
finds in the "cunning locutions" of his addressee. Bobrov remarked,

---

[30]   Cited and translated in Catherine Ciepiela, *The Same Solitude: Boris Pasternak and Marina Tsvetaeva* (Ithaca, NY: Cornell University Press, 2006), 45.

[31]   Markov, *Russian Futurism*, 234.

for instance: "Now, it seems, artists who love the past (*starinu*), who are occupied with it, for some reason do not themselves go further than a cheap and vulgar stylization of these guileless masterpieces, not understanding, not sensing the massive painterly value of them. But Russian purists, having seen all this value, abide with them, enter into their very souls" (43). In Bobrov's view, the statuary and the other primitive and archaic artifacts comprising his menagerie of native antiquities could serve as a counterweight to a Symbolist aesthetic that had placed more emphasis on metaphysics than on physics and on mass, the qualities that Bobrov and Goncharova had valued in primitive forms.

Perhaps one final image can best serve as the transition from this section to the next. Another parallel between Bobrov's poem and "The Bronze Horseman" is found in the rhyme *ruku* (arm / hand) and *muku* (torment). After the fateful encounter with the Bronze Horseman, Pushkin describes Evgenii: "To his chest, / He hurriedly pressed his hand / As though bridling his torment" (*K serdtsu svoemu / On prizhimal pospeshno ruku / Kak by ego smiriaia muku*), while Bobrov describes the statuary as it stands "Upon the gigantic torment of the stump. / It will raise to the sad land / its untiring arm" (*V gigantskuiu obrubka muku. / Podnimet na pechal'nyi krai / On neoslabnuvshuiu ruku*). The rhyme invites a comparison between the stone *baba* and Evgenii. But if the *baba* were to raise its untiring arm, it would thereby assume the pose of the Bronze Horseman, while Evgenii, beleaguered and crazed, hand pressed close to his chest, makes a gesture that marks him as the iconological antithesis of the Bronze Horseman. The pose of the *baba*, by contrast, adopts that of the Bronze Horseman, and its roar channels the Horseman's sound as it chases after Evgeny. Both the *baba* and Evgenii, however, are figures of defiance, and perhaps part of the statue's challenge is leveled against the Horseman as a symbol of imperial Petersburg. The *baba*, that is, forms another source of challenge, one that comes from the East rather than from the little man represented by Evgenii, and one that comes at a moment of "twilight grandeur" that could allude to the apocalyptic fears of the time and to the fate of the empire itself. Even though the statuary settles back upon the kurgan in the final stanza, it continues to "severely survey the steppe," which suggests that it remains animate even as its threatening mobility is deferred until such time as it is itself recognized as a poet.

ii. Indigenous Cubism

Bobrov included an essay entitled "On the New Illustration" ("O novoi illiustratsii") in *Gardeners*. In it, he envisions a new relationship between poems and their illustrations that would break free of the "impressionistic chatter" (*impressionisticheskaia boltovnia*) that he alleges was all too prevalent in earlier work. Goncharova's illustrations, according to Bobrov, furnish the pictorial means for readers to understand his central aesthetic aims. The illustrations are liberated from any subordination to thematic elements and are focused instead on matters of form. To that end, Bobrov asserts, Goncharova captures the "lyrical movements" of his *poèma* (the generic designation he uses for his collection as a whole) through her emphasis on "the chain of transverse and longitudinal lines, introduced into painting by the Futurists."[32]

Bobrov's essay reminds us that we cannot just harness Goncharova's lithograph to the poem. The lithograph does not illustrate the poem in any traditional sense, but, rather, offers a way of comparing two distinct treatments of the statuary. In the lithograph, Goncharova employs a far more Cubist mode in rendering the *baba* than she had deployed in her previous work on the statuary in such paintings as *Pillars of Salt* (*Solianye stolpy*, 1908), *Still Life with Pineapple* (*Natiurmort s ananasom*, 1908), and *God of Fertility* (*Bozhestvo plodorodiia*, 1908–09),[33] where she retains the statuary's iconic pose with its hands holding the vessel. In the lithograph, by contrast, the *baba* appears fractured between multiple planes, its canonical pose diagonally transecting the drawing, while multiple visages are distributed throughout the upper half of the drawing (figs. 4.4 and 4.5).

[32] Bobrov, *Vertogradari*, 156.

[33] For more on Goncharova's work on the statue see Sharp, *Russian Modernism*, 159-61; Parton, *Larionov*, 98-100.

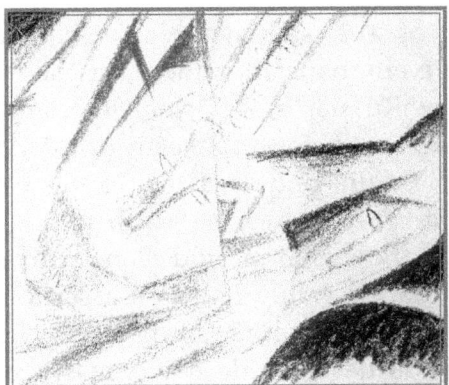

Figure 4.4.

Detail of figure 4.1.

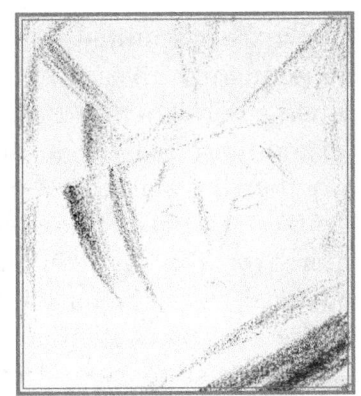

Figure 4.5.

Detail of figure 4.1.

The poem gave Goncharova another occasion to return to the subject of the statuary and the question of Cubism, which she had begun incorporating into her paintings in 1908. Jane Sharp's study of Goncharova has provided the fullest account of the artist's engagement with the *babas*. In her words, "the complexity and mystery of the statuettes' origin and ritual function clearly appealed to Goncharova and provided ample room for her to interpolate a history that answered to her needs."[34] Goncharova not only painted the statuary on various occasions but, like Bobrov, used it as a central term in elaborating her artistic visions and her sense of how to mediate between Russian national traditions and the influence of Western Europe. Livshits records a speech Goncharova gave at an exhibition of the Jack of Diamonds, a rival group to the Donkey's Tail:

> "Cubism," Goncharova continued, "is a good thing, but not entirely new. The Scythian stone *babas*, the painted wooden dolls sold at fairs: these are also Cubist creations. True, they aren't painting[s], but sculpture, but even in France, the motherland of Cubism, the monuments of Gothic sculpture served as the departure point for this movement."[35]

[34]   Sharp, *Russian Modernism*, 161.

[35]   Livshits, *Polutoraglazyi strelets*, 363.

Goncharova's initial alignment of the statuary with Cubism subsequently gives way to a more emphatically nationalist claim, when she refers to the statuary as "Russian stone *babas*,"[36] a claim all the more striking in that Goncharova does not seem to worry whether the statues are Slavic in origin, only that they could be claimed as part of Russia's artistic heritage. It is worth noting, moreover, the slight differences in how Bobrov and Goncharova advance their claims for the statuary's value. Bobrov's assertion at the congress essentially rests upon a discourse of discovery, in which the statuary and other antiquities provide new vistas and models for art. Goncharova, by contrast, makes a more indigenizing claim. She polemically interprets the statuary in terms of Cubism, which furnishes her with newly established formal values—mass, facture, disproportion—for reassessing artifacts from the past, while concomitantly retrojecting these new formal values into Russia's past, "discovering" in the past an archaic precedent. Whatever their differences, Bobrov and Goncharova reevaluate the formal features of the *babas* while incorporating the statuary into a Cubist genealogy whose roots they transplant from the Seine to the Russian steppe. Both the artifact and the painterly tendency of Cubism, in effect, become one's own antiquity.

Goncharova's lithograph makes a more explicit case for reading the poem in terms of Cubism. If we were to interpret Bobrov's poem vis-à-vis the "new illustration" model, then we might see the kind of fracturing Goncharova employs in her work as the visual analogue to the fractured perspectives within the poem. We find various shifts between multiple perspectives: stanza one commands the addressee to look upon the idol, and so both the lyric poet and the addressee share a perspective. Stanza two focuses on the idol's perspective on the landscape, and so the poet shifts his angle of vision from looking at the statuary to looking from the statuary's angle upon the steppe. Stanza three restores the angle of vision we encounter in stanza one, but introduces the theme of the idol's possible movement. Such perspectival fractures might decouple the

---

[36]   Sharp, *Russian Modernism*, 161.

statue's phantasmatic movements in the poem away from a Symbolist critique of sense perception toward a Cubo-Futurist aesthetic that seeks to render the possibility of movement on canvas by representing objects from simultaneous viewpoints.

Bobrov's poem encodes a similar effort, but does so by taking up a specific tendency within Cubism, namely, the juxtaposition of primitive statuary with forms from classical antiquity or the heritage of canonical Western European art.[37] It is this kind of juxtaposition that adds another dimension to our understanding of why the Bronze Horseman is so central to Bobrov's assertion of the aesthetic value of the *baba*. Here, we might recall two aspects of Bobrov's characterization of the statuary. First, he says that it will raise its arm (*Podnimet na pechal'nyi krai / On neoslabnuvshuiu ruku*) — and, second, he refers to the statuary as a *gigantskuiu obrubka muku*. As we saw above, these lines refer us back to "The Bronze Horseman" and the Falconet statue, but the very device of combining two forms of statuary together arguably refers us to a range of primitivist and Cubist paintings in which we find a similar grafting, both gesturally and compositionally, of the primitive onto recognizable models from the antique or neoclassical past.

There are two possible models for this gesture of which Bobrov could have known, and which perhaps even appealed to him given the frequent references in *Gardeners* to paintings from the Renaissance up to the present day. With respect to painting, Bobrov was just as broad-ranging, even eclectic, in his embrace of all manner of styles and periods as he was with poetry.[38] The

---

[37] One way to approach the linking of the statuary to Cubism in Bobrov would be to identify a possible common historical genealogy between Bobrov and Picasso. Goncharova, in fact, provides one; in the same letter in which she links the statuary to the Scythians, she indicates a possible, if ambiguous, connection to Picasso and Bely. "The fact that the cubist Picasso is a great artist," she wrote, "only confirms that pathetic snails will stick to any great ship. In his manifesto, Andrei Belyi has spoken very well to this regarding petty, decadent men of letters." Sharp speculates that the unnamed manifesto to which Goncharova alludes is probably Bely's "Symbolism," and, in particular, the section on "The Magic of Words." Goncharova, moreover, had displayed her work at a lecture on Bely, delivered at the Society for Free Aesthetics. Sharp, *Russian Modernism*, 103.

[38] Alongside the writers to whom he alludes, other poems in *Gardeners* frequently refer to

first painting directly relevant to "The Stone Woman" is Henri
Rousseau's *The Dream* (*Le Rêve*) from 1910, to which he refers in
another poem in *Gardeners* entitled "The Dream" ("Son," 82-83).
The poem draws its epigraph from the poem Rousseau wrote
to accompany the painting: "Yadwigha dans un beau rêve." It is
Bobrov's most explicit reference to primitivist painting in *Gardeners*,
and it is notable because Rousseau's painting references the long
tradition of the reclining nude. Both Yadwigha's pose—her raised
arm gestures outward toward the forest—and the title of the poem
resonate with the last stanza of Bobrov's "The Stone *Baba*": another
indication that the poem's forays into the fantastic were nothing but
a "momentary dream" (*mgnovennyi son*).

The second painting that provides a notable counterpoint
for Bobrov's poem is Picasso's *Three Women* (1908). Art historians
suggest that works by Larionov and Goncharova were in dialogue
with those of Picasso from 1908 on,[39] and Bobrov could well have
known of Picasso through the two Russian painters, his colleagues
in the Donkey's Tail, or independently, given his own interest in
painting. The latter is thoroughly evident in his speech at the 1911
congress, where he discusses a range of French painters including
Picasso.[40] Like many of his contemporaries, Bobrov had access to
Picasso's paintings (primarily works of ca. 1908–10) in the Picasso
Hall in the mansion of the industrialist and art collector Sergei
Shchukin, which was open to the public on Sundays (fig. 4.6). The
mansion was one of the main venues where an entire generation of
Russian avant-gardists could see the extraordinary collection that

painters or take particular paintings as their subject matter. There is a poem set in a museum ("V muzee," 70); a poem on a portrait of Tiutchev ("K portretu F. I. Tiutchevu," 130); and
poems that cite specific painters: Cranach ("Istochnik iunosti"); Mikhail Larionov (68-69);
and Velázquez, which also revealed his interest in rhyme and tropological forms, when
he rhymed (perhaps for the first time in world literature) "Velázquez" with *katakrez*
(catachresis).

[39] Parton, *Larionov*, 58-59.

[40] Bobrov also refers to Picasso in *Gardeners* where he describes his poetic method. He writes of
Picasso that he was more "metonymical than Manet" (*Pikasso metonimichnee Mane* [*Vertogradari*,
155]), when Bobrov attempts to divide the arts of poetry and painting according to their
metaphorical or metonymic predispositions.

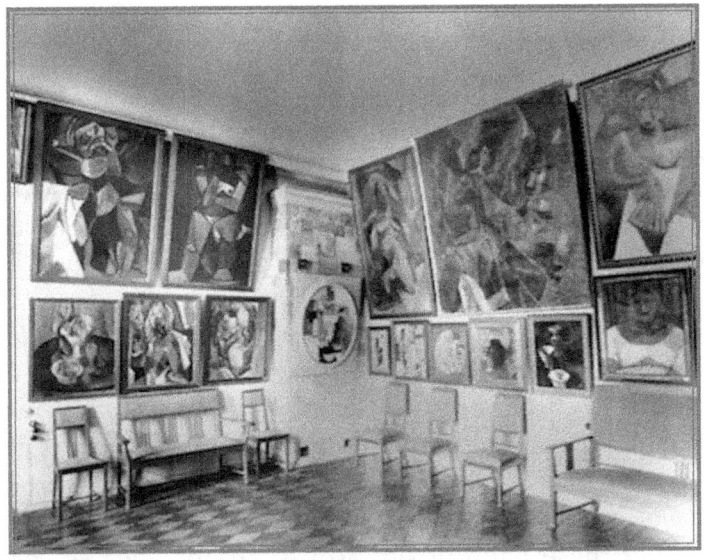

Figure 4.6.

Photograph of the Picasso Hall in Shchukin's mansion. The painting in the top row,
second from the right, is *The Three Women*; third from the left is *The Dryad*.
Photo courtesy of the Pushkin State Museum of Fine Arts, Moscow.

Shchukin had amassed, and, in particular, the paintings of such figures as Paul Gauguin, Henri Matisse, and Vincent Van Gogh, as well as Picasso.[41]

At 78 3/4 x 70 1/8 inches, *Three Women* held a prominent position in the Picasso Hall. As the art historian Elizabeth Cowling has characterized it, the painting is "distinctly sculptural," with the poses of the three women refering to various "European models," now merged with Picasso's understanding of the formal features of tribal art.[42] Hence, the viewer was asked to perceive those models in relation to the disposition of the figures in the work. At the same time, to again cite Cowling,

---

[41] See N. Iu. Semenova, *Moskovskie kollektsionery: S. I. Shchukin, I. A. Morozov, I. S. Ostroukhov; Tri sud'by, tri istorii uvlechenii* (Moscow: Molodaia gvardiia, 2010), 10-135; idem, *Zhizn' i kollektsiia Sergeia Shchukina* (Moscow: Trilistnik, 2002).

[42] Elizabeth Cowling, *Picasso: Style and Meaning* (London: Phaidon, 2002), 188-90.

The large geometric facets describing volumes of the bodies look
as if they have been formed with a flat-bladed tool, and the jerky,
irregular rhythm set up through the abrupt shifts in tone, and the
collision of so many diagonal lines and so many tipping planes,
evokes the sensation of sawing, hacking, chopping, and chipping.
The overall effect is uncouth. . . . A more polished effect would
have resulted in the diminution of the raw, earthy power Picasso
wanted.[43]

This passage could well serve as an apt description of the formal
features, aesthetic aims, and descriptive features we find in Bobrov's
poem: the statue roars, it is hunchbacked (*gorbatyi*), and Bobrov
likens the idol to an *obrubok*, or stump. It is a human form, made not
by chisel, nor out of marble, but by an axe. In the eighteenth century,
Pallas called such statues "rough hewn." Bobrov would agree.

Whether these paintings by Rousseau and Picasso served Bobrov as actual reference points or provide us with contemporaneous
counterpoints for interpreting "The Stone *Baba*," they illuminate
the multiple levels on which the poem operates. On one level,
the conflation of the statuary and the Bronze Horseman mediates
between modernism and the Russian literary tradition—and thus
between modernist primitivism and neoclassicism, just as Western
models, Cubist forms, and African sculpture all work together in
Picasso's painting. On another level, the very gesture of juxtaposing
the two statues might also be seen as quintessentially avant-gardist,
since the grafting of primitive artifacts onto various models of
greater cultural authority and iconological legibility carries with it
the very sign of what a modernist primitive should do. That is to
say, we could regard the poem's conjoining of the stone *baba* and
the Bronze Horseman as a kind of modernist device, a signature
move, which Bobrov may have gleaned from Picasso and to whom
he may now gesture in employing the device.

The art historian Anthony Parton has noted the particular irony
of Western European primitivism's influence on the work of such
figures as Larionov and Goncharova and what we are seeing take

43   Ibid., 190-91.

place in Bobrov. It was Western European precedent, he argues, that both inspired and legitimized Larionov's and Goncharova's investigations of the primitive, especially evidenced by their "interest in their indigenous sculptural forms," from which Parton singles out the stone *babas*.[44] In this view, Western influence threatens once again to cast Russian Neo-Primitivism into the established pattern of Russian belatedness and backwardness precisely at the moment when the "primitive," the indigenous, and the "backward" were being positively reevaluated. A painful irony indeed!

Parton's observation is true—indeed, as we saw above, neither Bobrov nor Goncharova shied away from acknowledging the influence of France, while in the same breath seeking to overcome it. But we should also note that the scholars at the 1911 congress were trying to move away from any claim to complete originality like that underpinning Parton's account. The congress itself presented versions of Russian art not solely in terms of its autochthonous development, but rather as the product of a range of influences that could help in its search for style. "The integrity of national culture (*tsel'nost' narodnoi kul'tury*)," Ainalov remarked, "which so attracted the populists (*narodniki*), does not exist. Something entirely different and more valuable emerged in place of this integrity and singularity: centuries of reworking these various inheritances."[45] This view, in turn, involved a no less robust reminder of how cultures are made: "Not a single state in Europe praises its originality (*samobytnost'*) in the spirit of the Slavophiles; everywhere, there is the history of influences, borrowings, repetitions (*perepevov*), and imports (*zanosov*) of styles and forms, but only the adoption and reworking of them gives a new and original style."[46] This is a remarkable rejoinder to any claim to autochthony and originality, which stands at the opposite end of the gradient from the reworking of "repetitions" and "imports." In fact, it reminds us that Picasso was a Catalan painter who was trying to establish himself in Paris, and

---

[44]   Parton, *Larionov*, 99.

[45]   Ainalov, "O nekotorykh sovremennykh techeniiakh," 6.

[46]   Ibid.

that modernism was itself constantly being invented and reinvented in the interactions between centers and peripheries.[47]

Where to map the various Russian avant-garde tendencies along this gradient can pose quite a challenge, given the internal differences between them. But Bobrov's "The Stone *Baba*" could be seen in this context to mediate simultaneously between the authority of the literary tradition and the influence of the West, while also promoting the statuary as a native antiquity. That is, the poem looks back into Russia's own tradition for a recognizable model—the Bronze Horseman—that could serve not only as the functional equivalent of Picasso's Western European models, but also as the absolute center of Russian literary authority, into which Bobrov could thereby interpolate the statuary. It is not a parodic gesture, or not just parodic; the move resonates as a kind of avant-garde device at the core of Picasso's Cubist enterprise in 1908. Bobrov's project kept one eye on the Russian past and another on the West, while seeking to radically expand the idea of what objects could comprise a "native antiquity."

By way of conclusion, I want to return to Shchukin's Picasso Hall, which offers us a notable convergence of the themes discussed in this and the preceding chapter on ancient terrors. As discussed in an art-historical study of this period in Russian modernism, it was the painting that hung to the left of *Three Women*, Picasso's *The Dryad*, which attracted far greater attention, from the leading art critic Iakov Tugenkhol'd to the philosophers Nikolai Berdiaev and Pavel Florenskii.[48] Much like Prince Myshkin in Dostoevsky's *The Idiot*, who stood before Hans Holbein's *The Body of the Dead Christ in the Tomb* and thought that it could make a person lose his or her faith, those who stood before *The Dryad* detected within the painting a sense of the end of man, the crisis of Western culture, or sheer metaphysical dread. From Nicoletta Misler's admirable

[47]   See, for example, Partha Mitter, "Decentering Modernism: Art History and Avant-Garde Art from the Periphery," *Art Bulletin* 90, no. 4 (December 2008): 531-48.

[48]   These responses are recorded in Nicoletta Misler's excellent reconstruction of the reception of the painting in her essay "Pavel Florenskii as Art Historian," in *Beyond Vision: Essays on the Perception of Art* (London: Reaktion, 2002); see esp. 56-61.

reconstruction of the history of Russian responses to the painting, we know that figures such as Sergei Bulgakov said that Picasso's painting possessed an "atmosphere of mystical terror verging on horror," while Nikolai Berdiaev remarked: "Beyond the captivating beauty of woman [Picasso] sees the horror of decomposition and pulverization."[49] What is particularly relevant here is that Tugenkhol'd, who published an extensive catalogue essay on Shchukin's collection in 1914, likened several of Picasso's paintings to the stone *babas*. In Misler's words, "Tugenkhol'd identified [the stone women] with *The Dryad*. . . . [He] saw them as a universal stylistic metaphor corresponding to the canons of both primitive monumentality and Cubism, and recognized this in Picasso's paintings such as *Peasant Woman* (*La Fermière*) and *Three Women* (*Trois Femmes. Etude pour le grand tableau de Stein*)."[50] Bobrov and Goncharova did much the same, except that neither was inclined to see the paintings in terms of horror, as did Bunin before them. Bobrov and Goncharova were primarily thinking about form, about how new formal tendencies can be culled from the past or projected back into that past; and it was on the basis of the formal features of the statuary that Bobrov staked his aesthetics. What he further shared with the Picasso of *Three Women* is that, alongside "primitive monumentality and Cubism," Bobrov sought a way to negotiate the authority of cultural tradition while asserting the value of a new, if hitherto unrecognized, antiquity.

The fact that the poem appeared in 1913, the so-called annus mirabilis of Russian modernism, makes it all the more symptomatic of the tensions generated by so many crosscurrents.[51] Considered in these contexts, the negotiation between traditions and novel tendencies marks a crucial shift in the status of the statuary. In Bobrov's and Goncharova's hands, the stone *babas* are made to

---

[49]   Cited in ibid., 57.

[50]   Ibid.

[51]   John Bowlt, "The Year 1913: Crossroads of Past and Future," in *Moscow and St. Petersburg, 1900-1920: Art, Life, and Culture of the Russian Silver Age* (New York: Vendome Press, 2008), 319-46; Clark, "Imperial Petersburg, 1913," in *Petersburg*, 54-73.

mediate competing visions about Russian art and its cultural history. For this purpose, the statuary was both the perfect emblem and vehicle for entering into a conversation about Russian art, inasmuch as it embodied an indigenous antiquity to which both Bobrov and Goncharova could lay claim as they confronted two essential features of their own status as modernists: first, their peripheral status in national art, and, second, their sense of Russian modernism's marginal status relative to Western European modernism. It is in the negotiation of these various marginal positions, cultural and geographical, that the fate of the steppe statuary became intimately bound up with that of the modernist artist.

Chapter Five

VELIMIR KHLEBNIKOV, POET OF THE STONE BABAS

In 1968 the archaeologist German Fedorov-Davydov published a book for a popular audience entitled *Kurgans, Idols, Coins* (*Kurgany, idoly, monety*),[1] in which he discusses the history and cultural value of various archaeological artifacts found in the Soviet Union. Fedorov-Davydov occasionally strikes a personal note in the work, nowhere more so than when he describes his encounters with various stone *babas*: "While studying the history of the Polovtsy," he writes, "I travelled to nearly all the regional museums of our South in pursuit of these stone statues. I searched for them in Rostov, Novocherkassk, Azov, Krasnodar, Stavropol. Whichever southern city I visited— these 'babas' were already waiting for me (*menia uzhe zhdali eti 'baby'*) in the courtyard of the local museum" (24). Like Nikolai Veselovskii before him, Fedorov-Davydov informs his readers of the various peoples once thought to have created the statuary—the Scythians, the Huns, the Mongols, among others— but he dismisses such conjectures, ascribing them to the Polovtsy.

Although the statuary was now firmly ensconced in museums, and the question of the provenance of the *babas* relatively settled, their story still included themes of neglect and indifference. As Fedorov-Davydov remarks:

> One *"baba"* ended up in the courtyard of the Rumiantsev Museum, the present-day Lenin Library. Indifferent patrons, always rushing about, have passed by it many times, and have rarely stopped to admire this absurd stone mass, with a protruding stomach, gigantic feet, flat face, and stooped shoulders. And it stands

---

[1] G. A. Fedorov-Davydov, *Kurgany, idoly, monety.* Nauchno-popularnaia seriia (Moscow: Nauka, 1968). All citations will appear in the text.

silently, dumbfounded (*ostolbenev do nemoty*), having seen with its stone eyes what modern man is no longer fated to see. (27)

Some of the poetic commonplaces Fedorov-Davydov employs here are familiar: the artifacts attest to an insuperable divide between the past and present; they languish, hidden in plain sight, suffering from an unrequited relationship with indifferent, busy moderns; they are emphatically silent. In fact while the theme of silence is a commonplace, the specific phrasing Fedorov-Davydov uses in the passage—"*ostolbenev do nemoty*"—which also serves as the epigraph to his chapter "Idols" is taken from a poem by Andrei Voznesenskii, "You Sit Pregnant, Pale" ("Sidish' beremennaia, blednaia," 1958). The poet, traveling by train, sees several women whom he compares to stone women: "И от Москвы до Ашхабада, / Остолбенев до немоты, // Стоят, как каменные, бабы, / Луне подставив животы. ("And from Moscow to Ashgabat, / Dumbfounded // They stand, like stone, women, / their bellies exposed to the moon."[2])

Even as Fedorov-Davydov thereby alludes to a recent poem in which the statues appear briefly in a resonant simile, the archaeologist goes on to note that there is indeed a poetic tradition in which they were the object of more sustained aesthetic attention than merely serving as a simile. Looking back into the past, he directs his readers' attention to Velimir Khlebnikov, the poet with whom the statues had broken their silence and upon whose poetic authority the archaeologist can establish the cultural value of "these absurd stone masses":

There lived a man with whom these stone statues also began to speak . . . This was the poet Velimir Khlebnikov. And for Velimir Khlebnikov the silent stone blocks (*glyby*) became speaking things (*govoriashchie*). Of course, the scientific side of the question did not interest him: who erected these idols and when; to what end, etc. These dead statues awakened his poetic perception of antiquity (*starina*), of paganism, and of ancient cults: and they, these silent centuries, began to speak with him. (28)

[2]   Andrei Voznesenskii, "Sidish', beremennaia, blednaia." http://www.ruthenia.ru/60s/voznes/antimir/beremennaja.htm, accessed May 12, 2013.

In these lines, the history of archaeology and literature intermingle. Other chapters in this book trace the interaction of archaeology and aesthetics in Russian modernist culture, often in terms of the modernist imagination's receptivity toward archaeology, but Fedorov-Davydov presents one of the few cases when a Russian or Soviet archaeologist relies on literary authority to establish the value of archaeological objects located in Russia.

Another such advocate for the relevance of literature to archaeology was Aleksandr Formozov, as we saw in chapter two, who similarly drew upon the work of the Nicholas Roerich and Viktor Vasnetsov, and promoted them to the status of Russia's equivalents of Johann Joachim Winckelmann. With Fedorov-Davydov, the *baba* is as much archaeological as it is poetic. His account enshrines Khlebnikov as the premier poet of the statuary, for whom they were central to his invention of an indigenous antiquity and his interest in paganism. No less significant, it was with Khlebnikov that they finally broke their silence, the supreme symbol of overcoming the gap between the present and the past.

Fedorov-Davydov was not alone in promoting Khlebnikov as the poet of the statuary in the 1960s. That same decade, Sergei Bobrov (whose poem on the statuary we discussed in the previous chapter) participated in the series of extraordinary interviews conducted by the literary scholar Viktor Duvakin, who recorded Bobrov's testimony on the generation and movement to which he had belonged.[3] In the interview, Duvakin inquires into Bobrov's life in the years since the eclipse of modernism and the interviews. During that time, Bobrov had published several more books of verse, joined the ranks of the Futurists with Boris Pasternak in the group called Centrifuge, and later translated several works from French into Russian. Duvakin goes on to ask for Bobrov's thoughts

---

3   V. D. Duvakin, "Interview with Sergei Bobrov," July 6, 1968. The transcript of the interview can be found in "Velimir Khlebnikov v razmyshleniiakh i vospominaniiakh sovremennikov (po fonodokumental'nam V. D. Duvakina 1960–1970 godov)," in *Vestnik obshchestva Velimira Khlebnikova*, vol. 1 (Moscow: Gileia, 1996), 44-66. For a history of Duvakin's interviews, see Dmitrii Sporov, "Zhivaia rech' ushedshei epokhi: Sobranie Viktora Duvakina," *Novoe literaturnoe obozrenie* 74 (2005): 454-72.

on Khlebnikov: "Did you see Khlebnikov, did you know him?" In his response, Bobrov first mentions Hylaea, and then turns to Mayakovsky and Khlebnikov:

> So, Hylaea was mainly Mayakovsky and Khlebnikov. They left a profound trace upon Russian literature, while Kruchenykh did not and would not have any significance. . . . In the first place, it was the renaissance of ancient Russian verse and life— that was Khlebnikov: the Stone *babas* of Russian literature. An artist unusually sensitive to the word (*eto vozrozhdenie russkogo starinnogo stikha i byta: eto byl Khlebnikov: Kamennye baby russkoi literatury. Khudozhnik neobyknovenno chutkii k slovu*).[4]

It's a remarkable comment. What Bobrov had once called "our native antiquity," he now deems the "renaissance of ancient Russian verse and life." And the program to recuperate the past, which we saw Bobrov advocate in 1911, he now sees fulfilled by Mayakovsky and Khlebnikov. Where he had once promoted the stone *babas* to the status of the leading artifacts of that antiquity, he now names both poets—and Khlebnikov in particular—not only as the pioneers of that very renaissance, but also its monuments; together, they are "the Stone *babas* of Russian literature," but Bobrov's focus seems ultimately to point toward Khlebnikov in this regard.

Khlebnikov's image as *the* poet of the statuary rests upon three works: a prose piece, "Lialia Rides the Tiger" ("Lialia na tigre," 1916); "The Stone Woman" ("Kamennaia baba," 1919), an unfinished *poèma*, or long narrative poem, published posthumously in 1929; and "A Night in a Trench" ("Noch' v okope"), another *poèma* written around 1919-20 and published in 1921. Khlebnikov's status as the poet of the statuary should not, however, overshadow how he could have encountered the statuary on both page and canvas prior to his sustained attention to them. He likely inherited the *babas* already mediated by previous modernist accounts, ranging from the Burliuks' "sculpture gallery" in Chernianka to the work of Natal'ia Goncharova, with whom he had collaborated on

---

4   Duvakin, "Interview with Sergei Bobrov," 51.

"A Game in Hell" ("Igra v adu," 1912). Perhaps he also knew Bobrov's poem.[5]

He shared with Bobrov and Goncharova, for example, the idea that the statuary could serve as an emblem of one's poetic values. We find in "Lialia" a point of departure for examining his poetic texts. Like many of the programmatic pieces on the nature of poetry Khlebnikov wrote throughout his career, "Lialia" advances a philosophy of time and space, his innovative views on poetic language, and his musings on Russia's relationship to other countries and cultures. It is within this context that the statuary makes a brief but evocative appearance, when Khlebnikov imagines it as a monument in which he invests his poetic and philosophical values:

> We know with absolute conviction that we will not be repeated on Planet Earth. We mean to leave a monument to ourselves — we don't want people to say "they vanished like the Obry" — so we have established the government of time (a new stone woman of the steppes of time: she is crudely carved, but she is powerful [*novaia kamennaia baba stepei vremeni; ona grubo vysechena, no ona krepka*]), and we propose to the governments of space either to accept its existence peacefully, and leave it alone, or to engage it in a struggle to the death. (*T*: 606; *CW* 1:330)[6]

Fashioning himself here as something of a poet-sculptor, Khlebnikov looks back into the past to find an aesthetic model, rough hewn and powerful, for a new poetic tendency. In his hands, the past gives the new age a deep ground. Appropriately, then, Khlebnikov's new monument — this newly fashioned "woman" (its gender is unclear in the passage but Khlebnikov frequently identifies the statuary as feminine) — is located in a "steppe" configured temporally, rather than spatially, perhaps because the very model for his monument transects multiple epochs; the *baba* serves as both the model and the guarantor for a modernist project that weaves together antiquity and

---

5   Vladimir Markov, *The Longer Poems of Velimir Khlebnikov* (Berkeley and Los Angeles: University of California Press, 1962), 131.

6   All references to Khlebnikov's works are cited as *CW* for *Collected Works*, trans. Paul Schmidt, 3 vols. (Cambridge, MA: Belknap Press, 1987); and *T* for *Tvoreniia* (Moscow: Khudozhestvennaia literatura, 1986).

novelty, recapitulating the past in the process of invention. Where "Lialia" thereby gives voice to the optimism of Khlebnikov's poetic project and to his aesthetic ambitions, the two later works in which the statuary figures no less prominently, find Khlebnikov freighting the statuary with a significance greater than that of serving as a monument. In both works, they act as vehicles for responding to the broader questions of Russian modernist poetic language and the nature of the modernist sign, but also as archaic counterpoints to the upheaval and carnage of his time.

i. "The Stone Woman" (1919): Modernist Metamorphosis

In "The Stone Woman" the statuary provides Khlebnikov an occasion to elaborate a modernist poetic rooted in morphology and metamorphosis. Over the course of its approximately one hundred lines, he touches on themes of archaic maternity, pagan cosmogony, and pastoral lament. The work's nimble rhymes and its folkloric and mythological tone are shadowed by a story of violence. The two central characters—the statue and a youth named "*pishi-pishi*" (felicitously translated by Paul Schmidt as "scribble-scrabble")— are anachronisms who find little refuge in a landscape where signs of the pastoral and of ancient myth are accompanied by allusions to martial violence. Where Khlebnikov had styled himself as a poet-sculptor in "Lialia," he is an incantatory poet-liberator in "The Stone Woman," freeing it through a bravura demonstration of the capacity of poetic language to transfigure the objects of the world.

The *poèma* begins in a setting marked by an enchanting quiet and by colloquies conducted in languages both human and arboreal. It contains direct addresses to the figure of an old man, who opens the work sitting upon a dead mammoth, and to the stone woman, whose liberation closes it. The poet notes the rustle of trees: "An ancient willow's bark resounds, / prattles tales in a human tongue" (*Shumit kora starinnoi ivy, / Lepechet skazki po-liudski*); the leaves of a "tender poplar" evoke a "conversational rustle" (*trepet razgo-vornyi*). Some of the cries are audible, yet inscrutable: "a tree prays to someone, / in the twilight field. / And cries and wails / in words without names" (*derevo komu-to molitsia / Na sumrachnoi poliane. / I plachetsia i volitsia / slovami bez nazvanii*). The poet everywhere "reads" the landscape, discerning its communicative patterns. He "reads" the statuary as well:

> А девы каменные нивы —
> Как сказки каменной доски.
> Вас древняя воздвигла треба.
> Вы тянетесь от неба и до неба.
> Они суровы и жестоки,
> Их бусы — грубая резьба.
> И сказок камня о Востоке
> Не понимают ястреба.
> Стоит с улыбкою недвижной,
> Забытая неведомым отцом,
> И на груди ее булыжной
> Блестит роса серебряным сосцом.

> The stone maidens of the field are
> Like the fairy tales of a stone slate.
> An ancient rite erected you.
> You extend from heaven unto heaven.
> They are fierce and cruel,
> Their necklaces are a rude carving.
> The hawks do not understand
> The stone's fairy tales of the East.
> She stands with an unmoving smile,
> Forgotten by an unknown father,
> And upon her cobblestone breast
> Dew glistens like a silver nipple.[7] (*T*: 255; *CW* 3:144)

The description of the statue's physical features — the necklace and the smile so frequently observed in writing on the statuary — and the epithets attached to those details — "severe" (*surovy*), "fierce" (*zhestoki*), and "rude" (*grubaia*) — reveal Khlebnikov's mimetic accuracy and, perhaps, his awareness of the commonplaces surrounding the *babas*. While rudeness is a quality he had associated

---

[7]   I have based my translations on Paul Schmidt's in *CW*. References are to this edition and are cited in the text.

with his desire to make a rough-hewn "new stone woman," that quality and the other physical aspects are now transfigured into fairy tales told in stone. In figuring the statuary in this way, he insinuates himself into the disjunction he observes between the eagles and the statuary. The former cannot comprehend the "fairy tales of the East" as can the poet, who notes the physical features of the statuary as signs of an origin story; the rhyme "*nevedovym otsom*" (unknown father) / "*serebiannym sostsom*" (silver nipple), emphasizes the statuary's generative abilities, revealing a kind of story of dispossession by a progenitor coupled with a narrative of maternal care.

These stories of dispossession and care anticipate the work's introduction of its second major figure, "scribble-scrabble," who, like the stone woman, is also dispossessed, but from the cosmos and from some kindred temporality:

> Сюда идет «пиши-пиши»,
> Златоволосый и немой.
> Что надо отроку в тиши
> Над серебристою молвой?
> Рыдать, что этот Млечный Путь не мой?
> «Как много стонет мертвых тысяч
> Под покрывалом свежим праха!
> И я—последний живописец
> Земли неслыханного страха.
> Я каждый день жду выстрела в себя.
> За что? За что? Ведь всех любя,
> Я раньше жил, до этих дней,
> В степи ковыльной, меж камней».
> Пришел и сел. Рукой задвинул
> Лица пылающую книгу.
>
> Here comes "scribble-scrabble,"
> Golden-haired and mute.
> What does the youth need in the stillness
> Above the silver murmur?
> To wail that this Milky Way is not mine?
> "How many thousands of dead groan
> Under the fresh cover of ashes!
> And I am the last painter
> Of the unheard-of terror of the land.

I wait each day to be shot.
Why? why? Loving everyone,
I lived before, until these days,
In the feather grass steppe, among the stones."
He arrived and sat.
He covered with his hand
The burning book of his face. (*T*: 255; *CW* 3:145)

Childhood innocence is lost as "scribble-scrabble" has become the synaesthetic "last painter of the unheard-of terror of the land." As a youthful foil to the poet, "scribble-scrabble" can likewise discern the communicative rustle within a landscape that terrorizes him as he awaits some future execution. The harmony with the steppe and stones he once enjoyed is lost, and he now finds himself in a landscape freshly covered in martial ash, an image set in contrast with the white eternity of the Milky Way.

While this landscape, which is replete with violence past and present, confronts both these anachronisms of "scribble-scrabble" and the statuary, the universe does show some pity on the youth:

И месяц плачущему сыну
Дает вечерних звезд ковригу.
«Мне много ль надо?
Коврига хлеба
И капля молока.
Да это небо,
Да эти облака!»
Люблю и млечных жен, и этих,
Что не торопятся цвести.
И это я забился в сетях
На сетке Млечного Пути.
Когда краснела кровью Висла
И покраснел от крови Тисс,
Тогда рыдающие числа
Над бедным миром пронеслись.

And to her crying son the moon
Gives a crust of evening stars.
"Do I need a lot?
A crust of bread

And a drop of milk.
And this sky,
And these clouds!"
I love both milky women, and these,
Which do not rush to flower.
And I took refuge in the nets,
In the mesh of the Milky Way.
When the Vistula reddened with blood
And the Tisza turned red from blood
Then the wailing numbers
Flew above the poor world. (*T*: 256-57; *CW* 3:145)

The interweaving of voices—of "scribble-scrabble" and the lyrical speaker—marks their shared experiences: a love of nursemaids and the need for refuge from the affairs of man, which they find in the heavens. This theme of refuge and liberation is the impetus for the second appearance of the statuary, in which the poet recapitulates the ritualistic theme from the opening lines of the poem and undertakes his own ritualistic incantation to liberate the stone woman:

И синели крылья бабочки,
Точно двух кумирных баб очки.
Серо-белая, она
Здесь стоять осуждена
Как пристанище козявок,
Без гребня и без булавок,
Рукой грубой указав
Любви каменный устав.

And the wings of the butterfly became blue,
Like the eyeglasses of the two totemic *babas*.
Grayish-white, she
Is condemned to stand here
Like an asylum for small insects,
Without combs and without pins,
Having shown with [her] rude hand
The stone code of love. (*T*: 256; *CW* 3: 145-46)

The reference to the statuary as "condemned" seems to harken back to an earlier moment in the poem, which had seemed like unintegrated mythological fragments. The poet recounts: "Here the flight of a dark-haired maiden / Awoke a night eagle, / Her scattered braids, / The silence of his horse's bit!" (*Zdes' devy skok temnovolosoi / Orla nochnogo razbudil, / Ee razveiannyie kosy, / Ego molchanie udil!*) One reading of these lines is that they allude to the kind of "fairy tales of the East" represented by the statue herself, and that the poet conjures a landscape suffused with fairy tales. Another reading is that this maiden is part of the story of the statuary, who perhaps committed some sort of infraction, as in Afanas'ev's version of the tale and later taken up by Remizov. In either case, Khlebnikov offers throughout the poem a mythopoeisis that is registered as a perception of the landscape and the statuary as a generative matrix, in which fairy tales are discerned and combined as he recasts his own liberation story for the statuary.[8]

In any case, the story of condemnation establishes the basic plot for the story of liberation:

> Глаза серые доски
> Грубы и плоски.
> И на них мотылек
> Крылами прилег,
> Огромный мотылек крылами закрыл
> И синее небо мелькающих крыл,
> Кружевом точек берёг
> Вишневой чертой огонек.
> И каменной бабе огня многоточие
> Давало и разум и очи ей.
> Синели очи и вырос разум
> Воздушным бродяги указом.
> Вспыхнула темною ночью солома?
> Камень кумирный вставай и играй
> Игор игрою и грома.
> Раньше слепец, сторож овец,
> Смело смотри большим мотыльком,
> Видящий Млечным Путем.

8   I rely here on Henryk Baran's discussion of Khlebnikov's mythopoetics in his "Poeticheskaia logika i poeticheskii alogizm Khlebnikova," in *O Khlebnikove: Konteksty, istochniki, mify* (Moscow: Rossiiskii gos. gumanitarnyi universitet, 2002); see esp. the section "Poet kak mifotvorets," 30–32.

The gray eyes of the slate
Are crude and flat.
And upon them a moth
Lay with its wings,
The huge moth covered [them] with its wings
And the blue sky of flickering wings,
Guarded with a lace of points
The small light, as though it were a cherry red line.
The dots of fire
Gave to the Stone Woman
Reason and eyes.
The eyes grew blue and reason grew
By the aerial decree of the wanderer.
Has a blade of straw caught fire in the dark night?
Stone idol, arise and play
A game of games and of thunder.
Earlier blind-one, a guardian of sheep,
Daringly look with big moth [eyes],
Who looks by means of the Milky Way. (*T*: 256; *CW* 3: 146)

In this passage, the motor of action is defined not by history, as it will be in "A Night in a Trench," but rather by poetic language. The deft rhymes and meters mark a shift in tone from the theme of martial violence, as it is with "scribble-scrabble," toward the themes of play and incantation. The poet's command to the statue—"arise and play / a game of games and of thunder"—is not a Pygmalionesque dream; the desire here is not amorous, but liberatory, ludic, linguistic.

Indeed, this metamorphosis of the statuary indicates that much of the drama of the second half of the poem consists of dazzling morphological permutations. This drama of poetic language is initiated at the beginning of the passage with the pun on *babochki* (butterflies) and *bab ochki* (eyeglasses of the *babas*), which furnish the scene with its two generative images. The wings of the butterfly (one the poet's beloved figures) overlay the statuary's rude and flat eyes, becoming the spectacles through which it later sees. So assertive is the pun, and so manifestly realized are both images, that the passage unfurls as a realized metaphor propelled by the logic of incantation. Where we saw in the previous chapter Bobrov counseling his addressee not to mistake the statuary's possible mobility for reality—with both the addressee and the statuary warned to remain rooted to the earth—Khlebnikov, by contrast, conjures a tale that envisions the unshackling of the statue from the earth, and even its liberation from being a statue at all.

Let me pause here to note two works germane to Khlebnikov's *poèma*: the first by Vladimir Mayakovsky and the second by Konstantin Sluchevskii, whose "The Stone Women," ("Kamennye baby," 1888) is singled out by commentaries as a reference point for Khlebnikov's work.[9] Bobrov, to recall, referred to both Khlebnikov and Mayakovsky as the "stone *babas* of Russian literature." In part, this was because he saw both as participating in the renaissance of ancient Russian literature (although the latter seems more of a Khlebnikovian project than a Mayakovskian one). Perhaps Bobrov had in mind the fact that Mayakovsky had once compared himself to a stone *baba* in the opening of *Vladimir Mayakovsky: A Tragedy* (*Vladimir Maiakovskii: Tragediia*, 1913):

> Милостивые государи!
> Заштопайте мне душу,
> пустота сочиться не могла бы.
> Я не знаю, плевок—обида или нет.
> Я сухой, как каменная баба.
> Меня выдоили.
> Милостивые государи,
> хотите—
> сейчас перед вами будет танцевать
> замечательный поэт?

> Kind Sirs!
> Darn my soul,
> The emptiness might trickle out.
> I don't know: is spit an offense or not.
> I'm dry, like a stone woman.
> They milked me dry.
> Kind sirs,
> Do you want a remarkable poet to dance
> before you now?[10]

---

9   Velimir Khlebnikov, *Sobranie sochinenii v shesti tomakh* (Moscow: Nasledie, 2000), 3:459

10   Vladimir Maiakovskii, *Vladimir Maiakovskii: Tragediia* (1913), in *Sochineniia v dvukh tomakh* (Moscow: Pravda, 1988), 2:437.

It is unclear whether Mayakovsky knew about the statuary's defiling of the gods by spitting at them (as in Afanas'ev and Remizov), since his version of the statuary is more bound up with his battle against the philistines who have "milked him dry." In any case, as Katherine Lahti has noted in her study on Mayakovsky and the statuary, one can detect in his use of the *baba* a Dionsysian "confusion of genders,"[11] in which the statuary stands in for the particular plight of the poet. His use of the statuary marks two forms of degradation, transforming the tragic poet into a petrified statue on the one hand, and, on the other, a dancer-entertainer. If Khlebnikov had these lines in mind, what his version of "The Stone Woman" presents is a different vision of the poet, one in which he exercises the overwhelming power of poetic incantation to free the statuary from its punishment—and from the sphere of the mundane altogether. Its dancing and play is a sign of that liberation.

In Konstantin Sluchevskii's 1888 poem "The Stone Women," by contrast, we find a story of the statuary in which it is eroded by natural forces rather than possibly pulverized by gunfire.[12] Sluchevskii's poem is dominated by two figures: the immobile statuary, scattered across the steppe on what Sluchevskii refers to as "steppe hills" (*stepnye kholmy*) which are likely kurgans, and

---

[11]   Lahti, "Living Statues," 453.

[12]   Konstantin Sluchevskii, "Kamennye baby," in *Stikhotvoreniia i poemy* (St. Petersburg: Akademicheskii proekt, 2004), 198-99. The poem was first published in *Stikhotvoreniia K. Sluchevskogo* (St. Petersburg, 1880), and again in the six-volume *Sochineniia K. K. Sluchevskogo* (St. Petersburg, 1898). Considered a late Romantic whose poetry provided a bridge between Romanticism and the Decadent movement, Sluchevskii is the least studied of the writers discussed here. Although his first published poetry from the late 1850s enjoyed the praise of Apollon Grigor'ev and Ivan Turgenev, he would endure withering criticism from the utilitarian critics, which led him to cease publishing his own poetry, and instead publish polemical brochures in "defense of pure art" until 1871, when he resumed his poetry (*A Handbook to Russian Literature*, s.v. "Konstantine Sluchevskii"). His poem "The Stone Women" appeared toward the end of the decade, which would also see Sluchevskii writing several lyric works devoted to a range of Russia's ethnographic features. While it is difficult to ascertain whether later writers knew Sluchevskii's poem, he was a significant enough presence in the early modernist scene to suggest they could have; Valery Briusov and Ivan Bunin, for example, attended Friday gatherings at Sluchevskii's from 1898 on, the same year in which volumes of his writings were published (Valery Briusov, *The Diary of Valery Briusov* [1893-1905], ed. and trans. Joan Delaney Grossman [Berkeley and Los Angeles: University of California Press, 1980], 75).

a heraldic wind, redolent of fairy tales, which communes with the statuary and brings word of the "miracles of the land":

На безлесном нашем юге
На степных холмах,
Дремлют каменные бабы
С чарками в руках.

Ветер, степью пролетая,
Клонит ковыли,
Бабам сказывает в сказках
Чудеса земли.

In our woodless South,
Upon the hills of the steppes
Stone women slumber
With cups in their hands.

The wind, sweeping along the steppe
Bends the feather grass
Telling to the women tales
Of the miracles of the land.

In subsequent stanzas, the poem furnishes the reader with a veritable catalogue of Russia's ethnographic and ecological "marvels": "how people far off in the North travel by sleds pulled by shaggy dogs even in the summer when there's no snow" (*Kak na severe, daleko, / na mokhnatykh psakh, / dazhe letom i bez snega / ezdiat na saniakh*); how Russia has "river estuaries so abundant with fish that not even God's angels could count them" (*Kak u nas v rechnykh limanakh / stol'ko, stol'ko ryb, / chto i angely Gospodni / schest' ikh ne mogli*); how one can find Kalmyks, "with heavy cheekbones, narrow eyes, thin hair" (*skuly tolsty, ochi uzki, / redki volosa*) as well as Tartars, that "shaven people" (*vybrityi narod*). Even though vast distances separate them, the statuary and the ethnic groups enumerated by the wind belong to a similar order of things; the wind does not, in other words, tell the statuary about St. Petersburg. To borrow a phrase from M. H. Abrams, the wind is quite literally a "correspondent," an elemental herald that performs the crucial role of informing the statuary of "news" from all parts of the country, thereby gathering and unifying the vast cultural, geographic, and topographic wealth contained within it.[13] The poem's trochaic meter—traditionally used to evoke the poetic world of the Russian folk, which had underpinned Gorodetskii's poem on the statuary—buttresses the sense that the poem approximates the fairy-tale nature of the wind's speech (*Babam skazyvaet v skazkakh*).

In the final two stanzas of the poem, the interplay between the elements of wind and earth, both personified throughout the poem, turns away from an initial sense of communion and becomes more ominous. The wind becomes an alluring but destructive force to which the statuary yields:

> Слышат каменные бабы
> С чарками в руках,
> Что им сказывает ветер,
> Рея в ковылях.
>
> И на сладкий зов новинки
> Шлют они за ним
> За песчинками песчинки . . .
> И пройдут, как дым!
>
> The stone women listen,
> With cups in hand
> To what the wind tells them
> Howling in the feather grass.
>
> And to the sweet call of novelty,
> They send after it
> Grains of sand after grains of sand
> And they shall pass, like smoke!

If the underlying drama of the poem rests upon the opposition between the statuary's immobility in the steppe and the vast

---

13 For Abrams, the metaphor of the "correspondent breeze," found throughout Western European Romanticism's "thoroughly ventilated" poems, employed the wind as both a "property of landscape, but also a vehicle for radical changes in the poet's mind." M. H. Abrams, "The Correspondent Breeze: A Romantic Metaphor," in *English Romantic Poets: Modern Essays in Criticism*, ed. M. H. Abrams (New York: Norton, 1975), 51.

cultural and topographical expanse the wind reports, then the final stanza resolves this opposition by presenting the statuary's self-willed disintegration. The grains of sand the statues release into the air are in fact pieces of their bodies; many of them were carved out of sandstone (*peschanik*).[14] Notably, Sluchevskii attributes the fragmentation of the statuary not to the erosive action of the wind but rather to the desire of the statuary itself. The intentional atomization of the stone women—their desire to become as mobile as the wind (while destroying themselves in the process)— suggests that the statuary's dispersal into the order of the new is due to its desire for an elemental metamorphosis. Erosion is thus figured as liberation (perhaps one theme the two works share), a desire to enter into the flux of time. These processes paradoxically undo the immobility and stasis of the artifact while presaging its disappearance and destruction.

Whether Khlebnikov had these works in mind while writing his *poèma* brings up one of the difficulties that besets any intertextual criticism.[15] But the comparisons nevertheless place into high relief how Khlebnikov combines the story of liberation and ludic play into a story of language and the realization of metaphor as a form of metamorphosis. According to Roman Jakobson, metamorphosis was a "beloved motif" of Khlebnikov's. Jakobson identifies several features associated with the device in Khlebnikov's poetry: "here we have the realization of the same trope, the projection of a literary device into artistic reality, the turning of a poetic trope into a poetic fact, into a plot element."[16] In the case of "The Stone Woman," the animation of the statue relates to the incantatory nature of the poem, gesturing back to Khlebnikov's "Incantation by Laughter" ("Zakliatie smekhom," 1908).

---

[14] *Entsiklopedicheskii slovar' F. A. Brokgauza i I. A. Efrona*, s.v. "kamennye baby."

[15] See David Bethea, "Whose Mind Is It Anyway?: Influence, Intertextuality, and the Boundaries of Legitimate Scholarship," *Slavic and East European Journal* 49, no. 1 (Spring 2005): 2-17.

[16] Roman Jakobson, "The Newest Russian Poetry: Velimir Khlebnikov," in *My Futurist Years*, ed. Bengt Jangfeldt and Stephen Rudy, trans. Stephen Rudy (New York: Marsilio Press, 1992), 182.

We could, however, also see the function of incantation and metamorphosis in another way: as shifting the terrain upon which the rhetorical and semiotic approaches to the question of literary statuary are typically elaborated.[17] Literary statues have long been bound up in a complex nexus of desire and threat, representation and reification. Borrowing again from Jakobson: to represent a statuary in literary form means skirting the brink of semiotic collapse: "The relationship of the sign to the object signified, and especially the relationship of the representation to the object represented, their simultaneous identity and difference, is one of the most dramatic semiotic antinomies."[18] In Khlebnikov, literary statuary operates within a framework of modernist paganism that upends much of the fear expressed in other literary accounts of statuary. Khlebnikov's poetic power, instead, reveals an investment in transmuting the sign, which links his themes of metamorphosis to what Yuri Tynianov described as his "infantilism, a pagan relationship to language."[19] Here the archaic statuary furnishes the occasion for Khlebnikov to coordinate the themes of vision and infantilism alongside a range of his poetic concerns. The statuary and Khlebnikov's views on poetic language thereby form a mutually reinforcing bond between an archaeological artifact and a newly forged modernist poetic.

ii. The Steppes of Time: "A Night in a Trench"

In Vladimir Markov's view, "The Stone Woman" and "A Night in a Trench" are "non-identical twins" produced out of the "same creative effort."[20] Where "The Stone Woman" depicts an incantatory and magical world that was shadowed by violence, the world of "A Night in a Trench," as its title suggests, is one in which warfare is the central theme. "A Night in a Trench" features the statuary

---

[17] Mitchell, "Ekphrasis and the Other," 151–81.

[18] Roman Jakobson, "The Statue in Pushkin's Poetic Mythology," in *Language in Literature*, ed. Krystyna Pomorska and Stephen Rudy (Cambridge, MA: Belknap Press), 337.

[19] Iurii Tynianov, "O Khlebnikove," in *Mir Velimira Khlebnikova: Stat'i, issledovaniia, 1911-1998*, ed. V. V. Ivanov. Z. S. Papernyi, and A. E. Parnis (Moscow: Iazyki slavianskoi kul'tury, 2000), 219.

[20] Markov, *Longer Poems*, 131.

and the kurgans woven into the work's complex temporal structure. Past and present intermingle throughout "A Night in a Trench." On one level, we find the Red and White armies, the singing of the *Internationale*, a Lenin figure who appears as the "face of the Siberian East" (*Litso sibirskogo vostoka*), the staccato of gunfire, the profanation of churches and relics, and mechanized warfare in the form of a "monstrosity made out of copper" (*chudovishche iz medi*), which appears in one of the work's extended tableaux.[21] On another level, we have the stone *babas* and two kurgans—that of "the Pagan Rogneda" and the Chertomlyk Kurgan, a major site for Scythian archaeology. The *babas* and the kurgans serve as archaic counterpoints to contemporary events, as memento mori, emblems of death and sources of lament. They reveal a steppe whose temporal element is marked by the perpetual repetition of the paradigm we saw the historian and archaeologist Zabelin call "the martial essence of the steppe." The latest recapitulation of that paradigm is the Civil War (1917–22).

In the case of the *babas*, they are also observers, even commentators upon the Civil War; as, for example, when they first appear in the opening lines of the work:

> Семейство каменных пустынниц
> Просторы поля сторожило.
> В окопе бывший пехотинец
> Ругался сам с собой: «Могила!»
> Объявилась эта тетя,
> Завтра мертвых не сочтете,
> Всех задушит понемножку.

> A family of stone anchoresses
> Kept watch over the spaces of the field.
> In the trench, a former infantryman
> Cursed to himself: "A Grave!"
> This auntie declared,
> Tomorrow there'll be too many dead to count,
> It'll strangle everyone little by little. (*T*: 275; *CW* 165)

---

[21] I follow here Markov's reading of the poem as composed of four "tableaux" (Markov, *Longer Poems*, 127).

The statues frame the work; in these opening lines they are associated with anchoresses, and in the work's concluding lines, with steppe goddesses. Just as they announce here the fate that will befall the infantryman—"A Grave!" (*Mogila!*)—they do so again at the conclusion of the *poèma* when they are asked—possibly by the infantryman or by the lyrical speaker—what will come of the war: "Typhus!" (*Sypniak!*) is their answer. In this regard, the primary symbolic function of the statuary as memento mori is also buttressed by its spatial position near the trench; the statuary's frequent location, perched upon kurgans, and the infantryman's location in the trench suggest the latter will become a grave soon enough.

The *poèma*'s multiplicity of times and variety of images and events—from the speaking statuary that open and close the work to the speech of the Lenin figure, to the cosmological and terrestrial visions projected within it—have prompted debates about its overall cohesiveness. It has been reconstructed to make the work cohere; while other readings have argued that the whole scenario is an emanation from the mind of the trench soldier, who cries out at the beginning of the poem in a typhoid delirium.[22] This reading, for example, rests upon a passage in the middle of the *poèma*, in which the speaker, presumably the infantryman, exclaims:

> Проклятый бред! Молчат окопы,
> А звезды блещут и горят . . .
> Что будет завтра — бой? Навряд.

> Damn, what a delirium! All quiet in the trenches,
> the stars above us shine and burn . . .
> What will tomorrow bring? A Battle? Hardly. (*T*: 277; *CW*: 163)

---

[22] N. L. Stepanov, for example, considered "Noch' v okope" to be a *poèma* lacking a siuzhet (*Zhizn i tvorchestvo Khlebnikova* [Moscow: Sovetskii pisatel', 1975)]. R. V. Duganov, by contrast, sought to eliminate the text's putative defects, citing the frequent textological problems attending Khlebnikov's works, in his "K rekonstruktsii poemy Khlebnikova 'Noch' v okope'," *Izvestiia Akademii nauk SSSR: Seriia literatury i iazyka* 38, no. 5 (1979); http://www.ka2.ru/nauka/duganov.html, accessed December 5, 2013. For a review of Duganov's work, see Valentina Morderer, "Retsenziia na knigu R. V. Duganov," in *Velimir Khlebnimov i russkaia literatura: Stat'i raznykh let* (Moscow: Progress-Pleiada, 2008); http://www.ka2.ru/nauka/valentina_2.html, accessed December 5, 2013.

Such a reading of the *poèma*—along with the fact that Khlebnikov himself had suffered from typhus—links everything to the infantryman's mind and suggests that none of the events in the poem actually happen: and certainly not the speaking of the stone women or the flowing of Scythian warriors in and out of the kurgans.[23] The interwoven times could thus be seen as pathological, with typhus causing the infantryman to slip in and out of consciousness, and thus in and out of his own time.[24]

Another way to approach these multiple temporalities, however, is to emphasize the particular function of the steppe artifacts. The image of the steppe accords with much of Khlebnikov's poetics, and his ambition to perceive various times together as a way to overcome, indeed to master time itself. In his story "Ka," for example, the eponymous spirit of the piece has "no barriers in time. Ka moves from dream to dream, cuts through time, and achieves a bronze (a bronze of time)" (*bronzy vremeni*) (*T*: 524). In his manifesto "To All! To All! To All!"("Vsem! Vsem! Vsem!") Khlebnikov refers to laws of time, which "are cut not from the stones of hopes and desires, but from the stone of time" (*T*: 635). Common to each work is the insistence that multiple times could be apprehended simultaneously. What he does, in essence in "A Night in a Trench," is to highlight a vision of the steppe as a space containing these various times indexed by peoples and artifacts. Whether the confusion in "A Night in a Trench" arises from the infantryman's slipping in and out of his delirium, rather than from an ability (like Ka's) to transgress any temporal border, the kurgans and the statuary anchor the temporal pattern of the work.

One way to register the differences between Khlebnikov's various accounts of the statuary is to consider the shifting status of the pastoral. Where "The Stone Woman" referred to the statuary

---

23   Morderer, "Retsenziia na knigu R.V. Duganova."

24   Morderer's argument that the work could be seen in terms of the infantryman's typhoid delirum is akin to Jakobson's observation that metamorphosis in Khlebnikov is often related to mental pathology. Such a view relies upon a reality principle whose basic law is to suspend the fantastical possibility of a statue speaking (Jakobson, "The Newest Russian Poetry," 181–86).

as the "guardian of sheep" (*storozh ovets*), the statuary in "Night"
guards the fields of the steppe, but it is a landscape now upheaved
by the Civil War. Khlebnikov, however, redistributes the pastoral
to other figures in "Night." In a brief episode, we find the soldiers
practically mocking their coming deaths: they announce: "We'll dig
ourselves a grave, in the silver feather grass" (*My sebe mogilu roem /
V serebristom kovyle*). To this, an old man growls:

Им мало дедовской судьбы!
Ну что ж, заслужите, пожалуй, —
Отцы расскажут, так бывало, —
Себе сосновые гробы,
А лучше бы садить бобы
Иль новый сруб срубить избы,
Сажать капусту или рожь,
Чем эти копья или нож.

Wasn't their grandfather's
                    fate enough!
Well, all you'll end up deserving, —
The fathers tell us, it's happened before, —
Are pine coffins, it'd be better to plant beans
Or cut frames for a hut,
Plant cabbage or rye,
Than a spear or knife. (*T:* 278-79; *CW* 3:164-65)

The opposition between the martial and pastoral themes is succinctly
encapsulated by the rhyme of *rozh'* with *nozh* (rye /knife). The
rhyme—and the values with which it is associated—are reminiscent
of Homer's epic similes, where martial events of war are linked to
pastoral scenes through similes of threshing. As Susanne Wofford
has argued, such similes in *The Iliad* often compare martial and
pastoral values, with the latter forming "a critique that can take the
form of an implicit counternarrative lodged in the representation
of heroic action."[25] The story of war in "Night," by comparison,
never seems to verge upon heroic action. As commentators have

[25] Wofford, *The Choice of Achilles*, 30.

suggested, the "old man" in the passage above discloses the poem's overarching sense of the "tragedy of historical recurrence," with his pastoral values in effect the victims of tragic repetition.[26]

The artifacts serve as reminders of the ceaseless repetition of violence and the inexorability of death. The Revolution may promise a transformation—those "who once were nothing will now be all" (*kto byl nichem, tot budet vsem*) (CW 3:160; T:276)— but the statuary and the kurgans indicate that the common fate of the Revolution's soldiers will be death, and that those who die will not be memorialized by kurgans or slain by arrows like the warriors of old—the trench will be their grave, and the slaughter inflicted by bullets: "Flowers are needed to cover graves, / And the grave reminds us: We are flowers, / And like them, ephemeral" (*Tsvety nuzhny, chtob skrasit' groby, / A grob napomnit: my—tsvety / Nedolgovechny, kak oni*) (CW 3:162; T: 227).

The various graves announced in these passages form the basic paradigm, for which the kurgans serve as archaic precedent. At times, they serve as the backdrop for the events of war, as for example, "the kurgan of the pagan Rogneda, which preserves the virgin bones" (*Kurgan iazycheskoi Rognede / Khranil devicheskie kosti*) and upon which feather grass grows. Khlebnikov immediately contrasts this setting, however, with the appearance of a "monstrosity of copper" (*chudovishche iz medi*). In Markov's estimation, "Khlebnikov's main achievement in ["Night"] is a highly successful juxtaposition of Civil War events and pagan antiquity."[27] Indeed, what we see in such scenes is both a juxtaposition of the archaic and the modern as typifying the work, and the slippage between the two temporal planes: Khlebnikov will go on to describe the "monstrosity" as "dressed in iron armor" (*odetoe v zheleznyi pantsyr'*), as though the tank were a medieval warrior, as it cuts down soldiers and moves through the landscape. These events give way to a momentary pause—"And again the desert seems as of old"—a reprieve from war, and restoration of a quiescent past, which Khlebnikov quickly

---

[26]   Khlebnikov, *Collected Works of Velimir Khlebnikov*, vol. 3, 254.

[27]   Markov, *Longer Poems*, 127.

undercuts in the following line with a "But a faithful machine gun, like a bell-man, echoed the prayers of a requiem mass" (*No sluzhit vernyi pulemet/ obedniu smerti, kak zvonar'*) (*CW* 3:163, *T*: 278). The scene, then, is one in which war enters in as a profanation of the past paradigms, as the sound of rifles substitute for those of a religious mass.

What adds still more poignancy to the fate of these steppe artifacts in "A Night" can be sensed when we turn again to the image of the kurgans. The *poèma* was one of several works in which Khlebnikov included mounds: for example, "Kurgan" ("Kurgan," 1915) where a fierce warrior for Zaporozh'e lies beneath a mound; and his "City of the Future" ("Gorod budushchego," 1920), with its "transparent kurgans" made of glass in a resplendent city, and also containing the promise of a more peaceful rapprochement between past, present, and future (*T*: 119). He spoke too, roughly around the same time as the two works central to these pages, of the "sands of stupidity" that buried him under a kurgan, in "A Cliff out of the Future" ("Utes iz budushchego," 1921-22). But it is his symbolically complex and programmatic essay "The Kurgan of Sviatogor" ("Kurgan Sviatogora," 1908), in which, in Thomas Seifrid's view, we find Khlebnikov elaborating a view of the "Russian language [as having] . . . a messianic role to play in all this utopian language-building."[28] The essay, moreover, reveals how Khlebnikov had signaled early on in his career how Russia's archaeological past would be central to the articulation of his aesthetic program: "We remain deaf to the voice of the land" he writes in the work. Presumably, the deafness would be overcome by the apotheosis of the poet, who suddenly becomes capable of hearing and channeling that voice.

Such voices from the land were being heard in various quarters. We have already seen the topos of the voice of the landscape as comprehensible only to certain poets in Chekhov and in Bunin, where either the steppe or the kurgans emanate, almost

---

[28] Thomas Seifrid, *The Word Made Self: Russian Writings on Language, 1860-1930* (Ithaca, NY: Cornell University Press, 2005), 69.

inaudibly, some secret language. Viacheslav Ivanov, too, speaks of the voice of the deep past emanating from "sepulchral crypts" in "Ancient Terror," which appeared a year after "The Kurgan of Sviatogor":

> As if from the depths of sepulchral crypts, we hear these hushed words about the earth's ancient tremors, about the cataclysms of the still-chaotic world . . . We all feel that we live at a time of the waning and taming of the world's elemental forces and humanity's elemental energies, but we still hear, somewhere below the level of conscious and superficial life, a distant, deep song of native chaos. (*SE:* 148)

By 1920, Khlebnikov had heard his "deep song" shattered by gunfire: the kurgans were not a source of words, but reminders of future deaths. The Chertomlyk Kurgan, for example, performs this function in "Night." The mound is the source for a band of mythological warriors who emerge and fill the air with a "bestial howl" (*s zverinym voem*). These figures belong to the paradigm of steppe warfare, terrorizing the folk. That pattern is recognized, but cannot be overcome.

Such oscillations of the multiple temporalities found in the steppe typify the work, as does the theme that the war violates the old orders and profanes the sacred. That violation is maximally realized in the profanation of ruins, which takes shape around the figure of Lenin: "The face of the Siberian East, / A massive forehead / worn out by troubles" (*Litso Sibirskogo Vostoka / Gromadnyi lob, izmuchennyi zabotoi*). He leads armies and sends "doctors" to disinter reliquaries:

> Когда врачами суеверий
> Мои послы во тьме пещеры
> Вскрывали ножницами мощи
> И подымали над толпой
> Перчатку женскую, жилицу
> Искусно сделанных мощей,
> Он умер, чудотворец тощий,
> Но эта женская перчатка
> Была расстрелом суеверий.

When, like doctors of superstitions,
My ambassadors, dissected relics with their
                                    scalpels in the dark of a cave,
And raised above the crowd a woman's glove,
An inhabitant of artfully made relics,

He died, the gaunt miracle-worker,
Yet this woman's glove
Was an execution of superstitions by firing squad.
                                    (*T*: 276; *CW* 3:161)

The Lenin figure is the poem's most zealous positivist, his
"ambassadors" conducting autopsies in order to assert the brute
materiality of the relics. Sanctity is gone; only matter remains. The
disinterment and display of relics to the public, a common program
of Bolshevik demystification, is "archaeology" at its most negative
and profane.

For all the story of profanation, however, the embodiments of
the old orders retain at the very least the ability to comment upon
the events. We have already seen this with the pastoral critique of
the war leveled by the old man. But it is the *babas* at the end of
the *poèma*, who are given the final word on this theme when they
emerge as the observers and judges of "human affairs":

Смотрели каменные бабы.
Смотрело
Каменное тело
На человеческое дело.
«Где тетива волос девичьих?
И гибкий лук в рост человека,
И стрелы длинные на перьях птичьих,
И девы бурные моего века?» —
Спросили каменной богини
Едва шептавшие уста.

The Stone Women watched.
The stone body
Watched
Human affairs.
"Where are the bowstrings of maidens' hair?
And the lithe bows the height of a man,

And the long arrows with bird feathers,
And the tempestuous maidens of my own era?" —
Asked the stone goddess's
Barely whispering lips. (*T*: 280; *CW* 3:166)

Notably, the "stone goddess" does not appear to lament war itself, but rather the loss of particular kinds of warriors—"the tempestuous maidens of my own era." She has emerged at a time when bows and arrows are long obsolete in the face of forms of mechanized warfare and forms of violence to which she is unaccustomed:

Тупо животное лицо
Степной богини. Почему
Бойцов суровые ладони
Хватают мертвых за виски
И алоратные полки
Летят веселием погони?
Скажи, суровый известняк,
На смену кто войне придет?
—Сыпняк!

The animal face
Of the steppe goddess is stolid. Why
Do the harsh palms of the warriors
Seize the dead by their temples
And the Red Army regiments fly
                with delight in the chase?
Tell us, harsh limestone,
Who will come in the wake of war?
—Typhus! (*T*: 280; *CW* 3:166-67)

Just as the statuary spoke at the beginning of the *poèma*, so, too, does it speak at the close. It is given the final word in the *poèma*, but the final linguistic act of the statuary is to talk in a language not of its own time: "Typhus!" (*Sypniak!*). There are many ways to approach this final utterance of the stone woman from the perspectives of both the *poèma* and the statuary's career in modernist letters. On one level, it recapitulates the theme of the inexorable deaths of the various warriors in the *poèma*, with the statuary again cast as a memento mori.

On another, it returns us to the question of voice. That the statuary speaks at all at several points throughout the work returns us to the centrality of voice, and the topos of its reticence or absence in accounts of the stone *babas* and of statuary in general. The statuary had refused to speak to the poet in Bunin's lyric poem, but spoke in Remizov's fantastical world. Fedorov-Davydov saw Khlebnikov as the first poet to whom the statuary spoke. However, what is notable, indeed poignant in Khlebnikov's use of the statues in "Night," is perhaps best grasped if we recall his desire to create a "new stone woman of the steppes of time." At the very moment that Khlebnikov wants to give them voice, the violence of the Civil War enters in and blocks out all other words. Violence now seems to be the fate of the statuary that Khlebnikov had hoped would serve as the model for his own aesthetic tendency, as the monument for his battle between time and space, and as the central icon of his mythology.

Moreover, "typhus" (*sypniak*) is a strange word to utter for this animal-faced steppe goddess. Addressed as a "harsh limestone" (*surovyi izvestniak*), the *baba* had just spoken of "the bowstrings of maidens' hair," a phrase and image perhaps more commensurate with her own time. *Sypniak*, however, is the colloquial form of *sypnoi tif*, or "trench typhus," and, in 1920, it was a word of recent vintage. In this sense, the final word uttered by the statuary is also the work's final anachronism, which belongs to a class of literary devices Jakobson designated as a "device of temporal shift," which he singled out as particularly significant for the poet.[29] The statuary, too, is something of an anachronism against the backdrop of mechanized warfare and the Civil War. And it is now made to speak anachronistically, serving as a commentator on the events occurring within its purview, but with a word not of its own time. The anachronism is all the more charged because it fulfills the rhyme of *izvestniak* (limestone), one of the stones out of which the statuary was made, with the new and grim colloquialism, *sypniak*.[30]

---

[29]   On the figure of "anachronism" as a device, see Jakobson, "The Newest Russian Poetry," 188.

[30]   *Entsiklopedicheskii slovar' F. A. Brokgauza i I. A. Efrona*, s.v. "kamennye baby."

The anachronism, however, also reveals a chilling symmetry of time, language, and fate, as though the *baba* was fated to utter the new word. History and an open future are foreclosed by a rhyme.

iii. The Grave of Khlebnikov

How one becomes the poet of a particular object or site is a difficult cultural mechanism to explain. But there are innumerable examples. Pushkin is the bard of the Bronze Horseman; Gogol, of Nevsky Prospekt and Gorod N; while Gavrila Derzhavin, Pushkin Akhmatova, and Annenskii perhaps vie for the title in relation to Tsarskoe Selo. Despite all his predecessors and followers, Khlebnikov is the undisputed poet of the Stone Women. If the general trajectory of this and the other chapters trace the transformation of the archaeological artifacts into aesthetic resources for the modernists—and its movement from the realm of archaeology into that of Russian arts and letters—then perhaps the best coda that can be provided here is to return to the moment when archaeology enshrined Khlebnikov as the poet of the statuary.

On the ninetieth anniversary of Khlebnikov's birth, a new monument for his grave was unveiled in the Novodevichy Cemetery. Every aspect of the endeavor was beset by challenges, even the effort to locate where Khlebnikov had been laid to rest in 1923. We know from Khlebnikov's nephew, M. Miturich-Khlebnikov, that several designs had been considered to adorn Khlebnikov's grave after its transfer to Novodevichy.[31] One proposal came from Aleksei Zelinskii, a student of Vladimir Tatlin, and another from the artist Viacheslav Klichkov (a relief featuring a young male nude adorned with a crown), but both proposals were rejected. Miturich-Khlebnikov, together with the poet Boris Slutskii and the literary scholar Nikolai Stepanov, the editor of a major edition of Khlebnikov's collected works, then decided that an appropriate

---

[31]   M. Miturich-Khlebnikov, "Gde umer i gde pokhoren Velimir Khlebnikov," in *Vestnik obshchestva Velimira Khlebnikova*, vol. 1 (Moscow: Gileia, 1996), 75-89.

monument for Khlebnikov would be a Stone Woman. What's more, the statuary should appear "as if it were not made by human hands, and coming from eternity," a reference to the Orthodox concept of the icon (*nerukotvornyi*) now extended to a pagan statuary.[32]

Finding an "available 'Stone Woman'" proved difficult, however, so they turned to an archaeologist, Georgii Fedorov. We know from Fedorov's account of this time that he searched for a "Stone Woman" for nearly ten years before one was eventually found:

> My colleague unearthed a "Stone Woman," brought it to Moscow, and turned it over to me. I gave it to the Union of Writers. The "Stone Woman" turned out to be uncommonly expressive. The features of the face were clearly Turkic. This was a humble, peaceful woman, with a pensive, mournful face. In her right hand is something resembling a circular vessel, but more likely it is a pomegranate fruit, which in the whole of the East is a symbol of the eternal cycle, of the interrelation and intersection of life and death. The sculptor, who carved her nearly fifteen hundred years ago, was a true artist.[33]

According to Miturich-Khlebnikov, this *baba* they found was not the kind of statuary they originally had in mind, but they decided to use it after all. (Quite likely, they had in mind one usually associated with the Polovtsy, which, as Khlebnikov described it in "The Stone Woman," was often adorned with a hat and necklace.) As Fedorov goes on to note, "we placed the statue upon Khlebnikov's grave. Here, she is located with the hope of preserving and suitably crowning the grave of the poet."[34] Perhaps it might have been better to call the statuary another "imaginary" Stone Woman, as the archaeologist Nikolai Veselovskii might have done. For it was here, at the grave of Khlebnikov, whose imagination made him into *the* poet of the statuary, that another imaginary Stone Woman, so often

[32]   Ibid., 79.

[33]   G. B. Fedorov, "Poet, khudozhnik i kamennaia baba," in *Dnevnaia poverkhnost'* (Moscow: Detskaia literatura, 1977), http://ka2.ru/nauka/baba,html, accessed on June 6, 2013.

[34]   Ibid.

found upon kurgans, was riveted to his marble tombstone. The cultural and aesthetic revival of the statuary had come full circle. A cultural poetics was incarnated in stone (fig. 5.1).

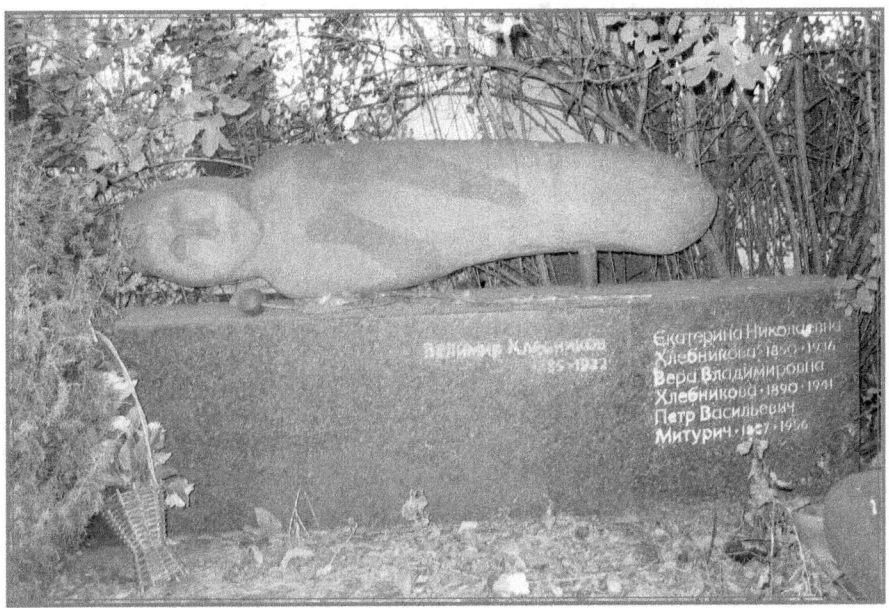

Figure 5.1.
The grave of Khlebnikov.
Photo courtesy of Jon Stone.

Chapter Six

The Landmarks of Time: Burial Mounds, Eurasian Necropolises, and Modernist Form in Boris Pil'niak's The Naked Year

In June 1919, in the aftermath of the Revolution and amid the Civil War, a writer and an archaeologist arrived at the excavation site at Uvek, one of the fortified cities of the Golden Horde situated along the banks of the Volga. The archaeologist was F. V. Ballod, who devoted an extensive section to the Uvek excavations in a work he published several years later entitled *The Volga "Pompeiis": An Essay on the Artistic-Archaeological Examination of the Zone on the Right Bank of the Volga near Saratov and Tsaritsyn* (fig. 6.1).[1] Ballod's book detailed the archaeological remains that he and other archaeologists had found in the region, a space crisscrossed for millennia by various nomadic peoples.

In the opening description of the Volga landscape as it stretches out before him, Ballod attunes himself to the recondite traces of the past. "Through the 'Great Gates of Peoples,'" he writes in the work's introduction,

> between the Urals and the Caspian Sea, innumerable waves of tribes have passed since the most ancient of times into the Volga steppes, and stopped, awaiting laggards at those natural barriers

[1] F. V. Ballod, *Privolzhskie "Pompei": Opyt khudozhestvenno-arkheologicheskogo obsledovaniia chasti pravoberezhnoi saratovsko-tsaritsynskoi privolzhskoi polosy* (Moscow: Gosudarstvennoe izd-vo, 1923). For contemporary scholarship on the excavations of Uvek (also known as Ukek), see, for example, L. F. Nedashkovskii, *Zolotoordynskii gorod Ukek i ego okruga* (Moscow: Vostochnaia literatura RAN, 2000).

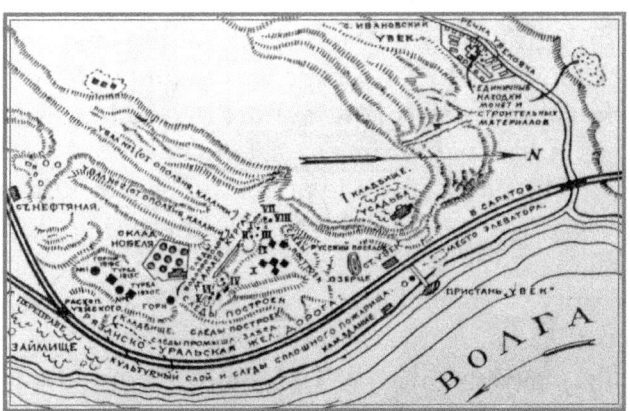

Figure 6.1.

Sketch of Uvek from
Ballod's *The Volga
"Pompeiis"* (1923),
indicating the main
sites of the excavation,
the Ural Railway,
and the Volga.

to carefree travel on the Volga. There, having gathered their strength, they crossed the river and established fortified sites on its right bank, and from there they wended their way further into the West and into the South-Russian steppes. The path of these movements was clear: from the Urals to the Volga, from the Volga to the Don and Dnieper: it lay partly through forests and partly through the steppe; it went along the steppe rivers, where horses and herds are not threatened by drought or thirst during the summer heat. . . . An observer, moreover, would not need to search out this path. Traces of the presence of man point toward it: sites with broken wares flung about, and landmarks of the road in the form of kurgans. The path is clear even to this day, for the chains of kurgans have stood in their places despite the work of later agrarian peoples, the fierce steppe wind, and the whole destructive hand of time.

Sometimes flat and eroded, a barely perceptible elevation of soil; sometimes stone mounds (*kamennye mary*); sometimes superbly intact hills (*sopki*) in the shape of overturned bowls, with the characteristic sepulchral stones on top: these are the landmarks of the trans-Volga path that present themselves as both the landmarks of time (*vekhi vremen*) and as monuments of the various cultures that have successively replaced one another. (i)

Ballod offers here nothing less than a hermeneutics of landscape. Sensitive to traces, he apprehends the "landmarks of time" before him as indices of the passage of peoples, time, and man's passage through life, since the majority of the landmarks are graves. What he found in the landscape was a story of movement, ruination, and the supersession of one culture by another. From this vantage point, he could traverse time at a standstill.

The other figure to arrive at Uvek in June of 1919—in fact, just a few days after Ballod—was the writer Boris Pil'niak. In 1919, Pil'niak was still several years away from becoming the "first celebrity of Soviet letters,"[2] a status he achieved with the publication in 1922 of *The Naked Year* (*Golyi god*), the first major prose work of the post-Revolutionary period. In a middle section of *The Naked Year*, Pil'niak gives an extensive description of the Uvek excavations that begins much like what probably transpired in June 1919. Three characters arrive at the "bald, stony mount" of Uvek: one is an artist, Gleb Ordynin, whose surname conjures up the Golden Horde (*Zolotaia Orda*); his sister Natal'ia, who becomes a Bolshevik and an archaeologist and from whose perspective the excavations are recounted; and her eventual lover, an archaeologist named Baudek:

> On the summit of Uvek people had noticed ruins and kurgans (*razvaliny i kurgany*)—the archaeologist Baudek and the artist Ordynin had come to excavate them with a detail of muzhiks. The excavations were in their third week and centuries were emerging from the earth. On Uvek they found the remnants of an ancient town, stone ruins of aqueducts lay in layers, the foundations of buildings, a sewer system—what was hidden by the loamy soil and black earth had remained not from the Finns, nor the Scythians, nor from the Bolgars—some unknown people came here from the Asiatic steppes in order to found a city and to disappear from history forever. But after them, after those unknown people, the Scythians were here, and they left their kurgans.[3]

<hr>

[2] Peter Alberg Jensen, *Nature as Code: The Achievement of Boris Pilnjak, 1915–1924* (Copenhagen: Rosenkilde & Bagger, 1979), 65, cited in Clark, *Petersburg*, 52.

[3] Boris Pilnyak, *The Naked Year*, trans. A. R. Tulloch (Ann Arbor, MI: Ardis, 1975), 91–92. All references to the novel will first include the page number to this edition, and then to Boris Pil'niak, *Sobranie sochinenii v shesti tomakh* (Moscow: Terra-Knizhnyi klub, 2003), 1: 91-92. The translations have been adjusted.

The aesthetic structure and the themes found in this remarkable passage are the central concerns of the present chapter. Similar to what Ballod later describes in the opening of his *Volga "Pompeiis,"* what Pil'niak delineates here are multiple epochs emerging from the ground, with each particular group—the unknown Asiatic tribe, then the Scythians, the Bolgars, the Finns—leaving behind some deposit in the space before him. Uvek becomes an emblem for a general feature of *The Naked Year*, in which artifacts from the deep past are perceived alongside a host of other eras simultaneously present within the Revolutionary moment. The Scythians and their burial mounds, Uvek as both a Eurasian necropolis and archaeological complex: these are among the deepest of the pasts to be found represented in *The Naked Year*, but they belong to a gradient of temporalities embodied in the present by wizards and Bolsheviks, syphilitic aristocrats and anarchists, pagans and Orthodox, burial mounds and factories, monks' cells and cinemas, incantations and Revolutionary slogans, thoroughly dead cities like Uvek and moribund cities such as the work's imagined Ordynin-Town.

It was this multiplicity of times and their correlated aesthetic forms in *The Naked Year* that provoked broad debate about the novel's representation of the Revolutionary epoch—just as so many of Pil'niak's later works would do (although the debates became ever more strident). Leon Trotsky, for example, highlighted this feature in a long essay on Pil'niak, in which he observed that *The Naked Year* reflected the disquieting dilemma of the past pervading the present:

> And although in present-day Russia, a sorcerer's incantations exist next to the Gviu and Glavbum, they do not exist on the same historical plane (*v odnoi istoricheskoi ploskosti*). The Gviu and the Glavbum, however imperfect, tend forward, while the incantations, no matter how "folk-like," are the dead weight of history.[4]

---

[4] Leon Trotskii, *Literatura i revoliutsiia* (1923; reprint, Moscow: Izd-vo polit. lit-ry, 1991), 75.

In Trotsky's view, Pil'niak heard these stump-words turned incantations—Gviu and Glavbum—but he did not bring his artistic vision
in line with the change Trotsky thought they symbolized: "The wind
wails in the Kremlin, in the side streets: Gu-vuu-zii-maa! And the roof
iron of the old houses roars: —gla-vbum!" (165/162). Instead, Trotsky
faulted Pil'niak for failing to delineate the differences between
these "historical planes": between the vital and the moribund, the
historical and ahistorical, the living and the dead. The novel gave
a spurious vision of the Revolutionary period—spurious, in Trotsky's
view, because *The Naked Year* founders in a synchronic perspective
on "present-day Russia" that reveals all the "particularities of the
historical development of Russia," to borrow a phrase Trotsky used
elsewhere, but leaves out the development.

In fact, other critics insisted the work went so far as to
repudiate development and modernization altogether, favoring
instead a retrogressive utopian ideal based on the peasants and
the primitive.[5] Not only do some characters in the work reject
modernization, they also hope the Revolution will jettison the entire
ballast of Western influence on Russia: a perspective that meant that
technological development, Peter the Great, and even Bolshevism
were iterations of the same paradigm: "And everything is dead,
sheer machinery, technology, comfort," says Gleb Ordynin, the
artist who accompanies Baudek to Uvek, in a lengthy conversation
with another character, the Archbishop Sylvester, which reveals
the novel's philosophical horizon: "The path of European culture
led to war, '14 [1914] was able to create this war. The culture of the
machine forgot about the culture of the spirit" (72/74). Such views
have led scholars to link the work to parallel intellectual currents in
the 1920s such as primitivism, Eurasianism, and Scythianism, and
to the accursed question of what historical path the Revolution had
set for Russia to travel along, pitted as it was between the symbolic
antinomies of East and West. Indeed, various characters in the work
seem more like embodiments of ideological perspectives rather than

---

5   Robert Maguire, *Red Virgin Soil: Soviet Literature in the 1920s* (Princeton, NJ: Princeton University
    Press, 1968), 103-4.

fleshed-out characters. These perspectives vie with one another; the Archbishop, for example, responds to Gleb: "Russia, you say?—but Russia—is a fiction, a mirage, because Russia is the Caucasus, and the Ukraine, and Moldavia! . . . Great Russia, it must be said is the regions of the Oka, Volga, Kama (Pooch'e, Povol'zhe, Pokam'e)" (73/75). This space where Sylvester locates "Great Russia" is where Uvek too is found and where much of the action in *The Naked Year* takes place. How might we understand those "historical planes" that were emphatically dead, that is, those planes represented by Uvek and the Scythian burial mound? And how can they be integrated into the novel's vision of the steppe landscape and of the ability of Russian history to negotiate between the archaic East and the modern West?

The scholar E. B. D'iachkova once observed that Pil'niak "loves the metaphor of archaeological excavations, the immersion in another time."[6] I want to expand on this observation by considering how archaeology served as a conceptual and aesthetic resource for Pil'niak. *The Naked Year* extends the present study's concerns into the post-Revolutionary period while maintaining the steppe and the Russian hinterland as the central arena in which the confrontation with the archaeological past takes place. As another character, Svirid, a local, says to Natal'ia, who has accompanied Baudek to the excavations, and whose contemplation of Russian history will be central to the pages to come:

> Now it's the night, Comrade Natal'ia, no chance to fall asleep, how about a cuddle! All the Communists are in the plants. Have you been to the excavators? (*kopatel'iam*)—they say they're excavating the town—these days everything's being dug up! (*vremia teper' takoe, do vsego dokapyvaiutsia*). (94/96)

The play here on the various words for "excavation," in the middle of the sequence describing the archaeological excavation, serves as Pil'niak's reminder that not only industrialization, but

---

6   E. B. D'iachkova, "Problema vremeni v proizvedeniiakh B. Pil'niaka," in *Boris Pil'niak: Opyt segodniashnego prochteniia* (Moscow: Nasledie, 1995), 66. My thanks to Ilya Kukulin for bringing this work to my attention.

also archaeology were forces exhuming the ground during the Revolution and Civil War. At the very moment when industrial modernization and the Revolution marked the upheaval of time and space, so, too, did archaeology destabilize the ground, pointing toward the archaic strata contained within or upon the land.

The following pages focus on two episodes in *The Naked Year* where we find Pil'niak offering period emblems to think through these twin upheavals, along with the convergence of archaeology, the Revolution, and modernist aesthetics. The first is the excavation of Uvek; the second, a sequence involving a train station named after a burial mound, "Loop Station Mar" (*"Raz"ezd Mar"* [the quotes are Pil'niak's; MK]), which can also be translated as "Loop Station Burial Mound," since *mar* is a local word for the Russian "kurgan" (which Pil'niak frequently uses in the novel). The two episodes are respectively structured according to two aesthetic principles of modernist stratigraphy and modernist topography, which highlight and juxtapose a range of times, historical planes, and forms of life simultaneously found in "present-day Russia."

With Uvek, we see the continual layering of temporal epochs one over the other, which allows these epochs to be perceived simultaneously, but which, as the sequence continues, open onto a range of other temporalities discernible within the country. And with Loop Station Mar, which punctuates the work, we find a reliance on a set of topographic juxtapositions in which the archaic and the modern enter into especially close proximity. At both sites, Pil'niak charts a range of temporalities present before him—just as we saw Ballod and Baudek doing in their surveys of the Volga steppe—and both reveal how time and narrative fracture in such spaces. These two episodes allow us to see how Pil'niak thought about archaeology not only in terms of its standard affiliation with metaphors of depth, but also in terms of contiguity and adjacency. This poetics of depth and of adjacency, in turn, structured Pil'niak's aesthetics of archaeology and his conception of a historical model for Russia.

i. Volga "Pompeiis"

"I am already terribly bored here," Pil'niak wrote his wife, Mariia Sokolova, in a letter during his sojourn in Saratov in June 1919. "But . . . I think I'll return toward July, so that I can perhaps gather more impressions. In a few days, I'll head to the excavations, the archaeological ones, and write a story—'Wormwood.'"[7] A day after Pil'niak sent this letter, the archaeologist Ballod also set off from Saratov to the excavations of the sites described in *Volga "Pompeiis,"* in the company of fifty people, many of whom were from the Historical-Philological Department of Saratov University.[8] It was this team and their excavations that probably served Pil'niak as the model for the description that first appeared in "Wormwood" ("Polyn'"), which he finished in July as planned, and published in his 1919 collection Long-Forgotten *Pasts* (*Byl'e*): "At the top of Uvek people had noticed ruins and kurgans; the archaeologist Baudek with a group of Tver muzhiks, who had earlier been barge haulers on the Volga, had arrived to excavate them."[9] To judge from the afterlife of this passage, Pil'niak found more than just relief from boredom.

In 1919, Uvek and other sites throughout the Volga region faced numerous threats. The construction of a railroad (see fig. 6.1,

---

[7]   Letter to M. A. Sokolova, June 9, 1919, in Boris Pil'niak, *Pis'ma v 2 tomakh* (Moscow: IMLI RAN, 2010), 1:303-4.

[8]   Ballod, *Privolzhskie*, 5.

[9]   Boris Pil'niak, "Polyn'," in *Byl'e* (1919; reprint, Munich: Wilhelm Fink Verlag, 1970), 43. Pil'niak scholarship, to my knowledge, has not linked "Wormwood" or *The Naked Year* to the actual excavation practices of the period, but scholars of archaeology in Russia have, albeit only in passing: the archaeologist A. A. Formozov observed that "Baudek" was based on Ballod, in his *Russkie arkheologi v period totalitarizma: Istoriograficheskie ocherki* (Moscow: Znak, 2004), 315, cited in N. M. Malov, "Sovetskaia arkheologiia v Saratovskom gosudarstvennom universitete (1918-1940): Organizatsionnoe stanovlenie, razvitie i repressii," *Arkheologiia vostochno-evropeiskoi stepi*, no. 4 (2006): 13, n. 49. Historians of the Volga Germans have also noted Pil'niak's close association with other archaeologists, especially with a certain Paul Rau, who is the protagonist of Pil'niak's story "A German Story" ("Nemetskaia istoriia," 1928). Natalie Kromm, "Povolzhsko-nemetskii sled v zhizni i proizvedeniiakh pisatelia Borisa Pil'niaka," in *Die Geschichte der Wolgadeutschen*, http://wolgadeutsche.net /biographie /Pilnjak_WD_Spuren_rus.htm, accessed May 30, 2013. See also N. M. Malov's article on Rau in *Nemtsy Rossii: Entsiklopediia*, s.v. "Paul Rau."

with the railroad partially encircling Uvek) provoked Ballod and other Saratov archaeologists associated with the local museum and university to worry about "the destruction of a series of monuments of Tatar culture, more or less intact in the depths of the earth."[10] Given the year, the Civil War generated other threats: Uvek was designated "one of the forts of the Saratov fortified region" and, as such, "military engineering projects threatened to destroy part of the monuments."[11] This sort of conjunction of an archaic site and contemporary developments particularly appealed to Pil'niak. "Wormwood," for example, concludes with a suggestive emblem: "at dawn, soldiers arrived from the city and placed cannons on Uvek."[12] On the one hand, the arrival of the cannons marks a new temporal overlay that seems starkly at odds with the archaic site. On the other hand, the cannons remind us of Uvek's strategic function, past and present, which collapses the differences in time into a single paradigm of steppe warfare. Just as kurgans could be reused for steppe warfare, so too could necropolises be repurposed and their strategic value reasserted. While this emblem is ultimately omitted in *The Naked Year,* Pil'niak offers up others to establish the paradigms by which he thinks through repeated patterns in both the steppe and Russian history.

Although the events of the Civil War lent urgency to Ballod's excavations, when he recorded his thoughts about Uvek and the other Volga "Pompeiis" in 1923, another argument emerges that makes explicit why these sites should be preserved:

> The beautifully equipped furnaces for the firing of ceramic wares, the homes with a complex system of central heating made of marble and decorative tiles, the water supply system, the geometrically arrayed streets and squares, the caravan sheds, the mosques and grandiose mausoleums, the silks and brocades

---

10 Ballod, *Privolzhskie,* 5.

11 Ibid. For more on the history of the Civil War and the destruction of monuments in the Saratov region, see Donald J. Raleigh, *Experiencing Russia's Civil War: Politics, Society and Revolutionary Culture in Saratov, 1917-1922* (Princeton, NJ: Princeton University Press, 2002).

12 Pil'niak, "Polyn'," 50.

from interments, the silver ladles, and the Venetian and Persian glass: all portray the population of the cities of the Golden Horde not as savages, but as a cultured people, engaged in manufacture and trade: they were not alien to dealings with the peoples of the East and West, and they broadly developed the applied arts.[13]

The Volga "Pompeiis," in other words, were sites of cultures past, not the gathering places of destructive hordes. Indeed, they were also spaces of interaction between peoples from East and West through commerce and trade.

This was in fact a fairly old argument. In promoting these Volga sites to the status of Pompeii, Ballod extended what was at least a half-century of debate over the provenance and value of the archaeological artifacts and sites found in the Volga steppes. One such case, as the historian Robert Geraci has shown, was the so-called "Bulgar controversy," which centered on the question of the origins of the Russian village of Bolgary, near Kazan.[14] The archaeologist Konstantin Evlent'ev, for example, compared the ruins of Bolgary to Italian ruins when he made his claim for their value: "Italy takes justifiable pride in the ruins of classical Pompeii. Russia also has its Pompeii—Bulgar on the Volga."[15] The ruins found at Bolgary included burial mounds and the remnants of buildings, for which the archaeologist was seeking support to excavate: "the Russian Pompeii has been forgotten by its compatriots and is unknown to educated Europe."[16]

Most striking here were claims by various scholars that Bolgary was Russian. But was Bolgary Russian by virtue of imperial possession, or by some claim of ethnic patrimony? As Geraci observes,

---

13   Ballod, *Privolzhskie*, 131.

14   Robert P. Geraci, *Window on the East: National and Imperial Identities in Late Tsarist Russia* (Ithaca, NY: Cornell University Press, 2001); see esp. "*Whose* Pompeii?: The Bulgar Controversy," 180-94. All further references are cited in the text.

15   Ibid., 180, citing K. G. Evlent'ev, "Ob uchrezhdenii arkheologicheskogo muzeuma v Bulgare Kazanskoi gubernii," in *Trudy pervogo arkheologicheskogo s"ezda* (Moscow, 1869), 1:90.

16   Ibid., 181, citing Evlent'ev, "Ob uchrezhdenii," 90.

the question about Bolgary was a question about the ethnicity of
its founders, and, by extension, who "bore chief responsibility for
its achievements" (183). Language, for instance, served as a notable
arena in which to contest the provenance of the site. Those who
wanted the Bulgars to be Russian divined Slavic roots in their
language, while those claiming they were Finns found Finnish
roots. It was possible, Geraci concludes, "to argue almost anything
one liked about the people of Volga Bulgaria" (183). Such was
the sentiment, to recall, expressed by the archaeologist Nikolai
Veselovskii about all the speculation on the stone *babas*.

We can discern a parallel drama of origins in Pil'niak's
characterization of Uvek. His description of the excavation, cited at
the beginning of this chapter, highlights the archaeological deposits
left by various peoples: the Finns, the Scythians, the Bolgars, and
"some unknown people [who] came here from the Asiatic steppes"
(93/91-92). Some of this accords with Ballod's findings, although
Pil'niak, on the whole, seems more interested in marking out a con-
glomerate of nomadic deposits in order to postulate that what lies
underneath everything in Uvek is Asia.

One reason this image of Uvek matters is that the site had been
the subject of a debate about its origins, just as had Bolgary. Where
archaeologists had linked some Volga sites to Pompeii, by at least
the 1890s, archaeologists had likened Uvek to "Troy and other cities
of the East and of Greece" not because it rivaled Troy in terms of
prestige, but because the assertion of its value and origins would
follow the same method pioneered by Heinrich Schliemann, when
he transformed *The Iliad* into a compendium of geographic clues,
rather than a storehouse of myths: that is, a text just as relevant
to archaeology and geography as to philology.[17] As I suggested
earlier, the text that mattered in this regard to Russian archaeologists was Herodotus's *Histories*, and, in particular, the chapters on
Scythia.

[17]   Marchand, *Down From Olympus*, 118-24.

In the case of Uvek, it was not only Herodotus, but also Homer, Hesiod, Strabo, Marco Polo, Ibn Fadlan, and Zabelin (in particular, his *History of Russian Life*), who all figured prominently in the work of Prince L. L. Golitsyn and S. S. Krasnodubrovskii in their research on the origins of Uvek (which they referred to by its earlier Tatar name "Ukek").[18] Indeed, the authors reminded their readers in 1891 that it was in Marco Polo's *Travels*, where one finds the earliest mention of Ukek, to which he and his brother traveled after leaving Bolgary.[19] (In the Russian translation of Marco Polo's *Travels*, it was referred to as "Ukak.") They had singled out the site as "an unhappy exception in the order of material monuments of our past (*nashei stariny*)" and reconstructed the mythologies surrounding it.[20] They recounted, for example, how Zabelin related in his *History* that travelers had once marvelled at Ukek's "beautiful castle," and that it had also once been referred to as "Sodom."[21] (We know from other sources that Russian inhabitants of Uvek told the English traveler Christopher Burrough, a member of the Hakluyt Society who traveled through the region in the sixteenth century, that the remains of Uvek had been "swallowed into the Earth by the justice of God, for the wickedness of the people that inhabited [the town]."[22])

All these details mattered to Golitsyn and Krasnodubrovskii because they wanted to establish a pre-Tatar origin of Uvek by relying on travel sources through the Volga steppe (61). Zabelin,

---

18   Prince L. L. Golitsyn and S. S. Krasnodubrovskii, *Ukek: Doklady i issledovanii po arkheologii i istorii Ukeka* (Saratov: Tipografiia Gubernsk. Zemstva, 1891), 2. The discussion of antique sources is on pp. 11, 54-55. Most further references are cited in the text.

19   Ibid., 60, n. 2. The two authors rely on a Russian translation of Marco Polo's *Travels*, which appeared in 1861.

20   Ibid., 1-6.

21   Ibid., citing Zabelin, *Istoriia russkoi zhizni s drevneishikh vremen*, 235.

22   *The Travels of Marco Polo: The Complete Yule-Cordier Edition*, 3 vols. (1903; reprint, New York: Dover, 1999), 8-9, n. 4. Yule and Cordier provide a useful gloss of the history of the toponym "Ukek/Uvek" in note four, along with the range of other toponyms for the site, which included "Ucaca," "Ukek," "Uwek," or "Uwesh." According to them, "Uwek and Uwesh [appear] in Russian documents of the 16th century" (8-9).

the two authors knew, had speculated that those origins could have been Greek, when he suggested that the town of Helon as described by Herodotus in the *Histories* lay beneath present-day Uvek. For their part, Golitsyn and Krasnodubrovkii had proposed that the founders of Uvek were the Budini, who, according to Herodotus, lived to the north of the Scythians; and the Geloni, who were "the great-grandfathers of Saratov Ukek [i.e., Uvek]." It was from Herodotus (via Zabelin's *History*) that the duo knew that the Budini "all have markedly blue-gray eyes and red hair; there is a town in their territory called Gelonus, all built of wood." This Gelonus was founded by the Geloni, who "occupied the Saratov Volga Area." The question hinged on the location of Gelonus, "whose walls, houses, and temples were all made of wood. In this city were the temples of the Hellenic Gods, built according to Hellenic custom." "The very site of Ukek," they proposed (hoping for support to confirm their hypothesis), "is itself composed of three cultures — the Greek, Burtass, and Tatar — and the site of the ancient settlement is composed of three layers (*iz trekh nasloenii*): of the Helons (*Gelony*), Burtas, and Ukek."[23]

But why might it matter that the nomadic Budini and the agrarian Geloni had come to live together? Because the Geloni "had settled with the Budini after their expulsion from the Greek trading cities of the Black Sea, Olvia, Pantikapei, among others."[24] And because others had conjectured that the Budini were proto-Slavs, this vision of the origins of Uvek also meant early contact between Greece and the earliest of Slavs. At the base of Golitsyn and Krasnodubrovskii's Ukek, then, was a possible story of the merger of the nomadic Budini and the Hellenic Geloni, meaning that underneath it all, one could find not only a story of archaic contact and trade, but also a connection with Athens. In their view, the cultural ambit of the antique world extended deep into the Volga steppe.

It is not entirely clear whether Pil'niak knew about the debates surrounding Uvek, but he, too, advances a vision of Uvek and its

---

23   Golitsyn and Krasnodubrovskii, *Ukek*, 2-4.

24   Ibid., 2.

origins. His Uvek, however, is Asian, and through this assertion of origins, he establishes the groundwork for the novel's broader consideration of the Asian theme. On one level, his insistence on the Asian origins of the site buttresses the idea that the deepest levels of time central to *The Naked Year* always point east. On another, he was gesturing to the reinvigorated interest in the Scythians in the immediate aftermath of the Revolution.

ii. Scythianism, 1918

The Scythian kurgans Pil'niak includes in his description of the Uvek excavations deserve special attention in light of the notable upsurge of the Scythian theme the year before he set off for the excavations. In 1918, right on the heels of the Revolution, this upsurge was heralded by the publication of several major statements on Scythians that form the immediate background for Pil'niak: Aleksandr Blok's poem "The Scythians" ("Skify");[25] Evgenii Zamiatin's "Are We Scythians?" ("Skify li?"),[26] a review of the journal *Skify*, edited by Ivanov-Razumnik, whose first issue appeared in 1917;[27] and *Iranians and Greeks in South Russia* (*Ellinstvo i iranstvo na iuge Rossii*), by the noted scholar of classical antiquity Mikhail Rostovtsev, devoted to the archaeology of ancient nomadic peoples, the Scythians prominent among them.[28]

"The Scythian" served as a counter-image to prevailing attitudes about "civilized" life. In that capacity, it operated in the manner of

[25]   For the purposes of this chapter, I am using the edition prepared by Ivanov-Razumnik, *Ispytanie v groze i bure: Skify-Dvenadtsat'* (Berlin: Skify, 1920). The edition is prefaced by Ivanov-Razumnik's essay on the poems.

[26]   E. I. Zamiatin, "Skify li?," in *Sochineniia*, 4 vols. (Munich: Neimanis, 1970-88), 4: 503-13.

[27]   Ivanov-Razumnik, eds., *Skify* (St. Petersburg: Skify, 1917-18). Ivanov-Razumnik's statement on the notion of the Scythians is in his introduction to volume one; see esp. pp. x-xii.

[28]   M. I. Rostovtsev, *Ellinstvo i iranstvo na iuge Rossii* (1918; reprint, Moscow: Knizhnaia nakhodka, 2002). Rostovtsev's magnum opus on the Scythians was published by N. Ia. Marr, after Rostovtsev's emigration, as *Skifiia i Bospor: Kriticheskoe obozrenie pamiatnikov literaturnykh i arkheologicheskikh* (Leningrad: Rossiiskaia akademiia istorii material'noi kul'tury, 1 925).

other civilizational "mirrors" such as the noble or ignoble savage, the nomad, the gypsy, or the Caucasian mountaineer. Much like Maksimilian Voloshin's concept that artists and poets transform archaeological artifacts into "multifaceted mirrors . . . in order to see in each facet a fragment of their own face," the Scythian served as an *archaic* mirror, in which contemporary issues and cultural and aesthetic values were reflected in the deep past.[29] In that regard, the Scythian could represent the quintessential predecessor of Russia, invoked as the model for a struggle with the West (Blok); the archetypal precursor of the modern artist, forever pursuing new aesthetic territory (Zamiatin); or a predecessor of the avant-garde artists and the Revolutionaries in a struggle against the petty bourgeoisie (Ivanov-Razumnik). Along with these ideologies of Scythianism, or *skifstvo*, 1918 also witnessed its reaffirmation as an archaeology, chiefly in the South of Russia and, in particular, the northern bank of the Black Sea, where one could find traces of their former dominance of the region and of their interaction with other peoples during antiquity (Rostovtsev).

There is some dispute over Pil'niak's relationship to Scythianism as a cultural ideology. Peter Jensen, for example, claims that Pil'niak's interest in Scythianism was "half-hearted and frivolous: he was happiest with the Scythian's pagan semantics" but "did not share the 'skify's' Messianic dreams of the Revolution as the gateway to a peasant paradise."[30] In contrast, Gary Browning argues that "Pilniak crafted his themes, style, composition, and narrative manner with a few rapid, powerful strokes of his Scythian axe. Here [in *The Naked Year*] he first produced a successful work parallel to the time-worn and pitted burial mound fertility statues and the rough,

---

29   The notion of the Scythians as an archaic mirror combines the ideas of several works: Hayden White, "The Forms of Wildness: Archaeology of an Idea," in *The Wild Man Within: An Image in Western Thought from the Renaissance to Romanticism*, ed. Edward J. Dudley and Maximillian E. Novak (Pittsburgh: University of Pittsburgh Press, 1972), 3-38; François Hartog, *The Mirror of Herodotus: The Representation of the Other in the Writing of History* (Berkeley and Los Angeles: University of California Press, 1988); and Yuri Slezkine, *Arctic Mirrors: Russia and the Small Peoples of the North* (Ithaca, NY: Cornell University Press, 1994).

30   Jensen, *Nature as Code*, 315.

soaked oak of his artistic ideal."[31] Katerina Clark has extended Browning's account—with its correlation between the rough-hewn *babas* and Pil'niak's literary style—in specifically arguing that what we find in *The Naked Year* is that "Scythianism involves marrying Romantic Anticapitalism to one of the myths of Russian particularity (its essentially Asian identity making it freer and more expansive than the dry and repressed 'logical' Europeans)." This view, she argues, is given acute expression in "the mandatory scorn for material possessions or comfort," which typifies many Pil'niak's heroes.[32] What can be underscored for our purposes is the manifestly archaeological dimension of the Scythian theme. Along with offering counter-models to bourgeois philistinism, Scythians and other nomadic groups provided Pil'niak—much as it had Khlebnikov—with a variety of sites and artifacts with which to think through the deep past of the steppe in conjunction with the upheavals of the Civil War.

One way to specify Pil'niak's relationship to those 1918 works is to consider him in regard to his two major modernist predecessors, Andrei Bely and Aleksandr Blok, and their own contributions to the archaeological theme of steppe artifacts and the Scythians. Andrei Bely, to recall, had also evinced an interest in the archaeological, the archaic, and the antique in his *Petersburg*.[33] Indeed, the novel is something of a compendium of a range of pasts. There are the Italian-made Greek deities who cower from "the tooth of time" in the Summer Gardens; the epilogue finds Nikolai Ableukhov, after the failed assassination of his father, in Egypt, doing research in the museum at Bulaq, visiting the "large piles at Gizeh," where he leans against one of the pyramids: "He is himself a pyramid,

---

[31]   Gary Browning, *Boris Pilniak: Scythian at a Typewriter* (Ann Arbor, MI: Ardis, 1985), 114. Browning's reference to "burial mound fertility statues" is his term for the *kamennye baby*, which pears frequently in Pil'niak's works. We will discuss his use of the statuary in greater detail in chapter seven, part two.

[32]   Clark, *Petersburg*, 52-53.

[33]   Bely, *Petersburg*, 97.

the summit of a culture which will crash into ruins."[34] His father, Apollon Apollonovich, too, had been linked to the archaic and the steppe through his fear of space: "O Rus, Rus! Is it you who have set the winds, storms, and snows howling across the steppe? It seemed to the senator that a voice was calling him from a solitary burial mound (*s odinokogo grobovogo bugra*). Only hungry wolves gather in packs out there. Undoubtedly, the senator had been developing a fear of space."[35] That space—the fearful, immeasurable steppe—is the central locus in which Pil'niak stages his continual engagement with the archaeological past, and the space into which he translates the modernist literary aesthetics he inherits from Bely and Blok.

Still, the direct engagement with the Scythian theme and archaeology in *The Naked Year* seems to be with that of the theme's apotheosis in Russian modernism, namely, Blok's "The Scythians" ("Skify"). When Blok proclaimed—"Yes, we are Scythians" (*Da, Skify my!*) in his poem, he was identifying Russia with both the barbarian and the nomad, in an admixture of apocalyptic Scythianism aimed at the West. As Ivanov-Razumnik interpreted the poem, the opposition Blok drew was, in fact, between the two enemies: Russian-Scythians versus the European petty bourgeoisie (*meshchanstvo*), whom he consigned to "Old Europe."[36] The "New Europe" could still embrace the Scythian paradigm and wipe away all the vestiges of its past. Blok's "Scythians," moreover, also comprised a general category, a paradigm for other Asiatic nomads, and his reference point in this regard was Vladimir Solov'ev, whose poem "Panmongolism" (1894) was written in a paroxysm of terror at the "Yellow Peril," and cast Russia again as under threat from the East.[37] Blok, who cites as the epigraph for "The Scythians" the first

---

[34]   Ibid., 292.

[35]   Ibid., 53. I have added several lines from the 1916 edition of the novel (*Peterburg* [Leningrad: Nauka, 1981], 76-77) to this section of Maguire and Malmstad's translation, which they based on the 1921 edition.

[36]   Ivanov-Razumnik, *Ispytanie*, 37.

[37]   On Solov'ev's "Panmongolism," see Harsha Ram, "Panmongolism and the Crisis of Empire," in *The Imperial Sublime: A Russian Poetics of Empire* (Madison: University of Wisconsin Press, 2003), 221-25.

two lines of Solov'ev's poem—"Panmongolism! Although the word is savage, it caresses my ear" (*Panmongolizm—khot' slovo diko / No mne laskaet slukh ono*)[38]—defiantly embraced the image of a threatening East, and enfolded Russia into the paradigm of the martial Scythians in a struggle against both the West and the Westernization of Russia.

One particular line of attack in "The Scythians" is especially relevant to these pages. Blok's Scythians directly aimed at European antiquities. "And the day will come," Blok proclaims, "[when] there will not even be a trace of your Paestums!" (*I den' pridet—ne budet i sleda / ot vashikh Pestumov, byt' mozhet*).[39] In this vision, Paestum, which contained both Greek and Roman antiquities, is destroyed by Blok's Russo-Scythian barbarians, who warn Europe that they will emerge to complete the work of their ancestors. As Olga Matich notes, his work expressed a "Eurasian apocalyptic fantasy [that] erases ancient historical sites," which recapitulates Chaadaev's topos of the tabula rasa and the desire for renewal by wiping the slate clean.[40]

The comparison with Blok's poem brings into greater focus an essential difference between Pil'niak and his modernist forerunners: in perceiving the Scythians and other nomads as an archaeology and thereby the steppe as a space containing artifacts from the deep past, Pil'niak could not entirely subscribe to the idea that one can wipe the slate clean. This is not to say that his novel does not have characters who are drawn toward the tabula rasa. The character Donat, a member of the Reds, returns to Ordynin, the town where he grew up, "full (of an evil memory!) of the remembrances of youth, full of hatred and of will. Donat did not know the new, Donat knew what was old, and he wanted to destroy what was old. Donat came to create—he hated the old" (29/34). Although such figures

---

38 V. S. Solov'ev, "Panmongolizm," in *Stikhotvoreniia i shutochnye p'esy* (Leningrad: Sovetskii pisatel', 1974), 104.

39 Blok, "Skify," in *Ispytanie*, 48.

40 Olga Matich, *Erotic Utopia: The Decadent Imagination in Russia's Fin de Siècle* (Madison: University of Wisconsin Press, 2005), 159.

embody these views of destruction and renewal, Pil'niak's interest in archaeology, among many other pasts, indicates that his narrative style continually focuses upon the former traces of the past, even when they have been destroyed. As the novel's first line announces: "On the town kremlin's gates was inscribed (now destroyed): Save, O Lord / This town and Your people. / And bless all those / who enter these gates" (19/25). This poetics of the incomplete erasure of the past finds its realization in the archaeological theme.

iii. Modernist Stratigraphy: Uvek, Site of Time

Perhaps the very toponym "Uvek" immediately suggested to Pil'niak a way to link time, space, and modernist aesthetics. A name of Turkic origin, "Uvek," by virtue of an interlingual pun, contains the Russian word *vek*, meaning "age" or "century," and thereby interweaves the story of the Eurasian steppe with the story of time: "And the centuries preserved for it its name—Uvek" (*I veka sokhranili za nim svoe imia—Uvek*):

> Вершина Увека, в камнях, облысела, серебряной пыльной щетиной поросла полынь, пахнула горько.—Века.—Века учат так же, как звезды, и Баудек знал радость горечи. Понятия археолога Баудека спутались веками. (92/92)

> The summit of Uvek, all in stone, had grown bald; like silvery, dusty bristle, wormwood had grown upon it, and it smelled bitterly.—The centuries.—The centuries teach just as the stars do, and Baudek knew the joy of bitterness. The concepts of the archaeologist Baudek were mixed up with the centuries.

On display here are the many features typifying the so-called ornamental style, weaving into the description a verbal patterning that discloses the multiple levels of linguistic signification.[41] *Vek, veka, vekami, Uvek, Uveka*: Uvek is as much a remnant of a bygone

---

[41]   For more on ornamentalism, see Gary Browning, "Russian Ornamental Prose," *Slavic and East European Journal* 23, no. 3 (August 1979): 346-52; Patricia Carden, "Ornamentalism and Modernism," in *Russian Modernism: Culture and the Avant-Garde, 1900-1930*, ed. George Gibian and H. W. Tjalsma (Ithaca, NY: Cornell University Press, 1976), 49-64.

time as it is a toponym that sounds in Russian as though one were in spatialized time: *u veka*. The name contains the Russian spatial preposition *u* with the nominative form of the word *vek* (century, age). This paronomasia is Pil'niak's Eurasian version of a modernist interlingualism perhaps better known by such examples as Osip Mandelstam's *more i Gomer* and *toska v Toskane*,[42] where a Russian word is "anagramatically" linked to a foreign word or place (in the case of the first, the Russian words for "sea" and "Homer"; in the second "yearning" and "Tuscany").[43]

If Mandelstam's "creative etymologies" seek to overcome the distance between Russia and Italy (*toska v Toskane*) and between Russia and the antique past (*more i Gomer*), and to point toward the "Hellenistic soul" of Russian,[44] Pil'niak's etymology interweaves Russia and Asia, time and space. No wonder, then, that Baudek's thoughts are "mixed up with the centuries" (*sputalis' vekami*). Baudek's experience of Uvek reveals what Mary Nicholas has aptly described as a central predicament of Pil'niak's works generally, namely, "a modern search for a cohesive point of view," which also recognized that such a point of view was both "paramount and relative."[45] Baudek must locate himself not just in space, but also in time: Not just where, but when am I?

Critics and scholars, then as now, have observed and often complained about the stylistic elements epitomized by this passage. The editor of *Krasnaia nov'*, Aleksandr Voronskii, who published sections from *The Naked Year* in the journal, objected: "the reader has to overcome the pages and persistently connect [them] for himself."[46]

---

[42] These two lines are, respectively, from Mandel'shtam's "Bessonnitsa: Gomer; Tugie parusa" (1915), and "Ne sravnivai: Zhivushchii nesravnim" (1937), in *Sobranie sochinenii v dvukh tomakh* (Moscow: Khudozhestvennaia literatura, 1991), 1: 104-05, 232.

[43] Clare Cavanagh, *Osip Mandelstam and the Modernist Creation of Tradition* (Princeton, NJ: Princeton University Press, 1995), 25.

[44] Ibid.

[45] Mary A. Nicholas, "Boris Pil'niak and Modernism: Redefining the Self," *Slavic Review* 50, no. 2 (Summer 1991): 411.

[46] A. Voronskii, "Literaturnye siluety: B. Pil'niak," *Krasnaia nov'*, no. 4 (1922): 268.

One had to struggle with *The Naked Year*, with its structure variously referred to as "a patchwork counterpane," "a regular anti-
system," "a literary montage," "a mosaic," and "a Cubist collage."
Such terms have been invoked to explain and to give coherence to the
work's radical attenuation of plot; its multiple orders of discursive,
ethnographic, and archaeological material, from eighteenth-century
decrees to pagan incantations; and its reliance on a structure of
motifs that requires constantly juxtaposing different parts of the
work in order to reconstitute its overall verbal patterning.

The work has also been deemed something of an incoherent
mess. Victor Erlich remarks that *The Naked Year* proceeds with
a "montage-like accumulation of heterogeneous detail, often
resulting in a virtual orgy of enumeration and apparently designed
to mimic the bewildering multifariousness of the new reality." But,
he goes on to note, this "should not be mistaken for a pluralistic
vision or a genuine sense of complexity."[47] Montage, in this view,
cannot salvage its putative incoherence. Indeed, a related criticism
regards the novel's shortcomings as overextensions of the modernist styles championed in such works as Bely's *Petersburg* and
Blok's "The Twelve": hence, Pil'niak is dismissed as their maladroit,
slavish epigone.

By contrast, to invoke "montage" and "collage" as unifying
metaphors for the text is to point toward a necessary reorientation
of modernist textual dynamics. Robert Maguire, for example, argues
that "Pil'nyak works, as he describes it, through 'associations of
parallels and antitheses,' not through an unfolding of a story line
in time and space. We must therefore read him as we read so much
modern poetry—vertically, as it were, piecing together a picture
from scattered clues."[48] While "verticality" is metaphorical in
Maguire's account, it structures the description of Uvek, where time
acquires shape and substance: "and centuries were emerging from
the earth." Baudek's mode of apprehending the excavation scene

47 Victor Erlich, *Modernism and Revolution: Russian Literature in Transition* (Cambridge, MA: Harvard
University Press, 1994), 139.

48 Maguire, *Red Virgin Soil,* 117.

glosses the approach to the novel Maguire advocates, with various temporal layers disclosed by the archaeologists. So many temporal frameworks coalesce in and around the excavation sequence that a reader might feel somewhat like Baudek in trying to parse them. For all the possible difficulty this might involve, one reason to track these various frameworks is that they reveal the greater crisis of thinking through the Revolution and the question of history that haunts *The Naked Year*.

During the excavation, for example, Pil'niak describes archaeological practice in detail. He orchestrates various responses to the excavations, which reveal how the archaic and the modern are centrally opposed throughout the sequence:

> Here on Uvek, the diggers used to wake up at the crack of dawn, boil water in a billy can. They would dig. At noon, lunch was brought from the commune. They rested. They dug again until sunset. . . . Beyond the river in the village, they plowed, reaped, ate, drank, and slept, to live—just as they did below the ravine in the commune and in the steppe among the sectarians, where they also labored, ate, and slept. And also, besides this, they drank a bit and wanted to imbibe peace and joy. (92/93)

The various forms of labor in the passage seem all of a piece, as though archaeological labor and agricultural life belong to a kind of pastoral idyll. Both practices seem out of sync with their time, especially in the context of the Civil War, since the narrative goes on to note how reports of military violence occasionally puncture the idyll, and the commune, we learn later, dies.

As Pil'niak proceeds to describe the excavation, other temporal signatures crop up that remind us that archaeology, too, is a practice of modernity, involving its own forms of disrupting the archaic past:

> Some were digging into the earth, the dry loam, which was mixed with flints and thunderstones; others carted it off in wheelbarrows, and sifted it through sieves. . . . They dug down to a stone entrance. The vault was dark and smelled of nothing. The tomb stood upon a platform. They lit lanterns. Sketched. They lit the place up with magnesium and photographed. It was

quiet and mute. They took down the covering, which weighed
ten poods and had turned green. Others at the precipice on a high
point were digging up the remains of a kind of circular structure,
the stones of which time had not yet bestrewn. (93/94)

We know from Ballod's descriptions of the excavations that Pil'niak
is being quite accurate here about the process of the excavation
(fig. 6.2) and the kinds of objects collected and studied in the
Volga "Pompeiis." Beyond mimetic accuracy, however, Pil'niak's
sense of archaeology in these lines registers the practice as the
encroachment of modernity into the space of the archaic.[49] The
very process of excavation and the media involved in documenting
the site—from the lighting of the magnesium to the sketching and
photographing—not only intrude into the kurgan and other sites,
but also usurp the function of the kurgan—which is, after all, to
preserve the objects within it. In effect, these objects will now be
preserved not in the kurgan, but rather in a new form, in a new
medium, the photograph or the sketch, made in situ before the
objects are ultimately dispersed, bestrewn not by time but by the
archaeologists themselves.

The cumulative effect of these details is to blur the line between
archaeological excavation and desecration. Pil'niak observes this
split of views on archaeology when the wizard Egorka arrives at the
excavation to admonish the archaeologists: "You have no business
digging up these places. Because this place, Uvek, is mysterious,
and it always smells of wormwood" (104/104). Uvek, in other
words, is not an archaeological site for Egorka—a space that can be
diagrammed (fig. 6.3), its contents catalogued and reconfigured in
a museum (practices such as we saw in chapter two [figs. 6.4 and
6.5]). Uvek, for Egorka, is a space of worship.

Such differing views on the excavations roughly map onto the
opposition drawn throughout the novel between secularization

49   On archaeology and modernity, see Julian Thomas, "Archaeology's Place in Modernity,"
      Modernism/modernity 11, no. 1 (2004): 17-34. See esp. 17-19, where Thomas differentiates
      between "addressing the archaeological" and "practicing archaeology" as a way to distinguish
      between various manifestations of excavation or collection throughout history.

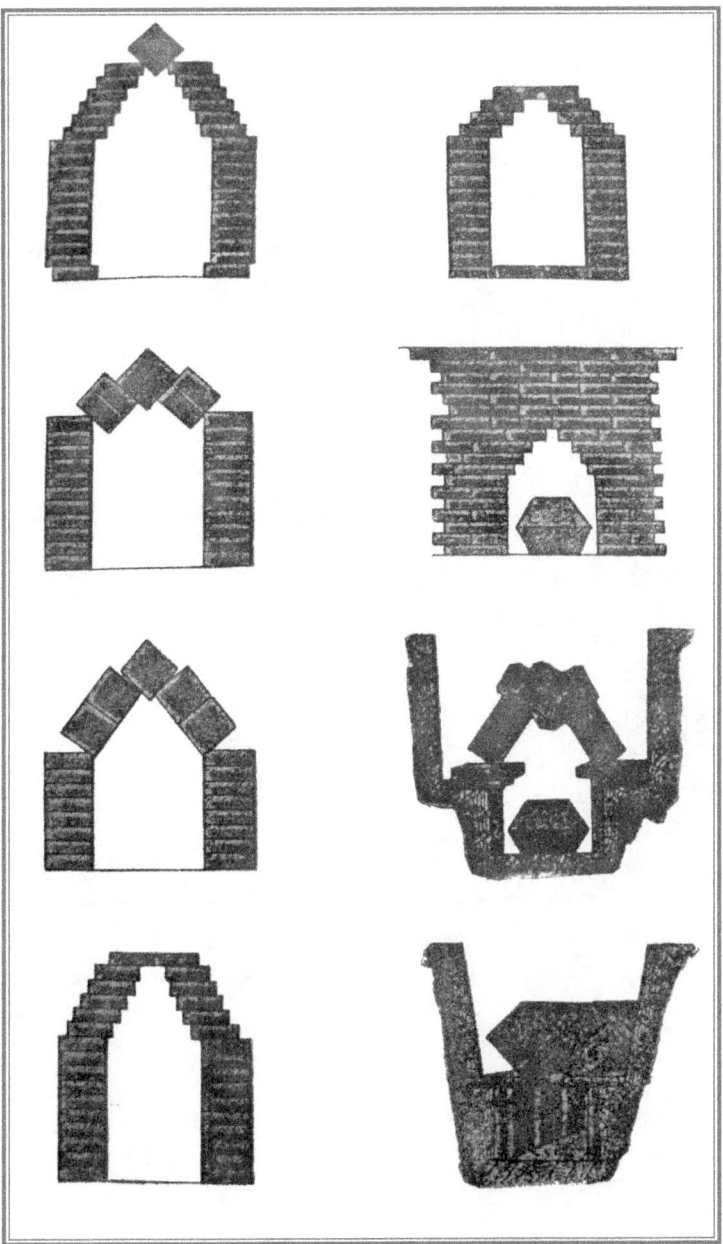

Figure 6.2.
Types of crypts found at Uvek.
Diagram in Ballod's *Volga "Pompeiis"* (1923).

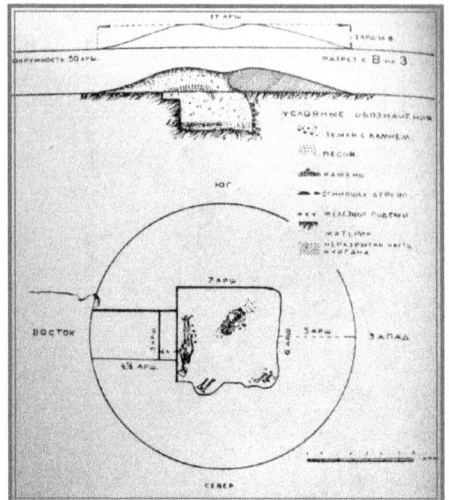

Figure 6.3.

Diagram of the kurgan at Ternovka, a site near Uvek, in Ballod's *Volga "Pompeiis"* (1923).

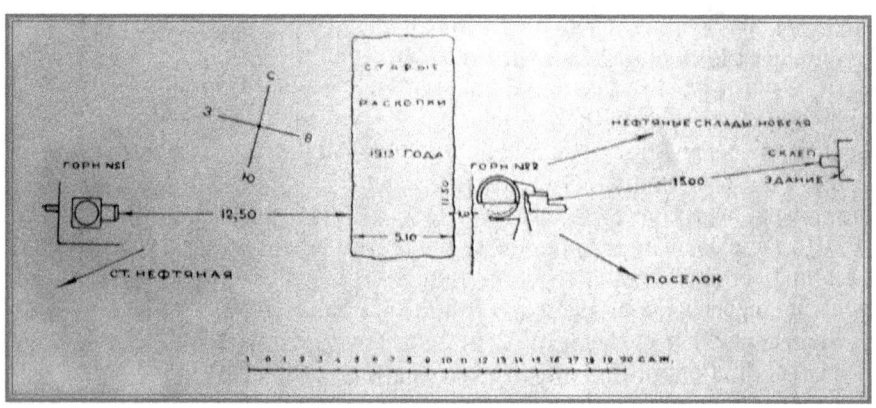

Figure 6.4.

Diagram of the Uvek excavations in Ballod's *Volga "Pompeiis"* (1923).

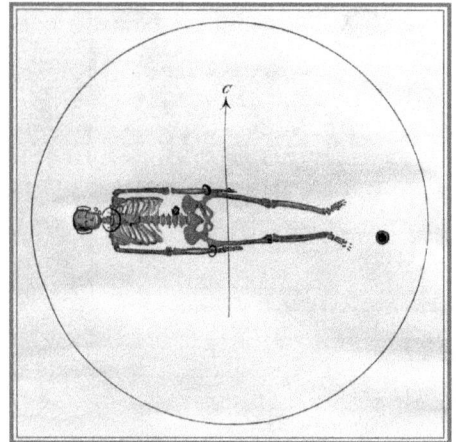

Figure 6.5.

"Kurgan 23." Diagram of an interior of a typical kurgan with a women's bones from the Uglichskii Uezd' (1862).

and sectarianism, and between different conceptions of time. These oppositions find one of their most explicit articulations during the excavation sequence, when Baudek and Natal'ia observe a pagan ritual in which a group of naked women appear and circumambulate the excavation site:

> They stopped to say goodbye and noticed: from the gully toward the excavations, from the other side, from Nikola [the church], naked women were running, in single file, with broad, unhurried gait, with disheveled hair, with the dark hollows of their pubic regions, with brooms of feather grass in their hands. The women ran silently to the excavations, ran around the circular ruin on the high point and turned to the ravine, the gully, raising wormwood dust. (93/94-95)

According to Egorka, the women worship the kurgans because of a folk belief that a Persian princess had been locked away in a tower that once stood there: "the girls at times jump naked for the Persian beauty, at night, at the solstice, in this season, but that is not known" (104/105). Like Egorka, the women signal the inter-connection between the Russian folk and archaeological sites, or rather, archaic sites for worship, since the kurgan is not archaeological for the women. For Baudek, the women represent temporal endurance and an object of desire. He trades the geological depth of the excavation scene for a physiological one: the "hollows of their pubic regions"; the libidinal charge seems to compensate for the weeks spent in the excavation, with the latter's excess of morbidity now suddenly met by a surfeit of vigor and of erotic and anarchic drives that well up at any given moment (which we will see Pil'niak continue to explore in chapter seven). From Trotsky's perspective, however, this seeming shift from death to life might be thought to valorize a false, pagan vitality, belonging to "the dead weight of history," just as much as Uvek does and the "sorcerer's incantations" do.

Pil'niak seems keenly sensitive here to the various ways that archaic sites can be perceived. As the art historian David Summers has remarked about burial mounds generally: "A mound demands acknowledgement, simple passage around, circumambulation, behaviours perhaps as ancient and widespread as burial mounds themselves."[50] The various practices around the kurgan—from the ritual to the excavation—reveal that the scene could also be perceived as a clash between the religious and the secular. Indeed, on viewing the scene of the women, Baudek makes a proclamation that reveals how these women directly challenge the ideology of modernization:

> Somewhere, there is Europe, Marx, scientific socialism, but here a superstition has been preserved that's a thousand years old. The girls run about their land, they cast spells with their bodies and their purity. This is the week of the Peter Solstice [*Petra solntsevorota*: another name for Peter the Athenite and the Solstice with which he is associated; MK]. Who will invent the Peter Solstice? This is more beautiful than excavations! Now, it is midnight. Perhaps they are the ones casting spells on us. This is the girls' secret. (94/95)

Pil'niak seemed to have realized he could extract more from this scene than he had initially planned. In the earlier version, from "Wormwood," the lines were: "Fifteen versts from here is a regional port city, but here a thousand-year-old superstition has been preserved."[51] While this earlier juxtaposition derives its force from the proximity of modernization—just fifteen versts, and one is plunged into the archaic—the later version in *The Naked Year* emerges as central to the novel's linking of modernization to a philosophy of history and its delineation of the various challenges posed to that philosophy.

"Somewhere, there is Europe, Marx, scientific socialism": the line announces the distinction between premodern and modern times as a central opposition in the work. One way to consider how the novel represents these various temporalities is to view Baudek's proclamation—"Somewhere there is Europe"—in terms of what Benedict Anderson would call a "transverse, longitudinal comparison." Such comparisons typify

---

50   Summers, *Real Spaces*, 186.

51   Pil'niak, "Polyn'," 39.

modern concepts of simultaneity that Anderson locates at the very root of an "imagined community."[52] With Baudek, the comparison juxtaposes simultaneous events not directly connected to one another (as, for example, one might find in a newspaper), but also simultaneously coexisting temporalities: scientific Marxism and the pagan rite, the clock and calendar of modernity and the ritual time of the premodern.

What Pil'niak discerns in Russia challenges various accounts we have of modernity as temporal homogeneity. In this regard, *The Naked Year* lends an added nuance to the conception of modern time we find in Anderson and the scholars upon whom he draws, since they link modernity to what they call a "simultaneity-in-time." This conception of simultaneity involves a "homogenous, empty time, in which simultaneity is, as it were, transverse, cross-time, marked not by prefiguring and fulfillment, but by temporal coincidence, and measured by clock and calendar."[53] The "clock and calendar" in this account finds an analogy in Baudek's sense of "scientific Marxism" and the temporal and historico-philosophical values associated with it.

Such forms of a modern temporality are opposed to those connected to the premodern, which features a different form of the simultaneous that Anderson, following Erich Auerbach, refers to as a "simultaneity-along-time." This conception of time relies on Auerbach's concept of *figura*, for which the sacrifice of Isaac is a classic example: the sacrifice of Isaac "prefigur[es] Christ, so that in the former the latter is as it were announced and promised and the latter 'fulfills' . . . the former": hence "a connection is established between two events which are linked neither temporally nor causally," but rather, "vertically linked to Divine Providence, which alone is able to devise such a plan of history and supply

---

52 Benedict Anderson, *Imagined Communities: Reflections on the Origin and Spread of Nationalism*, rev. ed. (London: Verso, 1991), 37.

53 Ibid., 24. The phrase "homogenous, empty time" is Walter Benjamin's ("Theses on the Philosophy of History," in *Illuminations: Essays and Reflections*, ed. Hannah Arendt, trans. Harry Zohn [New York: Schocken, 1978], 263).

the key to its understanding."[54] In contrast with these concepts of prefiguration, fulfillment, and verticality, Anderson argues that modernity witnesses a new kind of "simultaneity," the perfect expression of which is the word "meanwhile," which juxtaposes two simultaneously occurring events, not necessarily related to one another, but conceptually apprehensible together. "Every essential modern conception," Anderson argues, "is based upon this concept of time."[55]

The excavation and the pagan ritual gather their force from this concept of "meanwhile," but it is used to generate a different sense of time. While "meanwhile" underpins Baudek's exclamation, it serves to indicate that the real discovery here is not the homogenization of time-space into what Trotsky might call a single "historical plane," but, rather, the persistent heterogeneity of modern time. Indeed, to borrow from Bakhtinian terminology, Baudek inhabits a kind of *chronotope* of *chronotopes*, where he, as a subject of modernity, is aware of the multiple temporal models by which others organize their relationship to the world.

The transverse comparisons Pil'niak draws only continue as the events of the Civil War start to impinge upon the excavation scene. For example, another character arrives to report to Natal'ia on the events of the Civil War occurring somewhere beyond Uvek: "The woods and ravines are swarming with bandits. You can hear it— a deathly silence! Death. In the steppes there are villages, which have died out completely. Nobody buries the corpses. . . . The Russian nation!" (95/96). This comparison juxtaposes the excavation scene with the story of Civil War violence. It is a gruesome image. And things get worse; as the narrator later recounts, "The Reds and the Whites had been in the village of Staryi Kurdyum several times each; whole side streets lie burnt and plundered" (153/151). Essentially the juxtaposition points to the significance of not burying the dead,

---

54   Ibid., citing Erich Auerbach, *Mimesis*, trans. Willard R. Trask (Princeton, NJ: Princeton University Press, 1953), 73-74.

55   Ibid., 24, n. 34. Anderson refines this point in later pages of *Imagined Communities*, when he links temporal homogenization to print culture, which made possible "wholly new ideas of simultaneity" (37).

just when the excavation scene is revealing how archaic peoples had buried their own. These villages are, in effect, becoming Uveks, necropolises, but without the archaic depth, and without the burial rites signified by the kurgan. The "Russian nation" has become an open grave.

Pil'niak, to be sure, was not the only writer to use the archaic as a device to indicate past precedent. In this study, for example, we encounter at least three others—Leo Tolstoy, Isaac Babel, and Velimir Khlebnikov—all of whom see the site of a kurgan as presaging violence and death in the present. In Pil'niak, too, these formal features buttress this sense of archaic precedent being recapitulated during the Civil War; the transverse comparison of the excavations at Uvek with other sites of warfare are structured along a horizontal plane, stretching outward across the steppe. But the syntagms are actually paradigms, telling us how Uvek, the dead city, prefigures the fate of all those other now-dead villages.

Seeing all the destruction before her, the character Natal'ia perceives these Revolutionary events as a fairy tale: "The people are creating fairy tales, the people are creating the Revolution, and the Revolution has begun as a fairy tale. Isn't hunger like a fairy tale, isn't death? Aren't cities dying as they would in fairy tales, departing for the seventeenth century? Look around—it's all a fairy tale. It smells like wormwood because it's a fairy tale" (98/99). The smell of wormwood sparks a memory in Natal'ia (Pil'niak's version of the modernist interest in the mnemotechnics of smell): "In April, when they were chasing the Whites, at a small, steppe station, where there were sky, steppe, five poplar trees, rails, and a station hut, she noticed three people—two peasants and a child" (96/97). The three are pitiable; they also embody for Natal'ia a vision of the "Russian people" that has not created anything, and prompts her to ask: "A people without a history—for where is the history of the Russian people—a people who have created their own songs, their own tunes, their own fairy tales?" (96/97-98). The question is a fraught one for many of the characters in *The Naked Year*, who find in the Revolutionary moment the possibility that both Russia's history and future can be discerned. What is also notable about Natal'ia's question is the setting in which she poses it: "the very station, where she met [the peasants] for the first time, was called 'Loop Station Mar'" (97/98). The station is the quintessential emblem and site for the struggle over locating Russia's own history within this configuration of an archaic, Asiatic past, on the one hand, and a modernizing, Western future on the other.

iv. Modernist Topography: "Loop Station Mar" and the Poetics of Adjacency

According to V. I. Dal', *mar* was used primarily in the Southeast, and, along with *kurgan*, it was also synonymous with words such as *bugor*, *nasyp'*, and *prirodnaia sopka*.[56] The linguist Max Vasmer indicates that *mar* was used by the Mordva, a Finno-Ugric people, to whom Pil'niak refers at various points in the work. In fact, he cycles through these various terms when he describes an interaction between the duty man and the burial mound, which will be the primary focus of this section:

> "Loop Station Mar," at which trains never stop and where they don't change the signaling rod, disappears at once in the darkness. All around is emptiness and steppe. The duty man walks past the *mar*: the steppe kurgan is deathly and silent,—who, when, which nomads raised it here, and what does it protect?—the withered feather grass rustles at the kurgan. (144/143)

In this passage, Pil'niak first highlights *mar* as the local toponym, then provides a translation of the term (*kurgan*): "the duty man walks past the *mar*: the steppe kurgan is deathly and silent." He then links it back to the theme of nomadic archaeology, when the duty man ponders who might have built it.

With the "Loop Station Mar," Pil'niak could have again drawn his emblems from the local topography. We know from Ballod that *mar* (plural: *mary*) was a synonym of *kurgan*. He describes various *mary* in his *Volga "Pompeiis"*, including "The White Mound" ("Belyi mar"), which locals called "Van'ka Kain," and the "Stone

---

[56]   V. I. Dal', *Tolkovyi slovar' zhivogo velikorusskogo iazyka*, s.v. "mar."

Mound" ("Kamennyi mar"), which was also known as "Grishka Rasstrizhka."[57] The very topography of the region, too, may have provided him with the idea of the archaic artifacts being directly linked to modernization. Pil'niak may have noticed, when he arrived at Uvek, how the train tracks partially encircled the ancient site (the layout can be seen in fig. 6.1 in the lower portion of the diagram from Ballod). Farther afield, he might also have known of a certain Seven-Headed Mound-Loop Station (*Semiglavyi Mar-Raz''ezd*), located between Saratov and Ural'sk, in Kazakhstan.

Beyond attesting to Pil'niak's topographical accuracy, the station extends the novel's archaeological theme, but reorients the theme's axis of articulation. Pil'niak focuses here upon archaeology as it is distributed horizontally across space, much as we saw at the outset of the chapter with Ballod's description of the steppe landscape. Thus, the station marks a shift from the stratigraphic (vertical) to the topographic (horizontal), and from a poetics of depth—perhaps the primary signifying mode of archaeology— toward a poetics of adjacency.[58] Where the excavation sequence had posited a divide between modernization and the pagan ritual, the archaic and the modern are now parallel signs. The former testifies to the archaic movement of peoples and the latter to movement tied to industrialization. The station thereby asks us to consider a quintessential symbol of industrial modernity now affixed to the traces of the nomadic past, and how this link between the modern

---

[57] Ballod, *Privolzhskie*, 112.

[58] This shift toward the topographic would later acquire significant force in the history of archaeology, and in its reception by scholars of modernism. It was this shift, for example, that Annette Michelson marked as the salutary feature of the archaeological work of the great French prehistorian André Leroi-Gourhan, who moved from the stratigraphic toward the planographic (what I refer to as the topographic): "We recognize, then, in Leroi-Gourhan's digging technique, the exact and concrete grounding of theory in praxis, for the rotation of the digging axis, the replacement of the stratigraphic by the planographic, rehearses for us that privileging of synchronic over diachronic in relational analysis of cultural texts which characterizes the structuralist enterprise. And indeed, the sense of rigor and illumination generated by these readings mark them as significant documents of the era which saw the adoption of the linguistic model as central to that analysis" (Annette Michelson, "In Praise of Horizontality: André Leroi-Gourhan, 1911–1986," *October* 37 [Summer 1986], 4-5).

and the archaic forms a symbol for Pil'niak to think through the upheaval of the Revolution and the history of Russia.

Pil'niak clearly wanted his readers to ponder the significance of the station. Like Uvek and the novel's other recurrent sites such as China-Town (*Kitai-Gorod*), Ordynin-Town, and the dead town of Porech'e, the station punctuates the text, serving as the backdrop for various events in the novel and the site in which Pil'niak coordinates several themes. Along with providing the setting for Natal'ia to contemplate the prospects of Russian history, it appears again as a central site in chapter five, entitled "Deaths," and composed of three sections: "The Death of the Commune," "The First Dying," and "The Third Part of the Triptych (The Darkest)." In this last section, Pil'niak amplifies the significance of the station by correlating it with one of the novel's most famous sequences: the horrific journey of "Mixed Train no. 57," as it winds its way through the steppe bearing a load of wretched passengers.

The train ride registers all the privations suffered by the displaced populations of the provinces as they flee from the encroaching armies on both sides of the Civil War: "Mixed Train no. 57 crawls along the black steppe. People, human feet, arms, heads, stomachs, spines, a human cargo" (145/144). Pil'niak's fragmentary style is at its most effective throughout the passage. As Gary Browning has observed of the sequence, "one finds the most intensive negation of humanity—of man's capability to govern himself, to provide for basic physical needs, and to establish a climate for proper love and children."[59] We find throughout the sequence a brutal kaleidoscope of human figures fractured and dismembered within Pil'niak's stylistic abattoir, or the complete disintegration of the human subject. The narrator focuses on an unnamed person (who he will later suggest is either the character Andrei or Gleb) "burning with the last flush of consumption." The man experiences "thoughts about stoicism and honor, his small room, his pamphlets and books, hunger—all this has flown to the Devil. After many sleepless nights,

[59]   Browning, *Boris Pilniak*, 121.

the thoughts, like a man's with a fever, were differentiated, and the man felt his 'I' breaking into two, into three" (146/146).

The image of the train journey radicalizes a view on moderniza-tion conveyed earlier on in the novel, during the extended dialogue that lays out many of the philosophical questions posed throughout *The Naked Year*. Where the character Gleb Ordynin found the prevailing mechanization of the West to destroy the realm of the spirit, the East fares no better: "How was our great Russian state founded?" Archbishop Sylvester says, "the beginnings of our history lie in the destruction of Kievan Rus'—hiding from the Pechenegs, the Tatars, from the princes' out-and in-fighting in the woods with the Vyess and the Finns (*Chud'*)" (73/75). This debate bears upon the symbol of the station by indicating to us that one way to consider its symbolic import is to see how the Russian people are perpetually forced into movement, whether escaping from nomads, whose archaic signs are still present in the landscape, or being conveyed to an unknown future by the train of modernity. The "Loop Station Mar," in this sense, forms a perfect, if grim, emblem for the various oppositions within the work, inasmuch as it contains the modern, which is associated with trains and the West, and the archaic, associated here with the *mar* and the East.

What makes the various symbolic associations ascribed to the station difficult to ascertain is that it also serves as a backdrop for the characters Andrei and Gleb, the latter of whom accompanied Baudek to the excavation. There, they consider the nature of the self, of time, and of the Revolution. Pil'niak, however, makes their relationship to the station all the more difficult to parse, because the narrator breaks into the narrative to ask whether the duty man who we saw above pondering the kurgan, could be either one, or both of these characters:

> Now then. One question—in Dostoevskian fashion—a *little question*:—that station agent from "Loop Station Mar"—was he not Andrei Volkovich or Gleb Ordynin?—Put another way:— Gleb Ordynin and Andrei Volkovich—were they not that man, who was burning with the last flush of consumption?—such as our Russian Ivanushka the Fools, Ivanushka the Tsareviches? (157/154-55)

The instabilities that we have previously seen in the narrative now intrude at the level of the characters. This creates an additional interpretive challenge, requiring—as we saw Maguire observe above—the piecing together of the narrative lines of both Andrei and Gleb in an effort to understand not only their respective fates in the novel, but how the values they are associated with now coalesce around the station.

Just as Natal'ia was inspired to ask where Russian history was located against the backdrop of the station, so, too, do Andrei and Gleb consider the fate of their ideas there. The station is a space where one experiences both fear and malice: "The duty man walks along the platform from end to end, looks into the dark steppe and thinks maliciously:—Asia!" (144/147). Where the duty man now looks into a steppe full of malice, it was supposed to be a space of freedom, as both characters imagined: Andrei, the former noble turned anarchist; and Gleb, who with Baudek, wanted to pursue the sectarians. Indeed, both characters' respective dreams for freedom now seem to stall at the station: "the dreams of the young duty man are coming true. At 'Loop Station Mar' a barrage detail is stationed, internal customs. Now the trains stop here for days and nights. And day and night the campfires burn and around the station are crowds of people . . . It's impossible to walk two paces without stepping in human excrement. . . . And already long since the dark abyss, the red lights of the campfires have been blazing at the 'Loop Station Mar'—frightening, like a feverish image" (155/152).

In an essay on Pil'niak from 1925, Viktor Shklovsky revealed that he was not inclined to interpret the significance of the station, but, rather, pointed to the compositional problems it epitomized. In fact, he singled out the loop station and the aforementioned passage, as typifying the problems of the novel: the challenge to the "unity of a hero," and the series of motifs linking the work.[60] Shklovsky

---

[60] Viktor Shklovskii, "O Pil'niake," *Lef* 3, no. 7 (1925): 130. For an account of why Shklovskii's formal investments could not accommodate Pil'niak's own, see Mary A. Nicholas, "Formalist Theory Revisited: "On Sklovskij 'On Pilnjak,'" *Slavic and East European Journal* 36, no. 1 (Spring 1992): 68-83.

included the station in a list of examples of what he called the "device of repetition" (*priem povtoreniia*), which Pil'niak deployed in order to integrate the work. One reason Pil'niak needed those links, in Shklovsky's view, was to compensate for another principle by which the work was formed—and ultimately deformed: its combinatory principle, or *sbornost'*. Pieces of the works, fragments, and stories could be arranged and rearranged, cobbled together in any which way: "A novel by Pil'niak is the cohabitation of several novellas. It's possible to take apart (*razobrat'*) two novels and glue them into a third."[61] It was the cutting and pasting of modernist collage. One problem with such a technique, as Shklovsky saw it, was that the devices for linking the work were not sufficiently elaborated. Indeed, having compiled his list of repetitions, for example, Shklovsky warned his readers not to misconstrue the import of the list: "I have been constantly underscoring connections in the novel," he wrote, "and perhaps someone might therefore be under the impression that the novel is coherent [*sviazan*]. This is not the case."[62]

There was another difficulty Shklovsky observed. In attempting to unify these various parts, Pil'niak, in Shklovsky's view, revealed a distinct tendency to "pile on" (*nagromozhdat'*) material. Symbols and sites in the novel become so laden with meaning as to verge on meaninglessness. Pil'niak, for example, adds to his description of the station another detail central to understanding its significance in the lines almost right before the narrator's intrusion in the passage cited above. He notes:

> Behind the loop station in the steppe lies the kurgan after which the loop station is named. Once a man had been killed near the *mar*, and on the gravestone somebody etched out in clumsy letters:
> "I was what you are—
> But you will be what I am."

---

61 Shklovskii, "O Pil'niake," 127.

62 Ibid.

> The boundless steppe, the kurgan, are all buried under snow,
> and of the inscription on the gravestone only two words remain.
> "I was." (156-57/154)

If Uvek was a complex site of multiple nomadic pasts, this image suggests that the station is a hyperbolized memento mori: it is a steppe grave, affixed to the modernity of the train station, and to another grave that bears an inscription that expresses a consciousness at once retrospective and prospective. In the original form of the epitaph, it entraps its addressee into an awareness of endless repetition and the inexorability of death. But the latter part of the epitaph is now obscured by snow, which suggests the possibility of an open future. One question this begs is whether Pil'niak can imagine a way out of the closed circle of life and death he signals here? Perhaps the snow—which is the metaphor of the elemental forces associated with the Revolution, and which blankets the steppe, the kurgan, and the epitaph—is meant to suggest some new field upon which things can be inscribed all over again, another tabula rasa.

The problem, for Pil'niak, is that he can never quite seem to believe that one can start over. Indeed, *The Naked Year* concludes with a snowstorm, just as Blok's "The Twelve" does, but where the latter relies on an eschatological vision for renewal, Pil'niak ends with the mythological recapitulation of Ilya Muromets, a primary figure of the Russian tradition of the *bylina*:

> The forest stands stern like a stockade and the snowstorm hurls itself against it like the furies. Night. Is the saga-legend about how the knights died not about the forest and the snowstorm?— More and more snowstorm furies hurl themselves against the forest stockade, howling, yelling, shouting, roaring like wrathful women, dead animals fall, and after them the furies rush, they never decrease,—they increase like the snake's heads—two for each one cut off, and the forest stands like Ilya Muromets. (186/180)

Another myth emerges in these concluding lines, another possible antiquity. Pil'niak cannot work himself out of the structuring oppositions of his novel in order to find a convincing answer to the question Natal'ia asks: "Where is the history of the Russian people?" What he wanted, just like his modernist forerunners with their apocalyptic visions, was a way out of time and out of space that could transcend and overcome divisions, and start the world anew. What he kept on offering, through such figures as Uvek and the "Loop Station Mar," was the idea that the tabula rasa was itself a myth, and that the past could not be buried entirely, but often remained in overbearing proximity to the present. To be at the "Loop Station Mar" is to be bounded within the two paradigms that have structured Russian cultural history for so long—the East and the West, the archaic and the modern—two crushing paradigms between which Russia is left with little room to maneuver.

We might invoke here one particularly powerful counter-vision to what Pil'niak offers. When the fifth volume of the monumental *History of Russian Art*, edited by Igor Grabar', appeared in 1910, the author of the volume, Nikolai Vrangel', opened it with the following claim for both the Scythians and the kurgans:

> For two and a half thousand years, the Scythians, the Korsun masters, the Germans, Italians, Dutch, and French, all vying with each other, brought their treasures to the history of Russian culture, and the reflections of their creations have come to us from ancient to modern times. The kurgans of southern Russia, the Crimea, Georgia, Novgorod, Kiev, Rostov, Vladimir, and Moscow preserve the monuments of the beauty of the past. In the end, the mixture of various cultures gave rise to a new worldview, a new beauty. Artistic traditions were inherited from the Greek colonies from the banks of the Black Sea to Kiev, from Persia to eastern Russia, from the depths of Central Asia to Siberia and to the banks of the Danube.[63]

This is a vision of Russian art and culture as a historical admixture from which a "new worldview, a new beauty," can emerge. The vision unifies the vast temporal and spatial extensions of Russia's geography into an aesthetic and, indeed, a broader history no

---

[63]   Nikolai Vrangel', *Istoriia russkogo iskusstva*, ed. I. A. Grabar', vol. 5 (Moscow: I. Knebel', 1910), 5.

longer characterized by rupture and realignment, but by continuity and mutual contribution. It is a remarkable vision, conciliatory and syncretic. Pil'niak recognized this variety in *The Naked Year*, but could not reconcile them into a unified vision, a greater emblem. Whether this was due to his angle of vision or the aesthetic structure of the work is difficult to say. There was Ilya Muromets on the one hand, the Scythians on the other. There were Bolsheviks and wizards. There were too many parts, too many details pulling the work not just centrifugally into different spaces, but also into a range of irreconcilable times.

Chapter Seven

AREAS OF DEFORMATION

Part One: DZIGA VERTOV AND THE SCYTHIAN

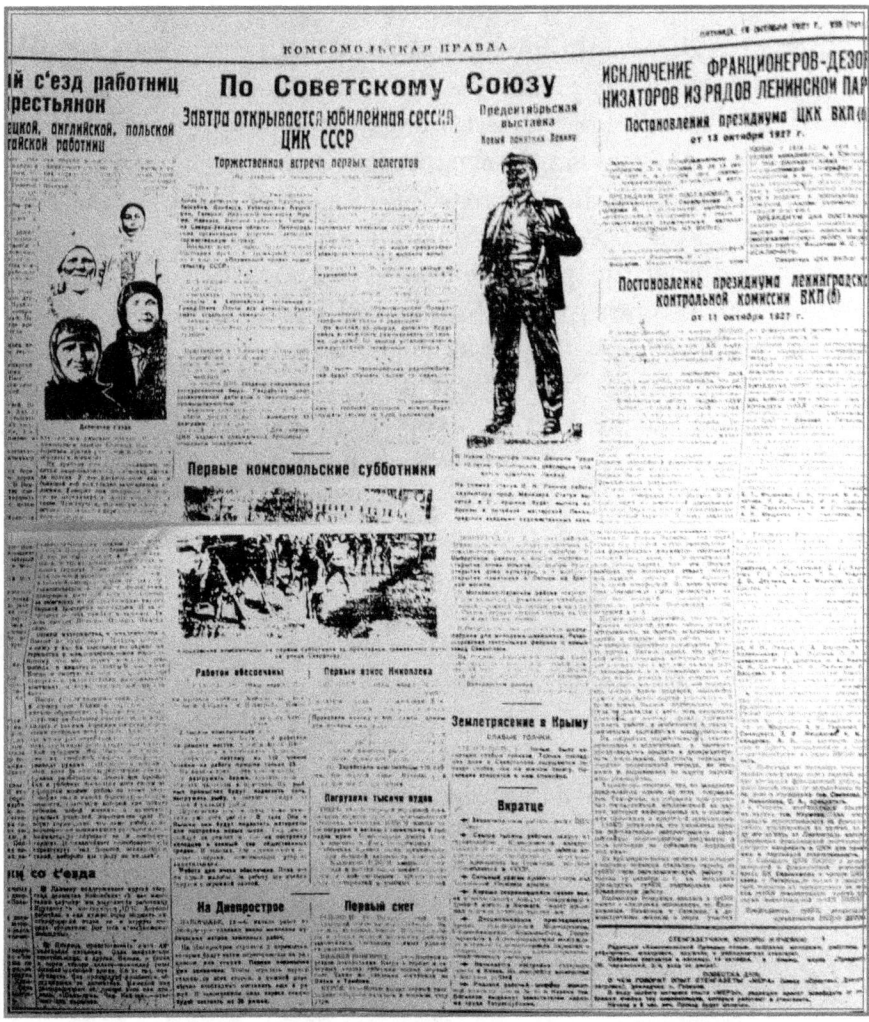

Figure 7.1.
Komsomol'skaia pravda, October 14 1927.

On October 14, 1927, a short article appeared in the newspaper *Komsomol'skaia pravda*, reporting on an archaeological discovery in Kichkas, Ukraine, a small town situated on the banks of the Dnieper river, which flows into the Black Sea (fig. 7.1):

> The well-preserved skeleton of a warrior and part of the skeleton of a horse were uncovered in an ancient grave in Kichkas. The skeleton was interred fifteen hundred years ago.[1]

Readers that day might have missed the article, a mere four lines long and tucked away into the "In Brief" section. Perhaps they would have found it of modest interest, equal in importance to the other reports of events in the section: workers arriving at an electric station, a hurricane, the construction of a sugar plant, disciplinary action against the director of a milk factory. Or perhaps they would have passed over the section entirely, and focused instead on the stories more prominently featured on the page: an earthquake in the Crimea or the unveiling of a new Lenin memorial in front of the Palace of Labor in the New Peterhof, the former palace of the tsars, on the occasion of the tenth anniversary of the October Revolution.

Someone who did not miss the article on the excavation that day was Dziga Vertov. Always keen on the kinds of spatio-temporal juxtapositions that seem to appear serendipitously on a newspaper page, Vertov, in fact, cut out the article from the newspaper and placed it in his journal, also recording in that entry his plan to visit the excavation while working on a new film.[2] Vertov and Mikhail Kaufman, Vertov's brother and cinematographer, were near the excavation because they were at work on a film on the construction of the Dnieper Hydroelectric Station, or Dneprostroi. As *Komsomol'skaia pravda* reported the same day, in an article just a few columns over, construction had begun a year earlier, not far from where the skeleton had been unearthed in Kichkas.

1   "Vkratse," *Komsomol'skaia pravda*, October 14, 1927, no. 235, 721.

2   RGALI, f. 2091, op. 2, d. 237. I want to express my enormous debt and gratitude to John MacKay for sharing with me his research on this part of Vertov's archive and journal.

Dneprostroi typified the visionary hydraulics of the era, ranking among the most celebrated of the *novostroiki*, or new construction sites, of the Five-Year Plans. Along with dams, these constructions included canal systems to link seas and rivers, irrigation systems to transform deserts into arable lands, and projects to reverse the course of rivers. The primary aim of these massive constructions was to establish the infrastructure of the future, yet also serving as laboratories in which the decade-old country tested, often at tremendous human cost, its models of citizenship, subjectivity, and modes of living—in short, where it put into practice its new civilizational ideals.[3]

Dneprostroi would harness the Dnieper for a hydroelectric dam, which, in keeping with the period's gigantomania, would be the world's largest, while also fulfilling Lenin's famous equation: "Communism is Soviet power plus the electrification of the whole country." It was under this slogan that the country was plunged into a second revolution, this time with the first Five-Year Plan, begun in 1928. Engineers, architects, writers, filmmakers, and other members of the cultural front gravitated to these sites to participate in designing and propagandizing for the socialist future. In this, the Dneprostroi differed from other *novostroiki* only in degree of interest, but not in kind. The writer Fedor Gladkov called it "one of the most cultured constructions of our state,"[4] and modelled the plot of his novel *Energy* (*Energiia*, 1932-38) on it; the architect Viktor Vesnin designed the dam; Boris Pil'niak also used the Dneprostroi as a model for his production novel *The Volga Falls to the Caspian Sea* (*Volga vpadaet v Kaspiiskoe more*, 1930), the subject of the second part of the present chapter; and filmmakers shot "hundreds" of films about the Dneprostroi.[5]

---

3   See, for example, Stephen Kotkin, *Magnetic Mountain: Stalinism as a Civilization* (Berkeley and Los Angeles: University of California Press, 1995).

4   Fedor Gladkov, "O rabote nad 'Energiei' (V poriadke samokritiki)," in *Sobranie sochinenii v vos'mi tomakh* (Moscow: Khudozhestvennaia literatura, 1958-59), 4:497.

5   For more on the construction, see Anne D. Rassweiler, *The Generation of Power: The History of the Dneprostroi* (New York: Oxford University Press, 1988), 3-4.

Vertov did more than just visit the excavation during his time at the Dneprostroi. He included an extended sequence on the archaeological site in a film he had hoped to contribute to the slate of films celebrating the tenth anniversary of the October Revolution. The so-called "anniversary year" of 1927 saw the release of Sergei Eisenstein's *October* (*Oktiabr'*), Vsevolod Pudovkin's *The End of St. Petersburg* (*Konets Peterburga*), and Esfir Shub's *The Fall of the Romanov Dynasty* (*Padenie dinastii Romanovykh*).[6] But Vertov's film was delayed, and when it finally appeared on screen in 1928, he had turned vice into virtue and entitled the film *The Eleventh Year* (*Odinnadtsatyi*, 1928) to mark the inaugural year of the country's second decade of existence.[7]

Dneprostroi provided Vertov with a site in which the past, present, and future entered into stark proximity. For someone so deeply invested in juxtaposing time and space, Vertov's aesthetic predilections had, in a sense, found an ideal situation wherein archaeology, industrial modernization, and avant-garde cinema could all be thought of together. Even as the film points toward the future, it negotiates with the persisting past, indeed, with the deep past. The first fifteen minutes of the roughly fifty total minutes of the film (the primary subject of the pages to come) present us with a past under excavation and a future under construction. This combination is a preeminently Vertovian concern, and comprises one of the two concluding episodes for this book's story of archaeology and modernist aesthetics, when archaeology comes directly into contact with industrialization.

This conjunction presents an occasion in which modernist aesthetics, here through the medium of avant-garde cinema, elaborates various models for grappling with the persistence of the archaeological past, and indeed, of archaeology itself as

---

6 For more on the tenth anniversary of the Revolution, see Jay Leyda's standard account, "The Anniversary Year," in *Kino: A History of Russian and Soviet Film* (Princeton, NJ: Princeton University Press, 1983), 222-44.

7 Dziga Vertov, *The Eleventh Year* (*Odinnadtsatyi*) (VUFKU, Kiev, USSR, 1928). I have consulted various versions of the film, but the most readily available is the edition prepared by the Österreichisches Filmmuseum, Wien (DVD, 2010).

a practice. In this regard, Vertov's silent film reconfigures the elemental importance of indigenous antiquity examined in the previous chapters. These archaeological artifacts no longer needed to be recuperated—at this point, they could hardly be avoided—and it was the ambiguous power now ascribed to them with which the film grapples, and, as we will see, a power for which Vertov was himself responsible. What makes that past unavoidable is the very thing that threatens to lay waste to it: the forces of industrialization, which are not only set in an indeterminate relationship with the past, but also unearth the past itself. It is archaeology not by the spade, but by dynamite; archaeology with a hammer.

The next three sections will track these various dimensions of the film. The first borrows a term from the archaeological parlance of the period—the "area of deformation" (ploshchad' deformatsii)—to describe the relationship between past and present in Vertov; the second provides a close examination of Vertov's account of his time at the excavation, in particular, his description of the unearthed "warrior," which he published in the journal Sovetskii ekran in 1928; and the third considers the formal device of superimposition as both the cinematic correlative of the area of deformation and a solution to the problem of a past obdurately refusing to go away.

i. Areas of Deformation

Among the lesser-known stories of the novostroiki is that they were also worksites for Soviet archaeologists. While workers and engineers wanted to establish the groundwork of the coming utopia at the novostroiki, it was also at these sites that a form of systematic excavation practice sought out the deep pasts contained within it. This was called, somewhat prosaically, the "archaeology at new construction sites" (arkheologiia na novostroikakh).[8]

---

[8]   Mykhailo Miller, Arkheologiia v SSSR. First series, no. 12 (1954): 53-56.

In the West, a similar practice has been designated more
dramatically as "salvage," "emergency," or "rescue" archaeology.[9]
The American archaeologist and director of the Peabody Museum
J. O. Brew defined the necessity of "salvage archaeology" in a 1961
article: "For millennia the centers of ancient civilizations have
watched the great buildings of earlier generations fall before the
tools of the wrecker to make way for the 'modern' structure so
sorely needed and so earnestly desired."[10]

The "archaeology at new construction sites," however, cannot
be easily assimilated into the category of salvage or emergency
archaeology. One reason is that the "wreckers" Brew vilifies were the
very figures valorized in early Soviet culture: the proletarians, shock
workers, Stakhanovites—in short, those battling for utopia against
nature, against obdurate matter, and against the many forms of the
persisting past. Another reason is that by the end of the 1920s, and
more decisively at the beginning of the 1930s, Soviet archaeology was
itself under various kinds of ideological pressures. As Yuri Slezkine
observes, by the early 1930s archaeologists had changed the name
of their vocation and become "historians of material culture." They
had convinced themselves that "the existence of archaeology under
any name was 'tantamount to the anti-Marxist and anti-Leninist
attribution of a special form of [dialectical] development to mere
artifacts.'"[11] Denigrated as the mindless worship of the past and its
artifacts or, in the most extreme cases, as a counter-revolutionary

---

9   J. O. Brew wrote in 1961: "It [salvage archaeology] has built a museum in the middle of what was
     once the Zuider Zee. It is turning the major river valleys of the world into vast archaeological
     laboratories. It delayed the construction of new buildings in the centers of the bombed-out cities
     of Europe while archaeologists deciphered the remains of the earliest life in those cities. . . .
     It has caused a natural gas pipeline company to devote space in its monthly house magazine
     to illustration and description of archaeological excavations which the company itself had
     made" ("Emergency Archaeology: Salvage in Advance of Technological Progress," *Proceedings of
     the American Philosophical Society* 105, no. 1 [1961]: 1-2). The practice of salvage archaeology
     escalated and expanded its purview throughout the twentieth century, ranging from such
     celebrated projects as those of Abu Simbel in the 1960s to the Three Gorges Dam in the 2000s.

10   Ibid., 2.

11   See Yuri Slezkine, "N. Ia. Marr and the National Origins of Soviet Ethnogenetics," *Slavic Review* 55,
     no. 4 (Winter 1996): 846.

force, archaeology could no longer argue for the intrinsic value of the artifacts of the past.

In this, too, Dneprostroi was only one, albeit particularly exemplary site where industrialization and archaeology were jointly at work. Construction sites such as the Moscow-Volga Canal and the White Sea-Baltic Sea Canal, as well as Magnitogorsk, Gidroelektoproekt, Giprogor, Glavzoloto, and Soiuzzoloto, were sites where archaeologists had excavated objects dating from as far back as the Upper Paleolithic era.[12] Dneprostroi, however, differed in degree from these other examples of "archaeology at new construction sites" because of the region's accumulated significance for Russian archaeology as it had been established by the middle of the previous century, when Greek and Scythian artifacts began to be systematically excavated.[13] Mykhailo Miller, one of several archaeologists working at Dneprostroi, later wrote of the site that it marked "the first, and possibly the largest of the archaeological expeditions at new construction sites."[14]

Indeed, the town of Kichkas, where Vertov headed in pursuit of the excavated warrior, had figured in the history of Russian archaeology ever since the middle of the nineteenth century. Count Aleksei Uvarov, whose work on the stone babas we discussed earlier, had included Kichkas in the resplendent array of illustrations— Collection of Maps and Drawings toward the Study of the Antiquities of Southern Russia and the Black Sea Coast (fig. 7.2)—he presented to the tsar to garner further support to excavate regions in the Russian South.[15]

---

[12]   These various excavation sites are discussed in the two issues of the series Izvestiia gosudarstvennoi akademii istorii material'noi kul'tury imeni N. Ia. Marra, vols. 109-10, entitled Arkheologicheskie raboty akademii na novostroikakh v 1932-33 gg. (Leningrad: Gosudarstvennoe sotsial'no-ekonomicheskoe izd-vo, 1935).

[13]   A recent history of archaeology in the south of Russia is Tunkina, Russkaia nauka o klassicheskikh drevnostiakh iuga Rossii. On the archaeological artifacts specifically located around Dneprostroi, I rely on Miller, Arkheologiia, and on S. M. Liashko et al., Kurgannye mogil'niki dneprovskogo nadporozh'ia (Zaporozh'e: Dikoe pole, 2004).

[14]   Miller, Arkheologiia, 53. All further citations are in the text.

[15]   See Lebedev, Istoriia otechestvennoi arkheologii, esp. the section "Osnovnye dostizheniia 'Uvarovskogo perioda' (1846-1884)," 130-96.

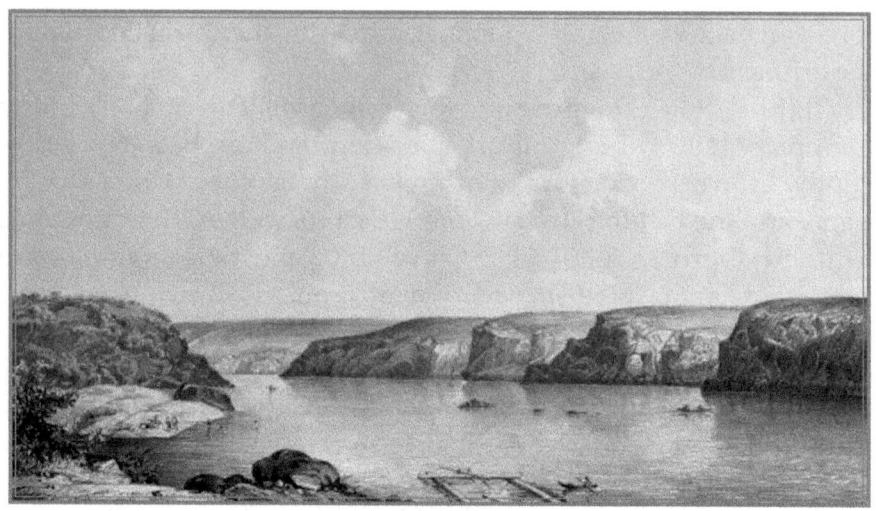

Figure 7.2.
"The Crossing at Kichkas,"
plate CXIII in *A Collection of Maps and Drawings toward the Study
of the Antiquities of Southern Russia and the Black Sea Coast* (1851).
Collection of the New York Public Library.

Given this history of archaeology in the region, the excavation of kurgans and the discovery of would hardly have been a novel occurrence. What was new—and perhaps what struck Vertov most—was that excavation now fell under the shadow of the Soviet industrializing project.

Vertov could find there a stunning example of what Gilles Deleuze has characterized as one of the filmmaker's abiding concerns, namely, "all the (communist) transitions from an order which is being undone to an order which is being constructed."[16] Vertov caught Kichkas and the region precisely at this transitional moment, prior to Dneprostroi's transformation of the region,

---

[16] Gilles Deleuze, *Cinema 1: The Movement-Image*, trans. Hugh Tomlinson and Barbara Habberjam (Minneapolis: University of Minnesota Press, 1986), 39.

when sites of archaeological value would be inundated. As Miller describes it:

> The primary task of the construction included building a dam with turbines at the lower rapids, at the colony of Kichkas, which would cut through the entire Dnieper, from bank to bank. Owing to the building of the dam, the waters in this location would rise to 40 meters high, as a result of which the Dnieper, above the dam, would turn into a lake, in a space up to 12 kilometers wide. (53-54)

The threatened space was, as Miller called it, an "area of deformation":

> The entire area subject to inundation was called the "area of deformation," and large-scale, detailed maps were made of this area. The upper part of a large elevation on the left bank of the Dnieper also entered into the territory of deformation, below the dam. This elevation was subjected to leveling and transformation into a completely even area for the construction of a few factories. Large earthworks were also executed on the right bank of the Dnieper, close to the dam, where the area was also leveled for the construction of the electric station. (54)[17]

Archaeologists had already excavated a "massive quantity" of artifacts from the Stone and Bronze ages, including eighty kurgans, the majority of which were located on the right bank. These were very likely the kurgans Vertov read about that day in October 1927, and whose contents he later depicted in *The Eleventh Year*.

An "area of deformation" is a resonant term. Miller himself was somewhat open as to its meaning, while insistent on using it. He speaks not only of the "area" and "territory" of deformation, but also of the process of the deformation (*deformatsiia*) in the archaeological zone on the one hand, and of "special archaeological expeditions that formed (*formirovalis'*)" at the *novostroiki* on the other. On one level, then, this phrase designates both the archaeologically valuable zone under threat of detonation or deluge, and the practice that takes shape precisely because of those threats.

---

[17]   The typesetting leaves unclear whether Miller wanted to place quotes around "area of deformation" or "deformation" alone.

On another level, the term can be extended metaphorically to consider the kinds of deformation we find throughout Vertov's film since "formation" and "deformation" recall the process the Russian Formalist Yuri Tynianov identified as central to the relations of past and present in literary change. As he writes in the essay "The Literary Fact," from 1928, "the need for incessant dynamism causes an evolution, since every dynamic system necessarily becomes automatized, and an opposite constructive principle dialectically comes into being. The specificity of a literary work of art . . . is in its 'formation,' that is, essentially, the deformation of the material."[18] I want to bring together these twin "deformations" — those of archaeology, and of material — to consider Vertov's juxtaposition of archaeology and industrialization. Why is it that the deep past held so much attraction at a transitional moment where all around were preparations for the deep future, for the bright prospects of revolutionary utopia? In Vertov's hands, the past, present, and future are all curiously deformed. Deformation is not destruction; the past is not obliterated by the new, but dialectically necessary to it. Within the *area of deformation* Vertov constituted a space where the signs of the past are not just juxtaposed with signs of the future, but where they supercharge one another, the deep past becoming all the more legible because the deep future is everywhere at stake.

The Sequence

The archaeological past is everywhere on offer in the opening fifteen minutes of the film. Like Uvek and the kurgans in Boris Pil'niak's *The Naked Year*, the artifacts and sites Vertov focuses upon belong to various pasts in the region. The opening shots — taken from onboard a boat traveling along the Dnieper — include "The Seat of Catherine," "The *Bogatyr'* Cliff," and "The Cliff of Love" (figs. 7.3-7.5), each a site described in various travel guides and archaeological studies of the region. D. I. Evarnitskii, for example, a leading authority on

---

[18]   Iurii Tynianov, "Literaturnyi fakt," in *Poetika, istoriia literatury, kino* (Moscow: Nauka, 1977), 261.

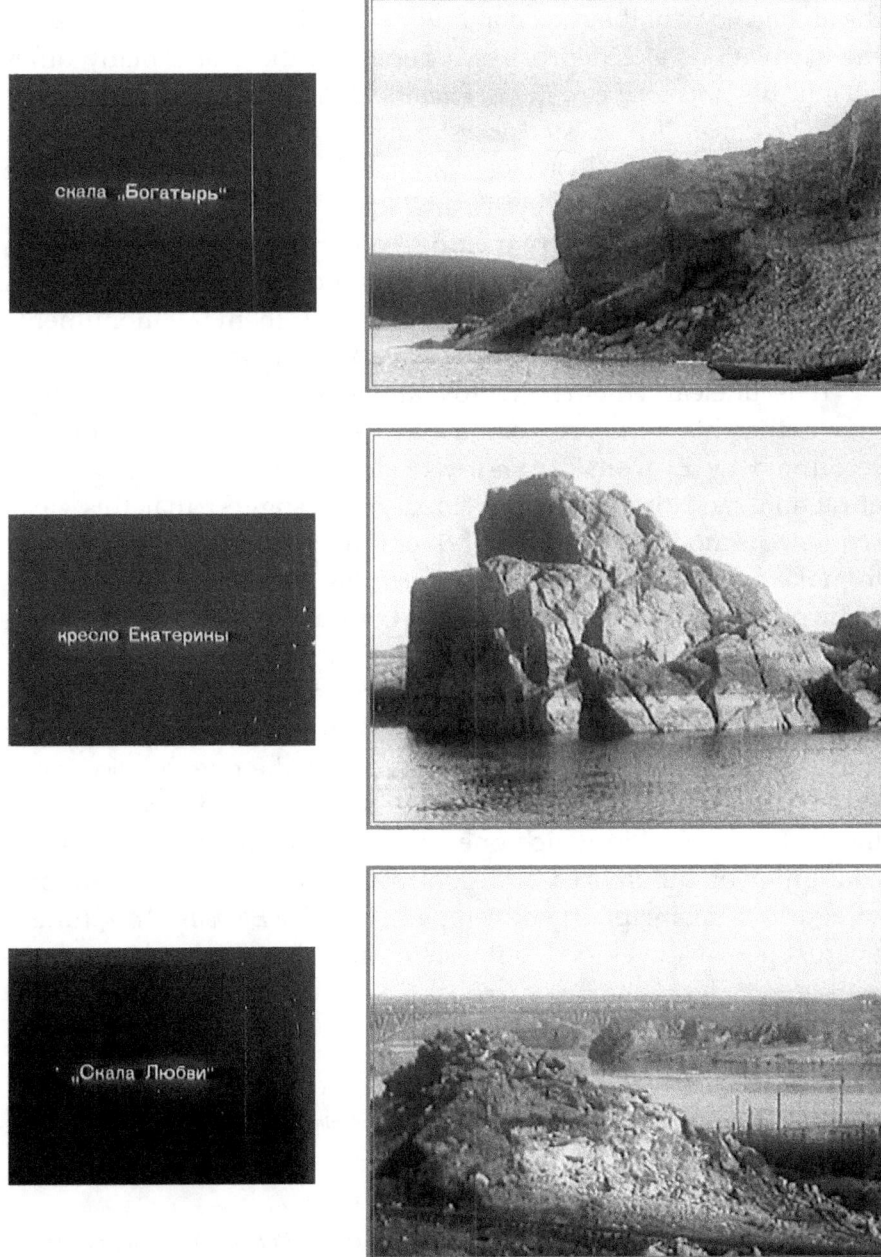

Figures 7.3-7.5.

The "archaeological" sequence of Vertov's *The Eleventh Year* (1928).
The intertitles read: "The *Bogatyr'* Cliff," "The Sea of Catherine," and "The Cliff of Love."

the archaeology of the region and who was charged with overseeing the excavations at Dneprostroi,[19] described these and many other sites in his *Zaporozh'e in the Remnants of the Past and the Sayings of Its Folk* (*Zaporozh'e v ostatkakh stariny i predaniiakh naroda*, 1888), a compendium of "historical, archaeological, and topographic information" about the region's artifacts.[20] Even during the time of construction, the sites were included on organized tours along the Dnieper. According to Miller, travelers would stop off at various "excavations, where archaeologists show[ed] them the monuments they were studying . . . and gave corresponding lectures."[21]

It is unclear whether Vertov attended any of those lectures or whether his audience would have known of the mythologies recounted by Evarnitskii. Vertov's selection of these topographic attractions and their depiction in the film suggest that this early sequence is modeled as a kind of river tour, betraying his initial plan to make a film entitled *Journey through the Ukraine*.[22] The relatively static nature of the shots—soon to be contrasted with the manner in which he depicts the construction—are no mere journey, however. His depiction of the landscape is polemical: industrialization will override both natural and archaeological time and bring the dynamic time of the revolution to the region. In this, the opening sequence is reminiscent of Mikhail Bakhtin's definition of the chronotope of the "travel novel," in which one encounters a "world [as a] spatial contiguity of differences and contrasts," and in which temporal categories remain "poorly developed."[23] In *The Eleventh Year*, time is not just poorly developed, but polemically absent from view.

---

[19] Miller, *Arkheologiia*, 54; Liashko, *Kurgannye mogil'niki*, 3.

[20] D. I. Evarnitskii, *Zaporozh'e v ostatkakh stariny i predaniiakh naroda* (St. Petersburg: Izdanie L. F. Panteleeva, 1888; reprint, Kiev: Veselka, 1985).

[21] Miller, *Arkheologiia*, 54.

[22] John MacKay, "Film Energy: Metanarrative in Dziga Vertov's *The Eleventh Year* (1928)," *October* 121 (Summer 2007): 43.

[23] Mikhail Bakhtin, "The Bildungsroman and Its Significance in the History of Realism (Toward a Historical Typology of the Novel)," in *Speech Genres and Other Late Essays*, trans. Vern W. McGee (Austin: University of Texas Press, 1986), 11.

Vertov shared this view on the region with other travelers to Dneprostroi in those late years of the 1920s. In July 1928, a few months after *The Eleventh Year* appeared on-screen, the writer Sergei Budantsev published an article on the construction in the "Soviet Land" section of the journal *Novyi mir.* Entitled the "Dnieper Construction" ("Dneprovskoe stroitel'stvo"), the article similarly described various aspects of the construction, from its geographic location to the preparations for energy production.[24] Although Budantsev and Vertov likely did not know one another's work, together they indicate a general problem posed by the landscape surrounding Dneprostroi, namely that industrialization was but

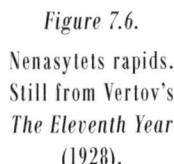

Figure 7.6.

Nenasytets rapids. Still from Vertov's *The Eleventh Year* (1928).

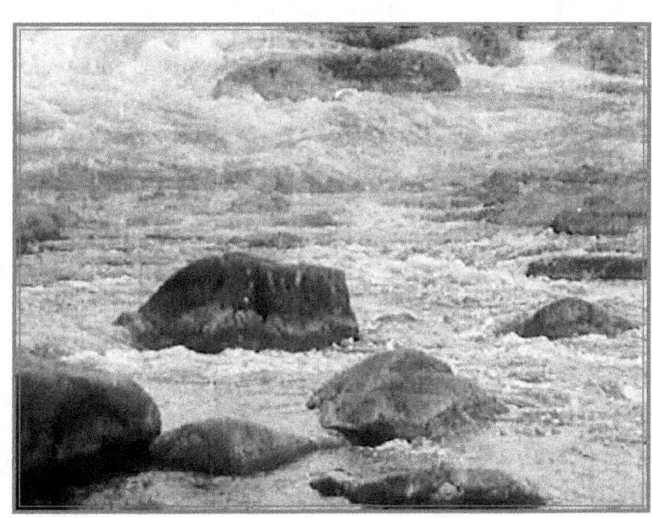

one of several competing sources of attraction for visitors there: for Bundantsev, another problematic source was nature.

He informs his readers about the Dnepropetrovsk-Kichkas-Zaporezh'e bus route, which travels along "the path of the Scythian steppe, wave-like and endless" (*shliakh skifskikh stepei, volnoobraznykh i beskonechnykh*).[25] This part of the steppe, Budantsev notes, was hardly untouched: "The steppe, that feather-grass ocean,

---

24   Sergei Budantsev, "Dneprovskoe stroitel'stvo," *Novyi mir* (1928), no. 7: 213-23.

25   Ibid., 213.

remained in name only. Now, it's a field, destroyed village springs, everything plowed and sown, even the kurgans, the innumerable and mysterious graves of history. To us, northerners, this landscape is wearying."[26] For all the transformations already present in the region, a concomitant transformation in spectatorship had not taken place; the landscape may be wearying to some northerners, but hardly to all visitors to the region. Budantsev observes that people still remained attracted to nature: "My fellow travelers, sentimental intellectuals, demanded that I delight in the powerful caprice of nature. But I felt irritation." In the Nenasytets rapids, which Vertov also highlights in the opening of the film (fig. 7.6), Budantsev could only discern "a fruitless noise, does not delight":

> Grand! You say, listening and pointing to the Nenasytets.
> —But have you heard how a propeller hums, with what infernal hissing, heat, and flame a Bessemer flask breathes in a metallurgical factory? No, no, not an urban man who's spent his life in Moscow. He knows no feelings or spectacles more keen (ostrye) and majestic, than this gurgling of water, which, having made use of it, it is necessary to destroy, as soon as possible.[27]

Nature, for Budantsev and Vertov, lacked purpose. Vertov also presents this dilemma about the attraction to nature, rather than to industry. To counteract that vestigial attraction to purposeless nature, when Vertov's tour down the river eventually arrives at Dneprostroi, the shift in location is accompanied by a significant shift in cinematic form; he renders the construction through various kaleidoscopic and split-screen effects, simultaneously capturing multiple areas of the construction or superimposing images of workers, magnified to Promethean proportions at work upon it (fig. 7.7). These formal features mobilize against the somnolent perception of the landscape that characterizes the first several minutes of the film and with which one might associate a touristic

[26]   Ibid.

[27]   Ibid.

gaze. Instead, the viewer is compelled to perceive the construction from multiple angles simultaneously (fig. 7.8). In that process, the viewer undergoes the cinematic equivalent of modernization, which seeks to dynamize space, and spectatorship.

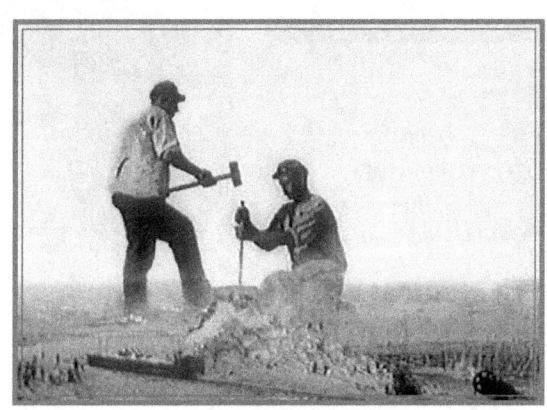

Figure 7.7.

Promethean workers. Still from Vertov's *The Eleventh Year* (1928).

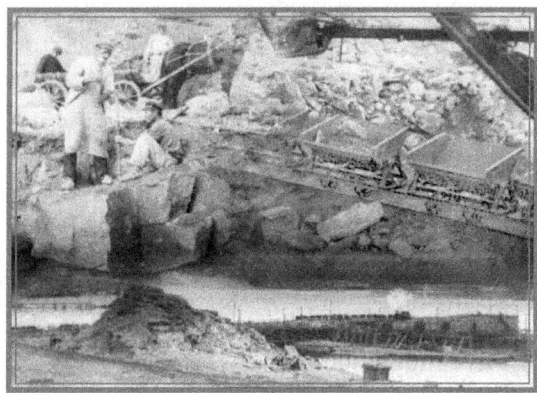

Figure 7.8.

Construction scene. Still from Vertov's *The Eleventh Year* (1928).

Alongside the competition between nature and industry we find in Budantsev, Vertov adds the spectacle of archaeology. In the midst of the construction's explosive clamor, Vertov introduces a "A Two-Thousand-Year-Old Scythian" (fig. 7.9). The image depicts a set of bones (in fact, a combination of two sets of bones) that Vertov forms into a composite image of an archaic warrior taken from various angles. The warrior could belong to one of various nomadic peoples found in the region, but Vertov ascribes it to the Scythians. He then proceeeds to alternate various images of this "Scythian"

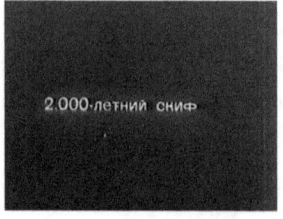

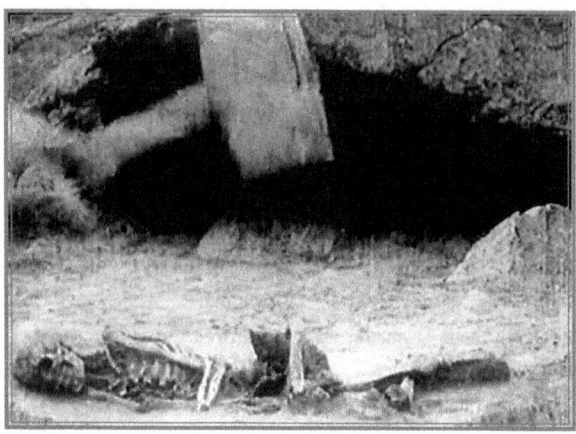

Figure 7.9.

The two-thousand-year-old
Scythian. Still from Vertov's
The Eleventh Year (1928).

with scenes from the construction. In doing so, the film establishes archaeology and industrialization as the central confrontation of its opening sequence. But what does the "Scythian" mean?

The appearance of the Scythian has provoked no minor interpretive debate. It ranks as one of the most curious sequences in Vertov's body of work. As the film historian Jay Leyda observed, the sequence is "one of *Eleventh's* most effective scenes," while also being a moment he found Vertov becoming "precariously virtuoso."[28] Both the effectiveness and precariousness of the sequence were due to a typically Vertovian excess of semantic possibility, with interpretations generally splitting along two lines: the first finds that the juxtaposition of the archaic past and the industrializing present marks the supersession of the Scythian epoch by industrial modernity; and the second views the juxtaposition as a way of pointing to the essential affinity between the two periods. The stakes of interpreting the entire sequence are high because it impinges on the larger question of what particular model of history and change underpins Vertov's film and how that model correlates with the cinematic techniques he employs.

Industrialization is so valorized in the film that one might well agree with a provincial reviewer from Tambov, who found that

---

[28]   Leyda, *Kino*, 250.

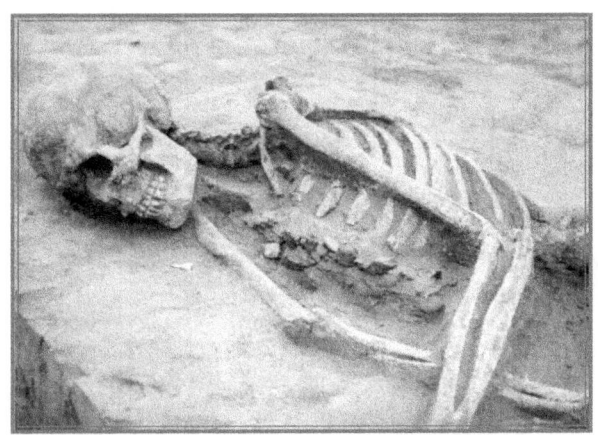

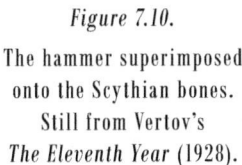

Figure 7.10.
The hammer superimposed
onto the Scythian bones.
Still from Vertov's
The Eleventh Year (1928).

"the play on the Scythian skeleton is interesting as a comparison of two different epochs: in the place where wild Scythians wandered in darkness two thousand years ago, the greatest achievement of culture, Lenin's electric lamp, is now shining brightly."[29] The central image for this view—namely, that industrialization will pulverize the archaic past—is a hammer superimposed onto the grave, which seemingly strikes away at the Scythian bones (fig. 7.10). According to Yuri Tsivian, the proper reading of the shot—or what he refers to as the "revolutionary metaphor" of the superimposed hammer[30]—is to see the hammer as a synecdoche of all those forces marshaled against the archaic past. Extending this view, one could say that the shot elaborates its hierarchy of value in the manner of a Russian icon, with the hammer—that central Soviet symbol and agent of pulverizing modernity—positioned above the scene, striking away at the archaic, benighted, and dark past below. The film, to be sure, readily invites readings such as that of the Tambov critic, given the oppositions it frequently draws between the old and the new, whether in the form of untamed and tamed nature; non-productive water and water made productive through the

29 "'Odinnadtsatyi,' *Tambovskaia pravda*, 7 June 1928," in *Lines of Resistance: Dziga Vertov and the Twenties* (Pordenone: Le Giornate del Cinema Muto, 2004), 306.

30 *Le Giornate del Cinema Muto XXIII edizione* (2004), s.v. "Odinnadstatyi." The reference to "revolutionary metaphor" is on p. 60.

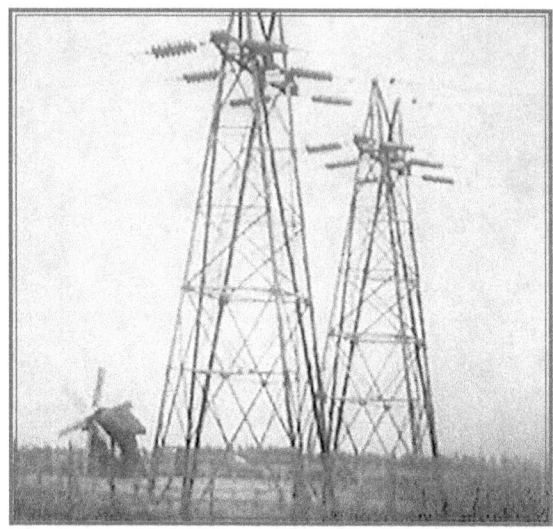

Figure 7.11.
Windmill and electrical wires.
Still from Vertov's
The Eleventh Year (1928).

hydroelectric station;[31] peasant and factory labor; or windmills and electrical wires (fig. 7.11).

Other interpreters have proposed different readings, seeing the juxtaposition of the Scythian past and the industrializing present as positing an affinity between the two epochs. Understood thus the power of Soviet industrialization is measured not by its ability to destroy the archaic past, but rather to revivify it. As John MacKay observes, "[the sequence] suggests that [the Scythian's] energies are stirred back to life by his successors, the warrior-builders of socialism."[32] MacKay finds support for his reading in Vertov's reference to the workers at the Dneprostroi as "proud warriors of peaceful building, warrior-builders of the proletarian country,"[33] which recalls the language of the *Komsomol'skaia pravda* report (the

---

[31]   Jeremy Hicks, *Dziga Vertov: Defining Documentary Film* (London: I. B. Tauris, 2007), 59.

[32]   MacKay, "Film Energy," 76-77.

[33]   MacKay takes the phrase "warrior-builders of socialism" from an article by Vertov in which he refers to the workers as "not the slaves of capital, but proud warriors of peaceful building, warrior-builders of the proletarian country." Vertov, "Stsenarnyi plan fil'ma '*Odinnadtsatyi*,'" in *Iz naslediia: Stat'i i vystupleniia*, ed. A. Deriabin and D. V. Kruzhkova (Moscow: Eizenshtein tsentr, 2008), 275.

"well-preserved skeleton of a warrior").[34] Indeed, the ambiguity of
the scene is amplified by that fact that Vertov does not invoke just
any past, but rather the specifically Scythian past of the region; it is
not a past coded as either imperial or Christian, and, as such, one
that possesses enough indeterminate value to make the Scythian
still available for extended consideration and recuperation. The
ground of the Dneprostroi is filled with warriors, dead and living. In
support of this view, one could also invoke the ambivalent status of
the Scythians in Russian modernist culture, which, as we have seen,
ascribed a positive value to them as mythological forerunners of the
contemporary warriors in a battle against the West (Blok) or of the
modern artist, in a battle with bourgeois philistinism (Zamiatin).

I would like to steer a middle course between the two views on
this scene, first in order to attempt to delineate why Vertov staged
a confrontation with the archaic past within the space of industrial
modernity. One possible reason he did so is that while ideas of
pulverizing or overcoming the old may hold true within the discrete
limits of the shot of the superimposed hammer, the Scythian skeleton
reappears even after that sequence. That continued presence means
that Vertov contends with categories such as temporal persistence
and repetition—and thus seems to acknowledge the threat the
archaeological artifact (and the energies bound up within it) pose to
clearing the ground for the future. The second reason is somewhat
simpler: Vertov was clearly fascinated by the Scythian. And it is in
part this fascination—in drafts of his account of the experience he
referred to the encounter as one of amazement—that indicates how
the Scythian would not just be an object pulverized or inundated
on the march toward the Revolutionary future, but cinematically
valuable.

ii. The Shooting Log

Vertov did not only race to the excavations or include "the Scythian"
in the film. He also accorded the bones a prominent place in the

---

[34]   MacKay, "Film Energy," 67.

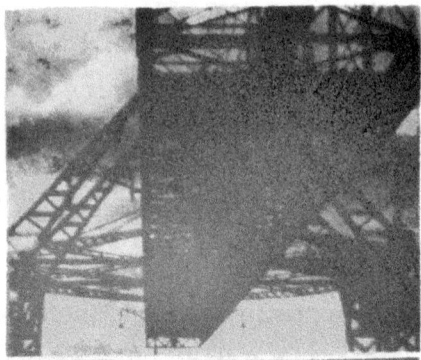
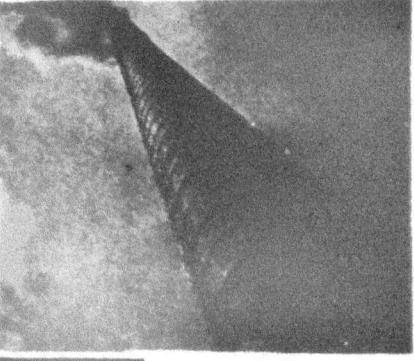

Figure 7.12.

The shooting log of Vertov's *The Eleventh Year* (1928),
as published in *Sovetskii ekran*, February 28, 1928.

excerpts from the shooting log he published in *Sovetskii ekran* in 1928 (fig. 7.12).[35] Indeed, the account of his encounter with the warrior's skull in the first of the three sections of the log (the second section shifts toward an account of a metallurgical scene; the third describes the end of the day's work) merits close attention in its own right. Vertov deploys a range of rhetorical devices in generating the ambiguous significance of the Scythian, and prompts the question of how he imagined an affective relationship with the bones. That Vertov devoted so much rhetorical effort to describing the archaeological encounter should indicate at the very least that the skull meant more to him than just some handy artifact to tell a story of superannuation.

Here is the first section of the log quoted in full:

A trumpet sounds the signal. A pause. The workers disperse. Horsemen patrol the area of the explosions. The striking of a bell. A pause. A slow roll call of bells. Little (from a distance) men prepare to light fuses. A fast ringing of bells. The men light fuses and run to dugout shelters. An explosion. Another follows. A series of explosions, one after another. A fountain of rocks and sand.

Fragments fly into the distance . . . over the rails, over rail-lorries, over a crane. They drum on the lorry beneath where we've taken shelter.

They fly as far as an opened grave where a Scythian has lain asleep for the last two thousand years. Beside his skeleton lie a spear and bronze arrowheads, pierced to hold poison. A cracked earthenware cup. At the head of the grave are some sheep's bones (food) and the skeleton of a warhorse.

The Scythian stares from his eye sockets, through the black holes of his skull. As though he's listening to the explosions. Above him are sky and clouds. Rails run right beside the grave. Along the rails, freight trains pass, and forty-ton cranes roll. Behind the rails are the scaffolding of a pump house under construction, quarries, rail-lorries, and thousands of men armed with hammers and picks.

[35]   Dziga Vertov, "'Odinnadtsatyi' (Otryvki iz s"emochnogo dnevnika)," *Sovetskii ekran*, no. 9 (February 28, 1928). A version of the text is included in Vertov, *Iz naslediia*, 140.

The Scythian in his grave—and the din of the new offensive.
The Scythian in his grave—and the cameraman Kaufman focusing [in amazement] on a silence of two thousand years![36]

The scene is replete with material fragments—ones that fly through the air and are linked to the concussive, sonorous din of industrial modernity; others that are found, still and quiescent, within the space of the grave. These fragments indicate how archaeology and industry form two sources of attraction in the scene. Indeed they seem to comprise two zones whose borders are demarcated by the industrial fragments; their trajectory marks the range of their explosive force because they stop oddly just short of the Scythian's grave. For some reason that Vertov leaves indeterminate, industrialization does not enter into the grave: the fragments do not fly in, and the "rails run right beside the grave." Industrialization, in the description, minds its borders, even when it is at its most explosive and transformative.

While the fragments don't enter the grave, Vertov does. And along with him, his brother, the cameraman, and the camera, too. They peer inside to catalogue its contents. Inside the grave, Vertov finds hardly just dead matter or mere empirical detail: the spear, arrowheads, warhorse, and earthenware cup were commonly found in the region's burial mounds. Vertov, in fact, goes so far as to surmise that the sheep's bones—"sheep's bones (food)"—were there for the afterlife. (Perhaps he did attend one of the archaeological lectures conducted at Dneprostroi, after all.) These archaeological objects hold his attention, and, what's more, they allow him to elaborate a relationship between the archaic, the project of industrialization, and the potentialities of film.

Vertov's catalogue of objects could also furnish a catalogue of personifying devices that he brings to bear upon the scene—none more significantly than the Scythian skull that emerges at the passage's conclusion. The skull is inert, yet animate. Absent

---

[36] Dziga Vertov, "Fragment from a Shooting Log," in *Kino-Eye: The Writings of Dziga Vertov*, ed. Annette Michelson, trans. Kevin O'Brien (Berkeley and Los Angeles: University of California Press, 1984), 169. Translation adjusted.

its flesh, it remains sensate to both the spectacle and the din of industrialization. It can see: "The Scythian stares." It can (almost) hear: "as though he's listening to the explosions." The "as though" marks Vertov hedging back from too much figurative excess when it comes to hearing, but that hedging back also seems to naturalize the possibility that the Scythian sees. The sockets of the Scythian's absent eyes and ears especially intrigue him; he emphasizes their absence twice: "The Scythian stares from his eye sockets, through the black holes of his skull." Absent, but still sensate "eyes" seem like a commonplace—where would one begin a taxonomy of the skulls in art and culture that awaken an atavistic fear that the dead (or undead) can survey the living?

Why might Vertov want these absences to remain organs of sensation despite their manifest decomposition? Flouting the boundary between the animate and the inanimate is a typically Vertovian gesture. In other films, he suggests that objects can come to life; he even credited the kino-eye with the power to reanimate the dead. In the most emphatic display of that power in his *Kino-Eye* (*Kino-glaz*, 1924), he ran the film backwards to revivify a disemboweled bull, in an act where the display of cinematic technique slipped over into the mystical or transcendent: "the bull com[es] back to life," the kino-eye proclaimed. Still, the apotheosis of Vertov's propensity to animate and (re-)vivify was the kino-eye itself. It possessed not only sight, but also sentience and voice. When the kino-eye debuted on the Soviet cultural scene, for example, it declared: "I am the [kino-eye]. I am the mechanical eye. I, the machine, show you the world as only I can see it."[37]

As Anne Nesbet has observed, it was precisely this contest over the eye, mechanical or organic, that revealed a broadly diffused concern in Soviet avant-garde film theory. In her words, "the new

37 D. Vertov, "The Cine-Eyes: A Revolution" (1923), in Richard Taylor and Ian Christie, eds., *The Film Factory: Russian and Soviet Cinema in Documents* (London: Routledge, 1993), 93. We might recall here those tropes that rhetoricians have identified in the ascription of animacy to inanimate things—anthropomorphism, personification, and prosopopeia—that structure Vertov's discursive account of his encounter with the Scythian. Where those tropes are primarily invested in the rhetoric of voice, the sequence in the film points out the cinematic correlate of a "rhetoric" built primarily around the fiction of sight.

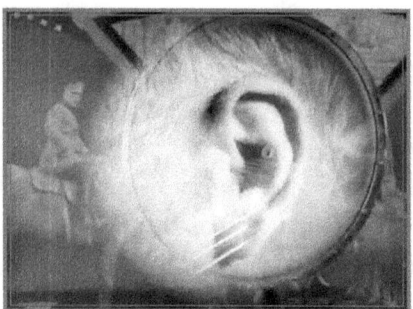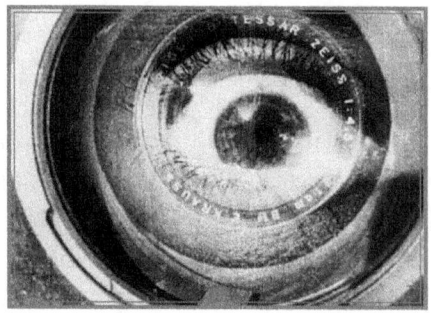

Figures 7.13 and 7.14.
Stills from Vertov's *Man with a Movie Camera* (1929).

'eye' of Russian modernism is a strange organ: part machine, part meat, it oscillates between these incompatible identities without finding any comfortable compromise between them."[38] The effort to distance the mechanical usurper as far as possible from the usurped human organ signaled a basic fear: "When examined closely, however, the 'kino-glaz' turns out to be haunted by the flesh it would leave behind."[39] The Scythian skull, whose sockets are morphologically similar to the cinematic apparatus, makes this fear over origins doubly the case; its power, Vertov imagines, is that it can see even without flesh. It can, in fact, also possibly hear. The skull, in this sense, possesses all those attributes to record scenes that Vertov would continue to explore throughout the 1920s, especially in his *Man with a Movie Camera,* where the kino-eye reveals itself overcoming both the human eye, and the human ear (figs. 7.13 and 7.14). This concern over eyes and ears is now recast as a confrontation between the archaic eye of the Scythian and the kino-eye itself; together, they generate much of the drama in the last line of the passage: "The Scythian in his grave—and the cameraman Kaufman focusing [in amazement] on a silence of two thousand years!"

What this line asks us to consider is what would be the proper response to the presence of the Scythian. Vertov implicitly poses

[38]   Anne Nesbet, *Savage Junctures: Sergei Eisenstein and the Shape of Thinking* (London: I. B. Tauris, 2003), 46.

[39]   Ibid., 31.

this as a problem in the shooting log, though he coordinates it through the response of his brother, "the cameraman Kaufman," to the Scythian skull. The question is made more difficult to answer by the textual variants in the available versions of Vertov's shooting log. In the version published in *Sovetskii ekran*, Vertov concludes the passage with an exclamation point. In his journal, by contrast, he had originally included the adverb *izumlenno* (in amazement) to characterize Kaufman's response to the discovery: "The Scythian in the grave and the cameraman Kaufman, focusing in amazement upon a two-thousand-year-old silence!"[40] While both versions were exclamations—Vertov and his cameraman are clearly excited by their encounter—the adverb "in amazement" dropped out when the log was published, with some later editions including it, and others following the version published in the journal.

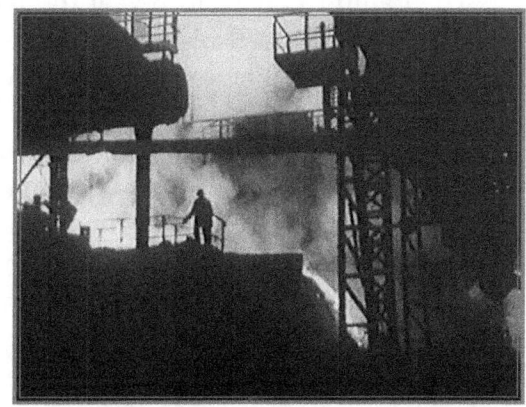

Figure 7.15.
Factory scene. Still from
Vertov's *The Eleventh Year*
(1928).

The disappearance of the adverb is key, and symptomatic of the general problem posed by the Scythian in the film. One way to think about why *izumlenno* might have disappeared is to look at a later section of the published shooting log where Vertov shifts from the

40 The various published accounts of the log can be found in the 1927 *Sovetskii ekran* version and two later editions: one is the edition prepared by S. V. Drobashenko, *Dziga Vertov: Stat'i, dnevniki, zamysly* (Moscow: Iskusstvo, 1966), which served as the basis for the translations in *Kino-Eye: The Writings of Dziga Vertov*. Another is the edition prepared by A. Deriabin; see Deriabin and Kruzhkova, *Iz naslediia*, 140. *Izumlenno* does not appear in the 1927 *Sovetskii ekran* version, but it did appear in Vertov's journals, which Drobashenko used in preparation for his edition.

archaeological site to a metallurgical one, where his technophilic
fantasy is given free reign. The scene Vertov describes is infernal
(as it is in the film; fig. 7.15), replete with "rivers of fire": a "flashing
wire, which, as though alive, rises up, curves, turns, cuts through
the air like lightning, and, finally, obediently (*pokorno*) dashes into
a spiral in proper bundles." What is this industrial zoomorph,
born of fire (but mostly of figuration), obedient *to*? And why
"obedient"? *Pokornost'*, whether translated as "obedience" or
"submission," might best be seen as the endpoint of the figurative
excess of Vertovian animation: cycling through enchantment
and disenchantment, through mystification and demystification,
through an excess of figuration and then figuration's requisite
regimentation, Vertov incites matter to a state of unruliness only to
then demand of it obedience.

The gambit is both to reveal the force contained in matter, in
things—whether as threat or as pure potentiality—and then to
control or channel that force. Perhaps this incitement and obedience
of matter also implicates spectatorship. The viewer's amazement
(*izumlenno[st']*) is provoked and ultimately counteracted by the
obedience or submission (*pokorno[st']*) of the thing that amazes. To
leave "in amazement" in the text would have made the relationship
between Kaufman and the skull transactional, indicating the power
of the skull to override Kaufman's rational processes, and thereby to
affirm the skull's power not only to vie with the industrial spectacle,
but also to have equal power over the scene, a power tied to the
gaze of the Scythian.

Vertov's use of the Scythian extends the function of Scythianism
deeper into the Soviet period, while also providing a caveat to one
notable account of its cultural function in Russian modernism. In her
perceptive account of the historiography of Scythianism, Ekaterina
Bobrinskaia writes: "The Scythian subject (*siuzhet*) in culture at
the beginning of the century became its own type of metaphor
for these unconscious aspirations [for revolution],"[41] but "fairly

---

[41]   E. A. Bobrinskaia, "'Skifstvo' v russkoi kul'ture nachala XX veka i skifskaia tema u russkikh
futuristov," in *Rannii russkii avangard v kontekste filosofskoi i khudozhestvennoi kul'tury rubezha
vekov: Ocherki* (Moscow: Gosudarstvennyi institut iskusstvoznaniia, 1999), 55.

quickly after 1917, these revolutionary-mystical moods [associated with the 'Scythian mythologeme'], in a manner of speaking, are again plunged into the depths of the cultural consciousness."[42] In *The Eleventh Year*, Vertov emphatically literalizes what happens to Scythianism in Bobrinskaia's account. The film does indeed capture the descent of Scythianism as a discourse "into the depths"—not so much the depths of "cultural consciousness," however, but the depths of the rising floodwaters in the area of deformation. To do so, the film might be seen to modulate Bobrinskaia's account: going beyond Scythianism requires more than psychological suppression; in Vertov's film it requires a conscious use of material force.

Still, Vertov was also invoking the whole discourse of post-Revolutionary Scythianism—in part through the very fact that he called the bones "the Scythian"—which meant that the bones could function not only as a source of possible mythological models for the period, but also that they could still generate a sufficiently ambiguous field offering Vertov time and space in which to maneuver and contemplate the archaic past. In the shooting log, what Vertov both entertains and tries to foreclose is an archaeology conjoined to the project of industrialization in order to indicate and control the disruptive force of the Scythian: its power to amaze. In this, he was like other modernists internationally who found a similar power here; when an archaeological object is "dug out and ripped from its matrix, the old object holds the potential of producing the effect of the new, by virtue of its very remoteness and alterity, its singularity. The process is one of estrangement, re-collection, recovery."[43] While Vertov commits himself to technological change, he also locates a counter-proposal for the enduring necessity of the archaic past in aesthetic terms: the juxtaposition of old and new acquires force in proportion to the disparity in time and space of its constituent parts; the greater the difference, the more striking, the more threateningly

---

[42] Ibid., 82.

[43] Jeffrey Schnapp, Michael Shanks, and Matthew Tiews, "Archaeology, Modernism, Modernity: Editors' Introduction to 'Archaeologies of the Modern,'" *Modernism/modernity*, 11, no. 1 (2004): 4.

"amazing" the force of their juxtaposition. In the case of *The Eleventh Year*, the threat of archaeology is not just that it destabilizes the idea of progress, but also that by some curious inversion, the deep past itself becomes a novelty that offers serious competition to the energetic novelty of the *novostroiki*.

It is not that Lenin's "electric lamp" forms the synecdoche of socialist enlightenment—as the Tambov critic had it—but that light and the cinema shine upon the deep past. The fact that Vertov lingers for so long on the Scythian grave and the Scythian's bones— in both log and film—indicates the value they acquire, precisely because they are set in relation to the industrialization. But so, too, does the converse hold: industrialization acquires an increased charge precisely because it has a counter-force against which it can be measured. In this regard, what is "amazing" about the encounter is not just that Vertov and Kaufman themselves see the skull, but, rather, that the scene involves an encounter between the kino-glaz and the skull, that is, between the archaic eye of the past, and the technological-eye of the future.

Here, we might compare the page layouts of *Komsomol'skaia pravda* and *Sovetskii ekran*. The former tucks the report on the archaeological discovery into the "In Brief" section, whereas the film journal accords the skull such prominence on the page that one could reasonably presume—having not even seen the film—that this juxtaposition of archaic past and industrializing present is the most important confrontation in the film. What the shooting log did not do—and perhaps could not do, given the exigencies of space limits and page layouts—was find a way out of the juxtaposition it placed so prominently on the page. In other words, the layout encodes a general problem. Nowhere in the log does Vertov indicate what would happen to the skull. There are no transitional passages. In this regard, the shooting log is something like a draft analysis of the problem Vertov leaves to the film to solve: How does one shift from static juxtaposition to chronological progress? And what can one do with a past that won't go away? The shift from page to screen, as we will see next, found a solution in the formal device of superimposition—a solution that in its own way reinscribes archaeology into the very structure of the shot.

iii. The Archaeology of the Superimpositions

The sequence of superimpositions is among the most celebrated in *The Eleventh Year*. Its images of rising tides inundating the region are at once mythologically resonant with themes of biblical renewal and a tour de force of cinematic technique. Superimposition belongs to the class of devices Vertov employed to demonstrate and experiment with cinema's ability to control time and space,[44] while serving as the film's premier aesthetic correlate to the area of deformation. By tying archaeology and aesthetics together, superimpositions enabled Vertov to construct an image of the future inundation, but also to give cinematic form to the multiplicity of temporal orders with which he was grappling as he sought to project an image of overcoming the stubborn persistence of the past.

The sequence extends over several minutes, and shows what appear to be the rising waters of the Dnieper superimposed over the images of various landscapes, each of which contains signs of antiquated modes of economic production, daily habits, and religious belief (fig. 7.16). Since the hydroelectric dam on the Dnieper opened only in 1932, four years after the film, Vertov's viewers would probably have understood that the superimpositions they saw in the film were glimpses into the future. Indeed, they may have guessed that Vertov was redeploying earlier footage of the Volkhov Dam (1918-27) to construct his image of Dneprostroi.[45]

Verisimilitude is not really at issue—such chronological and geographical displacements were nothing new in Vertov's work. Instead, the superimpositions deform the images of time and space. They testify to both the fungibility of the cinematic sign and the

---

[44]   As Annette Michelson observes, "The heady delights of the editing table . . . offer the sense of control through repetition, acceleration, deceleration, arrest in freeze-frame, release, and reversal of movement that is inseparable from the thrill of power . . . the euphoria one feels at the editing table is that of a sharpening cognitive focus and of a ludic sovereignty, grounded in that deep gratification of a fantasy of infantile omnipotence open to those who, since 1896, have played, as never before in the world's history, with the continuum of temporality and the logic of causality" ("The Kinetic Icon in the Work of Mourning: Prolegomena to the Analysis of a Textual System," *October* 52 [Spring 1990]: 38).

[45]   MacKay, "Film Energy," 67.

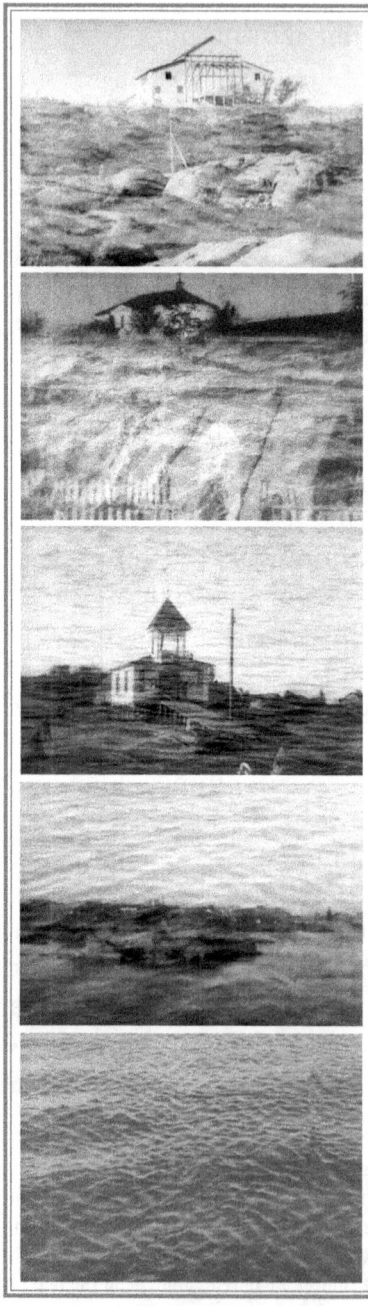

Figure 7.16.
Superimpositions. Stills from Vertov's
The Eleventh Year (1928)

power of cinema to create complex spatio-temporal images that convey what Mikhail Bakhtin once called, in a different context, *oshchushchenie vremeni*, the "feeling" or "sensation of time," which is elaborated and cultivated in this case within the medium of film.[46] The layering of images one upon the other collapses spatio-temporal boundaries, and transforms the temporal signatures within each layer. The very process of layering images places signs and their signifieds into a constant state of spatio-temporal crisis and flux. The grafting of images of the rising tides onto the image of a church, for example, functions somewhat like the kaleidoscopic scenes deployed early on in the construction sequence and again later in the film, with its scenes of crowds seemingly watching the construction of the dam. But where the components of those images were drawn from the chronological and spatial parameters of the construction—and, on occasion, suffused those images with the mythological paradigms and proportions of

[46] Mikhail Bakhtin, "Forms of Time and of the Chronotope in the Novel: Notes toward a Historical Poetics," in *The Dialogic Imagination*, ed. Michael Holquist, trans. Caryl Emerson and Michael Holquist (Austin: University of Texas Press, 1981), 206.

Promethean workers (see fig. 7.3)—the superimpositions of the flood seem to dilate time: they refer to a present as though it were past and project images of a future not yet in place. It is a space permeated by times past while being imagined as the space of the future.

The superimposed images, in this sense, radicalize archaeology, insofar as they operate within a signifying mode that continually asks the viewer to be aware of cinematic layering, understanding how each particular layer—or image—can be forced to have multiple temporal references simultaneously. Anne Nesbet has argued in her reading of Eisenstein's *The General Line / Old and New* that we must take "an archaeological approach" to that film in order to delineate "layer after layer of superimposed lines (or official ideologies); the new cannot merely liquidate the old, and the disquieting traces of the old are to be felt everywhere."[47] In *The Eleventh Year*, Vertov's experiments with superimposition make emphatically literal this link between archaeology and the aesthetics of cinema, a radically oscillating dynamic of old and new in the "cinematic archaeology" of the 1920s.

While the superimposed layers may thereby be seen to conjoin a modernist aesthetic investment in signs and signification with the archaeological investment in stratigraphy, they also serve as a solution to the problem of the persistence and repetition of the past. This problem can be seen in its most acute form if we return to the Scythian. One basic challenge the Scythian continues to pose is that for all the attempts to get rid of it, it keeps on reappearing. It reappears, for example, after the scene of the explosion; it reappears after the scene in which the hammer strikes away at it; and it is seen for a third time, right before Vertov depicts the inundation of the landscape. Why would the film, which is so much about the promise of chronological progress, incorporate a structure of repetition by which the Scythian continually threatens to reappear? After all, the first-time viewer could not be sure that the Scythian would *not* reappear, once again, even after the inundation.

[47]   Nesbet, *Savage Junctures*, 97.

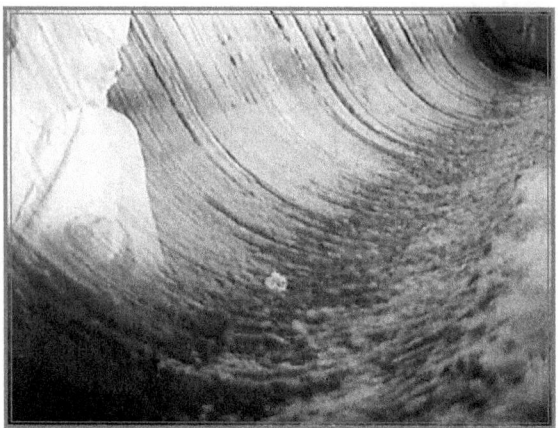

Figure 7.17.

Lenin superimposed on the waters. Still from Vertov's *The Eleventh Year* (1928).

The superimposed images are thus a curious metaphor: the Scythian skull, first unearthed at the site, is now ostensibly "buried" again—while the viewer is left with the knowledge that something still lurks beneath the surface of the waters. Vertov opts here not for pulverization—as the hammer promised—but inundation. It is a classic, almost ostentatious repression of the past, which threatens a return. If the skull's reappearance poses the problem, then the solution to that problem lies in the appearance of another figure superimposed over the waters: Lenin (fig. 7.17). Lenin's appearance here makes him into something of the master emblem of spectatorship, a figure surveying the waters and placing a seal upon the past. The skull is supplanted by the promise that Lenin, though dead, still observes and safeguards the living, the guarantor of Year Zero, the sign of an absolute point of origin from which a new chronology can be inaugurated.

Vertov's reliance here on Lenin would, in turn, pose a problem later on. According to Annette Michelson, Vertov's *Three Songs of Lenin* (1934) presents the dilemma of how to conclude the mourning for Lenin himself. "The function of the monumental," she observes, "is not only to commemorate, but definitively to inter and block the return of the dead."[48] The question of *The Eleventh Year*, by contrast, was: which dead—the Scythian or Lenin? What would become

---

[48]   Michelson, "Kinetic Icon," 38.

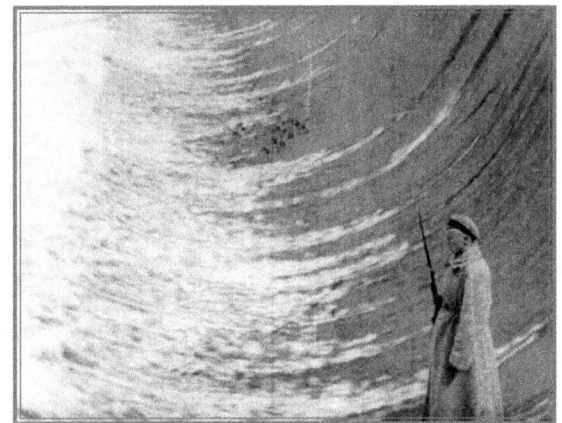

Figure 7.18.
On guard. Still from Vertov's
The Eleventh Year (1928)

a problem in *Three Songs*—namely, how to bring to a conclusion the ceaseless, traumatic repetition of mourning for Lenin—was still a solution in *The Eleventh Year*. Lenin need not be interred; he inters the Scythian and a whole array of pasts within the landscape. Vertov's dependence on inundation rather than pulverization might explain why the figures who appear after the Lenin emblem are cast both marveling at the construction of Dneprostroi, and as standing guard over the waters. Vertov shifts from spectatorial enthrallment, linking a myriad of peoples from the whole of the Soviet Union, toward spectatorial vigilance, in the face of the multifarious threats lurking either beneath the waters or beyond the borders (fig. 7.18).

iv. Archaeology with a Hammer

Archaeology appears in the film as a set of artifacts but nowhere as an actual practice. Still, several shots of the Scythian betray the hand of the archaeologist and the story of the "archaeology at new construction sites." These shots reveal that there are actually two excavated skeletons, although Vertov only refers to the "Scythian" in the singular in both the shooting log and the film. The first to be shown is the skeleton with the skeleton of a horse above it, which is probably the one he describes in the shooting log; and the second, a human skeleton laid on its side, is the one over which Vertov superimposed the hammer. Both were probably found among

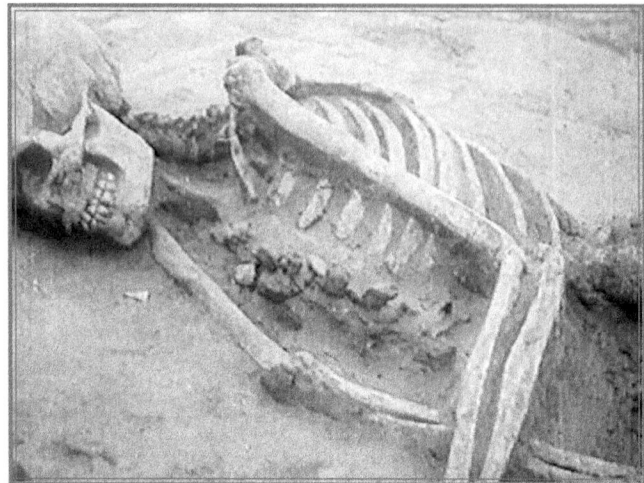

Figure 7.19.
Grave I. Still from
Vertov's *The Eleventh
Year* (1928).

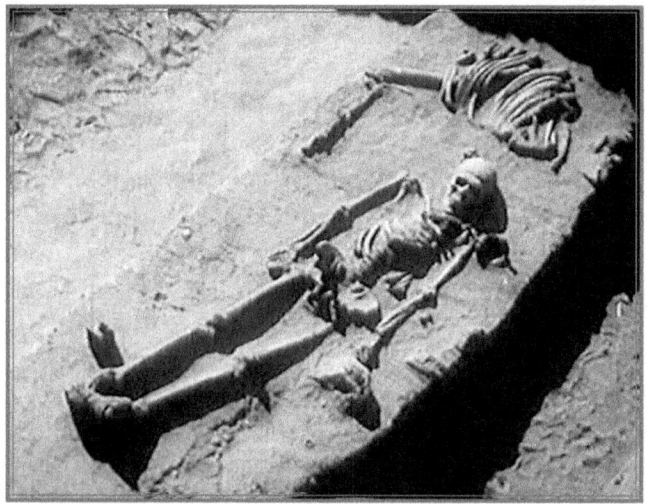

Figure 7.20.
Grave II. Still from
Vertov's *The Eleventh
Year* (1928).

the eighty or so kurgans that were excavated, according to Miller, during the construction. Judging from both images (figs. 7.19 and 7.20), the skeletons seem carefully tended.

Perhaps one reason to exclude the work of the archaeologists from the film is that it would indicate that the excavations were purposeful and that the skeletons were not a random find. Instead, the film seems to insist on treating the find as an accidental discovery of the archaic within the construction site—a discovery laid bare by virtue of the processes of industrialization, the very same ones that would pulverize or inundate the archaeological strata of the region. If, as the art historian T. J. Clark has observed, "modernity means contingency" and "points to a social order which has turned from the worship of ancestors and past authorities to the pursuit of a projected future,"[49] then what can we make of this ostensibly contingent, suggestively accidental discovery of an archaeological artifact at the very moment when the film is depicting the preparations for the coming industrialized future? From this perspective, the discovery of the Scythian(s) is something of a quintessential emblem for the early Soviet period, an essential sign under which Vertov inserts this episode into a narrative of Soviet modernity: industrial construction makes accidental discoveries that threaten the constitution of the future by forcing a confrontation with a deep past whose energies must be contained, harnessed, or annulled at the very moment when other energies, such as electrification, are preparing the ground for the future. The problem, in short, is how time can go confidently forward—an eleventh year, following a tenth, to be followed by a twelfth, and so on into the future—when establishing the ground work for the future unearths a past in such close proximity to it. Such a discovery plunges the utopian subject back into retrospection rather than encouraging utopian anticipation. One must prepare the way to the future, but those efforts create fissures and fractures through which fragments of the deep past emerge from the ground and are recorded for all to see (again and again), preserved in the flickering light of the cinema screen.

Perhaps another reason to avoid showing archaeological work is to promulgate another modernist myth—something like a Soviet primal scene—where industrial modernization unearths a challenge from the past in order to assert its own force in overcoming and containing that past: an archaeology with a hammer, an archaeology with dynamite. Or, perhaps it elides archaeology because actually showing the work would encode into the film the systematic

49 T. J. Clark, *Farewell to an Idea: Episodes from a History of Modernism* (New Haven, CT: Yale University Press, 1999), 7.

preservation of these artifacts, and thereby constitute an alternative future for them other than inundation.

In this light, we might return to the story of "archaeology at new construction sites." Many of the artifacts excavated in the region were indeed preserved, and excavations continued in the region throughout the twentieth century.[50] Mykhailo Miller reports that when he was serving as the deputy in charge of the archaeological expeditions at Dneprostroi, "archaeologists collected nearly 40,000 objects and shot 6,000 photographic negatives," with many of the artifacts being transferred to the Historical and Archaeological Museum of the Dnepropetrovsk Region, whose collection radically expanded in 1927 when archaeologists, headed by D. I. Evarnitskii (whose work at Zaporozh'e was discussed above), began to transfer objects from the area of deformation to the museum.[51] The collection was expanding in the very year the warrior's bones were discovered in Kichkas and Vertov began shooting *The Eleventh Year*.

When Dneprostroi finally opened in 1932, Miller reports that the excavated artifacts were gathered together for an exhibit entitled *From the Stone Axe to Dneprostroi*, which opened during the inaugural ceremony. The exhibit proved to be such a hit that Miller reported: "On the day of the inauguration, while solemn words in praise of the Party and the government were being pronounced and compulsory meetings for expressing gratitude were being held, the entire audience escaped to the archaeological exhibition, which was visited by 10,000 people on the first day of the inauguration."[52] Relishing the power of archaeology to retain its attraction for the audience, Miller concludes, with sly understatement: "For that reason disapproval was expressed to the organizers of the exhibition."[53] The title of the exhibition hints at the troubled relationship of the deep past to the present and future that we also find in *The Eleventh Year*. As a rival spectacle to the newly completed dam, the title

50   Liashko, *Kurgannye mogil'niki*, 3.

51   Miller, *Arkheologiia*, 55.

52   Ibid.

53   Ibid., 56.

discloses a sense of continuity between epochs by presenting an ongoing story of human tool making. It was this kind of attempt at establishing continuity between the archaic and the modern, which, as we shall see next, underpinned Boris Pil'niak's attempt to marry together the archaeological past with the Communist future, when he, like Vertov, imagined another area of deformation.

Chapter Seven

Areas of Deformation

Part Two: Boris Pil'niak's *The Volga Falls to the Caspian Sea* and the Courage of Farewell

Just as Dziga Vertov visited the Dneprostroi in search of a master emblem of Soviet industrialization, so too did Boris Pil'niak. Reporting in the 1930 miscellany *How We Write* (*Kak my pishem*), Pil'niak relates how he had finished a novel entitled *The Volga Falls to the Caspian Sea*: "To write the novel I read around thirty books about hydro-technology, researched, and met hydro-technical engineers, and traveled to the Dneprostroi."[1] The construction served as the model for the "Monolith," the massive hydraulic works whose construction underpins the plot of *Volga*.[2] And just as Vertov found a parallel story of archaeology proceeding in tandem with the construction, Pil'niak did as well. He writes early on in the novel:

> A young river was being built here, created not by geology, but made by man. The Moscow, the Oka, the Cis-Okian basin. The river was reconstructing geology. The river was destroying not only villages and history but also archaeology. The villages had left for new places. The engineers bored and dug up the subsoil. Archaeologists were bidding farewell to millennia.

---

[1] B. Pil'niak, "Bor. Pil'niak," in *Kak my pishem* (Leningrad: Izd-vo pisatelei v Leningrade, 1930), 128-29.

[2] The novel was completed in 1929, and published by Nedra in 1930. The translations used in the chapter are adapted from *The Volga Falls to the Caspian Sea*, trans. Charles Malamuth (New York: Cosmopolitan Book, 1931). All citations are cited in the text, with the first reference to the Malamuth translation, and the second to the edition of the novel published in volume four of Pil'niak's *Sobranie sochinenii v shesti tomakh* (Moscow: Terra-Knizhnyi klub, 2003).

Archaeologists, in their groups and by their excavations, roved over tens of square kilometers, which would be forever inundated by water, searching out camps of primitive man, the cities of ancient Meshchera, the kurgans, and graves—they were collecting prehistory. When the sluices freed the depths of the Oka river, archaeologists searched for the centuries that had been submerged in the waters.

The engineers knew, they knew very well the courage for the birth of the new (*bodrost' rozhdeniia novogo*), which attends every construction project. The archaeologists knew the courage of farewell (*bodrost' proshchaniia*). (31/258)

A key word in this remarkable passage is *bodrost'*, which conveys the senses of courage, enthusiasm, vigor, and cheer. What Pil'niak calls the *bodrost' rozhdeniia novogo*, or "courage for the birth of the new," he gears to *Volga*'s generic orientation toward the production novel. This form of courage is associated not only with the engineers in the novel, but also encompasses such other themes as the Prometheanism of the period, the domination of nature, the superannuation of various modes of living, and the desire for effluvial control—all themes Pil'niak shares with Vertov. More than the latter, however, Pil'niak emphatically addresses the practice of archaeology as it comes under the physical and ideological pressure of industrialization (fig. 7.21). He extends *bodrost'* to the archaeologists who must summon the *bodrost' proshchaniia*, or "courage of farewell," which they bid to the centuries and millennia of the world of artifacts now threatened by inundation.

In criticism of the novel, what has always shadowed such passages is the difficulty of determining where Pil'niak's own enthusiasms lay. According to the scathing assessment of Max Eastman, it was a failure of Pil'niak's own courage that lead to the enthusiasm for socialist industrialization we find in the novel. That enthusiasm became all the more emphatic—and in Eastman's reading, all the more suspicious—after the publication of "Mahogany" ("Krasnoe derevo," 1929), which had been greeted with a paroxysm of critical scorn. In the aftermath, the editor Ivan Gronskii advised Pil'niak to write a novel that would serve as a "form of propaganda for socialist construction and the five-year

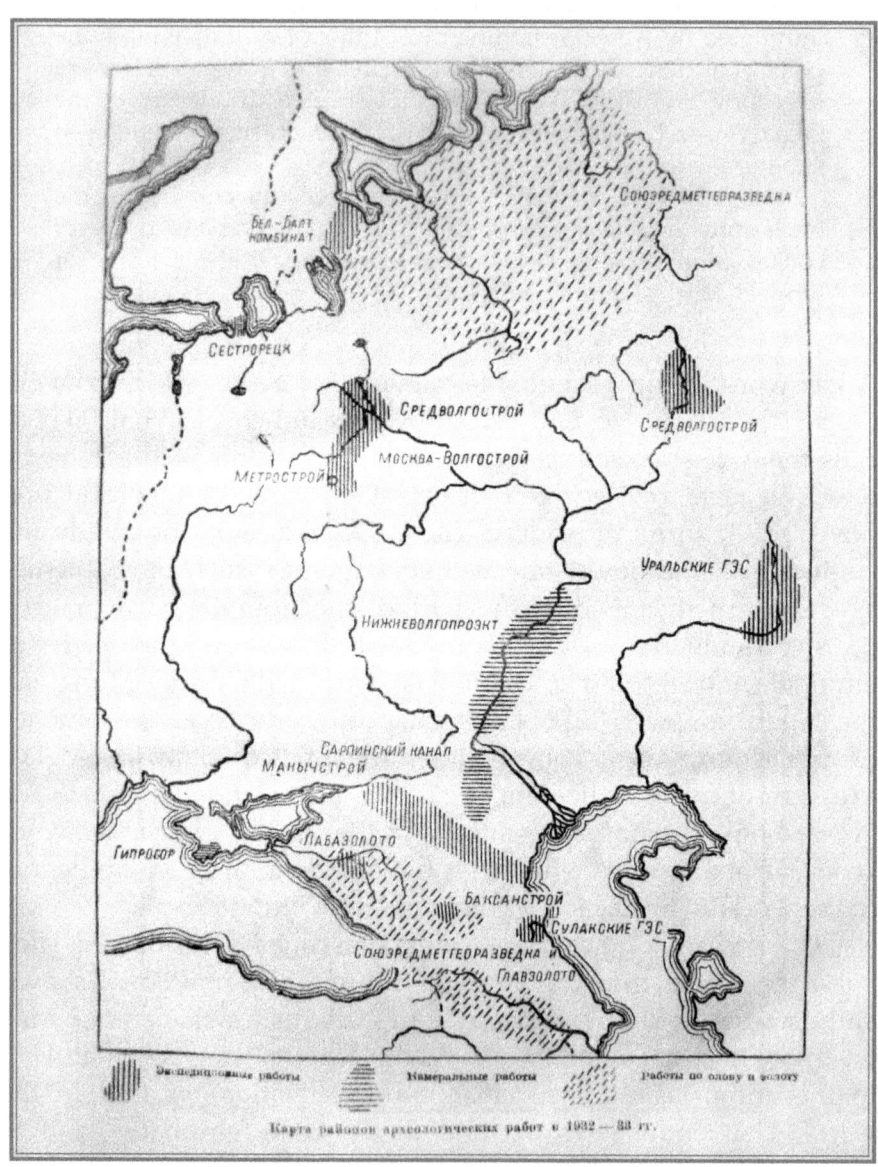

Figure 7.21.
Map of archaeological excavations at Soviet construction sites (1932-33).

plan."[3] Eastman's blistering appraisal initiated the line of criticism of the novel that has seen it as a work of appeasement: "probably no work of art in the world's history was ever completed in more direct violation of the artist's conscience, or with a more unadulterated motive of self-preservation."[4] Against this view, several scholars have pointed to both the manuscript history of *Volga* and to numerous textual sources, in elaborating an account of the work as far more complex than one of authorial appeasement.[5]

Archaeology and archaeological artifacts present the sort of ambivalence in the novel that makes the idea of appeasement too facile. Lodged in the passage cited above, for example, is a small detail that exemplifies how archaeology complicates any idea of the transformative potential of socialist industrialization—and, by extension, of Pil'niak's representation of and commitment to it in the novel. The "birth of the new," it turns out, inadvertently uncovers the old: "When the sluices freed the depths of the Oka river, archaeologists searched for the centuries that had been submerged in the waters." What Pil'niak describes here is another "area of deformation," but whereas *The Eleventh Year* consigns the past to the abyss, Pil'niak sees the destruction of one archaeological zone generating another as the water moves from one area to the next. Other industrializing processes do so as well: as Pil'niak writes shortly after the passage: "The foundation pits laid bare the river bottom as the centuries of archaeologists. Archaeologists were seeing off the centuries" (32/259).

While *The Naked Year* had earlier juxtaposed archaeology and the Revolution and Civil War at a remove, in *Volga* industrialization is accidental archaeology. It transforms the landscape, destroying

3   Max Eastman, *Artists in Uniform: A Study of Literature and Bureaucratism* (New York: Knopf, 1934), 121. Cf. Nicholas, "Boris Pil'niak and Modernism: Redefining the Self," 415, n. 23.

4   Eastman, *Artists in Uniform*, 125.

5   For two accounts rejecting the view of *Volga* as appeasement, see Kenneth N. Brostrom, "The Enigma of Pilnjak's *The Volga Falls to the Caspian Sea*," *Slavic and East European Journal* 18, no. 3 (Autumn 1974): 271–98, one of the most robust repudiations of this reading; and Irene Masing-Delic, "Boris Pil'niak's *The Volga Falls to the Caspian Sea* as Trotskyite Sophiology," *Slavic and East European Journal* 52, no. 3 (Fall 2008): 414-38.

one archaeological zone, while expanding rather than entirely annulling the range of artifacts to which archaeologists must summon the "courage of farewell." These simultaneous acts of destruction and discovery oscillate throughout the book. Characters are pulled between the past and the future, between the two forms of "courage" for novelty and farewell, and they must grapple with the fact that the past can actually proliferate in the face of the new. This tension variously affects characters in the novel: those who oversee the construction, those who work on it, and those who sabotage it; as well as those who profit from the past, like the antiquarian Bezdetov brothers. They all negotiate a relationship to the past and the future, the ancient and the modern. How they do so determines their fate in the novel.

Two of *Volga*'s positive characters embody these twin impulses: the archaeologist Liubov Poletika and her father, Pimen Poletika, the engineer who plans and supervises the construction of the Monolith. Both are Janus-faced in relation to time, at once looking backward and forward: "Liubov was digging into the ages in order to give them to the future. The world of this girl, who was overburdened with work, was pure and clear. The red March sunsets reminded Liubov of the daybreak of mankind in the steppes, and of the dawn of revolutions around the globe of the earth" (119-20/314). Liubov arrives in Kolomna to conduct various excavations and to study the Tower of Marina Mnishek — one of the novel's primary emblems of the past, the tower where Marina was supposedly imprisoned in the seventeenth century after her involvement in the failed coup led by the False Dmitry. Liubov excavates kurgans, salvages artifacts before and after inundation, and, most notably for the story of this book, unearths and studies the *kamennye baby* (which are primarily identified as feminine in the novel, hence my translation of them in the coming pages as "stone women"). Her archaeological project, as Pil'niak repeatedly emphasizes, is conducted in service to the revolutionary future.

Liubov's father, Pimen, by contrast, embodies the zeal for construction and the disdain for the past. He looks forward: "This was a battle for socialism, in the sense in which Professor Poletika understood socialism, when human labor, reconstructing rivers by the sheer force of its will, washes away the refuse of serfdom with these rivers and creates new labor relations" (22/252). Pimen's emphatically liquidationist vision to transform the landscape is expressed in his own self-deification as an engineer whose plan aims at nothing less than renewing the world through a socialist Flood.[6] He cannot, however, help but look backward, and he cannot liberate himself and the world from various temporal cycles. These cycles are historical, in the form of the rise and fall of empires; natural, in the processes of cultivation and desertification; and biographical, in, for example, the theme of cuckolding in Pimen's marriage and that of the first marriage of another positive character, Fedor Sadykov, in which both men's wives go off with the same man, the womanizer, Edgar Laszlo.

Such cycles belong to Pimen's worldview, which is characterized by his belief in the "recurrence of phenomena" (*povtornost' iavlenii*). Recurrence is made explicitly manifest in his name, which references Pushkin's *Boris Godunov* (to which the Tower of Marina Mnishek also alludes) and a range of other "Pimens," who extend back into the past and upon whom Pimen Poletika frequently meditates. Poletika, for example, visits the cave-monastery of "St. Pimen," experiencing there the full burden of the past: "As a boy, Poletika was always overcome by helplessness in those caves, and everything seemed pointless. Icon lamps and candles burned there, rooted in eternity, and the candles confirmed the horror and pointlessness of everything, beginning with those caves" (19-20/250). This early scene forms Pimen's initial trauma, the feelings of helplessness in the face of the deep past now propelling his desire to overcome the past and transform the world.

Yet Pimen ultimately cannot reconcile himself with his own time, or free himself from the concept of historical repetition. Instead, he affirms a resolution of the contradictory impulses of retrospection and utopian anticipation that split him through blessing his daughter's marriage to Sadykov, a worker who becomes an engineer. Pimen finds him vigorous and authentic: "Sadykov

6   Brostrom, "Enigma," 276.

smelled of the earth, the open shirt revealed his collarbones, he looked like a master mechanic, and he was not followed by secretaries. Professor Poletika loved this man of straightforward ideas and direct actions" (36/261). As Mary Nicholas has aptly observed, the relationship between Liubov and Sadykov "helps resolve inherent contradictions between the past and the present, prehistorical existence and future industrial development, passion and reason, and even women and men."[7] As Sadykov succinctly states the differences between him and Liubov: "I build the future, the new river—you dig up antiquities for the future" (229/386). In marrying Liubov to Sadykov, however, Pil'niak marries the past to the future; as Pimen says to him near the end of the novel, "I shall give you my projects, maps, plans, drawings, calculations. Our government will help you. . . . And you will see to it that they are carried out. . . . Liubov will go along with you to dig there, too, for the centuries" (349/469).

Pimen's proclamation is curious. Why should antiquities be preserved for the revolutionary future? Why do antiquities retain, perhaps even acquire greater power when the promise of the revolutionary future seems so bright? And why marry archaeology to industrialization, the deep past to the deep future? These questions guide this chapter. *Volga* instantiates the dialectic we previously saw in Vertov—namely, how the deep past and the deep future supercharge one another at moments of transition. Much like *The Eleventh Year*, *Volga* charts the clash between the two as the novel grapples with how the persistence of the past acquires heightened legibility in the pursuit of the revolutionary future. Pil'niak's commitment to archaeology in *Volga*—indeed, his effort to salvage the practice—not only relies on the marriage plot. To broker this rapprochement between archaeology and industrialization, Pil'niak triangulates the two with a third term, antiquarianism, which comprises another central theme of the novel. This rapprochement marks the recognition that the past is

---

[7]   Mary A. Nicholas, *Writers at Work: Russian Production Novels and the Construction of Soviet Culture* (Lewisburg, PA: Bucknell University Press, 2010), 188.

both necessary and unavoidable, capable of troubling utopian conviction without a proper frame. It also marks Pil'niak's attempt to negotiate the twin forms of courage as he reassessed his own concept of art and archaeology over the course of the 1920s.

i. All That Was Solid Did Not Melt into Air: Persisting Things

The encounter with archaeological artifacts typified a pervasive anxiety throughout the 1920s that all that was solid was *not* melting into air. Marx's great axiom was not proving axiomatic enough for the post-Revolutionary generation, who discerned the obdurate persistence of the past everywhere in the landscape and suspected revanchist threats lurking in the order of things. Such vestiges could differ in terms of their mode of manufacture, age, or the domain with which they were associated—the kitchen, the peasant household, the shop—or, by extension, the particular class with which they were affiliated—the peasantry or the bourgeoisie, pastoralists, or hunter-gatherers. And these vestiges could even proliferate as new pasts amid the shifting geographical and chronological coordinates of a given utopian vision. In all their variety, these vestigial forms shared an acute ability to trouble a utopian consciousness always on guard against such things, but perhaps also susceptible to them. Whatever guise the past assumed—vodka, samovars, relics, stone women—such remnants retained their power to awaken the lingering atavistic longings of people whose revolutionary convictions were especially weak.

We have various scholarly accounts of how figures in the 1920s sought to deal with objects whose stubborn refusal to disappear provoked a range of disturbances—psychic, ideological, political. Focusing on the NEP period, Eric Naiman, for example, has promoted the Gothic as a mode for encompassing these various disturbances: "The Gothic nature of NEP is most obvious in the relationship of early Soviet ideology to the past. It is not surprising that people who viewed themselves as utopia-bound should have targeted the concept of history for elimination. The past, when linked to the present, provides a conduit for contamination of the future."[8] The past refuses to stay past; it slips through the necessary divide between the pre- and post-Revolutionary periods. Rupture was desired, but return and persistence haunted the era, rendering all the more difficult the urgent task of inaugurating Year Zero. It was this threat for which Gothic repetition proves so apt. "The Gothic mode," Dale Peterson keenly observes, "affirm[ed] the vulnerability of chronological progress to disruption by anachronistic or atavistic events. It is true, though, that the author of a Gothic narrative may choose either to exercise or to exorcize those uncanny forces that threaten to make history repeat itself."[9] While this oscillation between the exercise and the exorcism of these disruptive forces is not limited to the NEP era alone, and signals an ongoing predicament in Russian modernist culture as a whole, the political ramifications of failure continued to grow, with different solutions to the problem of the persistence of things set forth.

Vertov's exercising and exorcising of his uncanny Scythian and Pil'niak's myriad encounters with antiquites in *Volga* exemplify these period dilemmas. Both disclose the typifying modes by which artists sought to grapple with the problem of persistence, of both things and various forms of life. In this, they join up with two tendencies of Russian modernist culture. While its most widely influential concept is arguably Viktor Shklovsky's *ostranenie*, or "defamiliarization,"[10] Russian and later Soviet modernists were hardly less aware of an order of things that did not need to be "defamiliarized." All too familiar, these objects were the saboteurs of any innovation in the realms of art, the spirit, technology, or politics. These were the things belonging to the category of *byt*, the humdrum banalities that choke off life and experiment. As Roman Jakobson writes: "opposed to this creative urge toward a transformed future is the stabilizing force of an immutable present, overlaid, as this present is, by a stagnating

---

8   Eric Naiman, *Sex in Public: The Incarnation of Early Soviet Ideology* (Princeton, NJ: Princeton University Press, 1997), 155.

9   Dale Peterson, "Russian Gothic: The Deathless Paradoxes of Bunin's *Dry Valley*," *Slavic and Eastern European Journal* 31 (1987): 38. Cf. Naiman, *Sex in Public*, 151.

10 Viktor Shklovskii, "Iskusstvo kak priem" (1917/19), in *Poetika*, 3:101-14.

slime, which stifles life in its tight, hard mold. The Russian name for this element is *byt*."[11] Jakobson's account was only one in a range of discourses on *byt*. Another line of attack—and one particularly relevant to the archaeological encounter in *The Eleventh Year* and to *Volga*—was Sergei Tret'iakov's charting of the persistence of *byt* not just in the world of objects, but in the sympathies of the people: "*byt* is a deeply reactionary force, that which in pivotal moments of social change prevents the organization of the will of a class for plotting decisive assaults. Comfort for comfort's sake; coziness as an end in itself; all the chains of tradition and of respect for objects that have lost their practical meaning, beginning with the necktie and ending with religious fetishes—this is the quagmire of *byt*."[12]

This "quagmire of *byt*" is represented in *Volga* in relation to both the world of objects and to modes of life threatened by modernization. To take one representative example of Pil'niak's insistent tracking of various forms of persistence:

> Such was the locality, where the country was delivering the battle to Old Russia—Roosha [*Rasseia*], Rus'—in the name of socialism. Three years ago in June men came to these pastures, they measured and bored the land, peered into the space and the future, dug into the Jura and the Perm epochs, walked near the rivers and on the pastures, burned woodpiles even as the nomads had probably done, and it became known that a battle for socialism would begin here, a battle that would remake history and geology; that there would be no more Bobrenovo, Parfenievo, Amerevo, and

---

11 Roman Jakobson, "On the Generation That Squandered Its Poets," in Jangfeldt and Rudy, *My Futurist Years*, 200.

12 Sergei Tret'iakov, "Otkuda i kuda?," *Lef*, no. 1 (1923): 200, as cited in Christina Kiaer, *Imagine No Possessions: The Socialist Objects of Russian Constructivism* (Cambridge, MA: MIT Press, 2005), 65–66. For more on the various perspectives on *byt* in the 1920s, see the section "Bolshevism and *Byt*: Can 'Everyday Life' Ever be 'New,'" in Kiaer, *Imagine No Possessions*, 53–71. For work on *byt* beyond the 1920s, see Svetlana Boym, *Common Places: Mythologies of Everyday Life in Russia* (Cambridge, MA: Harvard University Press, 1994), esp. "Mythologies of Everyday Life," 29–120; and Catriona Kelly, "*Byt*: Identity and Everyday Life," in *National Identity in Russian Culture: An Introduction*, ed. Simon Franklin and Emma Widdis (Cambridge: Cambridge University Press, 2004), 149–68.

Sergeevskaia and many other villages, for their lands would go
under water (30/257).[13]

The threat or the promise—depending on one's vantage point—
that socialism can inaugurate a new time through inundation is
undone throughout this passage and the details Pil'niak adds. As
with Kichkas in *The Eleventh Year*, *Volga* focuses on villages slated for
inundation. From the perspective of the inhabitants of Akatevo, the
construction workers who come to the region are like "nomads," that
is, yet another iteration of the many threats the villagers have faced
throughout their history. Pil'niak gives voice to these inhabitants:
one villager from Akatevo says, "We've lived here for thousands
of years, and now suddenly our life must come to an end. I think
they're lying about the river, though, as a matter of fact, they are
building. It is impossible to believe that not only shall we cease to
drive the rafts, but that even Akatevo itself will be plunged under
water just like Kitezh" (99/300). The reference to the mythological
city of Kitezh—saved from the Mongol hordes by being submerged
in water—encodes one challenge to the story of modernization,
since the reference denotes a shift in the mythological valence of
inundation from destruction to preservation. So, too, does Pil'niak
encode another detail on the endurance of the past a few lines later,
when he notes that the villagers will relocate, and the past will be
replicated: "the new arrivals had proposed to transfer Bobrenovo
and build it anew, in European fashion, as a model village. The
peasant women demanded that Bobrenovo should be transplanted
and reconstituted exactly as it had been before" (30/257). The past, in
other words, is not destroyed but displaced, and, indeed, replicated.
It's not only that nomads are a thing of the past, or that the new
"nomads" of migrating workers burn pyres like the nomads of old,
but also that the past itself is nomadic, eternally decamping and
encamping in the wake of new threats.

13   I follow Brostrom's translation here of the derogatory terms "Rasseia" and "Roosha." Brostrom,
      "Enigma," 277.

ii. The Fluids of History:
Archaeology and Antiquarianism

What place do archaeological artifacts have in this view of the past, and in this "quagmire of *byt*"? That they might be considered alongside everyday objects might seem odd given such disparities in age, but the archaeological artifacts are routinely ascribed the disturbing power to incite amazement or worship. In *Volga*, Pil'niak is centrally concerned with disentangling the multiple practices regarding objects so as to salvage archaeology within the broader project of socialist modernization. In doing so, he turns *Volga* into a remarkable case study of the broader opposition between antiquarianism and archaeology we find both locally in the Soviet 1920s and throughout modernism internationally.

The critic B. Aikhenval'd called attention to the image of antiquarianism Pil'niak fashions in a keen review of *Volga* published in *Krasnaia nov'* in 1931.[14] "Juxtaposed with the world of the Revolution," he writes, "is the world of *Mahogany*, of obstinate *byt*, and historical tradition, the world of antiquarians and restorers—the brothers Bezdetov, the two stern apostles of conservatism. . . . They are in love with the past, with undying things, which, by the riches of their form and style, represent the petrified dynamic of history."[15] This vision of antiquarianism makes the political problem of the persistence of *byt* ever more acute than a generalized opposition to worshipping the past that we find within international modernism, which typically opposed a "monolithic antiquarianism whose deeper logic is declared insidious because it locates the past at the very core of a conservative, continuity-based vision of the future."[16]

---

[14] For more on antiquarianism in the 1920s, see Anthony Anemone, "Obsessive Collectors: Fetishizing Culture in the Novels of Konstantin Vaginov," *Russian Review* 59, no. 2 (April 2000): 252-68; on antiquarianism generally, see Ackbar Abbas, "Walter Benjamin's Collector: The Fate of Modern Experience," *New Literary History* 20, no. 1 (Autumn 1988): 217-37.

[15] B. Aikhenval'd, "O romane Pil'niaka *Volga vpadaet v Kaspiiskoe more*," *Krasnaia nov'*, no. 4 (1931): 181. All further references are given in the text.

[16] Schnapp, Schanks, and Tiews, "Archaeology," 4

Embodying the antiquarian impulse, the Bezdetov brothers are the so-called "knights of the antique" (27/255). They scour homes of the déclassé for objects they can traffic in the fetid vestiges of a market system. The "courage of farewell" scarcely applies to them. They instead maintain a deep and sordid longing for the objects of antiquity. Pil'niak describes the type:

> He is an antiquarian—a restorer of antiques (*stariny*). In the attic of a Mos-cow home, in a pawnshop, in some district town, in the shed of a country estate yet to be burned down, he would find a chair, a trellis, or sofa—in the style of Catherine, Paul, or Alexander— and he'd spend months rummaging over them in his cellar, smoking, thinking, measuring with his eyes, in order to restore the living life of dead things. He is a restorer. He looks backwards, into the time of things. (50-51/270)

The Revolution may have forced the tsars from political power, but in the realm of the antiquarian, the tsars retain authority over taste and style. And just as the tsars thereby enjoy a posthumous authority in this realm of antiquarian objects, so, too, do antiquarian things enjoy a posthumous life.

At once manufactured and immortal, the object of antiquarianism gains ever more force by virtue of its persistence and its opposition to the new. It is immune to historical change and, more than that, it can freeze time in its tracks:

> Their basement stopped time, crammed full with the antiquities of the Alexanders, Pauls, and Catherines. The brothers—like emperors themselves—knew how to talk about antiquity and craftsmanship. In their basement breathes antiquity, which one could love and buy. (327/454)

This is a central passage in the ongoing story of the Russian modernist encounter with various forms of "antiquity," now recapitulated in the post-Revolutionary period. But now, in 1929, their posthumous existence reaffirms a relationship to the past evincing no creative impulse. Antiquarians do not create, they restore and preserve objects whose "fluids" lack vitality, bring history to a halt, and disclose no link to the future.

As if this posthumous life of things did not pose enough of a problem, Pil'niak also notes an increasing taste for antiques, and the fact that this taste was sanctioned in state markets.

> In the year 1929, antique shops arose in Moscow, Leningrad, and the district towns, where old things were bought and sold through state pawnshops, the state trading company, the state fund, and by private traders. In the year 1929, there were many people who collected "fluids" (*fliuidy*); people who bought the ancient things after the thunders of the Revolution, cherishing antiques (*starina*) in their homes, inhaled the living spirit of dead things, revived the dead past with things that survived it. (326-27/454)

Many of the objects described in this passage could have served as "antiquities" for various modernists, but they are now keyed to the problem of persistence and caught up in the question of what, if anything, should be preserved.

One notable consequence of the overriding desire to construct the future and liquidate the past is that it renders moot the question of whether Russia possesses an antiquity, or antiquities. Indeed, antiquities—and as in the aforementioned passage, *antiques*—suffuse the landscape presented in *Volga*:

> The most ancient Russian lands—the Cis-Okian districts, the Riazan Country, the old Tartar lands, the lands of ancient Muscovy, and the robber highways—the history of Russia from the time of Murom, Meri, Riazan, Meshchera, from the feudal period up to the railways . . . and previous to this, before there was a Russia, the Sarmatians, the Alani, the Finns, the Scythians, the Stone and Bronze ages. A landscape immemorially Russian. (29/256-57)

The description typifies much of the landscape in the novel. Spaces are characterized as "revel[ing] in their antiquity" (72/283); reminders of the past crop up everywhere—"stone monuments of murders and centuries and gray stones of kremlins" (45/267). Indeed, even the question as to whether Russia possessed antiquities on a par with Greece or Rome is rendered moot in the face of a socialist offensive and its opposition to "Old Russia." Pil'niak, at one point in describing the Bezdetovs, simply lists the various antiquities one could find: "Elizabeth, Catherine, rococo, baroque, Paul the Maltese, Paul the Severe, severe restfulness, darkly polished mahogany, green leather, black lions, griffins, Alexander, Empire, the classic, the Hellene. People were dying, but things lived, and from the things of the past come the 'fluids' of antiquity, of bygone years" (326/454). In a novel about effluvial control, the "fluids" of these antiquities is associated not with historical progress, but with the continuing authority of the past and its objects.

Such forms of persistence link the novel to other works from the period such as Andrei Platonov's *Chevengur*, which grapples with the challenge, in David Bethea's words, of "the possibility of effecting *any* change over the expanse known as the steppe. Here space becomes the chief obstacle to the apparent changes wrought in historical time by the revolution."[17] In *Volga*, the question of whether change can happen extends beyond the steppe to anywhere "Old Russia" holds sway, or where antiques proliferate. What archaeology adds to this account is that it points to the multiple temporal layers Pil'niak envisions have amassed within the landscape and that emerge during the very process of industrialization. These objects force the question of how, if at all, the past will be integrated into historical time.

In this, both characters in *Volga* manifest a general antagonism toward antiquity among the more committed cultural modernizers. In the journal *Novyi LEF*, to take one example, the poet Nikolai Aseev published sections of a travel diary he kept during his visit to Italy, where he found everywhere a "comedy of human ruins."[18] Aseev aims directly at the typical tourist who insists upon the preservation of the old and decries any sign of modernization. "Is it possible," he asks, "that I do not have the right to juxtapose this 'feeling for the antique' (*chuvstvo antichnogo*) with my own 'feeling for modernity' (*chuvstvo sovremennosti*) out of fear that

---

[17] Bethea, *Shape of Apocalypse*, 175-76. Cf. Thomas Seifrid, *Andrei Platonov: Uncertainties of Spirit* (Cambridge: Cambridge University Press, 1992), 228-29.

[18] N. Aseev, "Zagranitsa (iz dnevnika puteshestviia)," in *Novyi LEF*, no. 2 (1928): 3.

I will be taken for an ignoramus and a superficial person?" "I am glad," Aseev continues, "that a construction fever seems to be the chronic disease of the new Italy. I am glad that 'new buildings are rising up in Rome with such rapidity that few can justify whether they are necessary.'"[19] Adamantly opposed to the "divinization of ruins," Aseev shares with other revolutionaries this "feeling for modernity"—a version of which Pil'niak calls the "courage for the birth of the new"—inspired by various signs of modernization.

Various characters in *Volga* share Aseev's mindset, in particular Pimen, who expresses a similar drive toward modernity. But Pil'niak's grappling with the theme of modernization through Pimen reveals how industrialization unwittingly generates shocks of the past:

> Poletika looked angrily at the sky and thought that man, mankind, was called upon, not only to reconstruct the nature of things, but to drive back the flow of rivers, to solder monoliths to geology; but man, indeed mankind, also builds up monoliths of conceptions, digging up history and the subconscious element in man, building new human relations. (339/463)

Pimen's account of industrialization recapitulates the theme we saw at the outset of this chapter, namely, the discovery of the past by the processes of modernization; industrialization, Pil'niak makes explicit here, digs up the subterranean zone of the "subconscious element" in man. The question Pil'niak seems to pose is what happens to that element, once uncovered and unleashed.

In this, Pil'niak presents a remarkable local instance of what was a broader reassessment of archaeology in modernist circles in Western Europe. Where we find a general antagonism toward antiquarianism, we also encounter throughout West European modernism a desire to tap "into 'prehistoric' instinctualisms, violence, savagery, sacrifice, and sacrality. Instead of feeding necrophilia, this modernist archaeology purports to operate in the

---

19   N. Aseev, "Spor s putevoditelem," in *Novyi LEF*, no. 5 (1928): 15-23. The "guidebook" with which Aseev is quarreling in this article is Pavel Muratov's *Images of Italy* (*Obrazy Italii*), which served as a central guide to Italy in Russia.

service of life. It unburies life forms resistant or hostile to Culture and Civilization."[20] In Pil'niak's case, his contemporaries, such as Aleksandr Voronskii, had recognized early on that such forms of discovery and engagement with the past typified Pil'niak's writing. In an exceptional passage on Pil'niak and others of his generation, Voronskii notes:

> In various articles and in various connections we have had to note more than once the attraction of modern writers, artists, poets, and publicists to the primitive, to the simplified and uncomplicated life . . . The Russian Revolution, uncovering the depths of elemental forces, has thrust onto the arena of history the *muzhik*, the worker, the people of the Taiga, of the forests and steppes, with their healthy, fresh, direct relations to their surroundings. The war and the Revolution have shown the modern intellectual the significance of things as such, and the value of life in its simple, rude, primitive [state].[21]

In ascribing to the Revolution the responsibility for having uncovered "the depths of elemental forces," Voronskii establishes the basic template by which to understand how Pil'niak extends his sense of elemental drives to the world of objects, radically destabilizing and compulsively enthralling. The problem in *Volga*, at least with respect to archaeology, was how to make the past enter into the service of life and the Revolution. Pil'niak does not explicitly clarify this. He approaches the topic apophatically, that is, he reveals at the very least what the relationship to the past should not be: the transformation of the past into objects of antiquarian desire, which we see, in fact, with Pil'niak's account of the stone women.

20   Schnapp, Schanks, and Tiews, "Archaeology," 4.

21   Voronskii, "Literaturnye siluety," 255-56.

iii. The Courage of Farewell:
The Return of the Stone Women

The Stone Woman was the one object that the critic Aikhenval'd singled out in his review because he could not give a full account of its significance. In fact, he did not think Pil'niak could do so either: "What did Pil'niak want to say with these stone Scythian women (*kamennye skifskie baby*), which the Communist Liubov Pimenovna excavates together with the departing centuries? . . . [The statues are] conveyed with such a striking exaggeration as with other similar images they must mean something profound, grand, and wise?"[22] His sarcasm notwithstanding, Aikhenval'd recognized the difficulty of squaring a reading of the statuary with his own account of antiquarianism. One reason for this is that Pil'niak continually subjects the statuary to debate between characters as to their meaning and provenance, while also revealing several shifts in his own thinking about the statuary over the course of his career.

Pil'niak had established his views on the relationship of the statuary to his own artistic project in his *Machines and Wolves (Mashiny i volki, 1925)*, where the statuary served as a central emblem by which to elaborate his aesthetic values:

> Along the dryvales they're again excavating in kurgans stone women covered in moss. For us artists, these *babas* are aesthetically beautiful (*prekrasnaia krasota*). But if the smallest insect were to crawl along the chest of a stone woman, and from the chest to the neck — the chest of the woman, the path of the insect, — would not all of this be in paths and pits, in the sultriness of the stone, in the suffocation of the moss, in weariness, in sweat, in the wilderness? One must be at the height of the stone woman to see that she is aesthetically beautiful, and then to bow before her, as once worshipped the Muromians, the Meshcherans, and the Vyess.[23]

True artists can discern beauty within the statues because they are different from other viewers, whom Pil'niak compares to insects,

---

[22] Aikhenval'd, "O romane Pil'niaka," 184.

[23] B. Pil'niak, *Mashiny i volki* (1925, reprint; Munich: Wilhelm Fink Verlag, 1971), 166.

the radically diminished perspectives of which cannot take in the entirety of the *babas*. The statues, in turn, supply an aesthetic value to the artist because they are uninterested in the comings and goings of the insect: "But, indeed, this stone woman from the excavations is aesthetic beauty! And she does not know, does not notice the thing crawling" upon her. As Mary Nicholas has observed of these lines, we here find an essential elaboration of Pil'niak's modernism: "the artist who would adopt her far-sighted perspective must emulate this indifference as well."[24]

In *Volga*, responses to the statuary range far beyond the central values of beauty and apathy Pil'niak attributes to it. The statues serve instead as an arena for contested opinions about aesthetics and culture, as they have for so many other writers and artists we have seen. They serve as mirrors for the characters in the novel, but also as vehicles for Pil'niak to revisit some of the views he asserted not only in *Machines and Wolves*, but also throughout his career in the 1920s. The stone women were a way for Pil'niak to think through the place of archaeology in the socialist future, and to assess his own career and concerns during the course of that decade.

The statuary serves as a primary point of reference for several of the novel's most significant scenes. Scholarly criticism of the novel has alluded to them frequently, relating them, for example, to Pil'niak's "organic and cyclical understanding of the texture of everyday life"[25] and to his soteriological vision.[26] They are a central object of Liubov's archaeological study—she studies a group of them at the Historical Museum in Moscow and she salvages one from the depths of the Oka—and so stand apart from the order of

---

24 Mary Nicholas, "Pil'niak on Writing," *Slavonic and East European Review* 72, no. 2 (April 1993): 228–29.

25 Nicholas, *Writers at Work*, 189.

26 Given the recurrent images of archaeology and the Stone Women in the novel, other works have, not surprisingly, addressed this topic, including Brostrom, "Enigma," 284; Masing-Delic, "Boris Pil'niak's *The Volga Falls*," 427–29; and Nicholas, *Writers at Work*, 188–90. Brostrom also notes, "Pil'njak's use of symbolic women in relation to the problem of faith extends throughout the 20's. Some of the more familiar are the *soldatka* (*Golyj god*, 1920), the stone baba (*Rjazan'-jabloko*, 1921), Lisa Kalitina (*Tret'ja stolica*, 1922), Milica and the babishcha (*Mashiny i volki*, 1924), and the Egyptian female mummy (*Ivan Moskva*, 1927)" (297, n. 13).

antiquarian objects, even though they are often grouped within the helter-skelter congeries of the object world depicted in *Volga*. Pil'niak places one in a local museum in Kolomna, another space in *Volga* besides that of the pawnshops and the Bezdetovs' cellar where the "time of things" reigns. Run by a character referred to as Griboedov, the museum is where the character Mariia Sadykova, the first wife of Sadykov who leaves him for Laszlo, encounters a stone woman, prior to committing suicide:

> Mariia Fedorovna at that hour was lying curled up on the Paulite mahogany sofa from the Tuchkov manor at the museum custodian Griboedov's, in whose study were scattered the surplices and stoles, and where the naked Christ sat. A candle burned next to the Christ, and behind the Christ stood the terrible, green ancient stone woman that had spent a thousand years on the bottom of the river Oka and now squinted with blind eyes. (236/392)

This is the statue that Liubov, who will eventually marry Sadykov, had excavated during the construction of the Monolith at the bottom of the Oka river. Now in the heap of objects located in the museum, it seems to judge Mariia, who says to Laszlo: "It is terrible here in this strange house. This Christ and this ancient statue have such eyes that they watch you all the time, however much you may try to turn away from them" (253/403). That the *baba* judges her speaks to the overdetermined power ascribed to artifacts in *Volga*, and to Mariia's own guilt-ridden consciousness, whose suicide sets off the mass reaction of the women laboring at the Monolith.

Indeed, such views on the statuary are often tied to a given character's typifying features. Like that of Mariia's guilty conscience, Poltorak's relationship to the statuary typifies his relationship to women throughout the story: "The stone women, studied by Liubov Pimenova, were Poltorak's ailment (*bolezn' Poltoraka*)" (132/322). Why the statuary can haunt these various characters comes into focus through the relationship between Poltorak and Liubov, and, in particular, in an extended passage on the statuary—indeed, one of the most extensive passages we find on the statuary in literature—when he describes Liubov's speculations on the statuary, which serve as counterpoints to Mariia's sense that it judges her and Poltorak's sense that it torments him. I quote the passage at some length because it recapitulates several themes central to *Volga*, to the career of the statuary, and to the themes essayed in this book:

> There are people who give their lives over to strange things. That March, the twenty-year-old Liubov Poletika, finding time from her Komsomol work, devoted her time and thoughts to the study of the shadowy history of the stone steppe women, which are excavated in ancient kurgans. In Moscow, these stone women are preserved in the courtyard of the Historical Museum, piled up, cumbersome, hundreds of poods, terrible, eaten away by time, wind, and earth. They consisted of cheekbones, breasts, and stomachs. Liubov Poletika searched for the era of the emergence of the statues, the people who had made them, and their history. She went to the Volga, to the archaeologist Paul Rau, to unearth the statuary, and to see the bare steppe landscape, which for centuries had preserved the statues, having lost the people who created them, and the time and the memory of them. . . . After the Volga, she went to the places where the forerunners of her stepfather had left for Hungary. . . . The women were actually terrible, slit-eyed, cow-bellied, bony-cheeked; Liubov Pimenova spoke about their grace (*Baby deistvitel'no byli strashny, skulastye, uzkoglazye, korovozhivotye, —Liubov Pimenova govorila ob ikh gratsii*). Liubov Pimenova spent hours speaking about the folds in the clothes of these women, about the dry outlines of their empty steppe eyes, about their low foreheads, about their breasts and stomachs that stuck out, symbols of fertility. These women emerged in confirmation of the matriarchate. Studying their aesthetics by the laws of their craftsmanship, Liubov thought how far humanity is now removed from that unknown people, who had left their art in these women. (118-19/313)

Liubov's aesthetic evaluation of the statues, which seems to straddle the incompatible values of terror and grace, parallels the ambiguity in the final line of the passage on how to understand the distance between the present and the past: "how far humanity is now removed (*kak daleko ushlo*) from that unknown people." Does the distance separating Liubov's time from that of the statuary's creation encode an idea of development, whereby objects of the past serve as measures of civilizational progress? In that case, is Liubov's archaeological work important for the revolutionary future because it furnishes that future with the indices by which to measure its own progress? Yet to see distance not wedded to concepts of progress is to discern aesthetic and civilizational value in the objects of the nomadic past even though they come down in the form of "cow-bellied" statuary. In this latter sense, Liubov's assertion that this unknown people has "left their art in these women" reads archaic artifacts as aesthetically valuable in their own right, which encodes an argument for the value of the past unwedded to ideas of progress.

Encompassing the seemingly irreconcilable responses of terror and admiration, Liubov's views on the statuary mark the artifacts as more than just primordial yardsticks by which to measure civilizational progress, but aesthetic testaments as well. No less significant, however, is her ascription of the statuary to a fertility cult and a matriarchate which directly contrasts with the interpretation of the statues given by Poltorak, who has tried to seduce Liubov (who ultimately marries Sadykov, who Mariia, also tormented by the statuary, had left):

> Liubov led Poltorak under the vaults of the Historical Museum, where the stone women had been preserved. Poltorak perceived these stone beams as the remnants of idolatry, of a Rozanovian mysticism of sex (*rozanovskoi mistikoi pola*), of Slavophile Scythianism. Poltorak wanted to believe that the girl gave her time to these antiquities (*drevnostiam*) in the name of mysticism; he was trying to convince himself and her about this, but this was not true for Liubov. Liubov dug into the centuries to give them to the future. (119/313-14)

On one level, Poltorak's views make clear how the statues are symbols of the gender and sexual ideologies in the novel, with Pil'niak coordinating these "readings" of the statuary with the nature of a given character: Liubov's chaste and maternal commitment to the Revolution; Poltorak's libidinal desire now ascribed to the statuary. As with Liubov's views on the statuary, Poltorak's interpretation of them as figures of idolatry, and embodiments of a "Rozanovian mysticism of sex" and "Slavophile Scythianism" are keyed to his persona.

These are quite loaded terms, however, because more than serving as mirrors for Poltorak, they also encode Pil'niak's own complicated position throughout the 1920s. In fact, Poltorak's views refer us to the very criticism the writer faced from early on in the decade. Pil'niak's readers might well have recalled the debates surrounding several of his early works, in particular one of the first of many critical paroxysms Pil'niak set off when he spoke of the "erotics" of the Revolution in his 1922 story "Ivan and Maria," which contained the notorious line: "I feel that the entire Revolution—the entire Revolution—smells of sexual organs."[27] This line, as Robert Maguire remarks, was one that "would ever dog" Pil'niak.[28] And it continues to do so in *Volga*. The line scandalized the more staid visionaries of the Revolution, in particular Aleksandr Voronskii, who castigated Pil'niak in a lengthy essay on the writer published in 1922, in which, it turns out, we find something of a source for Poltorak's vision of the stone women: "To whom and for what purpose is all this pathology necessary?" Voronskii asks of "Ivan and Maria": "The result is something like the Rozanovian mysticism of sex, or the conversion of the world into a brothel."[29]

Perhaps Pil'niak's readers, who had picked up *Volga*, might have remembered Voronskii's charge of the "Rozanovian mysticism of sex" now ventriloquized by Poltorak. They may also have remembered what Voronskii went on to say: "We have entered a period of a real and genuine reworking and inner rethinking of everything we have experienced over the past five years. The artist who fails to understand that will quickly find himself behind the 'spirit of the times.'"[30] Seven years after Voronskii's essay, Pil'niak was still groping for a way to join up with the spirit of the times, and to do so, he recapitulated the terms of this earlier criticism through

---

[27]   Voronskii, "Literaturnye siluety," 267; cf. Maguire, *Red Virgin Soil*, 108.

[28]   Maguire, *Red Virgin Soil*, 108.

[29]   Voronskii, "Literaturnye siluety," 267, cited in ibid.

[30]   Ibid.

Poltorak, while distancing himself from those views by offering Liubov's interpretation of the stone women as an alternative to his own earlier vision of revolutionary erotics. The success, or rather failure, of Poltorak's views on the sexual mysticism of the *babas* could be linked to his fate in the novel: he and Laszlo are killed off in the narrative.

Here, we might compare Pil'niak's use of the statuary with another object that emerged from the ground around the time that Pil'niak published his full version of *The Naked Year*. In 1922, French archaeologists reported the discovery of an artifact, fashioned in female form, which would later be called the Lespegue Venus, named after the area in which it was discovered. It was the Lespegue Venus that encouraged Georges Bataille to speculate that Upper Paleolithic man fashioned artifacts "as a response to sexual desire."[31] Bataille linked the presence of erotics in the deep past to anarchy, or what he referred to as "the chaos of eroticism" incited by objects made by prehistoric people. Such a link between the erotic and the archaic artifact of the stone *baba* was not made in *Naked Year*, although the anarchic and scandalous potential of erotics was never far from Pil'niak's mind. To recall, the naked women circumambulating the kurgan in *The Naked Year* compelled Baudek to see them as the persistence of the past, though perhaps they are a libidinal upsurge of the erotic as well. It was in *Volga*, however, where Pil'niak uses Poltorak to simultaneously link erotics to the archaic past, even though he seems at the very verge of doing so, to bid farewell to that very association. Indeed, where Pil'niak had earlier linked aesthetics and idolatry to the stone women in *Machines and Wolves*, he now seems to disentangle one from the other, giving Liubov's character the ability to aesthetically appreciate the *babas*, and leaving Poltorak with idolatry, Rozanov, and Scythianism.

Such a reading might seem to accord with critical views on the novel as a capitulation. However, the second term Poltorak attributes to the stone women—Slavophile Scythianism—generates

[31] Georges Bataille, *The Cradle of Humanity: Prehistoric Art and Culture*, ed. Stuart Kendall, trans. Stuart Kendall and Michelle Kendall (New York: Zone Books, 2005), 110.

its own ambiguity. When, for example, the stone women appear
again later in the work, they do so as a reference point for Nadezhda
Antonovna, Poltorak's mistress, who sees a procession of women
protesting that had been set off by the suicide of Mariia Sadykova
because of her affair with Laszlo, whom the women now want to
see punished:

> Listen: this ancient square, this ancient howling of bells—and
> these ancient women, these proletarian women! I've looked at
> them; they are made of stone, these *babishchy*. The tan of their faces
> is dove-colored, like that of a plum; their skin's not at all white.
> They wore garments that are a thousand years old—*plakhty* and
> *panovye*. They were barefooted. They're ancient, these *babishchy*.
> This was a procession of Scythians—and a procession as old as
> the ages. In front they carried the coffin—what antiquity (*starina*)
> must they be burying when they follow the coffin, these *babishchy*
> in their panyovas and their speechlessness. (143/230)

Instead of advancing the theme of erotics through the stone *babas*,
as it would for Poltorak, the Scythian statuary and women-turned-
Scythian now emerge as something of an emblem for the eternal
plight of women, a mythological paradigm for laboring women.

Other works from the 1920s reveal an early Soviet reinvigoration
of past traditions to serve as models for the proletariat, but they were
frequently masculine in origin. In Andrei Platonov's *Chevengur*,
David Bethea notes, one finds a "wish to tap into an older and richer
tradition, that of the Western knight errant (especially Cervantes's
hero) and that of the Russian *bogatyr'* (folk/epic hero)."[32] Vertov, too,
participates in this tendency toward recuperating past myths, with
his promotion of the *bogatyr'* in *The Eleventh Year*. In *Volga*, the stone
women serve as a paradigm for the women. But this promotion also
encodes a problem. Nadezhda Antonovna's question in the passage
above—"what antiquity must they be burying?"—is a curious one
because the women in the burial procession are likened to Scythians
and to "stone women." They, too, are the living embodiments of
an antiquity they also bury. The scene, then, reveals a typifying

[32] Bethea, *Shape of Apocalypse*, 175-76.

structure in the novel regarding circular models of time and history; in this case, the burial marks the self-interment of the past by the past, of antiquity by antiquity, with little to offer a way out of that cycle.

Part of the goal of the novel, then, seems to be to find ways out of this dilemma. In this regard, we could return to the character Pimen, who ultimately finds peace with his wife, who had, like Mariia, left him for Laszlo. Finding her in a garden, with her hands covered with soil, he reaches out to her: "Pimen Sergeevich kissed the earth on the hands (*potseloval zemliu na ruke*) of Olga Alexandrovna. . . . Life can begin and end at any hour, any minute" (344/466). Brostrom observes that Pil'niak echoes Sonia's admonition to Raskol'nikov in *Crime and Punishment*—"kiss the earth"—by kissing Olga's soiled hands, an act that not only reconciles him with her, but also with the world he has been so zealously seeking to transform.

In the context of this book, the line also calls to mind the stone woman from Remizov's eponymous tale, who had admonished the protagonists to do the same. (The line, to recall, later finds its way into Stravinsky and Roerich's *Rite of Spring* via the stone woman.) It is thus all the more curious that after this scene with Pimen, Pil'niak returns to a discussion between Liubov and Sadykov precisely over the stone woman that she had excavated in the Oka:

> Fedor, one has to look backward in order to see the future . . . At the bottom of the Oka river a Scythian stone woman was found,— several years ago I studied the history of these stone women. . . . How long had this figure lain under the water? (345/467).

In a novel devoted so intensely to her father's vision of the future, Liubov's statement is no less significant in presenting a parallel account of the relevance of the past to the present. One moves forward in time by looking backward. A future without a past and a past without a future: this is one of the crucial quandaries of the novel for which Liubov's archaeology and her marriage to Sadykov present a possible way out.

At the same time, Liubov's question serves as a reminder that the novel is as much about the persistence as it is about the recuperability of the past. In that regard, her question also serves to prefigure the novel's final image: the inundation of the Tower of Marina Mnishek, with its ostensible promise that the inundation caused by the Monolith will inaugurate a new era:

> Mishka ran to see how the water swamped the old water pump, how it was advancing and had advanced up to the Marina Tower, inundated the foot of it, then immersed this most ancient Kolomna monument, near which, for centuries, desolation had hovered in the shape of a crow, incarnating the soul of Marina, the tower in which Marina died and in which Rimma conceived. In the hour of Ozhogov's death the boy Mishka was near the Marina Tower. (353/472)

In this final tableau—with the death of Ozhogov, the revolutionary; the inundation of the tower; and the youthful Mishka witnessing the inundation—Pil'niak conjures a scene analogous to the superimpositions in *The Eleventh Year*. This final scene also leaves insecure the prospects of inaugurating Year Zero, when it is read against the status of archaeology in the novel. Both Liubov's question about the *babas* and much of the novel have prepared us to read the scene against its own promise of the inundation of the past. Things in the novel do not simply disappear. Perhaps the character Mishka will remember that something lay beneath the waters, or that Kolomna will recapitulate the paradigm of Kitezh, which Pil'niak had earlier mentioned. Perhaps the waters will one day recede and the inundated town and tower will be excavated by future archaeologists. Should that be the case, Pil'niak has prepared his readers to ask from the outset of the work: Will future archaeologists also have to summon the courage of farewell? And what will be the status of the Revolution when they do so? Pil'niak's suggestion here is that only archaeology married to industrialization can provide historical continuity between past, present, and future, so that one can move forward in time. Without such a rapprochement, he suggests, the future without a past does not know what it is condemned to repeat, while the past, bereft of a future, is condemned to endless interment.

iv. Coda

One way to understand the interrelation of archaeology and industrialization in Russian modernism over the course of the first three decades of the twentieth century is to turn to a passage from Ivan Bunin, who published a work he fatefully entitled "Epitaph" ("Epitafiia") in 1900. In this story, we find one polarity of the encounter with steppe artifacts—as the title suggests, it is a lament for the denuded steppe:

> Now people are appearing on the steppe. More and more, they are arriving from the city. . . . At night they light fires to chase away the darkness; shadows run far from them along the roads. At dawn they go out to the fields and pierce the earth with long drills. All around there are black piles of dirt that look like burial mounds. Pitilessly, they trample upon the sparse rye, which still grows in some places without sowing, because they are searching for the sources of a new happiness, and they search for it in the bowels of the earth, where the talismans of the future lurk.
>
> Ore! Perhaps the smokestacks of factories will soon belch forth smoke; iron rails will replace the old road; and a city will rise above the wild village. The gray cross that once blessed the old life has fallen to earth and will soon be forgotten. . . . But how will the new people hallow their new life? How will they bless their brisk and noisy work?[33]

Expressing here the longing and lament for a simpler life whose obliteration he is on hand to witness, Bunin testifies to a contemporary fear, echoed by ethnographers, mineralogists, botanists, and anthropologists, all of whom worried about the fate of the steppe.[34] Embedded in this passage is a striking image of industrialization and archaeology built on the analogy between the black piles of dirt and the burial mounds (*mogil'nye kholmy*—a synonym for the kurgans). Such an image can also be seen at the conclusion of *The Eleventh Year*, where the industrializing process

---

[33] Thomas Marullo, *Ivan Bunin: A Russian Requiem, 1885-1920* (New York: Ivan R. Dee, 1993), 81; citing *Sobranie sochinenii*, 2:197–98. Translation adjusted.

[34] See Sunderland, *Taming the Wild Field*, 199-204.

creates new mounds in place of the old. The visual similarity between
the two hardly elides their different origins and their vast disparity
in age; and in this mere semblance of dirt piles to the archaic past
Bunin's narrator finds the perfect image for his lament over the other
transformations of the steppe: the supplanting of the "old road" by
the rails, or the "wild village" by the city. In those "talismans of
the future," the railroad and the city, the narrator can only discern
a forthcoming crisis of sanctification and desacralization.

Of course, such an account of the steppe and its transformation
by industry could have been treated in entirely different ways. It
could have dispensed with the lamentation and simply cheered
on the impending future. Some thirty years after Bunin's story
"Epitaph" portended the death of steppe artifacts—after, that is,
the Revolution and the plunging of the country into the "second
revolution" initiated by Stalin's Five-Year Plans—we find an image
of the world Bunin had foreseen now celebrated in *Time, Forward!*
(*Vremia, vpered!*), Valentin Kataev's production novel and a key
work of Socialist Realism. In the novel, a kurgan makes one brief
appearance—its brevity all the more conspicuous when contrasted
with the considerable amount of time devoted to such archaeological artifacts by both Vertov and Pil'niak:

> There was the steppe. A kurgan. Grass was growing. Fragrant
> wild flowers bloomed. For a hundred years and perhaps even
> longer the mound had stood on the steppe.
> But then diggers suddenly arrived, threw off their clothes,
> spat on the palms of their hands, and as soon as they saw the little
> mound they removed it! Only one little column of earth remained
> in the middle of the trench. And this little column would stand
> there as an untouched bit of steppe until the very end of the work.[35]

A couple of short paragraphs is all the kurgan now deserves. Its
"removal" as an impediment to modernization, though, is an event
that is punctuated by an exclamation point—perhaps a signal of
Kataev's awareness that the kurgan's destruction does entail some

---

[35]   Valentin Kataev, *Time, Forward!*, trans. Charles Malamuth (Evanston, IL: Northwestern University
       Press, 1995), 43. Translation adjusted.

violation of the archaic past. The final detail of the passage—that the kurgan remains as a "little column" in the midst of the worksite until the bitter end—is a gesture toward the tenacity of that past even as it is doomed to disappear.

The story of the indifferent destruction of kurgans had been part of the literary representation of the kurgan for over a century, even as the means of its destruction may have changed from plows to tractors. But Vertov and Pil'niak, despite their differences, are positioned between Bunin and Kataev not just chronologically. Even as *The Eleventh Year* shares Kataev's euphoria about the prospects for modernization, Vertov nevertheless mediates between the views espoused by Bunin and Kataev. Not only does he linger over the Scythian skeleton and the other archaeological artifacts in the film, he also deploys a structure of juxtaposition whose configuration requires the deep past, the present, and the deep future to serve as indices of each other. And even as we find Pil'niak seeking to carve out some space in the future for the archaic past, he also demonstrates that modernization can never entirely rid itself of the past. What is inundated in the novel is either still known to linger beneath the waters, or to make possible further archaeological discoveries. With its stark conjunction between archaeology and industrial modernization, the "area of deformation" delineated in both Vertov's film and Pil'niak's novel identified a fragile state of affairs. It designated the eventual destruction or inundation of a space within which archaeological artifacts would also be destroyed. In their hands, however, this process was still in transition, the past not yet obliterated, the future not yet realized.

To be sure, it is not as if the story of archaeology ends here, or that these are the last kurgans. What's more, it was hardly just modernist writers who continued to explore the productive possibilities of thinking through archaeology during this period. The "material historians" at the State Academy of the History of Material Culture (GAIMK), for example, opened their two-volume report on their excavation work at *novostroiki* with their own brief for preservation. The editor of the report argued that the monuments of the past were "necessary to the very construction of a new life . . . revealing an authentic picture of all past periods made intelligible by the study of social life, upon the crumbling foundations of which the new arises."[36] By commending the educational benefits of a long chronological view of human development, the authors of the report hoped to establish a place for their artifacts in a Marxist-Leninist order of things, which they feared required a complete supersession of the past. For them, the Soviet worker could find an ancestor in the wielder of the stone axe, a fellow *Homo faber*, man the toolmaker. This antiquity of labor, however disparate the levels of technological sophistication, had a common enemy: nature.

It is for this reason that both *The Eleventh Year* and *The Volga Falls to the Caspian Sea* contain so much of the drama that we associate with international modernism's quandaries about time—and which Soviet modernity brought to a particular head. To cite one account: Raymond Williams once observed that "even the range of basic cultural positions within Modernism stretches from an eager embrace of modernity, either in its new technical and mechanical forms or in the equally significant attachments to ideas of social and political revolution, to conscious options for past or exotic cultures as sources or at least as fragments *against* the modern world, from the Futurist affirmation of the city to Eliot's pessimistic recoil."[37]

There is little doubt that Vertov partakes here, in *The Eleventh Year*, and elsewhere of the technophilia of the period, but no less did he carve out a time and space in which to enable the deep retrospection underpinning the "conscious options" entertained by some modernists. He did not shore up the ruins, as it were, of the Scythian's bones: to do so at that time would already have been something of a vestigial modernist romance, or else the province of archaeologists at new construction sites. What he and Pil'niak offer, instead, is a way to see that even as the creative partnership of archaeology and modernist aesthetics neared its eclipse, it remained eminently productive. What Kataev in *Time, Forward!* enables us to

---

[36]   I. I. Meshchaninov, "Predislovie," in *Arkheologicheskie raboty akademii na novostroikakh v 1932-33 gg*, 109:7.

[37]   Raymond Williams, *Politics of Modernism: Against the New Conformists* (New York: Verso, 1989), 43.

grasp is how this conjunction could have been imagined entirely otherwise.

But to return to Pil'niak for some concluding words. In a letter he wrote on June 16, 1927, Pil'niak provided another perfect emblem for the possibility of archaeological disruption. He writes here about his plans for another story, to be called "A German Story" ("Nemetskaia istoriia," 1928):

> I am thinking about a new tale, about the steppe, about the desert, about a lost kurgan (*poteriannom kurgane*) and about how some pioneer-colonizers dig a well and stumble upon the skull of a Sarmatian.[38]

A great fashioner of emblems, Pil'niak does not fully elaborate upon their significance. Why might it matter that the past always lurks in the ground? And why administer shocks of discovery, shocks of the past (a Sarmatian skull!) to these "pioneer-colonizers," these representatives of the future? The emblem suggests not only Pil'niak's penchant for sudden juxtapositions in a space-time where one must suddenly confront the archaic past, but also the abiding sense that the past always threatens to emerge at the very moment when the groundwork for the future is being laid.

[38] Pil'niak, letter of June 16, 1927, in *Pis'ma v dvukh tomakh* (Moscow: IMLI RAN, 2010), 2:324.

Abbas, Ackbar. "Walter Benjamin's Collector: The Fate of Modern Experience." *New Literary History* 20, no. 1 (Autumn 1988): 217–37.

Abramov, N. P. *Dziga Vertov*. Moscow: Izd-vo Akademii nauk SSSR, 1962.

Abrams, M. H. "The Correspondent Breeze: A Romantic Metaphor." In *English Romantic Poets: Modern Essays in Criticism*, edited by M. H. Abrams, 37–54. London: Oxford University Press, 1975.

Afanas'ev, A. N. *Poeticheskie vozzreniia slavian na prirodu: Opyt sravnitel'nogo izucheniia slavianskikh predanii i verovanii, v sviazi s mificheskimi skazaniiami drugikh rodstvennykh narodov*. 3 vols. 1865–69. Reprint, The Hague: Mouton, 1969–70.

Aikhenval'd, B. "O romane Pil'niaka *Volga vpadaet v Kaspiiskoe more*." *Krasnaia nov'*, no. 4 (1931): 178–86.

Alekseev, A. Iu., et al. *Chertomlyk: Skifskii tsarskii kurgan IV v. do n.e.* Kiev: Naukova dumka, 1991.

Anderson, Benedict. *Imagined Communities: Reflections on the Origin and Spread of Nationalism*. London: Verso, 1991.

Anemone, Anthony. "Obsessive Collectors: Fetishizing Culture in the Novels of Konstantin Vaginov." *Russian Review* 59, no. 2 (April 2000): 252–68.

Antsiferov, N. P. *Dusha Peterburga*. 1922. Reprint, Moscow: Kniga, 1991.

Arkheologicheskie raboty akademii na novostroikakh v 1932–33 gg: Izvestiia gosudarstvennoi akademii istorii material'noi kul'tury imeni N. Ia. Marra. Vols. 109–10. Leningrad: Gosudarstvennoe sotsial'no-ekonomicheskoe izd-vo, 1935.

Babel, Isaac. *The Complete Works of Isaac Babel*. Edited by Nathalie Babel, translated by Peter Constantine. New York: Norton, 2002.

Baboreko, A. *I. A. Bunin: Materialy dlia biografii s 1870 do 1917*. Moscow: Khudozhestvennaia literatura, 1967.

Bakhtin, Mikhail. "The Bildungsroman and Its Significance in the History of Realism (Toward a Historical Typology of the Novel)." In *Speech Genres and Other Late Essays*, edited by Caryl Emerson and Michael Holquist, translated by Vern W. McGee, 10–59. Austin: University of Texas Press, 1986.

Ballod, F. V. *Privolzhskie "Pompei": Opyt khudozhestvenno-arkheologicheskogo obsledovaniia chasti pravoberezhnoi saratovsko-tsaritsynskoi privolzhskoi polosy*. Moscow and Petrograd: Gosudarstvennoe izd-vo, 1923.

Bal'mont, K. *Izbrannoe: Stikhotvoreniia, perevody, stat'i*. Moscow: Khudozhestvennaia literatura, 1980.

Baran, Henryk. *O Khlebnikove: Konteksty, istochniki, mify*. Moscow: Rossiiskii gos. gumanitarnyi universitet, 2002.

— —. "Towards a Typology of Russian Modernism: Ivanov, Remizov, Khlebnikov." In *Aleksej Remizov: Approaches to a Protean Writer*, edited by Greta Slobin, 176–205. Columbus, OH: Slavica, 1986.

Barford, P. M. *The Early Slavs: Culture and Society in Early Medieval Eastern Europe*. Ithaca, NY: Cornell University Press, 2001.

Barkan, Leonard. *Unearthing the Past: Archaeology and Aesthetics in the Making of Renaissance Culture*. New Haven, CT: Yale University Press, 1999.

Barthes, Roland. *Mythologies*. Translated by Annette Lavers. New York: Hill & Wang, 1972.

Bataille, Georges. *The Cradle of Humanity: Prehistoric Art and Culture*. Edited by Stuart Kendall, translated by Stuart Kendall and Michelle Kendall. New York: Zone Books, 2005.

Bell, Michael. *Literature, Modernism, and Myth: Belief and Responsibility in the Twentieth Century*. Cambridge: Cambridge University Press, 1997.

Belyi, Andrei. *Peterburg: Roman v vos'mi glavakh s prologom i epilogom*. Leningrad: Nauka, 1981.

— —. *Petersburg*. Translated by Robert A. Maguire and John E. Malmstad. Bloomington: Indiana University Press, 1978.

Benjamin, Walter. *The Arcades Project*. Translated by Rolf Tiedemann. Cambridge, MA: Belknap Press, 1999.

— —. *Illuminations*. Edited by Hannah Arendt, translated by Harry Zohn. New York: Schocken Books, 1968.

Bethea, David M. *The Shape of Apocalypse in Modern Russian Fiction*. Princeton, NJ: Princeton University Press, 1989.

— —. "Whose Mind Is It Anyway?: Influence, Intertextuality, and the Boundaries of Legitimate Scholarship," *Slavic and East European Journal* 49, no. 1 (Spring 2005): 2–18.

Bobrinskaia, E. A. *Rannii russkii avangard v kontekste filosofskoi i khudozhestvennoi kul'tury rubezha vekov: Ocherki*. Moscow: Gosudarstvennyi institut iskusstvoznaniia, 1999.

Bobrov, Sergei. *Vertogradari nad lozami*. Moscow: Knigoizdatel'stvo Lirika, 1913.

— —. *Zapiski stikhotvortsa*. 1916. Reprint, Letchworth, England: Prideaux Press, 1973.

Bois, Yve-Alain. *Painting as Model*. Cambridge, MA: MIT Press, 1990.

Bordier, A. "Les Sciences anthropologiques à l'exposition universelle." *La Nature: Revue des sciences et de leur applications aux arts et à l'industrie*, no. 285 (November 16, 1878): 408–10.

Boris Pil'niak: Opyt segodniashnego prochteniia; Po materialam nauchnoi konferentsii, posviashchennoi 100-letiiu so dnia rozhdeniia pisatelia, IMLI im M. Gor'kogo RAN. Moscow: Nasledie, 1995.

Bowlt, John E. *Moscow and St. Petersburg, 1900–1920: Art, Life, and Culture of the Russian Silver Age.* New York: Vendome Press, 2008.

Boym, Svetlana. *Common Places: Mythologies of Everyday Life in Russia.* Cambridge, MA: Harvard University Press, 1994.

Brandenburg, N. E. "K voprosu o kamennykh babakh." In *Trudy 8-ogo s''ezda v Moskve*, 13–18. Moscow: Tip. Mamontova, 1897.

Brew, J. O. "Emergency Archaeology: Salvage in Advance of Technological Progress." *Proceedings of the American Philosophical Society* 105, no. 1 (1961): 1–10.

Briusov, Valery. "Mednyi vsadnik." In *A. S. Pushkin: Biblioteka velikikh pisatelei.* Vol. 3, 456–72. St. Petersburg: Brokgauz-Efron, 1907.

— —. *Sobranie sochinenii v semi tomakh.* Moscow: Khudozhestvennaia literatura, 1973–75.

Brostrom, Kenneth N. "The Enigma of Pil'njak's *The Volga Falls to the Caspian Sea.*" *Slavic and East European Journal* 18, no. 3 (Autumn 1974): 271–98.

Browning, Gary. *Boris Pilniak: Scythian at a Typewriter.* Ann Arbor, MI: Ardis, 1985.

— —. "Russian Ornamental Prose." *Slavic and Eastern European Journal* 23, no. 3 (August 1979): 346–52.

Buckler, Julie A. *Mapping St. Petersburg: Imperial Text and Cityshape.* Princeton, NJ: Princeton University Press, 2005.

Budantsev, Sergei. "Dneprovskoe stroitel'stvo." *Novyi mir*, no. 7 (1928): 213–23.

Bunin, Ivan. *Sobranie sochinenii v deviati tomakh.* Moscow: Khudozhestvennaia literatura, 1965–67.

— —. *Stikhotvoreniia, 1903–06.* St. Petersburg: Tipografiia Montvida, 1906.

— —. *Stikhotvorennia, 1903–06: Manfred Bairona.* 2nd, exp. ed. Moscow: Knigoizdatel'stvo pisatelei, 1912.

Carden, Patricia. "Ornamentalism and Modernism." In *Russian Modernism: Culture and the Avant-Garde, 1900–1930*, edited by George Gibian and H. Williams Tjalsma, 49–64. Ithaca, NY: Cornell University Press, 1976.

Castagné, Joseph. "Étude historique et comparative des statues babas des steppes khirgizes et de Russie en général." *Bulletins et mémoires de la société d'anthropologie de Paris* 1 (1910): 375–407.

Catalogue spécial de l'exposition des sciences anthropologiques. Paris: Impr. nationale, 1878.

Cavanagh, Clare. *Osip Mandelstam and the Modernist Creation of Tradition.* Princeton, NJ: Princeton University Press, 1995.

Chaadaev, P. Ia. *The Major Works of Peter Chaadaev*. Translated by Raymond T. McNally. Notre Dame, IN: University of Notre Dame Press, 1969.

— —. *Polnoe sobranie sochinenii i izbrannye pis'ma*. 2 vols. Moscow: Iz-dvo Nauka, 1991.

Chekhov, Anton. *Polnoe sobranie sochinenii i pisem v tridtsati tomakh*. Moscow: Nauka, 1974.

Clark, Katerina. "The Avant-Garde and the Retrospectivists." In *Laboratory of Dreams: The Russian Avant-Garde and Cultural Experiment*, edited by John Bowlt and Olga Matich, 259–76. Stanford, CA: Stanford University Press, 1996.

— —. *Petersburg: Crucible of Cultural Revolution*. Cambridge, MA: Harvard University Press, 1995.

Clark, T. J. *Farewell to an Idea: Episodes from a History of Modernism*. New Haven, CT: Yale University Press, 1999.

Clifford, James. *The Predicament of Culture: Twentieth-Century Ethnography, Literature, and Art*. Cambridge, MA: Harvard University Press, 1988.

Cowling, Elizabeth. *Picasso: Style and Meaning*. London: Phaidon Press, 2002.

Dashkevich, Iaroslav R., and Edward Tryjarski. *Kamennye baby prichernomorskikh stepei: Kollektsiia iz Askanii-Nova*. Wrocław: Zakład Narodowy im. Ossolińskich, 1982.

Davenport, Guy. "The Symbol of the Archaic." In *The Geography of the Imagination: Forty Essays*, 16–29. Boston: David R. Godine, 1997.

Deleuze, Gilles. *Cinema 1: The Movement-Image*. Translated by Hugh Tomlinson and Barbara Habberjam. Minneapolis: University of Minnesota Press, 1986.

Del'vig, A. A. *Polnoe sobranie stikhotvorenii*. Leningrad: Sovetskii pisatel', 1959.

de Man, Paul. "Autobiography as De-Facement." In *The Rhetoric of Romanticism*, 65–81. New York: Columbia University Press, 1984.

Demetrykiewirz, Wladimir. "Altertümliche steinerne Statuen, sog. 'Baby' Steinmütterchen, Becherstatuen in Asien und Europa und ihr Verhältnis zur slawischen Mythologie." *Bulletin international de l'académie des sciences de Cracovie* (1910).

D'iachkova, E. B. "Problema vremeni v proizvedeniiakh B. Pil'niaka." In *Boris Pil'niak: Opyt segodniashnego prochteniia*, 63–70.

Duganov, R. V. "K rekonstruktsii poemy Khlebnikova 'Noch' v okope.'" *Izvestiia akademii nauk SSSR: Seriia literatury i iazyka* 38, no. 5 (1979), http: //www.ka2.ru /nauka /duganov.html.

Duvakin, V. D. "Velimir Khlebnikov v razmyshleniiakh i vospominaniiakh sovremennikov (po fonodokumental'nam V. D. Duvakina 1960–1970 godov)." In *Vestnik obshchestva Velimira Khlebnikova*. Vol. 1, 44–66. Moscow: Gileia, 1996.

Erlich, Victor. *Modernism and Revolution: Russian Literature in Transition.* Cambridge, MA: Harvard University Press, 1994.

Epstein, Mikhail. "Russo-Soviet Topoi." In *The Landscape of Stalinism: The Art and Ideology of Soviet Space,* edited by E. A. Dobrenko and Eric Naiman, 277–306. Seattle: University of Washington Press, 2003.

Fabr, Andrei. "O pamiatnikakh nekotorykh narodov varvarskikh, drevne obitavshikh v nyneshnem Novorossiiskom krae." *Zapiski imperator-skago odesskago obshchestva istorii i drevnostei* 2 (1848): 36–46.

Fedorov, G. B. "Poet, khudozhnik i kamennaia baba." In *Dnevnaia poverkh-nost'.* Moscow: Detskaia literatura, 1977, http: //ka2.ru /nauka /baba.html.

Fedorov-Davydov, G. A. *Kochevniki vostochnoi evropy pod vlast'iu zoloto-ordynskikh khanov: Arkheologicheskie pamiatniki.* Moscow: Izd-vo Moskovskogo universiteta, 1966.

— —. *Kurgany, idoly, monety.* Moscow: Nauka, 1968.

Flam, Jack, ed. *Primitivism and Twentieth-Century Art: A Documentary History.* Berkeley and Los Angeles: University of California Press, 2003.

Fleishman, Lazar. *Boris Pasternak: The Poet and His Politics.* Cambridge, MA: Harvard University Press, 1990.

Florenskii, P. A. "Naplastovaniia egeiskoi kul'tury." *Bogoslovskii vestnik* 11, no. 6 (1913): 346–89. Translated as "The Stratification of Aegean Culture," in *Beyond Vision: Essays on the Perception of Art,* edited by Nicoletta Misler, translated by Wendy Salmond, 137–74. London: Reaktion Books, 2002.

Fore, Devin. "The Metabiotic State: Dziga Vertov's *The Eleventh Year.*" *October* 145 (Spring 2013): 3–37.

Formozov, A. A. *Ocherki po istorii russkoi arkheologii.* Moscow: Izd-vo Akademii nauk SSSR, 1961.

— —. *Russkie arkheologi v period totalitarizma: Istoriograficheskie ocherki.* Moscow: Znak, 2004.

Foucault, Michel. *The Archaeology of Knowledge.* Translated by Alan Sheridan. New York: Pantheon, 1972.

Frank, Joseph. *The Widening Gyre: Crisis and Mastery in Modern Literature.* Bloomington: Indiana University Press, 1968.

— —. "Spatial Form: Thirty Years After." In *Spatial Form in Narrative,* edited by Jeffrey R. Smitten and Ann Daghistany, 202–44. Ithaca, NY: Cornell University Press, 1981.

Garafola, Lynn. *Diaghilev's Ballets Russes.* New York: Da Capo Press, 1998.

Garshin, V. M. *Sochineniia.* Moscow and Leningrad: Khudozhestvennaia literatura, 1963.

Gasparov, Boris. "Introduction: The 'Golden Age' and Its Role in the Cultural Mythology of Russian Modernism." In *Cultural Mythologies of Russian Modernism: From the Golden Age to the Silver Age,* edited by

Boris Gasparov, Robert P. Hughes, and Irina Paperno, 1–16. Berkeley and Los Angeles: University of California Press, 1992.

Gasparov, M. L. *Russkie stikhi 1890-kh–1925-go godov v kommentariiakh.* Moscow: Vysshaia shkola, 1993.

— —. *Russkii stikh nachala XX veka v kommentariiakh.* 2nd, exp. ed. Moscow: "Fortuna Ltd.," 2001.

Gatrall, Jefferson J. A., and Douglas M. Greenfield. *Alter Icons: The Russian Icon and Modernity.* University Park: Penn State Press, 2010.

Geraci, Robert P. *Window on the East: National and Imperial Identities in Late Tsarist Russia.* Ithaca, NY: Cornell University Press, 2001.

Gere, Cathy. *Knossos and the Prophets of Modernism.* Chicago: University of Chicago Press, 2009.

Gershenzon, M. O. *P. Ia. Chaadaev: Zhizn' i myshlenie.* 1908. Reprint, The Hague: Mouton, 1968.

— —, and Viacheslav Ivanov. "A Corner-to-Corner Correspondence." In *Russian Intellectual History: An Anthology,* edited by Marc Raeff, 373–401. Atlantic Highlands, NJ: Humanities Press, 1966.

Gimbutas, Marija. "The Indo-Europeans: Archaeological Problems." *American Anthropologist* New series 65, no. 4 (August 1963): 815–36.

Gladkov, Fedor. *Sobranie sochinenii v vos'mi tomakh.* Moscow: Khudozhest-vennaia literatura, 1958–59.

Gnedich, N. *Stikhotvoreniia.* Leningrad: Sovetskii pisatel', 1963.

Goldwater, Robert. *Primitivism in Modern Art.* 2nd ed. Cambridge, MA: Belknap Press, 1986.

Golitsyn, Kniaz' Lev L'vovich, and S. S. Krasnodubrovskii. *Ukek: Doklady i issledovaniia po arkheologii i istorii Ukeka.* Saratov: Tipografiia Gubernsk. zemstva, 1891.

Gorodetskii, Sergei. "Pro kamennuiu babu," *Galchonok* 12 (1911): 43.

Greenleaf, Monika. *Pushkin and Romantic Fashion: Fragment, Elegy, Orient, Irony.* Stanford, CA: Stanford University Press, 1994.

Griffiths, Frederick T., and Stanley J. Rabinowitz. *Novel Epics: Gogol, Dostoevsky, and National Narrative.* Evanston, IL: Northwestern University Press, 1990.

Grigor'ev, V. P. *Budetlianin.* Moscow: Iazyki russkoi kul'tury, 2000.

Hartmann, August. "Becherstatuen in Ostpreussen und die Literatur der Becherstatuen." *Archiv für Anthropologie* 21 (1892–93): 253–303.

Hartog, François. *The Mirror of Herodotus: The Representation of the Other in the Writing of History.* Translated by Janet Lloyd. Berkeley and Los Angeles: University of California Press, 1988.

Hicks, Jeremy. *Dziga Vertov: Defining Documentary Film.* London: I. B. Tauris, 2007.

Iavornyts'kyi, D. I., and M. M. Oliinyk-Shubravs'ka. *Zaporozh'e v ostatkakh stariny i predaniiakh naroda.* 2 vols. Kiev: Veselka, 1995.

Ivanov, Viacheslav. "Ancient Terror: On Leon Bakst's Painting *Terror Antiquus*." In *Selected Essays*, edited by Michael Wachtel, translated by Robert Bird, 144–62. Evanston, IL: Northwestern University Press, 2001.

Ivanov-Razumnik. "Ispytanie v groze i bure." Foreword to A. A. Blok, *Dvenadtsat' / Skify*. Berlin: Skify, 1920.

Izmailov, N. V. "'Mednyi vsadnik' A. S. Pushkina." In A. S. Pushkin, *Mednyi vsadnik*. Literaturnye pamiatniki. Leningrad: Nauka, 1978.

Jakobson, Roman. *Language in Literature*. Edited by Krystyna Pomorska and Stephen Rudy. Cambridge, MA: Belknap Press, 1987.

——. "The Newest Russian Poetry: Velimir Khlebnikov." In *My Futurist Years*, edited by Bengt Jangfeldt and Stephen Rudy, translated by Stephen Rudy, 173–208. New York: Marsilio Press, 1992.

——. "On the Generation That Squandered Its Poets." In *My Futurist Years*, 209–45.

Jensen, Peter Alberg. *Nature as Code: The Achievement of Boris Pilnjak, 1915–1924*. Copenhagen: Rosenkilde & Bagger, 1979.

Kahn, Andrew. *Pushkin's "The Bronze Horseman."* London: Bristol Classical Press, 1998.

Kalb, Judith E. *Russia's Rome: Imperial Visions, Messianic Dreams, 1890–1940*. Madison: University of Wisconsin Press, 2008.

Kataev, Valentin. *Sobranie sochinenii v deviati tomakh*. Moscow: Khudozhest-vennaia literatura, 1968–72

——. *Time, Forward!* Translated by Charles Malamuth. Evanston, IL: North-western University Press, 1995.

Katz, Michael R. *The Literary Ballad in Early Nineteenth-Century Russian Literature*. London: Oxford University Press, 1976.

Kelly, Catriona. "*Byt*: Identity and Everyday Life." In *National Identity in Russian Culture: An Introduction*, edited by Simon Franklin and Emma Widdis, 149–68. Cambridge: Cambridge University Press, 2004.

Kel'siev, A. I. "O kamennykh babakh." *Trudy V-ogo arkheologicheskogo s"ezda v Tiflise, 1881*, 77–78. Moscow: Tip. A. I. Mamontova, 1887.

Kenner, Hugh. *The Pound Era*. Berkeley and Los Angeles: University of California Press, 1971.

Khlebnikov, Velimir. *The Collected Works of Velimir Khlebnikov*. Edited by Ronald Vroon, translated by Paul Schmidt. Cambridge, MA: Harvard University Press, 1997.

——. *Sobranie sochinenii*. 1928–33. Reprint, Munich: Wilhelm Fink Verlag, 1968.

——. *Sobranie sochinenii v shesti tomakh*. Moscow: Nasledie, 2000.

——. *Tvoreniia*. Moscow: Sovetskii pisatel', 1986.

Kiaer, Christina. *Imagine No Possessions: The Socialist Objects of Russian Constructivism*. Cambridge, MA: MIT Press, 2005.

Koretskaia, I. V. "Literatura v krugu iskusstv." In *Russkaia literatura rubezha vekov (1890-e–nachalo 1920-x godov)*, 131–190. Moscow: IMLI RAN Nasledie, 2000.

Kotkin, Stephen. *Magnetic Mountain: Stalinism as a Civilization*. Berkeley and Los Angeles: University of California Press, 1995.

Kromm, Natalie. "Povolzhsko-nemetskii sled v zhizni i proizvedeniiakh pisatel'ia Borisa Pil'niaka." *Die Geschichte der Wolgadeutschen*, http: // wolgadeutsche.net /biographie /Pilnjak_WD_Spuren_rus.htm.

Kruchenykh, A. *Nash vykhod*. Edited by V. Rakitin and A. Sarab'ianov. Moscow: "RA," 1996.

— —. *Our Arrival: From the History of Russian Futurism*. Edited by V. Rakitin and A. Sarab'ianov, translated by Alan Myers. Moscow: RA, 1995.

Kryzytski, Serge. *The Works of Ivan Bunin*. The Hague: Mouton, 1971.

Lahti, Katherine. "On Living Statues and Pandora, *Kamennye baby* and Futurist Aesthetics: The Female Body in *Vladimir Mayakovsky: A Tragedy*." *Russian Review* 58, no. 3 (July 1999): 432–55.

Lebedev, G. S. *Istoriia otechestvennoi arkheologii, 1700-1917 gg*. St. Petersburg: Izd-vo S.-Peterburgskogo universiteta, 1992.

Leroi-Gourhan, André. *Treasures of Prehistoric Art*. Translated by Norbert Guterman. New York: Abrams, 1967.

Leyda, Jay. *Kino: A History of the Russian and Soviet Film*. Princeton, NJ: Princeton University Press, 1983.

Liashko, S. M., et al. *Kurgannye mogil'niki dneprovskogo nadporozh'ia*. Zaporozh'e: Dikoe pole, 2004.

Livshits, Benedikt. *The One and a Half-Eyed Archer*. Translated by John Bowlt. Newtonville, MA: Oriental Research Partners, 1977.

— —. *Polutoraglazyi strelets: Stikhotvoreniia, perevody, vospominaniia*. Leningrad: Sovetksii pisatel', 1989.

MacKay, John. "Film Energy: Metanarrative in Dziga Vertov's *The Eleventh Year* (1928)." *October* 121 (Summer 2007): 41–78.

Maguire, Robert A. *Red Virgin Soil: Soviet Literature in the 1920s*. Princeton, NJ: Princeton University Press, 1968.

Maiakovskii, Vladimir. *Polnoe sobranie sochinenii v trinadtsati tomakh*. Moscow: Khudozhestvennaia literatura, 1955.

Makovskii, Sergei. "Talashkino" (1905). Translated by Wendy Salmond. *Experiment/Eksperiment: A Journal of Russian Culture* 7 (2001): 275–300.

Malov, N. M. "Sovetskaia arkheologiia v saratovskom gosudarstvennom universitete (1918–1940): Organizatsionnoe stanovlenie, razvitie i repressii." *Arkheologiia vostochno-evropeiskoi stepi* 4 (2006): 4–28.

Manifesty i programmy russkikh futuristov. Munich: Wilhelm Fink Verlag, 1967.

Mantel, A. *N. Rerikh*. Kazan: Izd-vo knig po iskusstvu, 1912.

Marc, Franz, Klaus Lankheit, and Wassily Kandinsky. *The Blaue Reiter Almanac*. Documents of 20th Century Art. New York: Viking Press, 1974.

Marchand, Suzanne L. *Down from Olympus: Archaeology and Philhellenism in Germany, 1750–1970*. Princeton, NJ: Princeton University Press, 1996.

Markov, Vladimir. *The Longer Poems of Velimir Khlebnikov*. Berkeley and Los Angeles: University of California Press, 1962.

— — . *Russian Futurism: A History*. Berkeley and Los Angeles: University of California Press, 1968.

Marullo, Thomas Gaiton. *Ivan Bunin: Russian Requiem, 1885–1920; A Portrait from Letters, Diaries, and Fiction*. Chicago: Ivan R. Dee, 1993.

Masing-Delic, Irene. "Boris Pil'niak's *The Volga Falls to the Caspian Sea* as Trotskyite Sophiology." *Slavic and East European Journal* 52, no. 3 (Fall 2008): 414–38.

Matich, Olga. *Erotic Utopia: The Decadent Imagination in Russia's Fin de Siècle*. Madison: University of Wisconsin Press, 2005.

— — . Petersburg/*Petersburg: Novel and City, 1900–1921*. Madison: University of Wisconsin Press, 2010.

Michelson, Annette. "In Praise of Horizontality: André Leroi-Gourhan, 1911–1986." *October* 37 (1986): 3–5.

— — . "The Kinetic Icon in the Work of Mourning: Prolegomena to the Analysis of a Textual System," *October* 52 (Spring 1990): 17–39.

Miller, Mykhailo Oleksandrovich. *Arkheologiia v SSSR* First series, no. 12 (1954).

Mir Velimira Khlebnikova: Stat'i, issledovaniia, 1911–1998. Edited by V. V. Ivanov, Z. S. Papernyi, and A. E. Parnis. Moscow: Iazyki russkoi kul'tury, 2000.

Misler, Nicoletta. "Pavel Florenskii as Art Historian." In *Beyond Vision: Essays on the Perception of Art*, 29–93. London: Reaktion Books, 2002.

Mitchell, W. J. T. "Ekphrasis and the Other." In *Picture Theory: Essays on Verbal and Visual Representation*, 151–81. Chicago: University of Chicago Press, 1994.

Mitter, Partha. "Decentering Modernism: Art History and Avant-Garde Art from the Periphery." *Art Bulletin* 90, no. 4 (December 2008): 531–48.

Miturich-Khlebnikov, M. "Gde umer i gde pokhoronen Velimir Khlebnikov." *Vestnik obshchestva Velimira Khlebnikova*. Vol. 1, 75–89. Moscow: Gileia, 1996.

Morderer, Valentina. "Retsenziia na knigu: R. V. Duganov." In *Velimir Khlebnikov i russkaia literatura: Stat'i raznykh let*. Moscow: Progress-Pleiada, 2008, http: //www.ka2.ru /nauka /valentina_2.html.

Naiman, Eric. *Sex in Public: The Incarnation of Early Soviet Ideology*. Princeton, NJ: Princeton University Press, 1997.

Nedashkovskii, L. F. *Zolotoordynskii gorod Ukek i ego okruga*. Moscow: Vostochnaia literatura RAN, 2000.

Nesbet, Anne. *Savage Junctures: Sergei Eisenstein and the Shape of Thinking*. London: I. B. Tauris, 2003.

Newton, Sam. *The Origins of Beowulf and the Pre-Viking Kingdom of East Anglia*. Cambridge: D. S. Brewer, 1993.

Nicholas, Mary A. "Boris Pil'niak and Modernism: Redefining the Self." *Slavic Review* 50, no. 2 (Summer 1991): 410–21.

— —. "Formalist Theory Revisited: "On Šklovskij 'On Pil'njak'." *Slavic and East European Journal* 36, no. 1 (Spring 1992): 68–83.

— —. "Pil'niak on Writing," *Slavonic and East European Review* 71, no. 2 (April 1993): 217-33.

— —. *Writers at Work: Russian Production Novels and the Construction of Soviet Culture*. Lewisburg, PA: Bucknell University Press, 2010.

Nietzsche, Friedrich. *The Birth of Tragedy*. In *Basic Writings of Nietzsche*, translated by Walter Kaufmann. New York: Modern Library, 1992.

Palestine and Syria with the Chief Routes through Mesopotamia and Babylonia: Handbook for Travellers. Leipzig: K. Baedeker; New York: C. Scribner's Sons, 1906.

Pallas, Peter Simon. *Travels through the Southern Provinces of the Russian Empire, in the Years 1793 and 1794*. Translated by Francis Blagdon. 2 vols. London: T. N. Longman & O. Rees, 1802–3.

Panova, L. G. *Russkii Egipet: Aleksandriiskaia poetika Mikhaila Kuzmina*. Moscow: Vodolei, 2006.

Parton, Anthony. *Mikhail Larionov and the Russian Avant-Garde*. Princeton, NJ: Princeton University Press, 1993.

Perloff, Marjorie. *The Futurist Moment: Avant-Garde, Avant Guerre, and the Language of Rupture*. Chicago: University of Chicago Press, 1986.

Peterson, Dale. "Russian Gothic: The Deathless Paradoxes of Bunin's *Dry Valley*," *Slavic and Eastern European Journal* 31 (1987): 36–49.

Pil'niak, Boris. "Bor. Pil'naik." In *Kak my pishem*, 128-29. Leningrad: Izd-vo pisatelei, 1930.

— — *Byl'e*. 1922. Reprint, Munich: Wilhelm Fink Verlag, 1970.

— —. *Mashiny i volki*. 1925. Reprint, Munich: Wilhelm Fink Verlag, 1971.

— —. *The Naked Year*. Translated by A. R. Tulloch. Ann Arbor, MI: Ardis, 1975.

— —. *Pis'ma v 2 tomakh*. Edited by N. V. Kornienko. Moscow: IMLI RAN, 2010.

— —. *Sobranie sochinenii v shesti tomakh*. Moscow: Terra-Knizhnyi klub, 2003.

— —. *The Volga Falls to the Caspian Sea*. Translated by Charles Malamuth. New York: Cosmopolitan Book, 1931.

Potts, Alex. Introduction to Johann Joachim Winckelmann, *History of the Art of Antiquity*, translated by Harry Mallgrave, 1–53. Los Angeles: Getty Research Institute, 2006.

Pushkin, A. S. *Mednyi vsadnik: Poèma*. Literaturnye pamiatniki. Leningrad: Nauka, 1978.

— —. *Polnoe sobranie sochinenii v desiati tomakh*. 3rd ed. Moscow: Nauka, 1962.

Raeff, Marc, ed. *Russian Intellectual History: An Anthology*. Atlantic Highlands, NJ: Humanities Press, 1966.

Raleigh, Donald J. *Experiencing Russia's Civil War: Politics, Society, and Revolutionary Culture in Saratov, 1917–1922*. Princeton, NJ: Princeton University Press, 2002.

Ram, Harsha. *The Imperial Sublime: A Russian Poetics of Empire*. Madison: University of Wisconsin Press, 2003.

Rassweiler, Anne Dickason. *The Generation of Power: The History of Dneprostroi*. Oxford: Oxford University Press, 1988.

Remizov, Aleksei. *Sobranie sochinenii*. Moscow: Russkaia kniga, 2000–2002.

— —. *Storona nebyvalaia*. Moscow: Russkii put', 2004.

Richards, D. J. "Comprehending the Beauty of the World: Bunin's Philosophy of Travel." *Slavonic and East European Review* 52, no. 129 (1974): 514–32.

Rigolot, François. "Ekphrasis and the Fantastic: Genesis of an Aberration." *Comparative Literature* 49 (Spring 1997): 97–112.

Rosenthal, Bernice Glatzer. *New Myth, New World: From Nietzsche to Stalinism*. University Park: Penn State Press, 2002.

Rostovtsev, M. I. *Ellinstvo i iranstvo na iuge Rossii*. 1918. Reprint, Moscow: Knizhnaia nakhodka, 2002.

Rubin, William Stanley, ed. *"Primitivism" in 20th Century Art: Affinity of the Tribal and the Modern*. 2 vols. New York: Museum of Modern Art, 1984.

Sadovskoi, Boris. "Sergei Gorodetskii: Iar'; Stikhi liricheskie i liro-epicheskie. Spb., 1907 g." *Russkaia mysl'* 5 (May 1907).

Salmony, Alfred. "Notes on a 'Kamennaya baba.'" *Artibus Asiae* 13, no. 1/2 (1950): 5–16.

— —."La Sculpture en pierre de l'est de la steppe eurasiatique." *Cahiers d'art* 12, 7, no. 1–2 (1932): 45–50.

Samokvasov, D. *Mogily russkoi zemli: Opisanie arkheologicheskikh raskopok i sobraniia drevnostei*. Moscow: Sinodal'naia tip., 1908.

— —. *Raskopki drevnykh mogil i opisanie, khranenie i izdanie mogil'nykh drevnostei*. Moscow: Sinodal'naia tip., 1908.

Schenker, Alexander M. *The Bronze Horseman: Falconet's Monument to Peter the Great*. New Haven, CT: Yale University Press, 2003.

Scherr, Barry P. *Russian Poetry: Meter, Rhythm, and Rhyme*. Berkeley and Los Angeles: University of California Press, 1986.

Schimmelpenninck van der Oye, David. *Russian Orientalism: Asia in the Russian Mind from Peter the Great to the Emigration*. New Haven, CT: Yale University Press, 2010.

Schnapp, Jeffrey, Michael Schanks, and Matthew Tiews. "Archaeology, Modernism, Modernity: Editors' Introduction to 'Archaeologies of the Modern.'" *Modernism/modernity* 11, no. 1 (2004): 1–16.

Schönle, Andreas. "Garden of the Empire: Catherine's Appropriation of the Crimea." *Slavic Review* 60, no. 1 (Spring 2001): 1–23.

Seifrid, Thomas. *Andrei Platonov: Uncertainties of Spirit*. Cambridge: Cambridge University Press, 1992.

Semenova, N. *Moskovskie kollektsionery: S. I. Shchukin, I. A. Morozov, I. S. Ostroukhov: Tri sud'by, tri istorii uvlechenii*. Moscow: Molodaia gvardiia, 2010.

— —. *Zhizn' i kollektsiia Sergeia Shchukina*. Moscow: Trilistnik, 2002.

Shaitanov, I. O. "Istoricheskie metafory Borisa Pil'niaka (*Krasnoe derevo i Volga vpadaet v Kaspiiskoe more*)." In *B. A. Pil'niak: Issledovaniia i materialy* (Kolomna: Kolomenskii pedagogicheskii institut, 1991), 1:47–56.

Sharp, Jane Ashton. *Russian Modernism between East and West: Natal'ia Goncharova and the Moscow Avant-Garde*. Cambridge: Cambridge University Press, 2006.

Shevelenko, Irina. "Modernizm kak arkhaizm: Natsionalizm, russkii stil' i arkhaiziruiushchaia estetika v russkom modernizme," *Wiener Slawistischer Almanach* 56 (2005): 141–83.

Shklovskii, Viktor. *O Maiakovskom*. Moscow: Sovetskii pisatel', 1940.

Slezkine, Yuri. *Arctic Mirrors: Russia and the Small Peoples of the North*. Ithaca, NY: Cornell University Press, 1994.

— —. "N. Ia. Marr and the National Origins of Soviet Ethnogenetics." *Slavic Review* 55, no. 4 (1996): 826–62.

Slobin, Greta. *Aleksej Remizov: Approaches to a Protean Writer*. Columbus, OH: Slavica Publishers, 1987.

Spasskii, G. I. "Dneprovskie kurgany." In "Korrespondentsiia," *Zapiski imperatorskogo odesskogo obshchestva istorii i drevnosti* (1844): 593–96.

Sporov, Dmitrii. "Zhivaia rech' ushedshei epokhi: Sobranie Viktora Duvakina." *Novoe literaturnoe obozrenie* 74 (2005): 454–72.

Starkina, S. V. *Velimir Khlebnikov*. Moscow: Molodaia gvardiia, 2007.

Stepanov, N. L. *Velimir Khlebnikov: Zhizn' i tvorchestvo*. Moscow: Sovetskii pisatel', 1975.

Stieda, Ludwig. "Die anthropologische Ausstellung in Moskau, 1879." *Archiv für Anthropologie* 14 (1883): 258–64.

Stoichita, Victor. *The Pygmalion Effect: From Ovid to Hitchcock*. Chicago: University of Chicago Press, 2008.

Sunderland, Willard. *Taming the Wild Field: Colonization and Empire on the Russian Steppe*. Ithaca, NY: Cornell University Press, 2004.

Taruskin, Richard. *Stravinsky and the Russian Traditions: A Biography of the Works through "Mavra."* 2 vols. Berkeley and Los Angeles: University of California Press, 1996.

Taylor, Richard, and Ian Christie. *The Film Factory: Russian and Soviet Cinema in Documents*. London: Routledge, 1988.

Thomas, Julian. *Archaeology and Modernity*. London: Routledge, 2004.

— —. "Archaeology's Place in Modernity," *Modernism/modernity* 11, no. 1 (2004): 17–34.

Tiutchev, F.I. *Stikhotvoreniia. Pis'ma*. Moscow: Sovetskii pisatel', 1972.

Tret'iakov, Sergei. "Otkuda i kuda?" *Lef*, no. 1 (1923): 192–203.

Trotskii, Leon. *Literatura i revoliutsiia*. 1923. Reprint, Moscow: Izd-vo polit. lit-ru, 1991.

Trudy vserossiiskogo s''ezda khudozhnikov v Petrograde. 3 vols. Petrograd: T-vo R. Golike i A. Vil'borg, 1912.

Tsivian, Yuri. *Lines of Resistance: Dziga Vertov and the Twenties*. Gemona, Udine: Le Giornate del cinema muto, 2004.

Tsvetaeva, G. A. *Sokrovishcha prichernomorskikh kurganov*. Moscow: Nauka, 1968.

Tunkina, I. V. *Russkaia nauka o klassicheskikh drevnostiakh iuga Rossii (XVIII– seredina XIX v.)*. St. Petersburg: Nauka, 2002.

Tynianov, Iurii. "Literaturnyi fakt." In *Poetika, istoriia literatury, kino*, 255–70. Moscow: Nauka, 1977.

— —. "O Khlebnikove," in *Arkhaisty i novatory*, 581–95. 1929. Reprint, Munich: Wilhelm Fink Verlag, 1967.

Uvarov, A. S. "Svedeniia o kamennykh babakh." *Trudy pervogo arkheologicheskogo s''ezda v Moskve*, 501–20. Moscow: V Sinodal'noi tipografii, 1871.

Vásáry, István. *Cumans and Tatars: Oriental Military in the Pre-Ottoman Balkans, 1185–1365*. Cambridge: Cambridge University Press, 2005.

Vertov, Dziga. *Dziga Vertov: Stat'i, dnevniki, zamysli*. Edited by S. V. Dro- bashenko. Moscow: Iskusstvo, 1960.

— —. *Iz naslediia*. Edited by A. Deriabin and D. V. Kruzhkova. Moscow: Eizenshtein-tsentr, 2004.

— —. *Kino-Eye: The Writings of Dziga Vertov*. Edited by Annette Michelson, translated by Kevin O'Brien. Berkeley and Los Angeles: University of California Press, 1984.

Veselovskii, N. I. "Mnimye kamennye baby." 1904. Offprint, St. Petersburg: Tip. P.P. Soikina, 1905.

— —. "Sovremennoe sostoianie voprosa o 'kamennykh babakh' ili 'balbalakh,'" *Zapiski imperatorskogo odesskogo obshchestva istorii i drev- nostei* 32 (1915): 412–50.

Viazemskii, P. A. *Stikhotvoreniia*. Leningrad: Sovetskii pisatel', 1986.

Vickery, John B. *The Literary Impact of "The Golden Bough."* Princeton, NJ: Princeton University Press, 1973.

Voloshin, M. A. *Liki tvorchestva*. Literaturnye pamiatniki. Leningrad: Nauka, 1988.

Voronskii, A. K. *Izbrannye stat'i o literature*. Moscow: Khudozhestvennaia literatura, 1982.

— —. "Literaturnye siluety: B. Pil'niak," *Krasnaia nov'*, no. 4 (1922): 252-69.

Voznesenskii, Andrei. "Sidish', beremennaia, blednaia," http://www.ruthenia.ru/60s/voznes/antimir/beremennaja.htm, accessed December 20, 2014.

Vrangel', Nikolai. *Istoriia russkogo iskusstva*. Vol. 5, *Istoriia skul'ptury*. Edited by Igor Grabar'. Moscow: I. Knebel', 1910.

Wachtel, Michael. *A Commentary to Pushkin's Lyric Poetry, 1826–1836*. Madison: University of Wisconsin Press, 2011.

— —. *The Development of Russian Verse: Meter and Its Meanings*. Cambridge: Cambridge University Press, 2006.

— —. *Russian Symbolism and Literary Tradition: Goethe, Novalis, and the Poetics of Vyacheslav Ivanov*. Madison: University of Wisconsin Press, 1994.

Walicki, Andrzej. *The Slavophile Controversy: History of a Conservative Utopia in Nineteenth-Century Russian Thought*. Translated by Hilde Andrews-Rusiecka. Notre Dame, IN: University of Notre Dame Press, 1989.

Wegel, M. "Bildwerke aus altslavischer Zeit." *Archiv für Anthropologie* 21 (1892–93): 41–72.

Weiss, Peg. *Kandinsky and Old Russia: The Artist as Ethnographer and Shaman*. New Haven, CT: Yale University Press, 1995.

White, Hayden. "The Forms of Wildness: Archaeology of an Idea." In *The Wild Man Within: An Image in Western Thought from the Renaissance to Romanticism*, edited by Edward J. Dudley and Maximillian E. Novak, 3–38. Pittsburgh: University of Pittsburgh Press, 1972.

Williams, Raymond. *Politics of Modernism: Against the New Conformists*. London: Verso, 1989.

Winckelmann, Johann Joachim. *History of the Art of Antiquity*. Translated by Harry Francis Mallgrave. Los Angeles: Getty Research Institute, 2006.

Wofford, Susanne. *The Choice of Achilles: The Ideology of Figure in the Epic*. Stanford, CT: Stanford University Press, 1992.

Zabelin, I. E. *Istoriia russkoi zhizni s drevneishikh vremen*. 1876. Reprint, The Hague: Mouton, 1969.

— —. *Skifskie mogily: Chertomlytskii kurgan; Zapiska*. Moscow: Tip. Gracheva, 1865.

Zamiatin, E. I. *Sochineniia*. Munich: A. Neimanis, 1970.

Zhivov, V. M. *Razyskaniia v oblasti istorii i predystorii russkoi kul'tury*. Moscow: Iazyki slavianskoi kul'tury, 2002.

Ziolkowski, Theodore. *Minos and the Moderns: Cretan Myth in Twentieth-Century Literature and Art*. Oxford: Oxford University Press, 2008.

INDEX *

A

About Mayakovsky (Shklovsky), 57–58

"About the Monuments of Several Barbaric Peoples, Formerly Inhabiting Contemporary Novorossiisk" (Fabr), 29, 42–44, 44n26, 45–46

Abrams, M. H., 187–88, 188n13

Acropolis, 137, 138

Aeschylus, 17, 119
    Bunin's poem on, 107–8, 109–10, 109n2, 111–12, 113–16, 114n12, 119–21, 124, 131, 133, 135, 137

"Aeschylus" (Bunin), 107–8, 109–10, 109n2, 111–12, 113–16, 114n12, 119–21, 124, 131, 133, 135, 137

aesthetics
    archaeology and, 25, 65, 98, 175, 271
    of the kurgan, 13–14, 65, 68, 80, 83–84, 86–87
    modernist, 100, 210, 222, 246–47, 273, 310–11
    of the stone *babas*, 13–14, 33, 35, 38–39, 40–42, 45–49, 50, 56–57, 59, 60–61, 109–10, 115, 124, 128, 133, 141, 158, 165, 174, 203, 297–98, 300–1, 303
    of "the primitive," 110, 129–30, 135, 158, 171

Afanas'ev, Aleksandr, *The Slavs' Poetic Views on Nature*, 52–53, 52n40, 133, 183, 186

Afanas'ev, Aleksei, 142–43

"Agni" (Bunin), 122

Aikhenval'd, B., 291, 297

Ainalov, Dmitrii, 142, 147, 169

Akatevo, 290

Akhmatova, Anna, 152, 201

Aleksandrovskii Kurgan, 55n46

Aleksei Mikhailovich, 142

All-Russian Congress of Artists, 139

"Ancient Terror" (Ivanov), 110, 115–16, 118–20, 128, 130–31, 135, 196–97

Anderson, Benedict, *Imagined Communities: Reflections on the Origin and Spread of Nationalism*, 230–32, 232n55

Annenskii, Innokentii, 152, 201

anthropology, 35, 46–48, 100, 117, 123, 124

Anthropology Exhibition (Moscow, 1879), 47n29

antiquarianism, 291
    in *The Volga Falls to the Caspian Sea*, 284, 286–87, 291, 292

antiquity
    classical, 165, 217
    Greek, 44n26, 74, 110
    indigenous ("native)," in Russia, 13–15, 18, 19–25, 138, 172, 175, 247
    See also "native antiquity"

Anuchin, Dmitrii, 46–47, 47n29, 55

apocalypse, 23, 152, 161, 220, 221, 241

Apollon, 15, 48n32, 139

"Apologia of a Madman" (Chaadaev), 20–21, 92

Archaeological Commission, 53

Archaeological Congress, 35, 50, 64
archaeology
    and aesthetics, 25, 65, 98, 175, 271
    in *The Eleventh Year*, 246, 247, 250,
        252, 257–58, 264, 269, 270, 271,
        273, 275–79, 280, 309, 310
    kurgan, 63, 90–100
    in *The Naked Year*, 209–10, 220, 222,
        225–26, 234, 235, 283
    at new construction sites
        (*novostroiki*), 247–49, 275,
        278, 310
    Russian and Soviet, 21, 28, 42, 74,
        91, 97, 117, 175, 211n9, 214, 247,
        248, 249–50
    and Russian modernism, 15, 25,
        58, 100, 104, 175, 246, 307, 310
    salvage, 248, 248n9
    in *The Volga Falls to the Caspian
        Sea*, 280–81, 283–87, 291, 294,
        295–96, 298, 305, 306, 309, 310
archaism, 18, 97, 104, 105, 139, 141
    Voloshin's essay on, 15–18, 16n6,
        23, 60–61, 116–17, 134–35, 218
"Archaism in Russian Painting"
    (Voloshin), 15–18, 16n6, 23,
        60–61, 116–17, 134–35, 218
"Are We Scythians?" (Zamiatin), 217,
        218, 261
Argonauts, 19
art
    Aegean, 124n21
    African, 16n7, 125n22, 168
    Egyptian, 124n21
    Greek, 37, 43n25, 45
    Russian, 46, 48–49n32, 139, 142,
        147, 169, 172, 201, 241
    Western European, 16n7, 148, 165
artifacts
    archaeological, 16, 98, 125n21, 173,
        190, 201, 213, 218, 247, 261, 277,
        283, 287, 291, 308, 309
    Scythian, 15, 93

steppe, 14, 49, 50, 106, 112, 193,
        196, 219, 307, 308
Aseev, Nikolai,
        148, 294–95, 295n19
Asia, 22n14, 206, 207, 214, 217, 219,
        220, 223, 234, 238
Asia Minor, 107
Athens, 111, 216
Auerbach, Erich, 231
avant-garde, Russian, 24, 99, 118,
        125n22, 138, 142n10, 146, 151,
        166–67, 168, 170
    film, 246, 265
Azov (Azof), 173
    Sea of, 41, 83, 86

B
babas (stone *babas*, stone women,
        statuary, stone statuary)
    aesthetics of, 13–14, 33, 35, 38–39,
        40–42, 45–49, 50, 56–57, 59,
        60–61, 109–10, 115, 124, 128,
        133, 141, 158, 165, 174, 203,
        297–98, 300–1, 303
    and/as fertility deities, 52, 53, 162,
        218–19, 219n31, 300, 301
    and anthropology, 35, 46–48, 100,
        117, 123, 124
    Bobrov's poem on, 143–72, 144n13,
        145n14, 165n37, 175, 177,
        184–85
    Brandenburg's essay on, 54, 55,
        55n46, 56, 64
    Bunin's poem on, 108–10, 109n2,
        111–12, 113, 116, 119–22,
        123–25, 127–28, 130, 134, 135,
        137, 138, 200
    and Cubism, 46, 146, 162, 163–64,
        165, 165n37
    designations for, 28, 30–32, 35
    destruction and dislocation of, 33,
        49–61, 173–74, 189
    gender of, 30–32, 124, 177, 186, 301

Goncharova and, 59–60, *146*,
    153, 161, 162–64, 165n37, 169,
    171–72, 177
Gorodetskii's poem on, 143–72,
    144n13, 145n14, 165n37, 175,
    177, 184–85
Khlebnikov as the poet of, 174–203
peasants and, 33, 51–53, 60, 144, 149
and primitivism, 109, 110, 120,
    124–25, 127, 128, 130, 133, 148,
    152, 154, 155, 158, 160–61, 171
Pushkin's poem on, 131
Remizov's poem on, 32, 53, 110,
    131–35, 131n25, *134*, 138, 183,
    186, 200, 305
Sluchevskii's poem on, 185,
    186–89, 186n12
uncertain provenance of, 13–14,
    28–29, 32–33, 44, 54, 61, 117–18,
    122, 127, 152, 173, 213, 297
Uvarov's essay on, *27*, 34–39, *36*,
    42, 44–45, 55, 64, 85, *151*, 249
Veselovskii's writings on, 28–29,
    28n2, 30, 32–33, 37, *38*, 39, *39*,
    40, 44, 53–54, 55–57, 59, 60, 117,
    135, 173, 202, 214
Babel, Isaac
    "Berestechko," 89–90, 96, 233
    Red Cavalry Stories, 89, 90
Babylonian Statuette, 39, *39*
Baedeker guides, 111
Baer, Karl, 91
Bakhtin, Mikhail, 106, 232, 254, 272
Bakst, Leon, 15
    Terror Antiquus, 115–16, *115*, 120
Ballod, F. V., 211n9
    *Volga "Pompeiis": An Essay on
    the Artistic-Archaeological
    Examination of the Zone on the
    Right Bank of the Volga near
    Saratov and Tsaritsyn, The*, 204–
    6, *205*, 207, 210, 211, 212–13,
    214, 226, *227*, *228*, 234–35

Bal'mont, Konstantin, 68
    "Feather Grass," 112
    "Poetry as Magic," 125
Baran, Henryk, 132, 132n29, 183n8
Baratynskii, Evgenii, 148
Barkan, Leonard, *Unearthing the Past:
    Archaeology and Aesthetics in the
    Making of Renaissance Culture*,
    19, 37, 121n18
Barthes, Roland, 84
Bataille, Georges, 303
Battle of Berestechko, 90
Battle of Borodino, 86–87, 88
Battle of Stalingrad, 88
"Bears, The" (Garshin), 49–50, 51, 56, 57
Belarus, 88
Belsk, 49
Bely, Andrei, 19, 146, 165n37, 219, 220
    Petersburg, 53, 131–32, 152–53, 219, 224
Benjamin, Walter, 19, 231n53
Benois, Alexandre, 99, 139, 153
Berdiaev, Nikolai, 23, 170, 171
    Russian Idea, The, 23
"Berestechko" (Babel), 89–90
Bertrand, Aloysius, 148
Bethea, David, 23, 294, 304
Birth of Tragedy, The (Nietzsche), 116,
    128, 136–37
Black Grave, *62*
Black Sea, 59, 63, 66, 70, 85, 86, 93, 100,
    216, 218, 241, 244, 249
Blok, Aleksandr, 152
    "Scythians, The," 20, 96, 217, 218,
    219, 220–21, 261
    "Twelve, The," 224, 240
Bobrov, Sergei
    "Dream, The," 166
    "Foundations of the New Russian
    Painting, The," 139, 140–43,
    142n10, 160–61
    Gardeners over the Vines, 143, *146*,
    147–48, 155, 160, 162, 165–66,
    165–66n38, 166n40

"Kamennaia baba" ("The Stone Baba"), 143–72, 144n13, 145n14, 165n37, 175, 177, 184–85
and Khlebnikov, 175–76, 177, 184–85
"Legacy," 160
"Love for Pushkin," 155
Notes of a Versifier, 155
"On the New Illustration," 162, 164
Body of the Dead Christ in the Tomb, The (Holbein), 170
bogatyr', bogatyry, 75, 77, 78, 79, 252, 253, 304
Bois, Yve-Alain, 16n7
Bolgars and Bolgary (Bulgars), 32, 206, 207, 213–14, 215
Bolsheviks and Bolshevism, 198, 206, 207, 208, 242
Bordier, Arthur, "Les Sciences anthropologiques à L'Exposition universelle," 46–49, 47, 48n32
Boris Godunov (Pushkin), 285
Borodino, Battle of, 86–87, 88
"Borodino" (Lermontov), 68, 87
Bosphorus, 107
Brandenburg, Nikolai, 64
"Toward the Question of the Stone Babas," 54, 55, 55n46, 56, 64
Brew, J. O., 248, 248n9
Bright Green (Gorodetskii), 128
Briusov, A. Ia., 125n21
Briusov, Valery, 110, 112, 124–25n21, 186n12
"Mednyi vsadnik," 153–54, 156
"On Easter Island," 124–27, 125n22, 128, 131
broadsheets, 142n10
Brokgauz-Efron
edition of "The Bronze Horseman," 150
encyclopedia, 55, 114, 114n12

Bronze Age, 24, 251, 293
"Bronze Horseman, The" (Pushkin), 145–46, 149–62, 150, 153n21, 165, 201
Bronze Horseman (Falconet), 131, 132, 145, 145n14, 147, 148–49, 150, 151, 152, 152n19, 153, 154, 157, 158, 159, 161, 165, 168, 170, 201
Brostrom, Kenneth N., 290n13, 305
Browning, Gary, 218–19, 219n31, 236
Budantsev, Sergei, "The Dnieper Construction," 255–56, 257
Budini, 216
Bugaev, B. N. See Bely, Andrei
Bulgakov, Sergei, 171
Bulgarians. See Bolgars and Bolgary
Bunin, Ivan, 68, 69, 107, 171, 186n12, 196, 309
"Aeschylus," 107–8, 109–10, 109n2, 111–12, 113–16, 114n12, 119–21, 124, 131, 133, 135, 137
"Agni," 122
"Epitaph," 307–8, 309
"In the Archipelago," 123
"On the Donets," 112–13, 113n11
"Sea of Gods," 137–38
"Stone Baba, The," 108–10, 109n2, 111–12, 113, 116, 119–22, 123–25, 127–28, 130, 134, 135, 137, 138, 200
travels of, to ancient sites, 110–11
burial mounds, 18, 87, 89, 213, 220, 229–30, 264, 307
in The Iliad, 70–72
in The Naked Year, 207, 209, 210, 218–19, 219n31, 234
naming of, 65
words for, 13, 76n23, 90–91n38
Burliuk, David, 57, 58, 99, 100, 103, 154, 176
Burliuk, Vladimir, 57, 100, 176
Burliuk family, stone baba belonging to, 57–58, 59

Burrough, Christopher, 215
bylina, 240
Byron, Lord, 114, 114n12
byt, 288–90, 291
Byzantium, 19, 56, 56n51, 92

C
Cahiers d'art, 31
Canary Islands, 47
Catherine the Great, 152, 252, *253*,
    292, 294
Caucasus, 209, 218
    stone *babas* from, 39, *41*, 48
Celts, 32, 44, 45
Central Asia, 241
Centrifuge, 175
Chaadaev, Petr
    "Apologia of a Madman," 20–23,
        92, 94, 221
    Philosophical Letters, 20–21, 91–92
Chekhov, Anton, "The Steppe," 12–13,
        59, 77, 84, 130, 196
Chernianka, 57, 58, 102, 176
Chernigov, *62*
Chertomlyk Kurgan, 55, 65, 93, 191, 197
Chevengur (Platonov), 68, 294, 304
Christianity,
        22, 37, 123n20, 131, 141, 261
chronotope, 81, 106, 232, 254
Chulkov, Mikhail, *The Mocker, or
        Slavonic Tales*, 73
Clark, Katerina,
        24, 151–52, 152n18, 219
Clark, T. J., 277
"Cliff out of the Future, A"
        (Khlebnikov), 196
collage, 151–52, 152n18, 224, 239
*Collection of Maps and Sketches toward
        the Study of the Antiquities of
        Southern Russia and the Banks
        of the Black Sea, A* (Uvarov and
        Vebel'), 85–86, *85*, 249, *250*
Colombia, 47

"Corner-to-Corner Correspondence,
        A" (Gershenzon and Ivanov),
        135–36
Cowling, Elizabeth, 167–68
Cranach, Lucas, 166n38
Crete, 17, 117
Crimea, 54, 83, 85, 241, 244
Crimean War, 88
Cubism, 103, 165, 168, 170, 171, 224
        stone *babas* and, 46, 146, 162,
        163–64, 165, 165n37
Cubo-Futurism, 165
Cumans. *See* Polovtsy
"Current State of the Question of the
        'Stone *Babas*' or '*Balbals*,' The"
        (Veselovskii), 28–29, 28n2, 30,
        32–33, 37, 39, 44, 53–54, 55–57,
        59, 173, 214
Czech Statue, Elizabeth, 39, *40*

D
Dal', V. I., dictionary of, 100, 234
Darius, 95–96
Davenport, Guy, 16
Decadent movement, 186n12
Deleuze, Gilles, 250
Del'vig, Anton, "Kurgan," 75, 83
de Man, Paul, 121–22
Derzhavin, Gavrila, 201
Desmet, Karl, 51
D'iachkova, E. B., 209
Dneprostroi, 244–45
        Budantsev's article on, 255–56, 257
        in *The Eleventh Year*, 244, 246, 250,
        255, 256–57, 260–61, 264, 271,
        275, 278, 280
        excavations at, 244, 246, 249,
        250–51, 254, 257, 261, 264, 278
        in *The Volga Falls to the Caspian Sea*,
        245, 280–81
"Dnieper Construction, The"
        (Budantsev), 255–56, 257
Dnieper River (Dniepr) region, 40, 92

and Dneprostroi, 245, 251, 255, 271
   in *The Eleventh Year*, 252, 271
   excavations at, 244, 254
   kurgans in, 63, 83, 93, 205
Donets River (Donetz), 40
   Bunin's poem on, 112–13, 113n11
Donkey's Tail, 139, 140, 143, 146, 147,
      148, 163, 166
Don River, 63, 205
Doolittle, Hilda, 16
Dostoevsky, Fyodor, 24, 237
   Idiot, The, 170
Dream, The (Rousseau), 166, 168
"Dream, The" (Bobrov), 166
Drobashenko, S. V., 267n40
Dryad, The (Picasso), *167*, 170–71
Duganov, R. V., 192n22
Duvakin, Viktor, 175–66
dvoeverie, 52

E
East, the, 103, 111, 179, 180, 183, 202,
      213, 214, 220, 237, 241
Easter Island, 125n22
   Briusov's poem on, 124–27,
      125n22, 128, 131
Eastman, Max, 281, 283
Egypt, 19, 111, 123, 124n21, 219,
      298n26
Eisenstein, Sergei
   General Line, The, 273
   October, 246
Ekaterinodar, 59
Ekaterinoslav, 53, 55n46, 59
Ekimov, Petr, 69
Eleventh Year, The (Vertov), 243–79,
      259, 260, 262, 267, 272, 274, 275,
      276, 283, 286, 289, 290, 304, 306,
      307–8, 309, 310
End of St. Petersburg, The (Pudovkin),
      246
Energy (Gladkov), 245
"Epitaph" (Bunin), 307–8

Epithets of Literary Russian Speech
   (Zelenetskii), 69, 72, 75
Epstein, Mikhail, 105–6
Erlich, Victor, 224
eschatology, 23, 106, 240
Essence of Christianity, The (Feuerbach),
      123n20
ethnography, 18, 38, 46, 47n30, 57n52,
      91, 133, 186n12, 187, 224, 307
Eurasia, 15, 20, 22, 30, 37, 63, 105, 117,
      207, 221, 223
   steppe of, 13, 25, 30, 222
Eurasianism, 208
Europe, 20, 22n14, 42, 44, 47, 110, 111,
      117, 147, 167, 169, 208, 213, 219,
      220, 221, 230, 248n9, 290
   responses to archaeological
      discoveries in, 15, 16n6, 17
   Western, 16n7, 47n30, 74, 148, 163,
      165, 168–69, 170, 172, 188n13,
      295–96
Evans, Arthur, 17, 117
Evarnitskii, D. I., 278
   *Zaporozh'e in the Remnants of the
      Past and the Sayings of Its Folk*,
      252–54
"Evening on the Volga" (Viazemskii),
      81–83
Evlent'ev, Konstantin, 213
excavations, 16, 17, 21–22, 37, 86, 213
   in *The Eleventh Year*, 244, 246, 247,
      249–50, 254, 261, 275, 276–77
   of kurgans (graves), 55, 62–68, 90,
      92, 93, 102, 250, 251, 276, 300
   in *The Naked Year*, 206, 209–10, 211,
      211n9, 214, 217, 224–30, 232–33,
      235, 237
   at Soviet construction sites,
      247, 249, 250–51, 254, 278–79,
      282, 309
   in *The Volga Falls to the Caspian Sea*,
      280–81, 284, 297–98, 299, 300,
      305, 306

Excavations of Ancient Graves, and the Description, Preservation, and Publication of Grave Antiquities (Samokvasov), 64–67, *65*

F
Fabr, Andrei, "About the Monuments of Several Barbaric Peoples, Formerly Inhabiting Contemporary Novorossiisk," 29, 42–44, 44n26, 45–46
Falconet, Étienne, Bronze Horseman, 131, 132, 145, 145n14, 147, 148–49, *150*, 151, 152, 152n19, 153, 154, 157, 158, 159, 161, 165, 168, 170, 201
Falk, Johann, 34
Fall of the Romanov Dynasty, The (Shub), 246
False Dmitry, 284
"Feather Grass" (Bal'mont), 112
Fedorov, Georgii, 202
Fedorov-Davydov, German, *Kurgans, Idols, Coins,* 173–75, 200
fertility deities, stone *babas* and/as, 52, 53, 162, 218–19, 219n31, 300, 301
Fet, Afanasy, 69, 148
Feuerbach, Ludwig, 123, 123n20, 128
Finns, 24, 32, 206, 207, 214, 234, 237, 293
Five-Year Plans, 245, 281–83, 308
Flam, Jack, 125n22
Florenskii, Pavel, 170
      "Stratification of Aegean Culture, The," 110, 116–19, 120, 128
folk art, 48, 99
folklore, 52, 132, 132n29, 178
Formozov, Aleksandr, 74, 98, 175, 211n9
      Pushkin and Archaeology, 76–77, 76n23
"Foundations of the New Russian Painting, The" (Bobrov), 139, 140–43, 142n10, 160–61

France, 35, 46, 48, 48n32, 87, 103, 140, 147, 163, 166, 169, 235n58, 241, 303
Frank, Joseph, 101–2n53
Frazer, James, *The Golden Bough,* 52n40
"From That Life That Raged Here" (Tiutchev), 79n27, 94–95, 95n44
Fry, Roger, 105

G
Galchonok, 129
"Game in Hell, A" (Goncharova and Khlebnikov), 176–77
Gardeners over the Vines (Bobrov), 143, *146,* 147–48, 155, 160, 162, 165–66, 165–66n38, 166n40
Garshin, Vsevolod, "The Bears," 49–50, 51, 56, 57
Gasparov, Boris, 101, 101n53
Gasparov, Mikhail, 159
Gauguin, Paul, 167
Geloni, 216
General Line, The (Eisenstein), 273
Geraci, Robert, 213–14
"German Story, A" (Pil'niak), 211n9, 311
Germany, 22n14, 34, 35, 40, 41, 241
Gershenzon, Mikhail, 21
      "Corner-to-Corner Correspondence, A" (with Ivanov), 135–36
Geschichte der Kunst des Altertums (Winckelmann), 43n25
Gidroelektroproekt, 249
Giprogor, 249
Gladkov, Fedor, *Energy,* 245
Glavzoloto, 249
Gnedich, Nikolai, Russian translation of *Iliad,* 69–80, 90n38
God of Fertility (Goncharova), 162
gods, Greek, 43, 44, 219
Goethe, Johann Wolfgang von, 114n12
Gogol, Nikolai, 53, 133, 201
Golden Bough, The (Frazer), 52n40

Golden Horde, 204, 206, 213
Golden Woman, 39
Goldwater, Robert, 47n30
Golitsyn, L. L., 215–16
Goncharova, Natal'ia, 99, 139
    and Bobrov (lithographs for
        Bobrov), 146–47, *146*, 148, 153,
        161, 162–64, *163*, 165n37, 166,
        168–89, 171–72, 177
    "Game in Hell, A" (with
        Khlebnikov), 176–77
    God of Fertility, 162
    Pillars of Salt, 162
    Still Life with Pineapple, 162
    and the stone *babas*, 59–60, *146*,
        153, 161, 162–64, 165n37, 169,
        171–72, 177
Gorky, Maxim, 107
Gorodetskii, Sergei, 110
    Bright Green, 128
    "Kamennaia baba" ("The Stone
        Baba"), 143–72, 144n13, 145n14,
        165n37, 175, 177, 184–85
Gothic, 163
Goths, 32
Grabar', Ilya, 99
    History of Russian Art, 241
graves. *See* burial mounds;
        Khlebnikov, Velimir, grave of;
        kurgans; Samokvasov, Dmitrii
Graves of the Russian Land
        (Samokvasov), 62–63, *62*, *66*, *67*
Greece, ancient, 19, 43, 44n26, 74, 97,
        110, 111, 137, 293
    art of, 37, 43n25, 45
    linking of stone *babas* to, 42–45,
        43n25, 44n26, 48
    linking of Uvek to, 214, 216
    See also Fabr, Andrei; Gnedich,
        Nikolai
Greenleaf, Monika, 44n26
Grigor'ev, Apollon, 186n12
Güldenstädt, Johann Anton, 34

H
Hagia Sophia, 107
Hakluyt Society, 215
Hawaiian Islands, 47
Heaney, Seamus, 18
Herodotus, 32, 92–93, 214, 215, 216
Hesiod, 100, 102, 215
Hisarlik, 17
Historical Museum, Moscow, 50,
        59–60, 105, 298, 300, 301
History of Russian Art (Grabar'), 241
*History of Russian Life from the Most
        Ancient of Times, The* (Zabelin),
        90–96, 90–91n38, 191, 215–16
Hoffmann, E. T. A., 148
Holbein, Hans, *The Body of the Dead
        Christ in the Tomb*, 170
Homer, 17, 102, 215, 223
    Iliad, 69–80, 90n38, 93, 118, 194, 214
Hörnes, Moritz, 118
How We Write (Pil'niak), 280
Huns, 32, 40, 41–42, 173
Hylaea and Hylaeans, 57, 100–1, 102,
        103, 154, 155, 176

I
Iazykov, Nikolai, 148
Ibn Fadlan, Ahmad, 215
icons, 99, 141, 142, 142n10, 145, 158,
        202, 259, 285
Idiot, The (Dostoevsky), 170
Iliad (Homer), 118, 194
    Gnedich's Russian translation of,
        69–80, 90n38
    Schliemann and, 93, 214
Images of Italy (Muratov), 295n19
"Imaginary Stone *Babas*"
        (Veselovskii), 28, *38*, 39, *39*, *40*,
        59, 60, 117, 135, 202
*Imagined Communities: Reflections
        on the Origin and Spread of
        Nationalism* (Anderson),
        230–32, 232n55

Imperial Russian Archaeological
    Society, 35
Imperial Society of Agriculture of
    Southern Russia, 51
Imperial Society of Friends of the
    Natural, Anthropological, and
    Ethnographic Sciences, 46
"Incantation by Laughter"
    (Khlebnikov), 125, 189
industrialization (industrial moder-
    nity, industrial modernization)
    and archaeology, 100, 210, 246,
        249, 250, 252, 258, 269, 270,
        276–78, 283–84, 286, 294, 295,
        306, 307–8, 309
    in *The Eleventh Year*, 246, 247, 249,
        250, 252, 254, 255, 258–61,
        264–65, 268, 269, 270, 276–78,
        307–8, 309
    in *The Naked Year*, 210, 235–36
    in *The Volga Falls to the Caspian Sea*,
        280, 281, 283–84, 286, 294, 295,
        306, 309
International Exhibition (Paris, 1878), 47
"In the Archipelago" (Bunin), 123
Iranians and Greeks in South Russia
    (Rostovtsev), 217, 217n28, 218
Irkutsk, 53
"Ivan and Maria" (Pil'niak), 302
Ivanov, Viacheslav, 148, 160
    "Ancient Terror," 19, 110, 115–16,
        118–20, 128, 130–31, 135,
        196–97
    "Corner-to-Corner
        Correspondence, A" (with
        Gershenzon), 135–37
Ivanov-Razumnik, 20, 217, 218, 220
Izmailov, N. V., 152

J
Jack of Diamonds, 163
Jakobson, Roman, 189, 190, 193n24,
    200, 288–89

Jensen, Peter, 218
Joyce, James, 16
"Joy in Art" (Roerich), 24, 98, 135

K
Kahn, Andrew, 153n21
"Ka" (Khlebnikov), 193
Kalmyks, 187
"Kamennaia baba" ("Stone *Baba*")
    (Bobrov), 143–72, 144n13,
    145n14, 165n37, 175, 177,
    184–85
"Kamennaia baba" ("The Stone *Baba*")
    (Gorodetskii), 129–30, 138, 188
Kandinsky, Wassily, "On the Spiritual
    in Art," 140, 140n4
Kataev, Valentin, *Time, Forward!*,
    308–9, 310–11
Kaufman, Mikhail, 244, 264, 266, 267,
    268, 270
Kazakhstan, 235
Kel'siev, Aleksandr, 46, 48–49, 50–51
Kenner, Hugh, 17, 105
Kerch, 85
Kharkov, 53
Kharkov University, 49, 50
Kherson, 34, 53
Khlebnikov, Velimir, 16, 20, 100, 155, 219
    "Cliff out of the Future, A," 196
    "Game in Hell, A" (with
        Goncharova), 176–77
    grave of, 201–3, *203*
    "Incantation by Laughter," 125, 189
    "Ka," 193
    "Kurgan," 68, 89, 196, 233
    "Kurgan of Sviatogor, The," 196,
        197
    "Lialia Rides the Tiger," 176,
        177–78
    "Night in a Trench, A," 176, 184,
        190–93, 191n21, 195
    as the poet of the stone *babas*,
        174–203

"Stone Woman, The," 176, 178,
    190–95, 192n22, 200, 201–3, 233
"To All! To All! To All!," 193
Kichkas, 244, 249–50, *250*, 255
    excavation of Scythian warrior in,
        244, 249–51, 278, 290
Kiev, 64, 76n23, 241
Kino-Eye (Vertov), 265
Kitezh, 290, 306
Klichkov, Viacheslav, 201
"Knowledge about the Stone Women"
    (Uvarov), 27, 34–39, *36*, 42,
        44–45, 55, 64, 85, *151*, 249
Kolomensky Palace, 142
Komsomol'skaia pravda, 243, 244,
    260–61, 270
Konevskoi, Ivan, 148
Koretskaia, I. V., 155
Kostrov, Ermil, 69
Kozlov, Ivan, 69
Krakow, 94
Krasnaia nov', 223, 291
Krasnodar, 173
Krasnodubrovskii, S. S., 215–16
Kruchenykh, Aleksei, 154, 176
    Our Arrival, 58–59
Kul'bin, Nikolai, 140, 140n4
"Kurgan" (Del'vig), 75, 83
"Kurgan" (Khlebnikov),
    68, 89, 196, 233
Kurgan of Glory, 88
"Kurgan of Sviatogor, The"
    (Khlebnikov), 196, 197
"kurganomania," 68, 84
kurgans
    aesthetics of, 13–14, 65, 68, 80,
        83–84, 86–87
    archaeology of, 63, 90–100
    Del'vig's poem on, 75, 83
    excavations of, 55, 62–68, 90, 92,
        93, 102, 250, 251, 276, 300
    Khlebnikov on, 68, 89, 196, 197, 233
    Pushkin on, 68, 74–77, 83

Roerich's essay on, and sketches
    of, 96–99, *96*
Tolstoi's poem on, 69, 75, 77–80, 83
uncertain provenance of, 13–14,
    66, 75, 91, 93
as a word, 69, 70–74, 86–87, 210
Zelenetskii's entry on, 69, 72, 75
See also burial mounds; "kurgano-
    mania;" *specific kurgans*
Kurgans, Idols, Coins (Fedorov-
    Davydov), 173–75, 200
"Kurgan" (Tolstoi),
    69, 75, 77–80, 83
Kutuzov, General, 87
Kuzmin, Mikhail, 19, 20, 148

L
Lahti, Katherine, 60, 186
La Nature, 47, 48
Larionov, Mikhail, 59–60, 99, 139, 166,
    166n38, 168–69
"L'Art populaire russe" (Mourey),
    48–49n32
Lay of Igor's Campaign, The, 113
Leberghe, Charles van, 148
"Legacy" (Bobrov), 160
Lenin, 244, 245, 248, 310
    "electric lamp" of, 259, 270
    in *The Eleventh Year*, 274–75, *274*
    figure, in "A Night in a Trench,"
        191, 192, 197–98
Lermontov, Mikhail, 148
    "Borodino," 68, 87
Leroi-Gourhan, André, 235n58
Leskov, Nikolai, 133
Lespugue Venus, 303
"Les Sciences anthropologiques à
    L'Exposition universelle"
    (Bordier), 46–49, *47*, 48n32
Levant, 111
"Lialia Rides the Tiger" (Khlebnikov),
    176, 177–78
Linnichenko, Ivan, 67–68, 84

*Literary Anthology of Works by Students
     of Petersburg University,*
     134, 135
"Literary Fact, The" (Tynianov), 252
Livshits, Benedikt, 96, 100, 155, 163
     One and a Half-Eyed Archer, The, 99,
          100–4, 155
     "People in Landscape," 103
Long-Forgotten Pasts (Pil'niak), 211
Lotman, Yuri, 23
"Love for Pushkin" (Bobrov), 155
lubok, lubki, 141, 142n10

M
Machines and Wolves (Pil'niak),
     297–98, 303
MacKay, John, 260–61
Magnitogorsk, 249
Maguire, Robert, 224–25, 238, 302
"Mahogany" (Pil'niak), 281, 291
Makovskii, Sergei, 99
     "Talashkino," 48–49n32
Malakhov Kurgan, 88
Mallarmé, Stéphane, 148
Mamaev Kurgan, 88, *89*
Mamontov, Savva, 60
Mandelstam, Osip, 19, 223
Man with a Movie Camera (Vertov),
     266, *266*
Markov, Vladimir, 122n22, 160,
     190–91, 191n21, 195
     Negro Art, 122n55
Marx, Karl, 287
Marxism, 230–31, 248, 310
Matich, Olga, 221
Matisse, Henri, 167
Mayakovsky, Vladimir, 57, 154, 176
Vladimir Mayakovsky: A Tragedy,
     185–86
"Mednyi vsadnik" (Briusov),
     153–54, 156
Megulovskii Kurgan, 55n46
messianism, Russian, 23, 101, 196, 218

Mexico, 47, 99
Michelson, Annette,
     235n58, 271n44, 274
Miller, Mykhailo, 249, 251, 251n17,
     254, 276, 278
Ministry of Internal Affairs, 53
Misler, Nicoletta, 170–71
Miturich-Khlebnikov, M., 201–2
Mnishek, Marina, Tower of,
     284, 285, 306
Mocker, or Slavonic Tales, The
     (Chulkov), 73
modernism, Russian
     and archaeology, 15, 25, 58, 100,
          104, 175, 246, 307, 310
     and mythology, 101–2
     and *ostranenie,* 97, 136, 288
     and primitivism, 18, 24–25, 99,
          125n22, 130, 133, 136, 142, 143,
          146, 147, 155, 160–61, 165–66,
          168–69
     and the Scythians, 220–21, 261,
          268–69
     and the search for a "native
          antiquity," 13–15, 18, 19–25
     and the stone *babas,* 28, 33, 58–61,
          110, 117, 141
Mongols, 22, 290
     linking of stone *babas* to, 32, 37, 40,
          63, 135n33, 173
montage, 152, 224
Mordva, 234
Morgan, E. Delmar, 84
Morozov, Petr, 153
Moscow, 35, 47, 47n29, 57, 58, 59, 87,
     174, 202, 241, 256, 280, 292, 293,
     300
     Historical Museum in, 59, 105, 298
Moscow-Volga Canal, 249
Mourey, Gabriel, "L'Art populaire
     russe," 48–49n32
Muratov, Pavel, *Images of Italy,* 295n19
Muromets, Ilya, 240, 242

Muromtseva, Vera, 110–11
mythology
    Greek, 43–44
    Russian and Slavic, 43–44, 52
    Russian modernism and, 101–2

N
Naiman, Eric, 287–88
Naked Year, The (Pil'niak), 204–42,
    211n9, 252, 283, 303
Napoleon, 87, 95, 96
Napoleonic Wars, 74, 88
*National Corpus of the Russian
    Language,* 73
nature, 43, 44, 49n32, 52, 88, 90, 94, 95,
    128, 133
    as enemy of industry and
        modernization, 248, 255–57,
        259, 281, 310
necropolises, 15, 111, 207, 212, 233
Negro Art (Markov), 122n55
Nekrasov, Nikolai, "Who Lives Well
    in Rus'?," 130
neoclassicism, 14, 25, 49, 60, 152,
    152n19, 154, 155, 165, 168
Neo-Primitivism, 146–47, 169
NEP, 287–88
Nerval, Gérard de, 148
Nesbet, Anne, 265–66, 273
Nicholas, Mary, 223, 286, 298
Nicholas I, 153
Nietzsche, Friedrich, *The Birth of
    Tragedy,* 116, 128, 136–37
"Night in a Trench, A" (Khlebnikov),
    176, 184, 190–93, 191n21, 195
Nogais, 32
Notes of a Versifier (Bobrov), 155
Novalis, 148
Novocherkassk, 59, 173
Novodevichy Cemetery, 201
novostroiki, 245, 247, 251, 270, 309
Novyi lef, 294
Novyi mir, 255

O
Oceania, 47
October (Eisenstein), 246
Odessa Society of History and
    Antiquity, 42
Oka River, 209, 280, 281, 283, 299, 305
Old Russia, 142, 289, 293, 294
Olenin, Aleksei, 74
One and a Half-Eyed Archer, The
    (Livshits), 99, 100–4, 155
"On Easter Island" (Briusov), 124–27,
    125n22, 128, 131
"On the Donets" (Bunin), 112–13,
    113n11
"On the Kurgan" (Roerich), 96–99
"On the New Illustration" (Bobrov),
    162, 164
"On the Spiritual in Art" (Kandinsky),
    140, 140n4
Operation Bagration, 88
"On Pil'niak" (Shklovsky), 238–40
Orenburg, 59
Orthodoxy, 20, 22n14, 131, 202, 207
ostranenie (defamiliarization), 97–98,
    103–4, 105–6, 288–89
Our Arrival (Kruchenykh), 58–59

P
Paestum, 221
pagan
    past, 63, 130, 131
    rituals, 229, 231, 232, 235
    statuary, 45, 52, 53, 202
paganism, 52, 130, 174, 175, 190
Pagan Rogneda Kurgan, 191, 195
Palestine, 111
Pallas, Peter Simon, *Travels through
    the Southern Provinces of the
    Russian Empire, in the Years
    1793 and 1794,* 40–41, 41, 42,
    45–46, 168
panchronism, 101, 102, 105
"Panmongolism" (Solov'ev), 220–21

Paris, 47, 102, 103, 169
Parton, Anthony, 168–69
Pasternak, Boris, 175
Peabody Museum, 248
peasants, 171, 208, 218, 233, 234, 260,
    287, 290
    stone *babas* and, 33, 51–53, 60,
        144, 149
Peasant Woman (Picasso), 171
Pechenegs, 32, 55, 237
"People in Landscape" (Livshits), 103
Petersburg (Bely), 53, 131–32, 152–53,
    219, 224
Peterson, Dale, 288
Peter the Great, 97, 208
    Falconet's monument to (Bronze
        Horseman),
        131, 132, 145, 145n14, 147,
        148–49, *150*, 151, 152, 152n19,
        153, 154, 157, 158, 159, 161, 165,
        168, 170, 201
    reforms of, 20, 22
philology, 64, 92, 214
Philosophical Letters (Chaadaev),
    20–21, 91–92
Picasso, Pablo, 165n37, 166, 167, 169,
    170, 171
    Dryad, The, 167, 170–71
    Peasant Woman, 171
    Three Women, 166, 167–68, *167*,
        170, 171
Pillars of Salt (Goncharova), 162
Pil'niak, Boris, 89, 308, 309, 310–11
    "German Story, A," 311
    How We Write, 280
    "Ivan and Maria," 302
    Long-Forgotten Pasts, 211
    Machines and Wolves, 297–98, 303
    "Mahogany," 281, 291
    Naked Year, The, 204–42, 211n9, 252,
        283, 303
    and Vertov, 280–81, 288–89, 304–5,
        308, 309–10

Volga Falls to the Caspian Sea, The,
    245, 279, 280–306, 280n2, 310
"Wormwood," 211, 211n9, 212, 230
Platonov, Andrei, *Chevengur*,
    68, 294, 304
poèmas. *See* "Bronze Horseman,
    The" (Pushkin); "Kamennaia
    baba" ("The Stone *Baba*")
    (Bobrov); "Night in a Trench,
    A" (Pil'niak); "Stone Woman,
    The" (Khlebnikov)
"Poetry as Magic" (Bal'mont), 125
Polo, Marco, *Travels*, 215, 215n19, 215n22
Polotvsy, 32, 42, 55, 56, 56n51, 173, 202
Pompeii, 213, 214
Popov, Igor, 133–34
Pound, Ezra, 105
primitivism (embrace/investigation of
    the primitive),
    16, 18, 44, 44n26, 47n30, 110,
    128–29, 130, 165
    Pil'niak and, 208–9, 281, 296
    and Russian modernism,
        18, 24–25, 99, 125n22, 130, 133,
        136, 142, 143, 146, 147, 155,
        160–61, 165–66, 168–69
    and stone *babas*,
        109, 110, 120, 124–25, 127, 128,
        130, 133, 148, 152, 154, 155, 158,
        160–61, 171
production novels, 245, 281, 308
Prokudin-Gorskii, Sergei, photo of
    Raevskii Kurgan, 88, *88*
Prometheanism, 256, *257*, 273, 281
Prussia, 39
Pudovkin, Vsevolod, *The End of St.
    Petersburg*, 246
Pushkin, Alexander, 24, 133, 147,
    153n21, 201
    Boris Godunov, 285
    "Bronze Horseman, The," 145–46,
        149–62, *150*, 153n21, 165, 201
    kurgans in, 68, 74–77, 83

"Shield of Oleg, The," 76n23
"Song of Oleg the Wise,"
    75–76, 79, *104*
"Stone Guest, The," 131
Pushkin and Archaeology (Formozov),
    76–77, 76n23

R
Rachinskii, Grigorii, 148
Raevskii, Sergei, 148
Raevskii Kurgan (Raevskii's Battery),
    87, 88, *88*
Rau, Paul, 211n9, 300
Red Cavalry Stories (Babel), 89, 90
Remizov, Aleksei
    Posolon', 132n29
    "Stone Woman, The,"
        32, 53, 110, 131–35, 131n25, *134*,
        138, 183, 186, 200, 305
    Toward the Ocean-Sea, 131, 132
Renaissance, 37, 121n18, 165
Repin, Ilya, 139
Rigolot, François, 132
Rimbaud, Arthur, 148
Rite of Spring, The (Roerich and
        Stravinsky), 24, 105, 134, 135,
        136–37, 305
Roerich, Nicholas,
        15, 23–24, 96, 139, 175
    archaeological sketches, 96, *96*
    "Joy in Art," 24, 98, 135
    "On the Kurgan," 96–99
    and Remizov's "The Stone
        Woman," 134–35
    Rite of Spring (with Stravinsky),
        24, 105, 134, 135, 136–37, 305
    sketch of stone woman, *134*, 135
"Romance"(Del'vig). *See* "Kurgan"
        (Del'vig)
Romanticism, 75, 186n12, 188n13, 219
Rome, ancient,
        19, 37, 92, 111, 221, 293, 295
Rostov, 173, 241

Rostovtsev, Mikhail, *Iranians and
        Greeks in South Russia*,
        217, 217n28, 218
Rousseau, Henri, *The Dream*, 166, 168
Rozanov, Vasilii, 301, 302, 303
Rubin, William, 16n7
Rubruquis, 56, 56n49
Rumiantsev Museum, 173
Rus', 19, 22, 130, 289
Russia
    cultural history of, 13, 151, 241
    cultural identity of, 15, 20, 22, 23
    Golden Age, 24, 154
    North of, 97, 134–35
    post-Petrine, 19
    post-Revolutionary,
        206, 209, 269, 287, 288, 292
    Revolutionary, 207, 208, 233
    South of,
        51, 53, 74, 77, 83, 85, 86, 97, 110,
        218, 241, 249, 249n13
Russian Civil War,
        53, 88, 96, 191–92, 194, 195–96,
        200, 204, 210, 212, 219, 225, 232,
        233, 236, 283
Russian Empire,
        22, 40, 43, 92, 93, 100
Russian Formalism, 59, 252
Russian Futurism,
        24, 57, 58, 99–100, 103, 147, 154,
        155, 162, 175, 310
Russian Idea, The (Berdiaev), 23
Russian Revolution (October
        Revolution, Revolution),
        20, 22, 111, 204, 208, 210, 217,
        218, 225, 233, 236, 237, 240, 244,
        246, 283, 291, 292, 293, 294, 296,
        301, 302, 306, 308

S
Sadovskoi, Boris, 128, 130, 148
Sakhalin Islands, 47
Salmony, Alfred, 30–31, 37

Samokvasov, Dmitrii
　　Excavations of Ancient Graves, and
　　　　the Description, Preservation, and
　　　　Publication of Grave Antiquities,
　　　　64–67, *65*
　　Graves of the Russian Land, 62–63,
　　　　62, 66, 67
Saratov, 53, 204, 211, 212, 216, 235
Sarmatians, 32, 293, 311
Schimmelpenninck van der Oye,
　　David, 22n14
Schlegel, Friedrich, 114n12
Schliemann, Heinrich, 33, 93, 214
Scottish Geographical Magazine, 84
"Scythian Graves: The Chertomlyk
　　Kurgan, The" (Zabelin),
　　55, 64, 93–94
Scythians
　　artifacts of, 15, 93
　　Blok's poem on, 20, 96, 217, 218,
　　　　219, 220–21, 261
　　in *The Eleventh Year,* 249, 255, 257–
　　　　70, *258, 259,* 265n37, 273–75,
　　　　277, 288, 309, 310
　　Herodotus on, 92, 93, 216
　　kurgans of, 66, 94, 191, 206
　　linking of the stone *babas* to,
　　　　32, 33, 42, 49, 50, 54–56, 56n51,
　　　　163, 165n37, 173, 297, 301, 304
　　in *A Naked Year,* 206–7, 209, 214,
　　　　217, 218–19, 220–22, 241–42
　　valorization of (Scythianism),
　　　　18, 20–21, 94, 103, 208, 217–19,
　　　　218n29, 220, 241, 268–69, 301,
　　　　302, 303, 304
　　in *The Volga Falls to the Caspian Sea,*
　　　　293, 297, 301–5
　　Zabelin on, 55, 93–94, 95–96
　　Zamiatin's essay on, 217, 218, 261
"Scythians, The" (Blok), 20, 96, 217,
　　218, 219, 220–21, 261
Sea of Azov (Azof), 41, 83, 86
"Sea of Gods" (Bunin), 137–38

Seifrid, Thomas, 196
Sevastopol, 85
"Sevastopol in August" (Tolstoy), 88
Severianin, Igor, 148
Sharp, Jane, 59–60, 147, 163
Shchukin, Sergei, 139
　　collection of, 166–67, *167,* 170–71
Shelley, Percy Bysshe, 114n12
"Shield of Oleg, The" (Pushkin), 76n23
Shifner, Anton, 91
Shklovsky, Viktor
　　About Mayakovsky, 57–58, 59
　　"O Pil'niake," 238–40
　　and *ostranenie,* 97–98, 288
shock workers, 248
Shub, Esfir, *The Fall of the Romanov
　　Dynasty,* 246
Siberia, 63, 142, 191, 197, 241
signboards, 99, 141
Simbirsk, 53
Simferopol, 59, 85
Skify, 217
Skorodumov, G. I., gravure of Bronze
　　Horseman, *150,* 153
Slap in the Face of Public Taste, A, 103,
　　154–55
Slavophiles, 20, 22, 22n14, 169, 301,
　　302, 304
Slavs, 32, 52, 133, 216
Slavs' Poetic Views on Nature, The
　　(Afanas'ev), 52–53, 52n40, 133,
　　183, 186
Slezkine, Yuri, 248
Sluchevskii, Konstantin, 186n12
　　"The Stone Women,"
　　　　185, 186–89, 186n12
Slutskii, Boris, 201
Socialist Realism, 308
Society for Free Aesthetics, 165n37
Soiuzzoloto, 249
Sokolova, Mariia, 211
Solov'ev, Vladimir, 148
　　"Panmongolism," 220–21

"Song of Oleg the Wise" (Pushkin), 75–76, 79, *104*

Sovetskii ekran, 247, *262*, 263, 267, 267n40, 270

Soviet Union, 89, 106, 173, 206, 245, 248, 255, 259, 265, 268, 275, 277, 287, 288, 291, 304, 310
  archaeology in, 175, 247, 248
  industrialization in, 250, 260, 280

Spain, 39

Spasskii, Grigorii, 56n49, 83, 86

St. Petersburg, 34, 53, 139, 150, 187, 246

Bronze Horseman as genius loci of, 145, 145n14, 151

St. Petersburg University, 28, 134, 135

Stakhanovites, 248

State Academy of the History of Material Culture (GAIMK), 309

statuary. *See babas*

Stavropol, 173

Stepanov, Nikolai, 192n22, 201

steppe
  artifacts, 14, 49, 50, 106, 112, 193, 196, 219, 307, 308
  Chekhov's poem on, 12–13, 59, 77, 84, 130, 196
  displacement and disappearance of stone *babas* from, 33, 49–61, 173–74, 189
  Eurasian, 13, 25, 30, 222
  monotony of, 13, 57, 80, 81, 83–84, 105
  signification, 84, 92, 106
  temporalities of, 81, 104, 105, 106, 177, 191, 193, 197
  Viazemskii's poem on, 80–81, 83, 106

"Steppe, The" (Chekhov), 12–13, 59, 77, 84, 130, 196

"Steppe, The" (Viazemskii), 80–81, 83, 106

Still Life with Pineapple (Goncharova), 162

Stone Age, 24, 134, 135

Stone Age, The (Vasnetsov), 105

"Stone *Baba*, The" (Bunin), 108–10, 109n2, 111–12, 113, 116, 119–22, 123–25, 127–28, 130, 134, 135, 137, 138, 200

stone *babas*. *See babas*

"Stone Guest, The" (Pushkin), 131

stone statuary. *See babas*

"Stone Woman, The" (Khlebnikov), 176, 178, 190–95, 192n22, 200, 201–3, 233

"Stone Woman, The" (Remizov), 32, 53, 110, 131–35, 131n25, *134*, 138, 183, 186, 200, 305

stone women. *See babas*

"Stone Women, The" (Sluchevskii), 185, 186–89, 186n12

Strabo, 215

"Stratification of Aegean Culture, The" (Florenskii), 110, 116–19, 120, 128

Stravinsky, Igor, *The Rite of Spring* (with Roerich), 24, 105, 134, 135, 136–37, 305

Summers, David, 90–91n38, 229–230

Sunderland, Willard, 57n52

Sutton Hoo, 18

Symbolism, 125, 146, 152, 160, 161, 165, 165n37

Syria, 111

T

"Talashkino" (Makovskii), 48–49n32

Tambov, 258–59, 270

Tartars (Tatars), 22, 51, 187, 212, 215, 216, 237, 293

Taruskin, Richard, 135, 136

Tashkent, 59

Tatlin, Vladimir, 16, 201

Tauris, 53, 57, 58, 100

Temriuk, *85*, 86

Ternovka, kurgan at, *228*

Terror Antiquus (Bakst),
    115–16, *115*, 120
"These Poor Settlements" (Tiutchev),
    94
Three Songs of Lenin (Vertov), 274–75
Three Women (Picasso),
    166, 167–68, *167*, 170, 171
Tiflis, 50, 59
Time, Forward! (Kataev), 308–9, 310–11
Tiutchev, Fedor, 68, 94, 147, 166n38
    "From That Life That Raged
        Here," 79n27, 94–95, 95n44
    "These Poor Settlements," 94
"To All! To All! To All!" (Khlebnikov),
    193
Tolstoi, Aleksei, "Kurgan," 69, 75,
    77–80, 83
Tolstoy, Leo, 24, 136
    "Sevastopol in August," 88
    War and Peace, 68, 85, 86–88, 90, 233
toponyms,
    57, 65, 89, 215n22, 222–23, 234
Toward the Ocean-Sea (Remizov),
    131, 132
"Toward the Question of the Stone
    Babas" (Brandenburg), 54, 55,
    55n46, 56, 64
*Travelogue through South Russia to
    Crimea, Odessa, and Beyond*
    (Vsevolozhskii), 54–55
Travels in the Caucasus (von Klaproth),
    34, 41–42
Travels (Polo), 215, 215n19, 215n22
*Travels through the Southern Provinces of
    the Russian Empire, in the Years
    1793 and 1794* (Pallas), 40–41,
    41, 42, 45–46, 168
travel writing, 34, 35, 40–41, 50, 54–55,
    84, 137–38, 215, 252–54, 294–95
Tret'iakov, Sergei, 68, 289
trizna, 75–76, 77, 78–79
Trotsky, Leon, 207–8, 229, 232
Troy, 17, 70–71, 93, 214

Tsarskoe Selo, 201
Tsivian, Yuri, 259
Tugenkhol'd, Iakov, 170, 171
Turgenev, Ivan, 186n12
Turks, 32
"Twelve, The" (Blok), 224, 240
Tynianov, Yuri, 190
    "Literary Fact, The," 252

U
Ukraine, 84, 209, 244, 254
*Unearthing the Past: Archaeology and
    Aesthetics in the Making of
    Renaissance Culture* (Barkan),
    19, 37, 121n18
Union of Youth, 125n22
Upper Paleolithic era, 249, 303
Ural'sk, 235
utopia, 20, 196, 208, 247, 248, 252, 277,
    285, 287
Uvarov, Aleksei, 35, 55n47, 64, 74
    *Collection of Maps and Sketches to-
        ward the Study of the Antiquities
        of Southern Russia and the Banks
        of the Black Sea, A* (with Vebel'),
        85–86, *85*, 249, *250*
    "Knowledge about the Stone
        Women," 27, 34–39, *36*, 42,
        44–45, 55, 64, 85, *151*, 249
Uvek
    debates on origins of, 214–16
    excavations at, and sites in, 204,
        205, 206, *207*, 210–13, 217, 225,
        226–29, *227*, *228*, 240
    in *The Naked Year*, 206–07, 208–9,
        210, 211, 214, 216–17, 222, 223,
        224–29, 232, 233, 235, 236, 240,
        241, 252
    as a toponym, 215n22, 222–23

V
Van Gogh, Vincent, 167
Varangians, 24, 97

Vásáry, István, 56n51
Vasmer, Max, 234
Vasnetov, Viktor, 105, 139, 175
    illustration for "Oleg the Wise,"
        104, 104
    Stone Age, The, 105
Vebel', M., Collection of Maps and
    Sketches toward the Study of the
    Antiquities of Southern Russia
    and the Banks of the Black Sea, A
    (with Uvarov'),
        85–86, 85, 249, 250
Velázquez, Diego, 166n38
Vertov, Dziga
    Eleventh Year, The,
        243–79, 259, 260, 262, 267, 272,
        274, 275, 276, 283, 286, 289, 290,
        304, 306, 307–8, 309, 310
    Kino-Eye, 265
    Man with a Movie Camera, 266, 266
    and Pil'niak, 280–81, 288–89,
        304–5, 308, 309–10
    Three Songs of Lenin, 274–75
Veselovskii, Nikolai, 135, 173
    "Current State of the Question of
        the 'Stone Babas' or 'Balbals,'
        The," 28–29, 28n2, 30, 32–33, 37,
        39, 44, 53–54, 55–57, 59, 173, 214
    "Imaginary Stone Babas,"
        28, 38, 39, 39, 40, 59, 60, 117,
        135, 202
Vesnin, Viktor, 245
Viazemskii, Petr
    "Evening on the Volga," 81–83
    "Steppe, The," 80–81, 83, 106
Villon, François, 148
Vladimir Mayakovsky: A Tragedy
    (Mayakovsky), 185–86
Volga Falls to the Caspian Sea, The
    (Pil'niak), 245, 279, 280–306,
    280n2, 310
Volga "Pompeiis": An Essay on the Artis-
    tic-Archaeological Examination of

    the Zone on the Right Bank of the
    Volga near Saratov and Tsaritsyn,
    The (Ballod), 204–6, 205, 207,
    210, 211, 212–13, 214, 226, 227,
    228, 234–35
Volga River region, 215–15, 249
    excavations of ("Volga Pompeiis"),
        82, 204–5, 205, 207, 209, 210,
        211, 212–14, 226, 227, 228,
        234–35
    Germans, 211n9
    Viazemskii's poem on, 81–82
    See also Volga Falls to the Caspian
        Sea (Pil'niak)
Volhynia, 84
Volkhov Dam, 271
Voloshin, Maksimilian, 68
    "Archaism in Russian Painting,"
        15–18, 16n6, 23, 60–61, 116–17,
        134–35, 218
von Klaproth, Julius, Travels in the
    Caucasus, 34, 41–42
Voronskii, Aleksandr, 223, 296, 302
Voznesenskii, Andrei, "You Sit
    Pregnant, Pale," 174
Vrangel', Ilya, 241–42
Vsevolozhskii, Nikolai, Travelogue
    through South Russia to Crimea,
    Odessa, and Beyond, 54–55

W
Wachtel, Michael, 76n23
Wanderers, 139
War and Peace (Tolstoy),
    68, 85, 86–88, 90, 233
West, the, 98, 103, 104, 151, 170,
    205, 218, 220, 221, 237, 241,
    248, 261
Westernizers, 20, 155
White Sea-Baltic Sea Canal, 249
"Who Lives Well in Rus'?"
    (Nekrasov), 130
Williams, Raymond, 310

Winckelmann, Johann Joachim, 33,
    49, 175
  Geschichte der Kunst des Altertums,
    43n25
Wofford, Susanne, 194
World War II, 88
"Wormwood" (Pil'niak), 211, 211n9,
    212, 230

Y
"You Sit Pregnant, Pale"
    (Voznesenskii), 174

Z
Zabelin, Ivan, 64, 74, 90, 104, 215
  *History of Russian Life from the Most
    Ancient of Times, The,* 90–96,
    90–91n38, 191, 215–16

"Scythian Graves: The Chertomlyk
    Kurgan, The" (Zabelin), 55, 64,
    93–94
Zamiatin, Evgenii, "Are We
    Scythians?," 217, 218, 261
Zaporozh'e, 196
  Evarnitskii's work on, 252–54, 278
*Zaporozh'e in the Remnants of the
    Past and the Sayings of Its Folk*
    (Evarnitskii), 252–54, 278
Zelenetskii, A., *Epithets of Literary
    Russian Speech,* 69, 72, 75
Zelinskii, Aleksei, 201
Zhukovskii, Vasilii, 153, 153n21, 154
Znanie, 107
Zolotoe runo, 28, 116
Zuev, Vasilii, 30n6, 34

www.ingramcontent.com/pod-product-compliance
Lightning Source LLC
Chambersburg PA
CBHW071710170526
45165CB00005B/1961